Peter J. Aicher

Rome Alive
A Source-Guide to the Ancient City

VOLUME I

Bolchazy-Carducci Publishers, Inc.

Mundelein, Illinois USA

This book made possible in part due to a generous contribution from
Joseph R. Salemi

General Editor: Laurie Haight Keenan
Contributing Editor: D. Scott VanHorn

Rome Alive
A Source-Guide to the Ancient City, Vol. 1

Peter J. Aicher

Bolchazy-Carducci Publishers, Inc.
1570 Baskin Road
Mundelein, Illinois 60060
www.bolchazy.com

Printed in the United States of America
2018
by Seaway Printing

ISBN 978-0-86516-473-4

Library of Congress Cataloging-in-Publication Data

Aicher, Peter J., 1954–
  Rome alive : a source-guide to the ancient city / Peter J. Aicher.
    p. cm.
Includes bibliographical references and index.
  ISBN 0-86516-473-8 (pbk.)
  1. Rome--Guidebooks. 2. Rome--History--Sources. I. Title.
DG13.A37 2003
914.5'6320493--dc22

                                                    2003023423

Parentibus almis
carissimisque

Contents
VOLUME I

[**Volume II** contains the Greek and Latin texts of all sources in Volume I.]

LIST OF FIGURES

Rome Alive

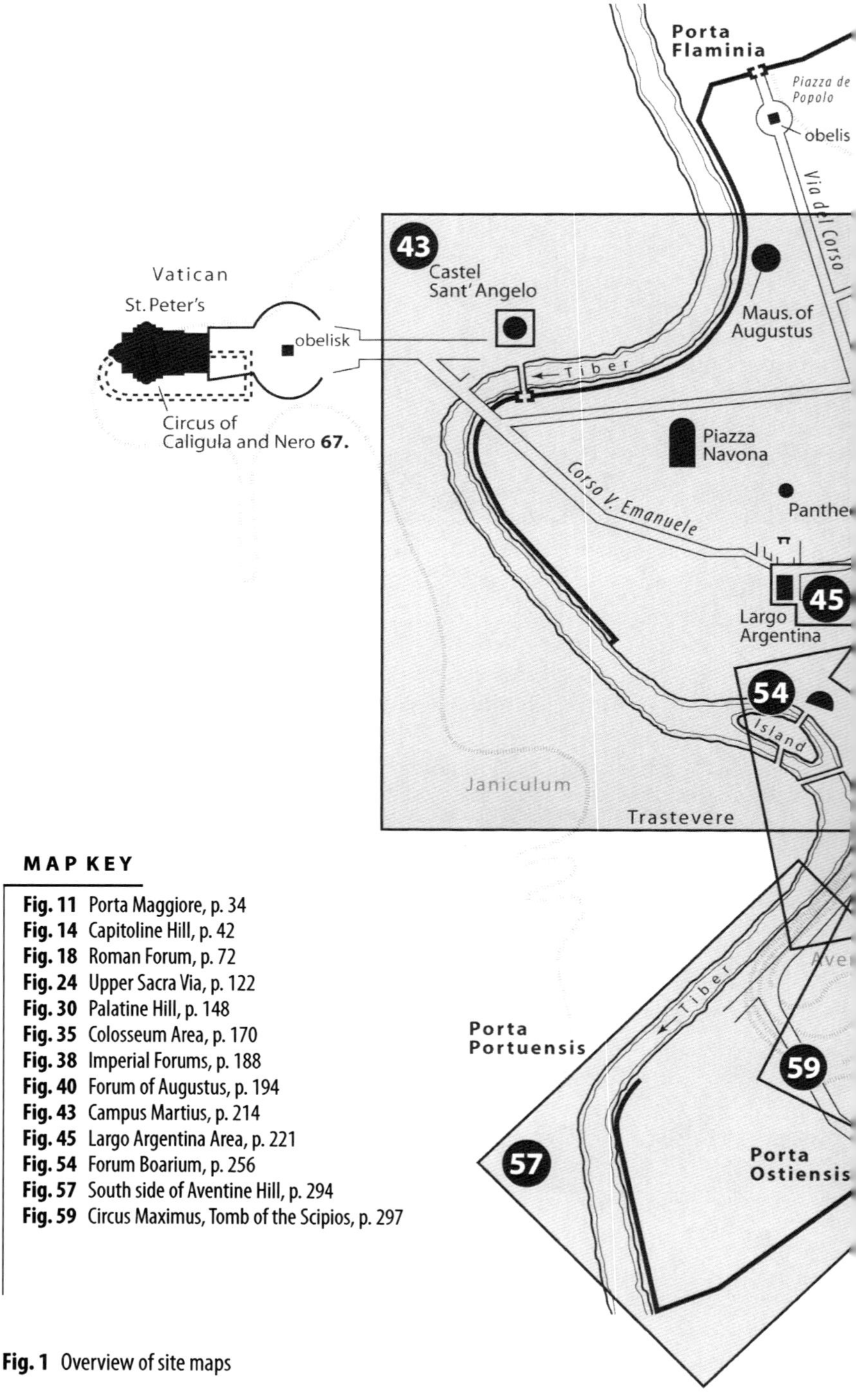

Porta
Flaminia

*Piazza de
Popolo*

obelis

Via del Corso

43 Castel
Sant' Angelo

Vatican

St. Peter's

obelisk

Maus. of
Augustus

Tiber

Circus of
Caligula and Nero **67.**

Piazza
Navona

Corso V. Emanuele

Panthe

45

Largo
Argentina

54

Island

Janiculum

Trastevere

Porta
Portuensis

Tiber

Ave

59

Porta
Ostiensis

57

MAP KEY

Fig. 1 Overview of site maps

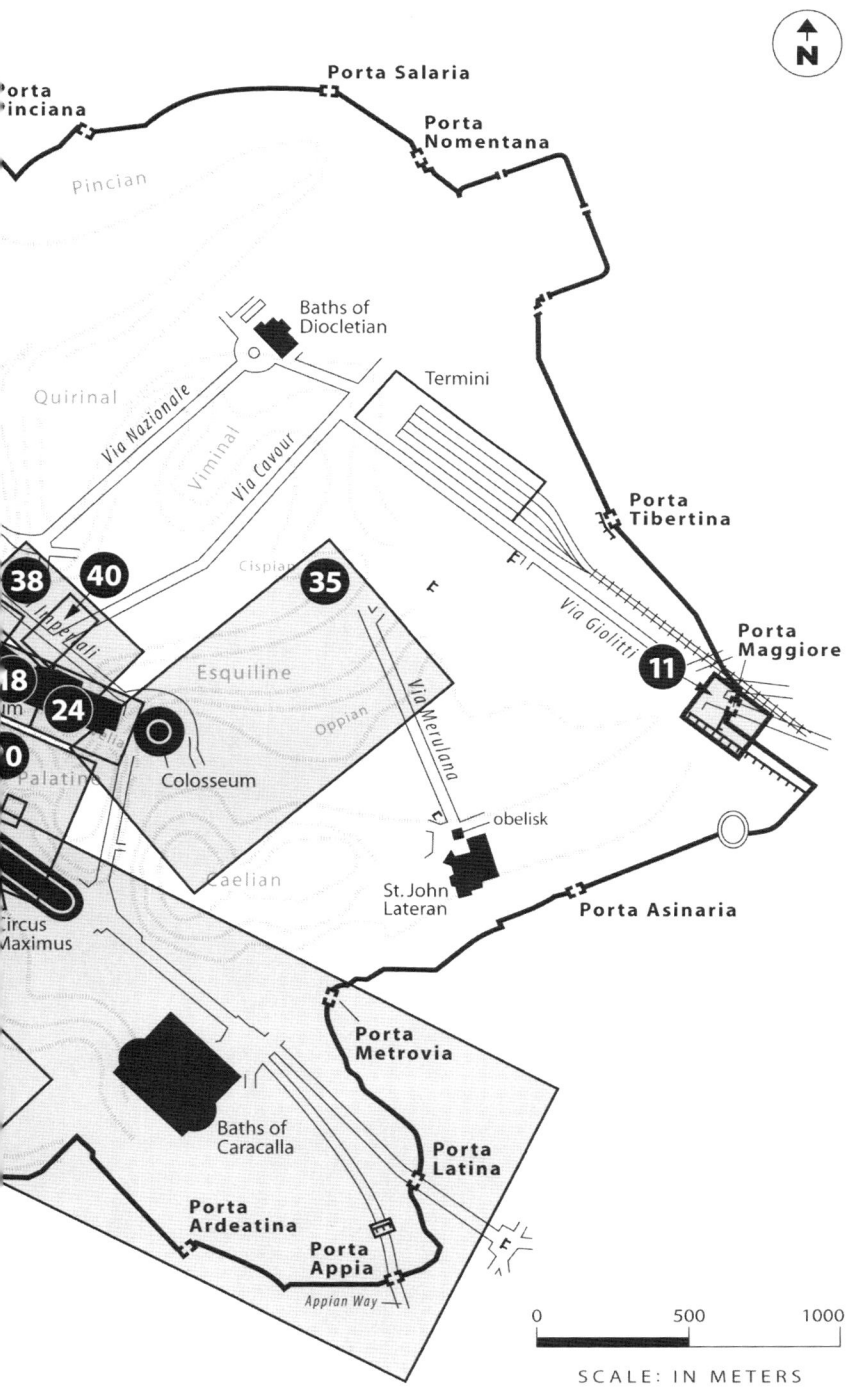

N

Porta Pinciana

Porta Salaria

Porta Nomentana

Pincian

Baths of Diocletian

Termini

Quirinal

Via Nazionale

Viminal

Via Cavour

Porta Tibertina

38 40

Cispian

35

Via Giolitti

Imperiali

Esquiline

Via Merulana

Porta Maggiore

18

11

24

Oppian

Colosseum

obelisk

Palatin

St. John Lateran

Porta Asinaria

Caelian

Circus Maximus

Porta Metrovia

Baths of Caracalla

Porta Latina

Porta Ardeatina

Porta Appia

Appian Way

0   500   1000

SCALE: IN METERS

Preface

Living briefly in Rome in 1906, the young James Joyce was clearly un-impressed: "Rome," he wrote to his brother on September 25, "reminds me of a man who lives by exhibiting to travellers his grandmother's corpse." Since Joyce in his great epics of recycling would go on to make a living doing much the same thing with Dublin, there is perhaps some envy mixed with his disdain. Like Finnegan, however, ancient Rome has refused to lie still, rising to life again in the inspirations of the Renaissance, in the aspirations of dictators and founding fathers, in the enthusiasm of movie audiences, and in the curiosity of countless visitors, scholars, and students who continue to be moved by its art, intrigued by the ancient city's distance and familiarity, and challenged by the complex puzzle of putting its pieces together again.

The ancient city of Rome was an urban fabric of extraordinary density. This is true not just in physical terms, although its million or so inhabitants in the time of Augustus made it seem a different species altogether from most cities of that time:

> The city that they call Rome, my friend, I foolishly thought
> Was similar to the market towns where we take our lambs;
> In the way the puppy resembles the dog, or the kid its mother,
> I likened the smaller to something bigger of its kind.
> Not so: that city lifts its head above all the others
> The way a cypress towers above the trailing yews.
> **Virgil**, *Eclogues* 1.19–25

The remarkable density of Rome's landscape was in its *meaning* as well as in its brick and mortar. A large portion of the city was devoted to a public architecture that not only physically assumed a larger function in most people's daily lives than public space does in our own cities, but that also encoded, with a pervasiveness and complexity that few or any urban areas now or since have matched, messages to its own populace and to the world that streamed in on its roads for entertain-ment or profit. Perhaps this sophistication and density of expression was abetted by Rome's long and continuous history, in combination with an intensely political public (if one allows that Roman politics included rioting and cheering as well as voting) and in the absence of such institutions as newspapers, screen media, and public schools that serve today to broadcast events and inculcate values. Whatever the causes, the building-types and architectural ensembles, the statues, reliefs, inscriptions, temple divinities, even the natural topography of the city itself that was woven into legend and myth, were all capable of speaking to the Roman not just impressionistically of power but quite specifically (if never univocally or determinately) of Rome's past, of individuals and ideals, of political programs and competing claims for authority.

The city of Rome, even narrowed to its ancient period, is of course many things to many people, and there are many ways both to approach and to present its shape and its meaning, each having its own limitations and strengths, its own particular uses. This book approaches the city through the writings of the ancient Greeks and Romans themselves, and it is the translated selections from these writers, most of whom were eyewitnesses to the ancient city, which form the book's core. I have arranged these selections, supplemented with commentary, maps, and illustrations, in the form of a topographical guide to the city. Volume II simply contains these ancient Greek and Latin selections in their original languages.

The limitations of this approach are obvious. From the written sources, we would not know that the Pantheon had a giant opening in its dome, or that the more utilitarian but equally fascinating Markets of Trajan even existed. And yet the written record on occasion provides irreplaceable evidence that supports and extends the archaeological and visual record, frequently giving us crucial information about the very identity of prominent ruins and about the very existence of structures that have vanished. The written sources are also a medium unequalled in their ability to link us to the varied experiences of those who lived among these buildings two thousand years ago. Accordingly, to take advantage of the close connection between topographical sources, historical narratives, and daily life in the ancient city, I have mixed texts that are (at least on the surface) blandly evidentiary and yet hold key information about a site, with texts whose virtue is to place the site or building in a larger context, whether that context is historical, political, social, or legendary. I have also not hesitated to include lengthy passages that cannot be pinned down to any one building, site, or even quarter of ancient Rome, but that nonetheless reveal worlds about what it was like to live there, to window-shop, to stroll, to attend a funeral, to live above a bath-house, to fear fires and go sleepless from the noise.

I should emphasize that the primary goal of presenting Rome in this book is not to determine the historical veracity of each ancient source, however useful many of the sources are in ongoing historical debates about the city (many of which are indeed touched on in the commentary and notes that accompany the sources), but rather to bring to the fore what the natural and architectural monuments meant to those who lived in the city or who read about it and felt its influence in distant regions of the empire. The Romans preserved and revered, for instance, a simple thatched hut on the Palatine which they considered and called the Hut of Romulus [62.], and Romulus appears in numerous sources as the founder not only of the city but of many of its institutions and structures, such as the city's first walls and the Temple of Jupiter Stator. That Romulus belongs to the world of legend, as do the next three kings of Rome's regal period, all of whom are more stereotypical models of kingship than historical figures, is agreed upon by virtually every modern historian. The Romans, however, believed that Romulus founded Rome, and their beliefs are important not only because they reveal much about the Romans as a people but because these beliefs, conveyed and expressed through monuments, physically affected the historical city. The Hut of Romulus was very real, even if its occupant never existed. Legend is further woven into and inseparable from documentable history when Augustus, who styled himself as a second founder of Rome, takes up residence on the Palatine near the Hut of Romulus, or when Cicero calls a meeting of the Senate at the Temple of Jupiter Stator [54.5] to deliver his second speech against the conspirator Catiline, involving by this choice of site the temple's foundation by Romulus during another moment of high crisis when the existence of the community was at stake (or so Cicero would want everyone to believe).

Varro, a Roman scholar whose treatise on the origin and relationships of Latin words is often quoted in the following pages, emphasizes in his discussion of the word *monumenta* the significance of monuments as *reminders*:

> The word *monere* ("to remind") is derived from the word *memoria* [Varro, as so often, gets this part wrong], as is the word *monumenta*, which are placed among the tombs and made visible on the roads, so that the dead might *admonish* passersby that they too once existed and that those who see the monument are mortal as well. From this usage, other things that are written or built for the sake of memory are also called *monumenta*.
>
> **Varro**, *The Latin Language* 6.49

What Varro stresses here is the importance of public architecture in its capacity to provoke memory, to occasion the exchange between past and present that was such a pressing concern for the Romans. It is interesting that Varro identifies tomb structures as the word's original sense; then as now, the primary function of tomb architecture is to remind, as our noun "memorial" stresses in a nice parallel to the Latin etymologies. But for the Latin speaker, the same word for a tomb memorial extends to other public architecture as well, defining their essential function as "memorials" of the past, even if, as is often the case, the dominant daily use of a structure—as an archive or treasury, for instance—tends to obscure this function. By focusing on the sources, which so often situate the monuments in the circumstances of their foundation (*the* crucial moment for Greeks and Romans), in the history of their times, and with the dramatic associations which accrued to them over the centuries, this particular power of the monuments can be restored to some degree. Clearly the visual remains are crucial in this attempt as well. The visual record is often in ruin, however, and ruins have a characteristic and peculiar power of suggestion *as ruins*, as memorials of a vanished civilization. The characteristic strength of literary sources is to stress the other layer of memory that these monuments were intended to provoke, not in an audience looking at the monuments in chance ruin, but by design in people who lived among them. I have also found that when faced with a ruin, one's first impulse is to rebuild that building mentally; confronted with sources, one's impulse is to rebuild a memory, a monument in Varro's sense.

The sources I have translated for this book are selections from literally thousands of others that refer to the city of Rome in general and to its hundreds of sites individually. A complete collection (which grows as new inscriptions are found yearly), even without translations and commentary, would fill many volumes. My selections and omissions, both of individual sources and of particular sites, reflect my own interests and ignorance to some degree, but are based as well on several criteria that take account of the wider interests of both scholars and tourists. I have attempted to include most of the sites that are well-known today, but was concerned to add to the traditional list some important sites (the temples of Diana, Hercules of the Muses, and Isis, for example) that are often neglected for the understandable reason that little or nothing of them remains (physically, that is). Other works on the city, cited below, were valuable in identifying sources crucial to scholarly debate, and I have eagerly included accounts of the famous legends, historical dramas, and Roman institutions that were associated with the topography of the city, some of which still have common currency. Romulus, Aeneas, and Horatius all have their topographical place in the city, as do Hannibal's siege, Caesar's assassination, Nero's "fiddling," and more generally triumphal processions, chariot races, Vestal Virgins, and famous imperial excesses. Occasionally the sources provide a rich picture of life in the capital but can be assigned to no particular location; rather than leave these free-floating or putting them under topical headings, I have placed them with a particular site by association. Thus, Seneca's vivid account of noises at a (nameless) Roman bath appears under the Baths of Caracalla, and Juvenal's account of urban dangers is placed in the Subura.

Historically, the period and person of Augustus are best represented in this guide, not only because the sources are comparatively rich, and because of the influence which Augustan Rome and Augustan literature came to have on later history from Dante to Mussolini, but because Augustan building in Rome strikes me as an uncommonly sophisticated attempt, even by Roman standards, to shape the city and encode its architecture with meaning. Many of the sources throughout the book stress the close connection between religion and military success (temple vows, temple financing, religious ritual involved in specific stages of war, etc.), but this frequency reflects something essential to Roman society, as does the concern in many sources with borders and boundaries, a concern one would expect in a community bent simultaneously on expansion and preservation of the past. As Rome grew from a tribal community into a city-state and then into an empire, and the borders expanded from a riverside town into a multinational empire, the landscape of the city and the rituals that were tied to it continued to be of vital importance in giving some sort of palpable, if increasingly symbolic, unity to the Roman world.

I have found it useful to make my own translations of all the sources, since there seemed something to be gained by having them stylistically constellated and differentiated by one sensibility, however much reliant on the translations and commentaries of others. This also allowed me to gloss obscure phrases (in this book, "the ridge of the parricide Telegonus" equals "the Alban Hills") and to make passages intelligible when taken out of their larger context, if only by the insertion of a person's proper name and title. I have enclosed the more overt of these glossed introductions in brackets, as well as BC and AD dating. When forced to choose between obscure fidelity to the letter (or even image or clause) and readable approximation of the spirit, I have tended towards the latter, except where specific topographical issues hang in the balance.

Though doubtful at first on whether to translate verse as verse, I concluded that for a work relying on a certain eyewitness immediacy of contact there was no way around it. The sense we get for Rome is not based solely on what is said, but also on how it is said, and the genre of a passage will influence the image or information we get from an author. A good example of this can be found in practically anything written by Juvenal, whose great satire on the City of Rome I have excerpted at length [77.6]. His poetry is filled with unforgettably vivid images and vignettes of life in the capital. That these descriptions occur in poetic satire does not necessarily mean that they are fabrications, but rather that they are artistically employed for purposes of entertainment and maximum dramatic effect. If they weren't believable descriptions by and large, the voice of the satire would lose plausibility. On the other hand, the picture we get in Juvenal has been manipulated, intensified, and compressed, expressing daily hassles and fears in dramatic worse-case scenarios (mangled feet, smashed heads, dismembered corpses, etc.). To take all of these scenes as slice-of-life descriptions or daily occurrences (as a prose translation would encourage) would be somewhat like concluding from an evening of television that car-chases and exchanges of semi-automatic gunfire are daily occurrences, when for many Americans they are just daily possibilities.

At any rate, verse will at least *appear* as verse by its formatting. I have also taken more liberties in translating the verse than the prose, primarily to reduce the need for explanatory notes but also for aesthetic reasons. Again, I have hewn closer to line when some detail of particular relevance to the urban landscape appeared.

Arrangment of Volumes I and II

Volume I begins with brief entries on each of the ancient writers whose descriptions of the city appear in this work. These writers are chronologically listed, and each entry includes the relevant works and genres of each author, some of the writer's historical circumstances and often some indication of the writer's familiarity with the city.

For each major division of the city, I have written short overviews, and have prefaced many of the individual sites as well with a commentary that provides some historical background, suggests something of the significance of individual sources, and occasionally fills in some of the major gaps in the written record that can be made good by the archaeological record. The ancient sources that follow the commentary are easily identified by a number before them and the citation of author and work at their tail. Sometimes "Notes" follow the sources, containing matter that I judged to be valuable but more technical than the commentary.

I have attempted to provide enough maps for a first-time visitor to understand Rome's basic topography, to locate the major sites in the city today, and to identify many of the ruins while joining them together on a walk. Sometimes, as in the case of the Forum of Augustus, a detailed ground plan is crucial to an understanding of the ancient sources. For general bearings, the master-map at the beginning of the book puts the individual site maps of each section in the context of the modern city; between the two, almost every ancient site can be located today, even if nothing remains to be seen. The site maps are keyed to the numbers assigned to each of the sources. When a Latin inscription can still be seen on site, I have located the Latin text in Volume I along with its translation.

Those whose Latin or Greek allows them to enjoy the translated passages in their original languages will want to take advantage of the original texts in Volume II, as will classics students using this book for a core collection of sources on individual monuments. For such use, the index may be the first place to turn to, leading backwards from original texts and perhaps on to the notes, translation, and commentary in Volume I. The notes also identify some of the current debates on the topography of Rome, and may be helpful in directing students to further exploration in the relevant resources mentioned below. In this fashion too, *pace* Joyce, the ancient city lives on, like his own texts, in unending debate.

In terms of resources, the new millennium is a good time to be studying the ancient city. Three recent works proved especially helpful in providing a picture of the current state of topographical knowledge and debate. Rather than citing them throughout the work, I refer the reader to them now both for their discussions on all the sites included in this book and for the bibliography they provide for further study (the full citations for the following titles and other works cited can be found in the back of this volume). In guide-format, there is Amanda Claridge's *Rome*, a well-written and richly illustrated guide book to the ancient city. Lawrence Richardson, Jr.'s *A New Topographical Dictionary of Ancient Rome* is organized alphabetically; each entry is followed by a bibliography, and there is an excellent overview of the sources of our knowledge in his introduction, which is at the same time a history of the topographical study of the city. The *Lexicon Topographicum Urbis Romae*, edited by Eva Margareta Steinby and appearing in five volumes between 1993 and 2000 (with indices in Volume VI), is also an alphabetized mother-lode of information about the ancient city and its bibliography. Its entries are primarily in Italian, but occasionally in English as well as German and French, and the numerous illustrations appended to each volume are themselves a treasure of information. Like Richardson's *Dictionary*, the *Lexicon* (abbreviated as *LTUR* in this book) frequently refers to written sources, and both publications were useful in deciding which sources to select, as I hope this book will be useful in turn in providing texts and translations for some of the sources that figure prominently in those works.

Also useful have been two previous collections of sources, Donald R. Dudley's *Urbs Roma: A Source Book of Classical Texts* and A. van Heck's *Breviarium Urbis Romae Antiquae*. Dudley's book (out of print as of 2003) includes both Greek and Latin texts in translations, as well as the Latin for some of the texts; though lacking useful maps, it has a good collection of photographs as well as much interesting commentary. The *Breviarium* has a larger collection of sources than either my own or Dudley's book (though dwarfed by the most complete collection of sources, Giuseppe Lugli's seven volume *Fontes ad Topographiam Veteris Urbis Romae Pertinentes*, 1952–1969), but includes neither translations nor any Greek sources, which frequently provide vital information about the city.

Although less directly influential in this work, the following writings are notable for their treatment of the ancient city and their creative use of sources: Catherine Edward's *Writing Rome: Textual Approaches to the City*, Diane Favro's *The Urban Image of Augustan Rome*, and Nicholas Purcell's essays on the city in volumes 9 and 10 of the *Cambridge Ancient History*. Edwards encourages sophisticated readings of literary texts about the city, Favro uses various disciplines and points of view to enter more vividly into the life of Augustan Rome, and Purcell breaks new ground in synthesizing the vast and scattered evidence to illuminate particular phases of life in the capital. John Stanbaugh's *The Ancient Roman City* also provides an interesting narrative combining topography, history, and daily life.

Acknowledgements

The origins of *Rome Alive* go back to the suggestions and encouragement of its publisher, Ladislaus Bolchazy. Laurie Haight Keenan provided much editorial assistance and further encouragement throughout the book's evolution. The anonymous readers of the manuscript greatly improved the text with their suggestions and corrections, as did Belinda Osier Aicher throughout the years of its preparation. Don Cyr, Susan Goodrich, Nicholas Humez, Lawrence Richardson, Jr., David Trobisch, and T.P. Wiseman provided valuable help along the way; Dawne Gilpatrick-Hall produced and patiently revised the illustrations.

A Faculty Senate Research Grant and sabbatical release time from the University of Southern Maine supported the preparation of this book.

Authors of the Ancient Sources Used in this Guide

In addition to the sources attributed to the writers chronologically listed below, many sources come from two major collections of Latin inscriptions: *ILS* (*Inscriptiones Latinae Selectae*), a five-volume selection by H. Dessau, and the more comprehensive *CIL* (*Corpus Inscriptionum Latinorum*). Where applicable, citations are to both collections.

Plautus (fl. 200 BC), Roman writer of verse-comedies whose plays are the oldest complete works of Latin literature to survive. Although the plays are set in a Greek world, Rome shows through, sometimes explicitly, as in his survey of characters to be found in specific parts of the Roman Forum [21.2].

Ennius (239–169 BC), Roman poet famous primarily for his *Annals*, a national epic of Roman history from its origins down to the great generals of his own day. His relationship with several leading Romans is classic example of the ties between client-poet and patron-leader that found architectural expression in the Tomb of the Scipios and the Temple of Hercules of the Muses.

Polybius (c. 200–after 118 BC), Greek historian who was deported to Italy, where he wrote a history explaining how "in the space of only 53 years [between 220 and 167 BC], most of the inhabited world fell under the rule of one power: Rome" (*History* 1.1.5). Being a tutor and companion to P. Cornelius Scipio Aemilianus, he was well placed to observe both the city of Rome and its aristocratic ceremonies such as the Forum funeral that he famously describes [21.3].

Diodorus Siculus (fl. 60 BC), Greek historian whose history (the *Bibliotheke*, "Library") in forty books (15 extant) covered Greco-Roman history from mythological times to 60 BC. Diodorus probably finished his history while living in Rome.

Catullus (c. 84–54 BC), Latin poet from northern Italy who lived in Rome. Many of his poems have a strong urban flavor and include vignettes of daily life in the city. He is excerpted here in connection with the Magna Mater temple on the Palatine and with her orgiastic rites [60.12].

Cicero (106–43 BC), prolific writer as well as a leading Roman statesman during the final years of the Republic. Cicero's statements relative to the city of Rome fall into many genres. Evocations of the city in his speeches can be very telling, in part because he often exploits the emotional value that he hopes various city sites will have in the hearts of his Roman listeners. The same distillation or framing of what Rome means occurs in the philosophical dialogues, where judgements about the city are attributed to characters known for their patriotic greatness. His private letters express a more critical and worldly attitude to the building projects that his equally ambitious but richer contemporaries are undertaking.

Varro (116–27 BC), Rome's most prolific scholar, although only two of his 75 works have survived (on agriculture and the Latin language respectively). Varro spent much of his time in Rome before his retirement after Caesar's assassination. In his treatise on the Latin language (c. 43 BC) he provides topographical information by way of explaining the etymologies of place-names (e.g., "forum" [21.1]).

Vitruvius (c. 80–18 BC), Latin writer of the only complete architectural treatise that has come down to us from antiquity. His discussions of architecture are preponderantly generic and prescriptive, but occasionally touch on Rome specifically.

Virgil (70–19 BC), poet from the north of Italy. Not especially fond of the busy public life of the capital, Virgil nonetheless gave classic expression to the legend of the city's origins, most topographically when Aeneas visits the site of Rome in Book 8 of the *Aeneid* [116.2].

Horace (65–8 BC), lyric poet and gentle satirist who had a greater tolerance for the capital than his friend Virgil, though frequently escaping to his beloved Sabine villa above Tivoli. His most extended passage in this book—his chance encounter with "the Boor"[21.7]—is an urban drama that hinges on the sites and activities of the Forum.

Strabo (64 BC–c. AD 25), Greek geographer whose *Geography* in 17 books described the geography of the Roman world and assessed its political implications. Since Strabo studied in Rome and returned several times, his accounts of the city and countryside are often first-hand.

Augustus (63 BC–AD 14), adopted heir of Caesar who ushered in the imperial period of Roman history. Of his writings, only the *Res Gestae* ("Achievements") survives, a long inscription which catalogues his major achievements, including a great number of building projects in Rome. The text was disseminated widely in the ancient world (the only copy that survived was carved in Greek and Latin on the walls of a temple in Turkey), suggesting that the geography and building activity in the capital were of universal significance, a topographical paradigm of civilized life.

Livy (59 BC–AD 17), Latin historian of the period from Rome's legendary founding to 9 BC. Only 35 of its 142 books remain, supplemented by later summaries of most of the missing parts. Besides giving much valuable information about the historical development of the city, Livy's narrative, especially in its treatment of Rome's foundation and early period, is a carefully-wrought and classic expression of what the Romans made of their landscape and the legends connected to it.

Dionysius of Halicarnassus (fl. 30–10 BC), Greek historian and literary critic who lived and taught in Rome under Augustus. He wrote a history of Rome from its origins to the First Punic War; only the section down to 441 BC survives.

Propertius (c. 50 BC–10 BC?), Roman writer of four books of elegiac poetry. In his earlier poems the world capital provided little more than scenery for assignations. His later poems turn to history and Roman themes while retaining some irreverence towards Roman tradition.

Ovid (43 BC–AD 17), Roman poet whose fascination with the city of Rome continued long after he crossed Augustus and was exiled to an undeveloped edge of the empire. The work by Ovid most quoted here, the *Fasti*, or "Calendar;" half-finished (January to June), is a day-by-day treatment of the religious year. Its many references to the monuments and landscape of the city show how closely religious observations and rituals were connected with Roman topography.

Velleius Paterculus (20 BC–c. AD 40), Roman historian whose work covers, in the space of two volumes, Rome from its legendary origins down to AD 29. He was familiar with the city and its rulers, but spent much of his life elsewhere in the empire.

Consolation to Livia (C1 AD), a poem of consolation nominally addressed to Livia, the wife of Augustus, for the death of her son Drusus in 9 BC, but probably a later literary exercise. The great imperial Mausoleum of Augustus, as the resting place of Drusus, makes an appearance in the poem [96.5].

Valerius Maximus (fl. AD 30), author, under the emperor Tiberius, of a handbook on (predominantly Roman) "Memorable Sayings and Deeds."

Seneca the Elder (c. 50 BC–AD 40), Roman rhetorician whose writings on the art of rhetoric provide interesting but scattered bits of information about the capital.

Lucan (AD 39–65), Latin poet educated in Rome. Lucan was first a favorite of Nero and then joined the conspiracy against him, committing suicide when detected. His surviving epic *De Bello Civile* recounts, with an atmosphere of horror, the civil war between Pompey and Caesar.

Seneca the Younger (c. AD 1–65), orator, senator, tragedian, and advisor the young emperor Nero. Seneca knew the city intimately, and an extract [128.4] from one of his 124 surviving letters provides us with a vivid depiction of Roman bathing.

Asconius (AD 3–88), commentator on the speeches of Cicero, with a detailed knowledge of the city of Rome.

Josephus (AD 37–after 93), Jewish priest and historian (in Greek) of *The Jewish Wars*, published c. AD 79. Initially resistant to Rome, he eventually sided with the Romans against the revolutionaries of his homeland before their resistance to Rome led to the capture of Jerusalem and destruction of the temple in AD 70. He eventually had a house in Rome, and witnessed the triumphal procession awarded to Vespasian and his sons for their victory over Judaea.

Pliny the Elder (AD 23–79), author of the comprehensive Encyclopedia (*Naturalis Historia*) in 37 volumes. Pliny devotes the last five books of his encyclopedia to metals and stones, especially as used in the arts and architecture, and in cataloguing and commenting on items of interest to him he locates many of Rome's famous works of art.

Frontinus (c. AD 30–c. 104), Roman senator appointed curator of Rome's water supply in AD 97. His handbook on the city's aqueducts (*De aquis urbis Romae*) is a valuable source of detailed information on the nine aqueducts that had been built by his day, and on the regulations, administration, and abuses of this utility.

Quintilian (c. AD 35–c. 90), Latin rhetorician whose only surviving work is a treatise on the education of an orator, in twelve books. From Spain, he taught in Rome for much of his professional life.

Statius (c. AD 50–c. 96), Roman poet who spent much of his life in Rome. His *Silvae* ("Occasional Poems") includes a poem thanking the emperor Domitian for inviting him to dinner in the great banquet hall of Domitian's new palace [64.4].

Martial (c. AD 40–103), Latin poet from Spain who moved to Rome c. AD 64 and lived there much of his life. His first book of poems celebrated the opening of the Colosseum under Titus, but his greatest claim to fame is the 12 books of epigrams, the majority of which have as their subject some element of city life. He joined Statius in currying favor from the despotic Domitian.

Pliny the Younger (AD 61–113), Roman senator, lawyer, and nephew of Pliny the Elder, known primarily through his literary letters. He held several important posts under emperors ranging from the tyrannical Domitian and the more liberal Trajan, including the management of the banks of the Tiber (*curator alvei Tiberis*, c. AD 104–6); his description of a Tiber flood [2.11] shows him in action as an artful letter writer and knowledgeable official.

Plutarch (c. AD 46–after 120), Greek philosopher and biographer who spent some time in Rome lecturing and teaching. His biographies of famous Greeks and Romans include notable Romans from the legendary Romulus to Mark Antony and Caesar, which are filled with references to the Roman settings of their lives.

Juvenal (fl. AD 125), Roman poet of 16 satires. Although we know next to nothing about Juvenal's life, his satires are set in Rome and filled with urban images. Satire 3 is a famous portrait of the city of Rome, told from the point of view of a city-dweller who pauses to talk to the poet before moving out of the city, sick of its social routines, inconveniences, expense, and dangers [76.6].

Tacitus (AD 56–c. 120), Latin historian who, in his *Annals* and *Histories*, chronicled Rome's history from the time of Augustus to the death of Domitian. Since he often focuses his attention on the emperors in Rome, the city often appears in his narrative.

Suetonius (c. AD 70–after 125), Latin biographer fond of lurid detail, most famous for his *Lives of the Caesars*, covering the emperors from Julius Caesar to Domitian.

Appian (fl. AD 160), Greek historian and admirer of Rome who wrote a history of Rome in 24 books, roughly a third of which survives.

Aulus Gellius (fl. late C2 AD), Latin "miscellanist" who wrote the rambling *Attic Nights*, a collection of notes on his reading. His topics are wide-ranging, and sometimes touch on details of Rome, where he spent most of his life.

Dio Cassius (c. AD 164–after 229), senator and Greek historian. With a busy career in the East, it is unlikely Dio spent much time in Rome, but his history of Rome from its foundations to AD 229, with its emphasis on the transformation of the Republic to the Empire, provides a picture of the major historical dramas that occurred in the city.

Tertullian (c. AD 160–c. 240), an early Christian polemicist from Roman Africa whose critiques of pagan social institutions contain interesting descriptions of entertainment in Rome.

Herodian (fl. AD 240), Greek historian and official in Rome who wrote a history of Rome in eight books, starting with the death of Marcus Aurelius and ending with Gordian (AD 180–238).

Arnobius (fl. AD 300), Latin rhetorician who converted to Christianity and wrote a defense of it in seven books.

Notitia (early C4 AD), catalogue or list of important monuments and landmarks in Rome in Constantine's time. The material, written in Latin, is organized by each of the fourteen Constantinian regions of the city, and is an informative (if fallible) source not only because it tells us what buildings were located in which region (and alternately helps define each region) but because within each region the sites are ordered by a rough spatial proximity.

Curiosum (C4 AD), an inventory of the buildings in Rome much like the *Notitia*.

Eusebius of Caesarea (c. AD 269–339), bishop, Church historian (in Greek), and the major literary source chronicling the life of the Emperor Constantine, whose vision before the battle at the Milvian bridge he recounts many years after the occurrence [71.2].

Ammianus Marcellinus (c. 330 AD–395), last of the great Latin historians in antiquity. His history in 31 books, finished in Rome in the mid-380s, covers the period between AD 96 and 378, treating the fourth century in greatest detail.

Aurelius Victor (C4 AD), pagan historian and biographer who was prefect of Rome in 389.

Festus (C4 AD), imperial official and writer of a synopsis of Roman history.

Imperial Lives, (*Scriptores Historiae Augustae*), collection of ancient imperial biographies, in Latin, of uncertain date (perhaps c. AD 400), authorship, and reliability. The work covers the emperors from Hadrian to Carus and his sons (AD 117–284).

Prudentius (AD 348–after 405), Christian Latin poet whose polemical verses against paganism and pagans occasionally touch on the topography of Rome, generally conceived as a battleground encoded with pagan values.

Symmachus (c. AD 340–402), senator from an old Roman family who led the pagan resistance against Christian imperial policies. Ten books of letters survive, which include his famous letter (*Relatio* 3) to the emperor Valentinian II arguing for the restoration of the Altar of Victory, which had been removed from the Senate house because of Christian opposition. Bishop Ambrose persuaded the emperor to uphold the altar's removal [28.5, 28.6].

Jerome (c. AD 347–420), Christian ascetic and translator whose empire-wide travels include two longer stays in Rome. His main interest for the topography of Rome comes from his Chronology, which lists, year by year though not without error, building activities and natural disasters in the city.

Augustine (AD 354–430), Latin rhetorician turned Christian theologian. Augustine was briefly employed in Rome as a teacher of rhetoric. His most famous text relating to the capital is a description of his friend Alypius's visit to the Colosseum games [70.11].

Macrobius (fl. AD 430), Roman official who wrote the *Saturnalia*, a collection of rambling dialogues set on December 16, AD 383, the evening before the festival of Saturn.

Procopius (c. AD 500–after 562), Greek historian on the staff of Justinian's general Belisarius during the latter's campaigns against the Persians, Vandals, and Goths. Procopius's account of these wars, in eight books, includes some eyewitness accounts of Rome when imperial and Gothic forces took turns besieging the city.

Chronology of Rulers

Kings (traditional dates)

Romulus	753–715 BC
Numa Pompilius	715–673
Tullus Hostilius	673–642
Ancus Marcius	642–616
Tarquinius Priscus	616–578
Servius Tullius	578–535
Tarquinius Superbus	535–Republic founded 509 BC

Emperors

Augustus	27 BC–AD 14
Tiberius	AD 14–37
Caligula	37–41
Claudius	41–54
Nero	54–68
Galba	68–69
Otho	69
Vitellius	69

continued on next page

Vespasian	69–79
Titus	79–81
Domitian	81–96
Nerva	96–98
Trajan	98–117
Hadrian	117–138
Antoninus Pius	138–161
Marcus Aurelius	161–180
Commodus	180–192
Pertinax	193
Didius Iulianus	193
Septimius Severus	193–211
Caracalla	211–217
Opellius Macrinus	217–218
Elagabalus	218–222
Severus Alexander	222–235
Maximius	235–238
Gordian III	238–244
Philip	244–249
Decius	249–251
Trebonius	251–253
Valerianus	253–260
Gallienus	253–268
Claudius Gothicus	268–270
Aurelian	270–275
Tacitus	275–276
Probus	276–282
Carus	282–283
Diocletian	284–305
Maximian	286–305
Constantius	292–306
Galerius	293–311
Licinius	311–323
Constantine	306–337

Rome Alive
VOLUME I

Fig. 2 Capitoline wolf (copy of original in Palazzo dei Conservatori)

Fig. 3 Italy

I. The Site and Foundation of Rome

Geographical Overview (see Fig. 3)

Rome's landscape is best understood as a plateau of soft rock (primarily tufa, a sedimentary rock of volcanic origins) that has been worn down by the Tiber River about 30 km. from its mouth. This erosion created, in the case of the Palatine, Aventine, and Capitoline, free-standing hills along the riverbank almost detached from the plateau. The other hills traditionally included in Rome's seven—the Caelian, Esquiline, Viminal, and Quirinal—are rather finger-like extensions of the plateau, all on the left bank; the Janiculum is a similar extension of the plateau on the right bank of the Tiber. Especially the free-standing hills were steeper in antiquity and previously had a greater elevation above the surrounding floor, which has risen between 5 and 10 meters since antiquity on ruins and sediment.

1. The Site of Rome

COMMENTARY

It was natural enough that the Romans, after becoming masters of the Mediterranean, should look back and find the signs that they were destined for greatness. The most grandiloquent conception of this greatness—that it was indeed destined by a higher power, an idea which found classic expression in Virgil's *Aeneid*—proved quite popular later among European Christians, who saw Rome as the chosen vessel for the spread of their religion. In the passages that follow, Vitruvius also has recourse to divine intelligence to explain Roman greatness, as manifested and operative, however, through the agencies of climate. The accounts by Cicero and Livy (put in the mouths of great Roman patriots, Scipio and Camillus respectively) mediate this destiny through the inspired insight of the founder Romulus, who recognized the strategic and economic advantages offered by the specific geography of the site. After such accounts, Strabo's skepticism is refreshing. Even his glowing account of the Roman Campagna's resources is largely accurate, and touches on a famous insight of antiquity: a city is not its walls and buildings, but its people. In the case of Rome, Strabo argues, it was the very lack of certain natural advantages (such as an easily defensible site) that was responsible for forming the character necessary for Rome's subsequent greatness.

SOURCES

1.1   It is a fact that southern nations, although keen in thought and extremely clever in strategy, give way when it comes to a contest of courage. This is because their spirit has been enervated by the hot sun. Conversely, people born in the frigid regions of the north, though better suited for the violence of warfare on account of their fearless courage, are slow of mind, and by rushing into things without reflection, these northern peoples fail to obtain their objectives because they take no thought of strategy.

   Since such differences between people are founded by the nature of things in geographical location, and since all other nations, north and south, are distinguished by an unbalanced mixture, Rome then manifestly occupies a territory that is in the middle of the world and is the mean point of land on earth. For the peoples of Italy are temperamentally balanced in each direction, having both physical strength and a mental vigor suited to their courage. ... Thus did divine intelligence situate the city of the Roman people in an extraordinary and temperate region, so that it might extend its empire across the world.

Vitruvius, Architecture 6.1.10–11

1.2   [Scipio Africanus the Younger begins his summary of Roman history.] "In choosing an advantageous site for his new city—a choice which requires careful consideration if you wish to found a lasting republic—Romulus showed great forethought by not placing his city directly on the coast. ... The primary drawback of a coastal location is a city's vulnerability to surprise attacks. In addition, maritime cities are more vulnerable to the corruption and degeneration of morals, since various languages and customs get mixed together in such cities.

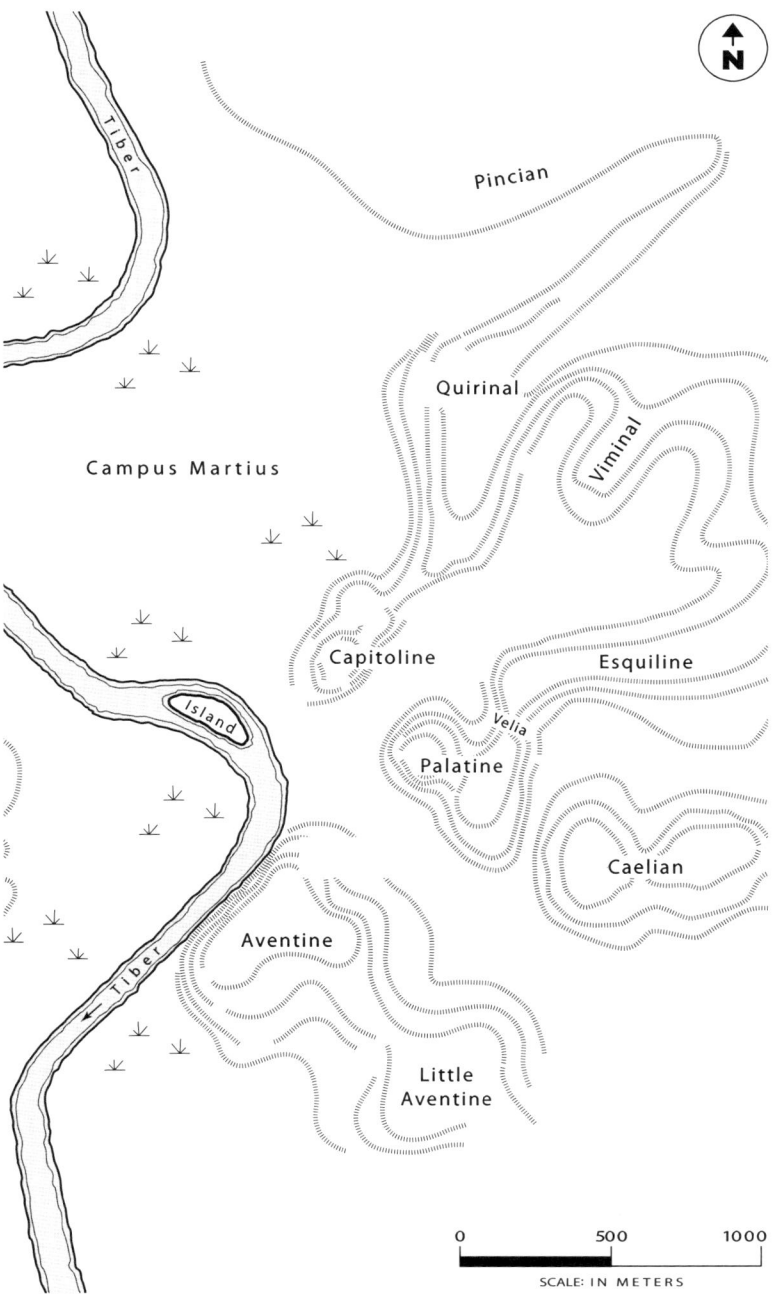

Fig. 4 Hills of Rome

Not only are goods imported from abroad, but ways of life as well, with the result that none of the traditional institutions can remain uncontaminated and pure.

[Seaside cities nonetheless enjoy one great advantage: convenience for importing and exporting goods.] Who then could show more divine guidance than Romulus, who was able to secure the advantages of seacoast cities and avoid their vices by founding Rome on the bank of a broad river that flows down to the sea with a smooth and unfailing current. … Even back then he must have divined that the city would one day furnish the seat and home of a mighty empire. In all probability, no other city located in any other part of Italy could have more easily secured such extensive power."

Cicero, On the Republic 2.5–10

1.3   [After the city was sacked and burned by the Gauls in 390 BC, the general Camillus persuaded the Romans not to relocate their city:] "With good reason did the gods and men choose this site for the founding of the city. Rome's hills provide a healthy environment, the Tiber is favorable for navigation upstream to inland crops and downstream to the sea, and the sea itself is close enough for trade and yet far enough that we are not in danger of invasion by foreign fleets. Consider too Rome's location at the center of Italy. This site is uniquely suited by nature for the expansion of a city—as is proven by the size itself of our city while yet so young."

Livy, History 5.54.4

1.4   After Numitor regained his rightful seat as ruler of Alba Longa, Romulus and Remus returned to their home to found the city of Rome. The site must not have been of their own choosing but rather dictated by necessity, since the location was not easily defended and comprised neither enough of the surrounding territory nor enough citizens to support a city. …

In my opinion, the founders of the city adopted a line of reasoning valid for both their time and for subsequent generations: the Romans ought to depend for their security and well-being not on their walls, but on their weapons and native valor. Walls, they reasoned, did not defend men, but men defended walls. Since in the beginning most of the fertile lands around them belonged to others, and the terrain of their own city was so open to attack, there is no reason to attribute any special good fortune to the site of Rome. But once the Romans acquired the territory around them by their own brave virtue and industry, there was an accumulation of resources that surpassed all natural advantage. …

The entire region of Latium is blessed with fertility, except for a few areas which are marshy and pestilential … and some other areas that are mountainous and rocky. Even these places, however, are not entirely barren and useless, since they provide abundant pasturage and wood, as well as some fruits that do well on marshy or rocky soil. ...

The Romans enjoy an amazing abundance of quarries and timber, as well as rivers that accommodate the transportation of such materials, such as the Anio.

Strabo, Geography 5.3.2; 5.3.7; 5.3.5

2. The Tiber River

COMMENTARY

As the passages above demonstrate, the Romans recognized the Tiber as a crucial factor in the location and prosperity of their city, but the inhabitants became increasingly vulnerable to its floods as they came down from the hills to develop the low-lying areas such as the Roman Forum, the Forum Boarium, and the entire Campus Martius. It is telling that a Tiber flood is integral to the city's foundation story, and is presumed by its chief icon, the wolf and twins. The travertine embankments constructed in the late 1800s have solved the flooding, but make it difficult to imagine the city's formerly intimate connection to the river, which, like all Greek and Roman rivers, had, or was itself, a divinity. Virgil's passage [2.2], in which the rivergod appears to Aeneas in a dream epiphany, helps restore some of Tiber's former personality, as does the reclining statue of the Tiber on the Capitoline in front of the stairs to the Palazzo Senatorio.

Virgil's "sky-blue" waters are as visionary as the rest of Aeneas's epiphany. Even the poets typically give the Tiber the epithet "tawny" or "yellow" (*flavus*), which it still is today when it runs high after storms; perhaps the flood-control dams upstream remove much of the colorful sediment under normal conditions. The same sediment that gave the river its color caused the channel and the harbors at the river's mouth to silt up.

The Tiber Island is in itself a significant piece of the city's topography. Just below where the island breaks the current, there was an early ford as well as the site of Rome's first bridge (treated in more detail under the Forum Boarium section [117.]). This easy crossing directed a good deal of traffic to the site of Rome long before there was a Rome. Although in antiquity the island did not form a break between upper and lower river traffic (as it does today with its rapids and the little weir nearby), this would have been a common place to off-load goods for surface transportation or for another stage of shipment by river.

Starting with Augustus there was a separate administrative post dedicated to the upkeep of the channel and its banks from Rome to

Ostia. Dio's passage attributes a board of five officials to Tiberius's initiative, but this could be a committee assigned specifically to the flooding problem. Tacitus in fact documents a board of *two* officials charged with investigating the possibility of diverting major upstream tributaries into other watersheds, an ambitious proposal which never came to pass because of local protests and the philosophical objection that nature knew what she was doing when she assigned rivers to their mouths (see *Annals* 1.76, 79).

About 120 boundary markers (called *cippi*) have survived that identified both the extent of the river bank under official control and the names of the officials themselves who were responsible for the improvements and regulation. The emperors Claudius and Trajan both responded to the inadequacy of the river's natural mouth as a port by building new harbors just north of Ostia, where the Fiumicino airport is today. Claudius's port was created by building breakwaters, whereas Trajan's port, still more protected, was excavated inland from Claudius's port. Flooding was also addressed by the new channels to the sea, which effectively added more mouths for the river's egress.

SOURCES

2.1   The Tiber was once called the Albula, on account of the milky (*albus*) color of its water. It got the name Tiber from Tiberinus Silvius, an Alban king who perished in the river.

Festus 4

2.2   When Aeneas finally slept, the god of the lovely river,
The ancient Tiber himself, appeared to the troubled hero,
Rising above the poplar leaves that lined his banks.
Veiled in a grassy cloak and shaded by a crown of reeds
He spoke, and with his words he calmed the hero's cares:

...

"Aeneas: I am the god himself of the rolling river
You see here tugging at the banks and cutting the fertile fields,
Sky-blue Tiber, of all the rivers, dearest to the gods.
My mansion is here by the shore, my source in mountain towns."

Virgil, *Aeneid* 8.31–35, 62–65

2.3   Some sections of the city walls are further fortified by the Tiber, which is about 400 feet wide and deep enough to carry large ships. It is also among the more rapid rivers, and generates large eddies.

Dionysius, *Early Rome* 9.68.2

2.4   Cicero sends greetings to Atticus: [July, 45 BC]
Capito happened to speak of the proposed expansion of the city:

Fig. 5 Statue of Tiber, with twins and cornucopia (Piazza del Campidoglio)

the Tiber, starting from the Milvian Bridge [upstream of the city], is to
be rechanneled alongside the Vatican Hills, and the Campus Martius
opened up to development. The Vatican fields in turn will become a
sort of Campus Martius. … "This law will be passed," Capito said;
"Caesar wants it."

Cicero, *Letters to Atticus* 13.33a

2.5   So that more people might become engaged in the administration of the government, Augustus thought up new offices, including
the Curatorship of the Tiber Channel.

Suetonius, *Augustus* 37

2.6   [Inscription on a boundary stone:] The Emperor Augustus,…
by decree of the Senate, marked off the boundaries of the Tiber [in
7 BC]. The next boundary stone [upstream] can be found at 206 feet,
direct measurement; another can be found at 205 feet downstream.

ILS 5924a = *CIL* 6.31542

2.7   [Omens abound:] We see the yellow Tiber,   [27 BC]
    Its raging waves flung back from the Tuscan bank,
Enter the Forum intent on toppling
    The monuments of Numa and Vesta's temple.

Horace, *Odes* 1.2.13–16

2.8   [In AD 15] the Tiber flooded much of the city, requiring people
to go around in boats. Many people thought this was an omen, as well

as the violent earthquake that shook down part of the city wall. …
The emperor Tiberius, however, took it as a sign that there was too
much surface water, and appointed by lot five senators to a permanent
board whose task was to ensure the Tiber flowed as steadily as possible
all year round, rather than flooding in the winter and drying up in the
summer.

Dio, *History* 57.14.7–8

2.9   [In AD 46] the Emperor Claudius, … while building a port for
Rome, freed the city from the danger of floods by constructing canals
that led from the Tiber into the sea.

ILS 207 = *CIL* 14.85

2.10   Gaius Pliny, a curator of the Tiber, its banks, and of the
city sewers … .

ILS 2927 = *CIL* 5. 5262

2.11   Gaius Pliny sends greetings to Caecilius Macrinus:
Here in Rome we have unceasing rains and frequent flooding.
The Tiber has left its channel and spills out high above the low-lying
banks. Even with the far-seeing Emperor Trajan's new canal draining it
into the sea, the river buries the valleys, flows across fields, and has
made a lake of the river plain. In addition, the streams, which nor-
mally empty into the Tiber as their common drain, are now backed up
as if by a dam, and flood fields that the river itself does not touch.
    The Anio, that most graceful of little rivers that so often gets
invited and detained, as it were, by the villas along its banks, has
uprooted and swept off a large part of the groves that gave it shade.
It undermines whole hillsides, which collapse and block its channel,
and the water, searching for a new way back to its bed, knocks down
buildings, submerges them, and carries them away. People trapped on
higher ground watch wealthy furnishings and heavy couches go
floating by, mixed in with farm equipment, yoked oxen, plows and
plowmen, and animals sent to pasture, all of this interspersed with
tree trunks, beams from villas, and whole roofs that are swept far across
the countryside.

Pliny the Younger, *Letters* 8.17.1–4

Notes: 2.4 Although a plan to move the Tiber rings true to Caesar's readi-
ness to break with Roman tradition (Garibaldi toyed with the same idea), it
isn't clear how serious the plan was or for what purpose. It seems from Cicero's
statement that it was primarily an issue of increasing land on the left bank of
the Tiber rather than a measure for flood control. As Cicero describes it, the
new channel proposed for the Tiber closer to the Vatican Hill could have
seamlessly joined the Campus Martius to the Vatican fields once the tradi-

tional Tiber channel had been filled in. This would have allowed the southern half of this area, the traditional Campus, to be developed, while the Vatican fields could take over the Campus's former function as the city's park-like exercise grounds.

3. The Foundation of Rome

COMMENTARY

The early stories about Rome's origins, even where they recede and ascend to mythic level, not only tell us much about how later Romans thought and felt about themselves as Romans, but mirror the archaeological record in two significant ways. First, they show that settlements in the area go back before there was a Rome. The stories of both Aeneas's visit to the site of Rome (traditionally C12 BC) and Romulus's youthful raids portray an area sparsely populated by simple settlements before either of the heroes arrived on the scene, and archaeological records find evidence of habitation in the area going back from the Iron and Bronze Ages into the Stone Age. But starting in the eighth century BC, when legend has Romulus's foundation of the city (753 BC), archaeology finds that there was a population increase in the whole area, and in Rome an urban boom that soon called for walls and a city center.

The names of Romulus and Remus are, in contrast to what the ancients thought, both probably derivatives of the name of the city rather than the other way around, and the myth is possibly no older than the 4C BC. The legends have been interpreted not only as anachronistic projections of the political and social realities of later writers who have incorporated (disputed degrees of) historical tradition, but as instances of wide-spread archetypes and patterns that include foundlings, floods, and rival twins.

Rome's foundation was celebrated on April 21, and this date is still recognized today with certain traditions (though with nothing nearly so elaborate as the anniversary ceremonies which marked this date under Fascist government of the city).

Another important foundational story of Rome, which expresses the later practice of incorporating other people into its system, is included in the Capitoline section [15.1].

SOURCES

3.1   [Thirteen generations after Aeneas's son Iulus (Ascanius) founded the town of Alba Longa in the Alban Hills, Numitor inherited the kingship.] Then his brother Amulius usurped the throne from Numitor and ruled Alba Longa. Piling crime on top of crime, Amulius wiped out all hope of a male heir to Numitor: under the pretext of honoring his brother's daughter Rhea Silvia, Amulius appointed her a Vestal Virgin, thinking to bind her to lifelong virginity and thereby put an end to Numitor's line.

But it was, in my opinion, fated that the great city of Rome should arise; fated, the beginnings of the mightiest power on earth after that of the gods. Though a Vestal, Rhea was raped, and gave birth to twins. She announced (whether she actually believed it, or simply thought that blaming a god lent stature to her misfortune) that Mars was the father of her uncertain offspring. But neither god nor man saved her or the infants from a king's cruelty: the priestess was bound and led off to prison, and the king ordered the boys to be cast adrift on the river.

By some divine chance the Tiber had just overflowed its banks. Since the quiet backwaters of the flood barred any access to the central current of the river, those charged with the task of exposure had to hope that the infants would drown as readily in stagnant pools as in the current, and they considered the king's command completed when they abandoned the boys at the margin of the flood, in the spot where the Ruminalis fig stands today (earlier called the "Romularis" fig, it is reported).

At that time the entire region was a wilderness. The story persists that a she-wolf, making her way down from the surrounding hills for a drink, heard wailing, and found the boys high and dry in their basket where the waters had receded. By the time a shepherd of the royal flocks happened by, the wolf was licking the babies and gently lowering her dugs to them. The shepherd—Faustulus by name—brought the boys home to his hut, and his wife Larentia took them in and raised them. Other people say, however, that the "she-wolf" was actually Larentia herself, who was given the nickname of she-wolf by the shepherds because she was a loose woman [*lupa* can mean both she-wolf and prostitute]. It was from this nickname, they say, that the miraculous legend later arose.

Such was the upbringing of Romulus and Remus. When the boys got older, after finishing with the day's chores at home and among the flocks, they would roam the woods hunting. Living such a life, the twins grew in strength and courage, and soon not only stood their ground against wild animals but would attack bandits loaded with booty, which they would then divide among the other shepherds. Their band of companions grew steadily, joining together in the celebrations of both serious and light-hearted occasions.

Livy, *History* 1.3.11–4.9

3.2   [With the help of the twins Romulus and Remus, the usurper Amulius was deposed.] When Numitor, their grandfather, was safely in place again as king of Alba Longa, Romulus and Remus became eager to found a city of their own, on the same site where they had been abandoned and brought up. An excess population of both Albans and Latins furnished emigrants; joined with the shepherd band led by the twins, they all had reason to hope that their new town would one day make Lavinium [founded by Aeneas], and even Alba Longa, look small in comparison.

Such concerns, however, were soon interrupted by the vice of their forefather—the lust for royal power—and an ugly struggle between the brothers broke out after a peaceful start. Since the brothers were twins and therefore age could not decide the issue, they let the gods, through bird-flight, decide which brother should take command and give the new city his name.

Each brother took up his station for marking out the augural lines of sight, Romulus on the Palatine Hill and Remus on the Aventine. Reportedly, the first sign came to Remus—six vultures—but they had no sooner announced the result than twice that number appeared to Romulus. Each of the camps claimed kingship for their leader, one side by virtue of priority and the other side by virtue of number. A fight broke out and in the heat of anger turned deadly: in the fracas, Remus was struck and killed.

A more common version of Remus's death is that he mocked his brother's new walls by jumping over them, whereupon Romulus killed him in a fit of anger and then added the threat, "The same fate awaits anyone else who jumps over my walls!"

In such fashion did Romulus gain sole power, and the city thus founded was named after him.

Livy, *History* 1.6.3–1.7.3

3.3   Calendar for April 21st:
After Amulius, brother of Numitor, paid for his crime,
    The band of shepherds was led by the twins in tandem.
To both the time looked ripe to unite the rustics, to found
    A city; the question remained: which brother would found that city?
"No need for a fight to decide the issue," said Romulus:
    "Much faith is put in the birds: let us then try the birds."
All approved, and one to the cliff of the wooded Palatine went
    at dawn to watch for birds, and the other climbed to the Aventine.
Remus saw six, but his brother a dozen. The twins' agreement
    Remained, and Romulus received the rule of the city.
A fitting day was chosen for him to plough the walls;
    When the festival of Pales arrived, the work began.

Ovid, *Fasti* 4.809–820

3.4   The city observed a holiday called the Feast of Pales,
    The anniversary of the day when the walls of Rome first rose.

Propertius, *Elegies* 4.4.73–4

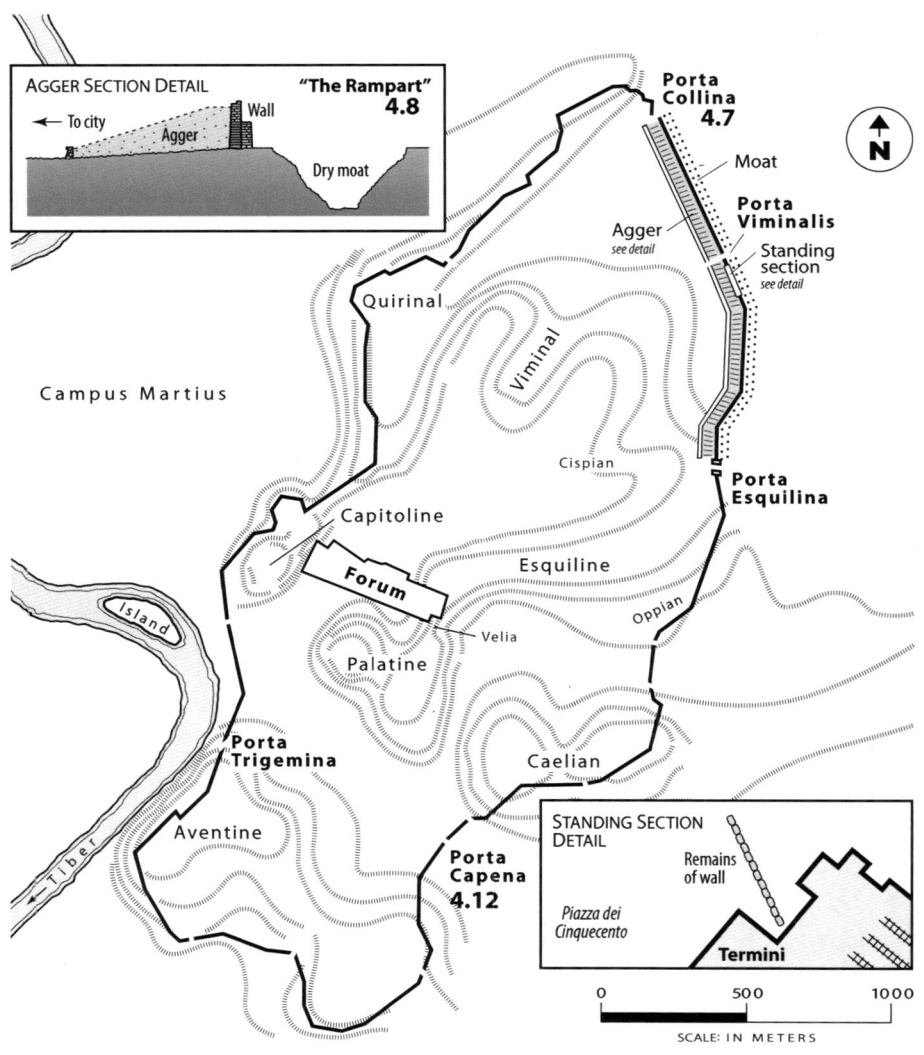

Fig. 6 Republican ("Servian") Walls

II. Walls and Aqueducts

4. The Republican Walls

COMMENTARY

Although Rome must have had some defenses from its very beginning, around the Palatine, which Livy and others attribute to Romulus's foundation, and certainly around the Capitoline Hill, which became Rome's last-stand defensive position, the Romans attributed the monumental Republican walls that enclosed all or part of all the major hills of the city to King Servius (dated traditionally to 578–534 BC), and these walls are often still called the "Servian" walls. The quotation marks, however, indicate a major failing of the literary record that the archaeological record can with some certainty correct. The key archaeological evidence concerns the primary stone of the Republican walls: their yellowish gray tufa (Grotta Oscura) comes from quarries of Veii, which would have been available only after Rome had conquered this town in 396 BC. The Gallic invasion a few years later (hardly time for such a wall to have been planned and built in the interim) no doubt provided a good impetus for the building of a massive and comprehensive wall to replace, and in places perhaps link together, the former defenses built at various times (the sources are conflicted) by a number of kings.

Perhaps Livy's reference [4.6] to repairs in cut stone in 377 BC could be a reflection of what was in reality the much more massive project of the Republican walls. At any rate, eleven kilometers in circumference, the Republican walls provided useful if increasingly decrepit protection into the C1 AD, by which time the borders of the empire were so distant and the threat of invasion so minimal that the capital was secure without them. In earlier centuries, however, they served not only to dissuade Rome's enemies from attack in the first place, but kept out her deadliest enemy Hannibal, who otherwise had both the means and the will to destroy the city. Livy's account of Hannibal at the gates of Rome, with its great story about the sale of the land where Hannibal was encamped [4.7], portrays in miniature the preparation, determination, and pride that saw Rome through this pro-tracted threat to its existence.

Much of the wall's exact course is uncertain, although stretches remain standing, including some significant ruins on the south side of the Aventine. The most interesting remnant of the Republican walls, however, is on display in front of the Termini train station (Fig. 6, in-sert). This section (the *Agger*, or "Rampart") was not freestanding, but part of a defensive system that, because unaided by any natural defen-sive escarpment of any sort for its run across the Esquiline, included a ditch on the outer side of it and a rampart on the inner side. The pas-sages from Juvenal and Horace show that this stretch of the wall was a popular place to stroll, no doubt for a fine view of the Sabine and Alban Hills as well as for the breezes on the top of the Rampart. Horace's "bleached bones" [4.8] is a reference to the mass graves that formerly occupied the land outside the walls here.

Of the many gates in the Republican walls, perhaps the most famous is Porta Capena, not only because it opened onto the "Queen of Roads," the Via Appia, but because Juvenal [4.12] and Martial [4.13] have given it character and identity: it was the "dripping Capena," due to the leaky channel of an elevated aqueduct (probably the Aqua Marcia) that crossed the valley between the Caelian and Aventine on top of or alongside the Republican wall.

SOURCES

4.1   [After gaining sole power] Romulus's first act was to build a wall around the Palatine, the place of his own childhood.

Livy, History 1.7.3

4.2   The first founders of Rome walled in the Capitoline, Palatine, and Quirinal Hills. ... The fourth king Ancus Martius extended the walls across the Caelian and Aventine Hills and the valley floor between them, ... and the sixth king Servius added the Esquiline and Viminal to Rome's walled area.

Strabo, Geography 5.3.7

4.3   [The census report undertaken by the king Servius in the C6 BC reported that 80,000 (sic) citizens lived in the city, many of them newcomers.] To address the needs of this population, it was clearly neces-sary to expand the city. Servius added two more hills—the Quirinal and the Viminal—and then enlarged the enclosed area of the Esquiline as well, where he himself took up residence to lend this quarter some status. He surrounded the city with rampart, trench, and wall, thus extending the pomerium.

Livy, *History* 1.44.3

4.4   Servius enlarged the city by the addition of two hills, the Viminal and the Esquiline. … This was the last king who enlarged the circuit of the city, adding two hills to the existing five … .

Today [c. 20 BC] the homes of the city spread far beyond the walls, unprotected and vulnerable to attack, should an enemy come. Indeed, the extent of the city is deceptive for any observer trying to determine where it begins and where it ends, since the urban area is closely intertwined with the countryside around it and gives the impression that the city stretches on forever. If however you judge the size of the city from the circumference of the walls (not an easy thing to do, since buildings are now incorporated into the walls for much of their course, leaving visible however some traces of their ancient structure), Rome would appear to be not much larger than the walled section of Athens.

Dionysius, *Early Rome* 4.13.2–5

4.5   The section of the wall between the Esquiline and Colline gates [see Fig. 6, inset] has been made stronger by engineering. In front of the wall outside the city a trench was excavated one hundred feet wide at the narrowest point and thirty feet deep. The wall rises above this trench and is supported on the inside by an earthen rampart that is so high and wide that the wall cannot be shaken apart by battering rams or undermined by sapping. This portion of the walls is a little less than a mile long and is fifty feet wide [including the banked earth].

Dionysius, *Early Rome* 9.68.3–4

4.6   Additional debts were incurred by the poor [in 377 BC] when the censors contracted to build a wall of cut stone.

Livy, *History* 6.32.1

4.7   [As Hannibal approached the city with his army in 211 BC, the Senate and consuls deliberated.] They decided on the following plan: the consuls would place their camps near the Colline and Esquiline gates; Gaius Calpurnius, the city praetor, would take command of the Capitoline and Citadel fortifications; and the full Senate would remain in the Forum in case there was a sudden need for their deliberation.

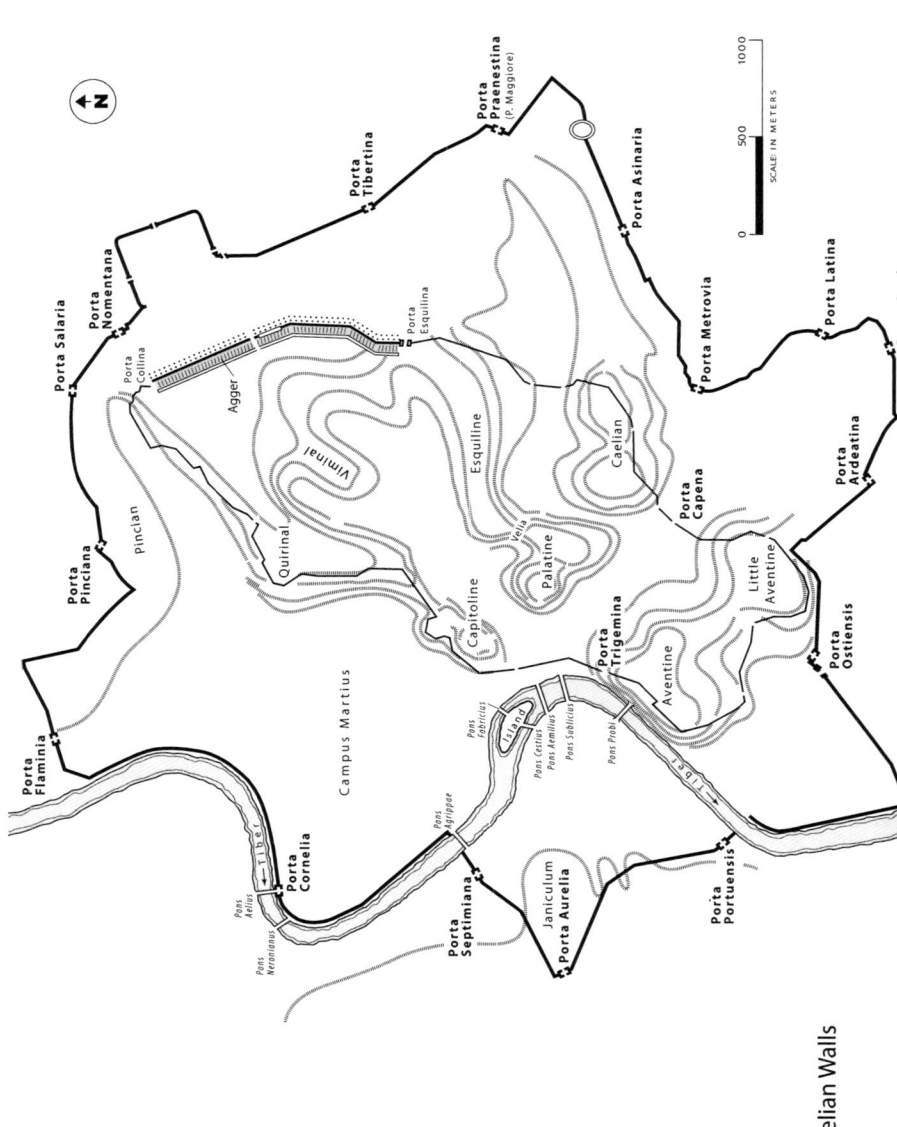

Fig. 7 Aurelian Walls

Hannibal, meanwhile, arrived at the Anio River and stationed a permanent camp there three miles from the city. Hannibal himself left camp with two thousand horse and rode towards the Colline gate, right up to the Temple of Hercules, and then rode along the walls as close as he could, studying the defenses and the terrain of the city. Hannibal's careful and leisurely review struck the consul Flaccus as such an insult that he sent out cavalry against him to drive the enemy back to their camp. …

A small incident soon occurred which helped to sap Hannibal's determination to take the city. He learned from a Roman who was taken prisoner that the very field upon which his army was encamped had just been sold to a new owner in the city, with no reduction in price.

Livy, *History* 26.10.2–5; 26.11.5–6

4.8 Today the Esquiline is wholesome enough for homes,
And one can stroll along the sunny Rampart, where lately
One gazed across a landscape littered with bleached bones.

Horace, *Satires* 1.8.14–16

4.9 [At dinner parties, the wealthy get served the choicest fruits]
While you're stuck with a rotten apple given to monkeys
Performing tricks on the Rampart in a shield and helmet …

Juvenal, *Satires* 5.153–4

4.10 [The rich go elsewhere to have their fortunes told]
But plebeian fates are told by the Circus and on the Rampart.

Juvenal, *Satires* 6.588

4.11 [You foolishly think that you yourself deserve some credit]
Because your mother glows with aristocratic blood
Instead of weaving for hire at the base of the windy Rampart.

Juvenal, *Satires* 8.43

4.12 When all my friend's possessions were packed on a single cart
He lingered by the ancient arcade and the dripping Porta Capena.

Juvenal, *Satires* 3.10–11

4.13 Where big drops rain from the Porta Capena…

Martial, *Epigrams* 3.47.1

5. The Aurelian Walls

COMMENTARY

By the middle of the third century AD, Rome was once again in need of a defensive wall, since the borders beyond the Alps and the

Fig. 8 Appia Gate in Aurelian Walls

defensive lines of northern Italy had become increasingly porous. The new walls, 19 km. in circumference and defending three times the area protected by the Republican walls (the course of which had been laid out for a much smaller city six centuries earlier, when the Campus Martius was little more than a field), were named after the emperor Aurelian, under whose principate they first arose starting in AD 271. The Aurelian walls were augmented in the early fourth century, probably by Maxentius, and more significantly under Arcadius and Honorius in the early fifth century, when their height was doubled from 8 to 16 m., with still higher square towers every 100 Roman feet (30 m.).

The Aurelian walls, with various modifications and repairs made over the centuries, continued to defend the city until Garibaldi breached Porta Pia in 1870. Significant stretches have been torn down since then, but two-thirds of their course is still standing. Major stretches exist either side of the Via Appia's Porta S. Sebastiano, which also houses a museum that provides access to the lower level of the walls.

SOURCES

5.1   Responding to the tribal invasions that occurred earlier under the Emperor Gallienus, the Emperor Aurelius expanded the walls of

Rome [in AD 271] after consulting with the Senate, although he did not enlarge the pomerium until a later date.

Imperial Lives, *Aurelian* 21.9

5.2   The Emperor Aurelian enlarged the walls of the city of Rome to such an extent that their circuit was nearly 50,000 feet.

Imperial Lives, *Aurelian* 39.2

5.3   Because our Illustrious [etc.] Emperors Arcadius and Honorius restored the walls, gates, and towers of the Eternal City [in AD 401] while removing massive quantities of rubble, as recommended by the distinguished … General Stilicho and carried out under the direction of the urban prefect … Longinianus, the Senate and the People of Rome set up these statues of the two emperors in lasting memory of their name.

ILS 797 = *CIL* 6.1189

5.4   Rome's new walls, built to the recent alarms of tribes
        That threatened our borders, have given a fresh young face to the city.
Thus was fear the father of beauty and a strange renewal:
        The city, grown old in peace, with war sloughed off its age,
Erecting sudden towers, rejuvenating all
        The seven hills of Rome with one continual wall.

Claudian, *On the Sixth Consulship of Stilicho*, 531–6 [AD 404]

6. The Pomerium

COMMENTARY

The pomerium was a line or band that marked the official limits of many Italian towns, including Rome—the town, however, considered not so much as an entity of brick and stone but as a ritually defined space inside which certain political, judicial, and religious behaviors and powers were allowed or forbidden.

The defensive walls of Rome did not necessarily coincide with its pomerium, but the foundation ritual and the etymologies (accurate or not) that Varro and others give to it, as well as Livy's description of the pomerium as the cleared space on either side of the city's defensive wall, all indicate that there was some ideal or original connection between the city's physical defense and its official augural limits. The Aventine, however, was within the Republican walls and yet not included within the pomerium until the time of Claudius, and several boundary stones designating Claudius's expansion of the pomerium were found north of today's Piazza del Popolo, far beyond the course of the Republican walls.

The most significant expansions of the pomerium can safely be attributed to Servius Tullius, Sulla, and Claudius, on the evidence of both the written and archaeological record. Sulla's expansion probably took in an additional swath of land on the Esquiline outside the Rampart. Since burial was forbidden inside the pomerium, Sulla's extension had the effect of reclaiming this area, which was notoriously unwholesome on account of its mass graves for the city's poor. Claudius's expansion, in addition to the Aventine, included much of the Campus Martius. The continued and subsequent presence of tombs and cremation sites in portions of the Campus Martius, as well as meetings of the military assembly (also forbidden inside the pomerium) suggest that certain parts of the Campus Martius lay outside of Claudius's expansion.

SOURCES

6.1 Many people in Latium founded towns using an Etruscan ceremony. In this rite, on an auspicious day in accordance with religious observance, they would yoke two cattle together, a bull and a cow, and plow a furrow around the town-to-be, with the plow folding earth to the inside so that they might be defended by both ditch and wall: the furrow was called the defensive ditch, and the turned-up earth on the inside represented the wall behind it. The ring created by this action was the limit of the city. Because this ring was outside the wall (*post murum*), it was called the "postmoerium," and it designates the outermost limits of the urban auspices.

Varro, The Latin Language 5.143

6.2 Those who look only at the word's etymological sense interpret the "pomerium" as being the strip "outside the walls" [*postmoerium*]. A better term would actually be "both sides of the wall" [*circamoerium*], since it is the space which the Etruscans, when founding cities, would ritually delimit on *both* sides of the wall that they intended to erect. The purpose of this was both to keep buildings away from the inside of the walls (although nowadays they are commonly even attached to the walls) and to preserve some space outside the wall cleared of cultivation.

Livy, History 1.44.4

6.3 Claudius also extended the pomerium of Rome [in AD 49], by an ancient custom whereby those who extended the empire might also expand the boundaries of the city. However, Rome's leaders, even those who greatly expanded the empire, had not availed themselves of this privilege, with the exception of Sulla and the deified Augustus.

The pomerium's expansion under the kings (whether in accordance with their vainglory or their true achievements) is variously reported, but I think that the beginning of Rome's foundation and the pomerium that Romulus established can be reliably traced as follows. From the point in the Forum Boarium where the bronze statue of the bull stands today (appropriately, since this is the species yoked to the ritual plow), a furrow was plowed to designate the city limits. It ran first to the Great Altar of Hercules [119.] and then along the base of the Palatine Hill, in a line preserved today by regularly spaced boundary stones. From here, the line extended to the Altar of Consus, then to the Old Assembly Grounds [*Curiae Veteres*] nearby, then to the Shrine of the Lares and on past the Roman Forum. Sources report that the Forum itself and the Capitoline Hill were not part of Romulus's original city but added by Titus Tatius. The pomerium was soon enlarged to keep pace with Rome's fortunes.

The boundaries of the pomerium as extended by Claudius are easy to recognize and also documented in the public records.

Tacitus, *Annals* 12.23-24

6.4   The Emperor Claudius, after expanding the boundaries of the Roman empire, extended and demarcated the pomerium [in AD 49].

ILS 213 = *CIL* 6.1231
(boundary stone near Monte Testaccio)

6.5   Lucius Sentius, son of Gaius, while praetor [in 83 BC] and in accordance with a decree of the Senate, oversaw the establishment of boundaries. May this act be propitious. It is forbidden to perform cremations inside the boundaries towards the city, or to dispose of dung or corpses here.

ILS 8208 = *CIL* 6.31614
(boundary stone near the Rampart)

6.6   It is forbidden that the Centuriate Assembly convene inside the pomerium, since an army can be commanded only outside the city; inside, there is no such right. Therefore the Centuriate Assembly is held in the Campus Martius.

Gellius, *Attic Nights* 15.27.5

6.7   On the meaning of "Pomerium": in the books that they have written about the auspices, the augurs of the Roman people define the pomerium in the following manner: "The pomerium is the area marked off from the surrounding fields by the augurs and ringing the entire city; it is behind the walls and limited by fixed boundaries. The pomerium forms the extent of the urban auspices." The oldest pomerium, established by Romulus, was limited to the base of the Palatine Hill. But this pomerium was extended several times as the Republic expanded, and it eventually surrounded many of the major hills. More-

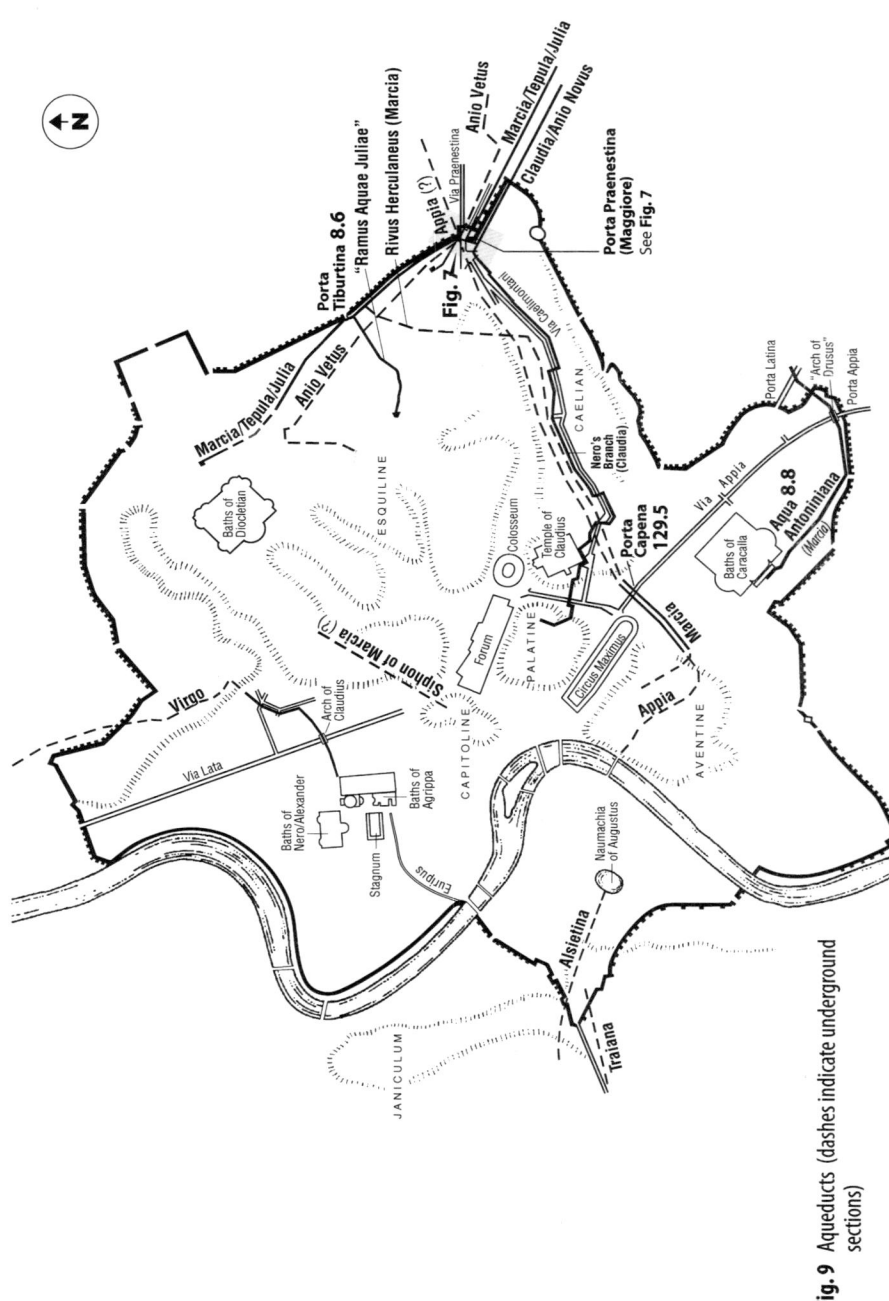

Fig. 9 Aqueducts (dashes indicate underground sections)

over, those who had increased the Roman people with the capture of land from the enemy had the right to extend the pomerium.

The question therefore arose—and still arises [in the C2 AD]—why, out of seven hills of the city, six lie within the boundaries of the pomerium and only the Aventine, which is neither far from the city nor sparsely populated, is excluded; also, why neither the king Servius Tullius, nor Sulla, who petitioned for permission to enlarge the pomerium, nor afterwards the deified Julius Caesar when he extended it, saw fit to enclose the Aventine within the augural boundaries of the city. ... I should however not pass up the following information about the Aventine which I found recently in the Commentary of the early grammarian Elys: there it is written that the Aventine was originally excluded from the pomerium, as I just mentioned, but was later incorporated inside it by the authority of the deified Claudius and has since then been regarded as lying within the augural boundaries of the pomerium.

Gellius, Attic Nights 13.14.1–4, 7

7. Rome's Aqueducts

COMMENTARY

The introductory passages by Pliny and Frontinus below suggest not only the engineering accomplishment of Rome's aqueducts—eventually 11 aqueducts totaling 500 kilometers, not including the elaborate and overlapping distribution network—but the passionate pride that the utilities of water supply and drainage could arouse in the Roman heart. Even the more sober and analytical Strabo ranks the aqueducts and sewers on par with the roads as Rome's greatest achievements.

The references to lead pipes by Ovid [7.5] and Vitruvius [7.6] support the archaeological findings, although most of the metal pipes in ancient Rome were eagerly scavenged and recycled by subsequent ages after the system fell apart. Ovid's striking simile (a water leak in a lead pipe = blood spraying from a wound) is a window into this poet's irreverent imagination as well as into the Roman world, combining a romantic Greek myth with an urban street scene and a Roman familiarity with spouting blood. In passing, however, it also illustrates an important feature of Roman aqueducts. After the water arrived in an open gravitational system (where it flowed in channels essentially as a stream with a cover) it entered an elevated water tank. From here the water ran under pressure in a closed system; pipes tapping the tank could take the water under streets and deliver it elsewhere to its original elevation. Although this pressure would have made it possible in lower neighborhoods to deliver water to upper stories of buildings, the Romans generally did not make use of this potential. Instead, water was made available at numerous public fountains, which, because of the pressurized plumbing, could be located at any elevation on any hill of the city, while many of the water mains could be buried beneath the streets.

Vitruvius's note of caution about the use of lead pipes for drinking water is interesting in light of modern concerns. In fact, the modern practice of using valves and stop-cocks, which lets the water sit in the pipes when not in use, only aggravates the problem. Although the ancient Romans occasionally used stop-valves, aqueduct water was generally left to run continuously through public and private fountains. As a result, their drinking water, even when it ran through lead pipes (as it often did), rarely paused to absorb the lead. In addition, Rome's water is heavy with minerals that quickly coated the pipes with deposits that acted like a sealant against the lead.

SOURCES

7.1   If anyone should carefully calculate the abundance of waters in Rome's public fountains, baths, pools, open canals, homes, gardens, and suburban estates, or the miles of delivery channels, the tall arcades, the tunnels under mountains and bridges across valleys, he would admit that there is nothing on earth more worthy of our wonder.

Pliny the Elder, *Encyclopedia* 36.123

7.2   [Frontinus has just finished his summary of the nine aqueducts that had been completed when he wrote his treatise in AD 97.] To so many indispensable structures of so many aqueducts compare, if you like, the idle pyramids or the many famous but useless monuments of the Greeks!

Frontinus, *Aqueducts* 16

7.3   [As a result of work carried out under the emperor Nerva in AD 97,] throughout the entire city most of the public water basins, new and old alike, have two supply lines coming from two different aqueducts. This way, a disruption to one of the aqueducts does not suspend service to the basin, which can be supplied by the back-up line.

The city herself, queen and mistress of the world, "Goddess of lands, who has no equal and no second," senses daily this devotion of her most dutiful Emperor Nerva, and the health of the Eternal City will improve on account of this increase in the number of tanks, supply lines, fountains, and basins. The benefits are spread among private individuals as well, due to an increase in the emperor's grants of water; those who once stole the water in fear can now enjoy it legally as a result of such grants. Not even waste water goes unused, channeled to flush away the sources of the city's once oppressive atmosphere.

The streets have a cleaner look, the air is purer, and the odor for which Rome was infamous in days gone by has vanished.

Frontinus, *Aqueducts* 87, 88

7.4 Whereas the Greeks have the reputation for choosing good sites for their cities, giving priority to natural beauty, natural defenses, harbors, and fertile soil, the Romans provided for matters little regarded by the Greeks: the paving of roads, water supply, and sewers able to wash the refuse of the city into the Tiber. Because their long-distance roads make use of rock-cuts through hills and of artificial embankments across hollows, the wagons that use them can carry as much freight as a ferry-boat, and their sewers, vaulted with cut stone, are in some places large enough to give passage to a hay wagon. As for water, the aqueducts deliver such quantities that rivers of it flow through the city and its sewers, and almost every habitation has cisterns, piping, and running fountains.

Strabo, *Geography* 5.3.8

7.5 [Thinking, wrongly, that his lover Thisbe was dead,]
    Pyramus grabbed the sword at his waist and ran himself through,
Then quickly pulled the reeking steel from the mortal wound
    And stretched out on his back: the blood leapt skywards
Gushing the way a faulty pipe that's made of lead,
    When cracked, will shoot a jet of water out a slender
Hissing hole, spraying the air with its pulsing pressure.

Ovid, *Metamorphoses* 4.119–124

7.6 Ceramic water pipes have the following advantages over lead pipes. First, if some defect is found in the work, it can be fixed by anyone. In addition, the water in ceramic pipes is much more wholesome than water that has run through lead pipes. A probable indication of lead's unhealthy effect on water is the toxic effect that cerussa (a white pigment made from lead) is said to have on human bodies. …

We can find further evidence for lead's harmful effects in the pale complexions of the people who make the lead pipes. The vapors that rise from lead when it is poured…rob the blood's strength from the limbs of the workers.

It would seem, therefore, that water should not be conducted in lead pipes if purity is a concern.

Vitruvius, *Architecture* 8.6.10–11

8. Rome's Individual Aqueducts and Frontinus

COMMENTARY

Aqueducts were a distinguishing feature of most Roman cities, one that was vital to basic needs, to social customs such as public bathing, and to displays of patronage. Rome, however, was exceptional for the complexity and size of its system. Extensive aqueduct archaeology in the last hundred years has revealed or elucidated a good part of the course of most of Rome's aqueducts (rendered obscure because aqueducts ran underground for most of their length), but we are also fortunate to have a remarkable account of the city's aqueducts written by Frontinus, a Roman senator who was appointed water commissioner in AD 97. Frontinus provides valuable information on numerous facets of the aqueducts, including the history, course, volume, elevation, and distribution network of the nine individual aqueducts that existed in his day (the Traiana and Alexandrina aqueducts had not yet been built), as well as information about the administration, laws, and maintenance of the aqueducts.

Inscriptions also testify to the need for the continual maintenance of the aqueducts, some of which, under the patronage of the Popes, continued running long after the western empire collapsed (wrongly, numerous modern accounts have all the high-level aqueducts falling into disuse after the Goths besieged the city in the C6 AD [8.24]). One aqueduct, the largely underground Aqua Virgo, never fully ceased running and provides water to fountains in the Campus Martius today, as testified by reliefs decorating the facade above Trevi Fountain, the terminus of the channel today.

Three of the inscriptions in the sources below [8.16–8.18] can be found at Porta Maggiore (Figs. 11 and 12), which is by far the best urban site to visit for an understanding and view of the ancient aqueducts. Called a "Gate" because it was incorporated in the Aurelian Wall in AD 271, for several centuries before the wall's construction this site was simply a monumental road-crossing for two high-level aqueducts, one riding on top of the other on a single arcade. A right-angle jog in the aqueduct where it turned to cross the ancient Via Labicana and Praenestina roads provided the opportunity to create a sort of triumphal arch to the conquest of nature and its conqueror, the emperor Claudius. The two channels of these aqueducts (the Aqua Claudia and Aqua Anio Novus) can be seen in cross-section running through the travertine attic over the roadways. The upper two inscriptions refer to repairs that for some reason needed to be carried out shortly after they were finished [8.17, 8.18].

Although there are impressive remains of the Claudia further out of town (especially at Romavecchia, near Cinecittà), nothing else remains to be seen of it and the Anio Novus in downtown Rome.

Nero, however, added an urban branch line to the Claudia, and notable ruins of this arcade [Fig. 13] can be tracked across the Caelian towards the Palatine, starting with the massive brick arcade abutting Porta Maggiore. This section has been heavily reinforced by later construction, including one in AD 201: "The Emperor Severus and Caracalla [etc.], at their own expense, repaired the Caelian Hill arches from the ground up, which in many places were weak and collapsing from age" (*ILS* 424). In addition, a remnant of the Aurelian wall flanking the Porta Maggiore preserves a cross-section of the Aqua Marcia with Tepula and Julia channels placed atop it (see Fig. 11). The lower, brick aqueduct boring through Porta Maggiore below the Claudia is the Acqua Felice, a papal aqueduct of the late 16th century.

In all, eight of Rome's eleven aqueducts (two of them below ground-level) approached Rome at or near Porta Maggiore. The four longest carried water from the Anio (today's Aniene) valley between Tivoli and Subiaco. In his summations below of each aqueduct's statistics, Frontinus gives the distance for each aqueduct under three categories: underground channel, elevated arches, and substructure (a solid wall, used for above-ground stretches of low elevation). From these figures, it is readily apparent that the Romans preferred underground channels to the more spectacular arcades that spring to mind when one imagines a Roman aqueduct.

[On the measurement of distances: 1,000 paces equals a Roman mile, which is about 100 yards shorter than an English mile.]

SOURCES

8.1   For 441 years after the Founding of the City [until 312 BC] the Romans were content to use what water they could draw from the Tiber, from wells, or from springs. The reverence for old springs exists to this day, since they are believed to restore health to ailing bodies, such as the springs of the Camenae [129.] … and of Juturna. Today [in AD 97], however, the following aqueducts bring water to Rome: the Appia, the Anio Vetus, the Marcia, the Tepula, the Julia, the Virgo, the Alsietina (also called the Augusta), the Claudia, and the Anio Novus.

Frontinus, Aqueducts 4

The Aqua Appia

8.2   In the consulship of Marcus Valerius Maximus and Publius Decius Mus [in 312 BC], the Aqua Appia was led into the city by Appius Claudius Crassus (later known as "the Blind") while he was censor – the same man who was in charge of building the Appian Way from the Porta Capena all the way to the city of Capua. …

The Appia takes its water from the Lucullan fields along the Via Praenestina … . The channel, from its source to its destination at the Salinae (near the Porta Trigemina), is 11,190 paces, 11,130 of which are underground; the remaining 60 paces are above ground on sub-structure and arches near the Porta Capena.

Frontinus, Aqueducts 5

The Anio Vetus (the "Old Anio Aqueduct")

8.3 [In 272 BC] forty years after the Aqua Appia was built, … the censor Manlius Curius Dentatus contracted for the Anio aqueduct (now called the "Old" Anio), which was paid for with the booty from the war with Pyrrhus. …

The Anio Vetus begins above Tivoli at the twentieth milestone beyond the [… ? name missing] Gate, where it supplies some of its water to Tivoli. The Anio Vetus is 43,000 paces long (winding a great deal to follow a gradient); 42,779 paces are below ground, and 221 above ground on substructure.

Frontinus, Aqueducts 6

The Aqua Marcia

8.4 [In 144 BC,] one hundred and twenty-seven years after the Anio Vetus was built, … the Senate, seeing that the Appia and Anio Vetus aqueducts were damaged by age and losing much of their water to ille-gal usage by private individuals, commissioned Marcius, who was a praetor for civilian cases at the time, to repair these aqueducts and reclaim their water. In addition, since the intervening growth of Rome was now judged to require a greater supply of water, the Senate charged him with the task of building another aqueduct. Marcius fixed the pre-vious two, and built a third with greater volume, which was named the Aqua Marcia after him. Fenestella [c. AD 20] tells us that Marcius was allotted 180,000,000 sesterces for the job … . At that time the Board of Ten, checking the Sibylline Books on another matter, are said to have found a prohibition against taking the waters of the Marcia (or the Anio, in a more common account) on to the Capitoline Hill … but each time the case was argued, Marcius Rex won, and water was chan-neled to the Capitoline.

The Marcia has its source at the 36th milestone of the Via Valeria, 3,000 paces down a side road to the right (as you come from Rome). It is 61,710 ½ paces long, 54,247 ½ of it below ground. Of the 7,463 paces above ground, 463 are on arches in the many places where the channel crosses valleys far from the city; closer to town, beginning at the 7th milestone, substructures carry the channel for 528 paces, and arches carry the channel for the remaining 6,472 paces.

Frontinus, Aqueducts 7

8.5 I restored the aqueduct channels that were collapsing from age in many places, and doubled the volume of the water called the Marcia by adding a new spring to its channel.

Augustus, *Achievements 20*

Note: The following three inscriptions can all be found at Porta Tiburtina/ S. Lorenzo, along the north side of the Termini train station. Here the channel of the Marcia crossed the road to Tivoli on a monumentalized archway that (like the Porta Maggiore, though much smaller) was later incorporated into the Aurelian Wall.

8.6   IMP. CAESAR DIVI IULI F. AUGUSTUS / PONTIFEX MAXIMUS COS. XII / TRIBUNIC. POTESTAT. XIX IMP. XIIII / RIVOS AQUARUM OMNIUM REFECIT.

The Emperor Augustus, son of the deified Julius, Pontifex Maximus, consul for the 12th time [etc.] repaired the channels of all the aqueducts [in 4 BC].

ILS 98 = *CIL* 6.1244

8.7   IMP. TITUS CAESAR DIVI F. VESPASIANUS AUG. PONTIF. MAX. / TRIBUNICIAE POTESTAT. IX IMP. XV CENS. COS. VII DESIG. IIX P. P. / RIVOM AQUAE MARCIAE VETUSTATE DILAPSUM REFECIT / ET AQUAM QUAE IN USU ESSE DESIERAT REDUXIT.

[In AD 79] the Emperor Titus [etc.] rebuilt the old and ruined channel of the Aqua Marcia and restored its water, which had ceased to run.

ILS 98 = *CIL* 6.1246

8.8   IMP. CAES. M. AURELLIUS ANTONINUS PIUS FELIX AUG. PARTH. MAX. / BRIT. MAXIMUS PONTIFEX MAXIMUS / AQUAM MARCIAM VARIIS KASIBUS IMPEDITAM PURGATO FONTE EXCISIS ET PERFORATIS / MONTIBUS RESTITUTA FORMA ADQUISITO ETIAM FONTE NOVO ANTONINIANO / IN SACRAM URBEM SUAM PERDUCENDAM CURAVIT.

[In AD 212] the Emperor Caracalla Antoninus [etc.] restored the Aqua Marcia, which had been disrupted by various damages, to the sacred city of Rome, after its source had been cleansed, mountains cut away and tunneled under, and its arcade rebuilt. In addition, he linked a new spring to the Marcia, the Fons Antoninianus.

ILS 98 = *CIL* 6.1245

The Tepula and the Julia

8.9   [In 127 BC] the censors Gnaeus Servilius Caepio and Lucius Cassius Longinus ... had the water called the Tepula brought from the Lucullan estates to Rome and the Capitoline. The Tepula has its source at the tenth milestone of the Via Latina, 2,000 paces down a side road to the right.

Agrippa, when aedile [in 33 BC], tapped new sources of water out by the twelfth milestone of the Via Latina, down a side road 2,000 paces to the right. This new channel, named the Julia by its builder, intercepted and took on the waters of the Tepula, but since the separate distribution system of the Tepula remained intact, so did its name.

… In the same year Agrippa restored the Appia, Anio Vetus, and Marcia aqueducts, which had almost fallen out of commission from disrepair, and with extraordinary devotion to duty he supplied the city with a great number of fountains.

Frontinus, *Aqueducts* 8, 9

The Aqua Virgo

8.10 [In 19 BC,] thirteen years after constructing the Aqua Julia, Agrippa … also built the Aqua Virgo, which (like the Tepula) began on the Lucullan estates and ended in Rome. … It was named the Virgo ["The Maiden"] because a young girl pointed out some springs to Agrippa's soldiers who were out looking for water sources. When the men dug deeper here, they discovered a huge supply of water. In the little shrine next to these sources, a painting illustrates this event.

The sources of the Virgo are at the 8th mile of the Via Collatina, in a marshy area where a cement enclosure has been built to collect the gushing springs. These sources are augmented by many other feeder lines along the way. The Aqua Virgo is 14,105 paces long; of these, 12,865 paces of the channel are below ground. The remaining 1,240 paces above ground are divided into 540 paces on substructure at several places and 700 paces on arches. …

The arches of the Virgo begin below the Gardens of Lucullus and end in the Campus Martius in front of the Voting Pens.

Frontinus, *Aqueducts* 10, 22

8.11 When he was aedile, Agrippa, besides adding the Aqua Virgo as well as repairing and augmenting existing aqueducts, built 700 basins, 500 fountains, and 130 distribution tanks (many of which were beautifully decorated), and adorned these installations with 300 bronze or marble statues and 400 marble columns. [Note: perhaps these columns refer to the boundary stones that marked the underground course of the aqueducts.]

Pliny the Elder, *Encyclopedia* 36.121

Note: The following inscription can be found on the travertine arches of the Virgo visible from Via Nazzareno, off Via del Tritone, behind the Bar Accademia. The arches proceed, now hidden by buildings, to the Trevi Fountain. A sculptural relief on the upper right side of the Trevi facade illustrates the story told by Frontinus in 8.10.

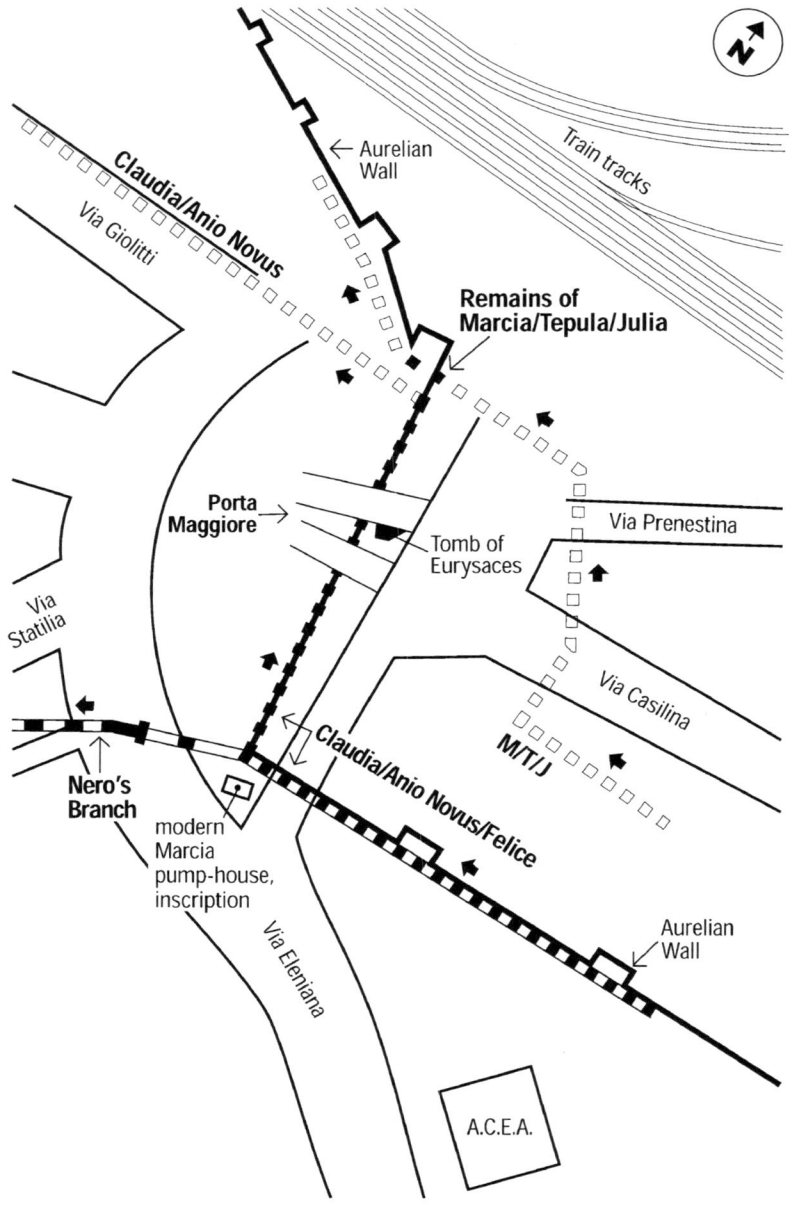

Fig. 11 Aqueducts at Porta Maggiore (ruins in bold)

Fig. 12 Porta Maggiore (an aqueduct road-crossing)

8.12 TI. CLAUDIUS DRUSI F. CAESAR AUGUSTUS GERMANICUS /
PONTIFEX MAXIM. TRIB. POTEST. V IMP. XI P.P. COS. DESIG. IIII /
ARCUS DUCTUS AQUAE VIRGINIS DISTURBATOS PER C. CAESAREM
/ A FUNDAMENTIS NOVOS FECIT AC RESTITUIT.

[In AD 46] the Emperor Claudius [etc.] rebuilt, from their foundations up, the arches of the Aqua Virgo that had been wrecked by his
predecessor Caligula.

ILS 205 = *CIL* 6.1252

The Alsietina

8.13 Whatever reasoning led Augustus, who was otherwise an emperor of careful planning, to build the Alsietina aqueduct escapes my
understanding. This water (also called the Augusta) has nothing to
recommend it, and is in fact of such poor quality that it is not distributed for public consumption. Perhaps Augustus, when building his
Naumachia [an artificial pond for mock sea-battles], did not want to
divert any wholesome water to fill it and therefore built a separate
aqueduct to supply it, granting the surplus water to adjacent gardens
and for private use in irrigation. Nevertheless, whenever the bridges
across the Tiber are being repaired and the aqueduct channels relying
on these bridges cease delivery across the river, out of necessity water
from the Alsietina is used to supply the drinking fountains in the
Transtiber region.

Fig. 13 Channel of Nero's Aqueduct

The source of the Aqua Alsietina is Lake Alsietinus, at the four-teenth milestone of the Via Claudia, six and one-half miles down a side-road to the right. The channel is 22,172 paces long, with 358 paces on arches.

Frontinus, Aqueducts 11

The Claudia and Anio Novus

8.14 [In AD 38,] in the second year of his reign, the Emperor Caligula, who had succeeded Tiberius, began construction on two new aque-ducts after it was apparent that the seven existing channels were no longer sufficient for public need and private luxury. His successor Claudius completed these aqueducts magnificently and dedicated them in the consulship of Sulla and Titianus [in AD 52]. One of the aque-ducts is called the Claudia, which delivers water from the Caerulean and Curtian springs, and which rivals the Marcia in purity. The other line built by Claudius and the highest of all the aqueducts has come to be known as the Anio Novus [the "New" Anio], since it is the second aqueduct to derive water directly from the Anio River. The former Anio aqueduct has subsequently become known as the Anio "Vetus" [the "Old" Anio], to distinguish the two more readily.

The sources of the Aqua Claudia are at the 38th milestone of the Via Sublacensis, within 300 paces down a side-road to the left. Here there are two large and beautiful pools of spring water, the Caeruleus ["Sky-Blue"] named for its color, and the Curtius. It also taps a spring called the Albudinus, which is of such purity that whenever the Aqua Marcia system needs to be supplemented, the addition of the Albudinus does not diminish the Marcia's quality. ...

The channel of the Claudia is 46,406 paces long, of which 36,230 are underground. Of the 10,176 paces above ground, 3,076 are on arches at various points in the upper portion of the route; near town, starting at the seventh milestone, 609 paces are on substructures and 6,491 on arches.

The Anio Novus is taken from the river at the forty-second milestone of the Via Sublacensis in Simbruine territory. Since the Anio flows through cultivated fields with rich soil, its banks erode quite easily, and as a result the stream flows muddy and turbid even without the added disturbance of rains. A settling tank was therefore constructed before the intake of the channel, where the water could form a still pool and clarify itself. Even so, whenever rainstorms pass over, unclear water is delivered to the city. ...

The channel of the Anio Novus has a length of 58,700 paces, of which 49,300 are underground. Of the 9,400 paces above ground, 2,300 are on substructures and arches at various points in the upper portion of the route; near town, starting at the seventh milestone, 609 paces are on substructures and 6,491 on arches. These are the highest arches, rising to a height of 109 feet in some places.

Frontinus, *Aqueducts* 13–15

8.15 The public works carried out by the Emperor Claudius are notable more for their size and usefulness than for their quantity. Among the most notable are the completion of the aqueducts begun by Caligula, the drainage tunnel for the Fucine Lake, and the harbor at Ostia. ... He conducted to Rome on stone arches both the Claudia's cold abundant springs (one called the Caeruleus and the other the Curtius and Albudignus) and the channel of the Anio Novus, and he distributed their waters in numerous basins of great beauty.

Suetonius, *Claudius* 20

Note: The following inscriptions are prominently displayed on the attic of Porta Maggiore (see above, and Fig. 12).

8.16   TI. CLAUDIUS DRUSI F. CAISAR AUGUSTUS GERMANICUS PONTIF. MAXIM., / TRIBUNICIA POTESTATE XII, COS. V, IMPERATOR XXVII, PATER PATRIAE, / AQUAS CLAUDIAM EX FONTIBUS, QUI VO-CABANTUR CAERULEUS ET CURTIUS A MILLIARIO XXXXV, / ITEM ANIENEM NOVAM A MILLIARIO LXII SUA IMPENSA IN URBEM PERDUCENDAS CURAVIT.

[In AD 52] the Emperor Claudius [etc.] had the waters of the Claudia brought to Rome from the springs called Caeruleus and Curtius at the 45th milestone, and likewise the Anio Novus from the 62nd milestone, both at his own expense.

ILS 218 = *CIL* 6.1256

8.17   IMP. CAESAR VESPASIANUS AUGUST. PONTIF. MAX. TRIB. POT. II IMP. VI COS. III DESIG. IIII P. P. / AQUAS CURTIAM ET CAERULEAM PERDUCTAS A DIVO CLAUDIO ET POSTEA INTERMISSAS DILAPSASQUE / PER ANNOS NOVEM SUA IMPENSA URBI RESTITUIT.

[In AD 71] the Emperor Vespasian [etc.] restored to the city at his own expense the Curtian and Caerulean waters, which had been led to the city by the deified Claudius but had fallen into intermittent use and disrepair for nine years.

ILS 218 = *CIL* 6.1257

8.18   IMP. T. CAESAR DIVI F. VESPASIANUS AUGUSTUS PONTIFEX MAXIMUS TRIBUNIC. / POTESTATE X IMPERATOR XVII PATER PATRIAE CENSOR COS. VIII / AQUAS CURTIAM ET CAERULEAM PERDUCTAS A DIVO CLAUDIO ET POSTEA / A DIVO VESPASIANO PATRE SUO URBI RESTITUTAS CUM A CAPITE AQUARUM A SOLO VETUSTATE DILAPSAE ESSENT NOVA FORMA REDUCENDAS SUA IMPENSA CURAVIT.

[In AD 81] the Emperor Titus [etc.] at his own expense, had the Curtian and Caerulean waters, introduced by the deified Claudius and afterwards repaired for the city by Titus's deified father Vespasian, restored with new structures, beginning from its source, after the aqueduct was ruined to its foundations from age.

ILS 218 = *CIL* 6.1258

Elevations of the Aqueducts

8.19   All the aqueducts reach the city at different elevations, such that some can deliver water to the higher quarters and others cannot (the hills too have gradually grown higher from the rubble of so many fires). Five of the channels are high enough to reach all parts of the city, but some with greater pressure behind them than others. The highest is the Anio Novus, followed in descending order by the Claudia, the Julia, the Tepula, and the Marcia. The sources of the Marcia are in fact the same elevation as the Claudia, but the earlier builders of aqueducts laid them at a lower level, either because they had not yet fully mastered the art of surveying, or because they purposely laid the channels below the ground so that they would be less readily cut by enemies, since the Romans then still waged frequent wars against the Italians. Today, however, there are places where, whenever the old channel is ruined by age, the new channel abandons its circuitous subterranean route and crosses over a valley on substructures and arches to shorten its route.

Seventh in height is the Anio Vetus, which likewise could have supplied the higher elevations of the city if it had been supported by substructures or arches in the places required by valleys and lower elevations. Next in height are the Virgo and the Appia; because these two originate in the fields not far from Rome, their elevation is limited from the start. The lowest line of all is the Alsietina, which supplies the Transtiber region and other low-lying locales.

Six of these aqueducts empty into covered settling basins this side of the seventh milestone on the Via Latina, where they take a fresh breath after their run, so to speak, and deposit their load of impurities. Here too the amount of their water is measured with gauges inside the basins. Three of the aqueducts—the Julia, Marcia, and Tepula— continue the journey after the basin on the same arches, one channel on top of the other. The highest of the three is the Julia, with the Tepula and then the Marcia below it.

After the settling basin the Anio Novus and the Claudia are carried together on the same arches (these higher than the triple-decker just mentioned), with the Anio Novus on top of the Claudia. This arcade ends behind the Gardens of Pallas, and from here their waters are distributed by pipes for use in the city. Just before this terminus, however, near the Temple of Ancient Hope, the Claudia diverts a portion of its water down another channel called the Neronian Arches [Fig. 13]. These arches extend along the Caelian Hill to end near the Temple of the Deified Claudius, and deliver water to the Caelian Hill itself as well as to the Palatine and Aventine Hills and the Transtiber quarter.

Frontinus, *Aqueducts* 18–20

Aqueduct Maintenance and Regulations

8.20 A few words should be said about the team of slaves assigned to the maintenance of the aqueducts. There are two of them, one the public's and the other Caesar's. The public body is older, bequeathed (as we said earlier) by Agrippa to Augustus, who handed it over to the state; it numbers about 240 slaves. The number of slaves on the

Emperor's team, which Claudius established when he built his aqueducts into the city, stands at 460.

Frontinus, *Aqueducts* 116

8.21   Many landowners who own fields along the route of the aqueducts illegally tap the channels, so that waters destined for public use end their journey in private hands, irrigating a garden.

Frontinus, *Aqueducts* 75

8.22   [Frontinus identifies and castigates various fraudulent practices that aqueduct workers engage in for money]. The income that the watermen collect for what they call "punctures" also has to stop. For long distances in several places, secret pipes run across the whole city under the pavement. I discovered that these pipes (which had been tapped in numerous places by a man called "The Puncturer") provided water to all the businesses along their routes, such that only a small amount of water got through for public needs. Just how much water has been saved in addressing this problem I judge from the considerable amount of lead pulled up in the eradication of the branch-lines of this sort.

Frontinus, *Aqueducts* 115

8.23   Damage to the aqueducts is frequently caused by the lawlessness of landowners, who injure the channels in a number of ways. First, they construct buildings or grow trees on the strip of land around or above the aqueduct that by senatorial decree should be kept vacant. Trees do the greater damage, since their roots break apart both the vaulted tops and the sides of the channels. People also build their village and country roads right down the track of an aqueduct. And recently, landowners have been denying maintenance workers right-of-way to the aqueducts. All of these problems have been anticipated in the following Senatorial Decree:

   "... [I]t has been resolved that a space of fifteen feet shall be kept clear on either side of aqueduct sources, walls, and arches; around the underground sections of aqueducts and around the conduit within the city or within the built-up area around the city, a space of five feet shall be kept clear on each side, such that no one is permitted from this time forward to erect a tomb or building in these zones, or to plant trees there. ... If anyone breaks these regulations, the fine will be 10,000 sesterces for each infraction, half of which will be paid to the person who brought the offense to notice, ... and half of which will be paid into the public treasury."

Frontinus, *Aqueducts* 126–7

Aqueducts and Goths

8.24   After the Goths had ringed Rome with their camps [in AD 537], they cut all the aqueducts so that as little water as possible might enter

the city. The aqueducts of Rome are fourteen [sic] in number, constructed long ago out of baked brick. Their channels are wide and tall
enough to ride through them mounted on a horse.

For his part, Belisarius [the commander of the imperial forces
being besieged by the Goths] arranged for the defense of the city. ...
He blocked as securely as possible each of the aqueduct channels with
stone walls, to prevent the enemy from entering the city by such a route.

Procopius, *Wars* 5.19.13,18

8.25   When the Goths wanted to damage the fortifications of Rome,
they first tried to gain entrance to the city by sending some men with
lamps and torches into one of the aqueducts at night, which had been
empty of water since the Goths cut them at the beginning of the war.
By chance, a guard stationed at the Pincian gate saw a glimmer of light
through a small crack in the channel where it ran along just above
ground level. He told some of the other guards, who said he must have
seen a wolf pass by and mistook the gleam of its eyes for a flame.

Meanwhile, the barbarians who were exploring the channel
reached the middle of the city and came upon an old passageway to
the surface, leading right up to a part of the Palatine Hill itself. A stone
wall, however, constructed as a precaution by Belisarius at the beginning of the siege (as I recounted earlier), blocked both their forward
progress and the passage leading to the surface. So they decided to turn
around, taking with them a small stone from the obstructing wall,
which they showed to their leader Vittigis when they returned and gave
their report.

On the following day, while the Gothic king Vittigis was busy
forming a plan with his chiefs, Roman soldiers guarding the Pincian
gate talked among themselves about the suspected sighting of the wolf.
When the story reached Belisarius, however, the general did not take
the matter casually, but immediately sent some of his best men, led by
his bodyguard Diogenes, down into the channel with orders to investigate everything at once. They found the lamps of the enemy and the
droppings of their torches all along the channel, as well as the gap in
the wall where the Goths had removed a stone. When Belisarius heard
their report, he personally assigned guards to keep the aqueduct channel under close watch. Learning of his precaution, the Goths gave up
this line of attack.

Procopius, *Wars* 6.9.1–11

Notes: For more on Roman aqueducts, see: P. Aicher, *Guide to the Aqueducts of Ancient Rome*; H. B. Evans, *Water Distribution in Ancient Rome: The Evidence of Frontinus*; A. T. Hodge, *The Roman Aqueducts and Water Supply*.

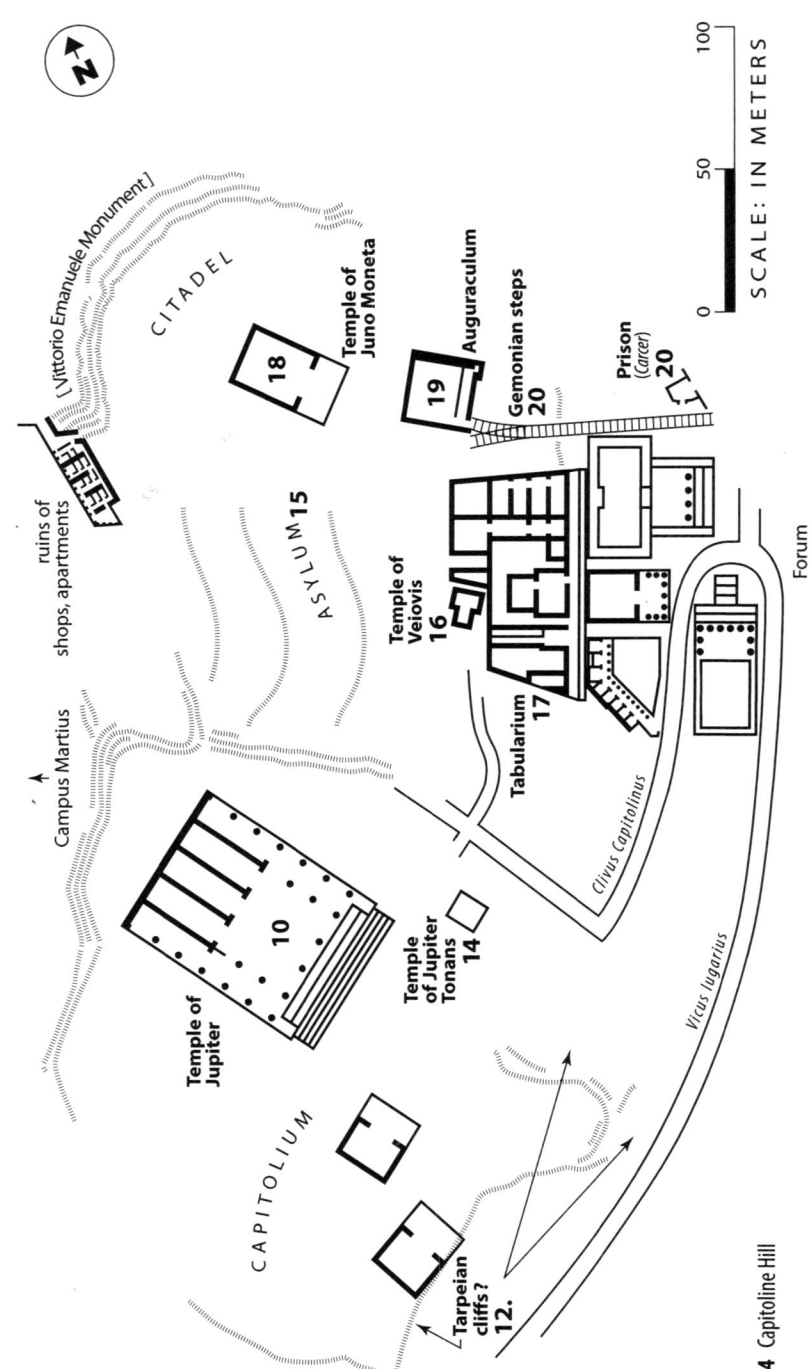

Fig. 14 Capitoline Hill

III. The Capitoline Hill

9. Overview of the Capitoline Hill

Although the smallest of Rome's seven hills in area, the Capitoline was in several important ways both the utilitarian and talismanic core of ancient Rome. Here were the early city's last-stand defensive walls as well as its chief place of contact with its tutelary imperial deity, Jupiter Optimus Maximus. Together with the hill's Asylum, the geography of the Capitoline gave topographical expression to the greatness of the state: the Temple, Asylum, and Arx respectively grounded Rome's power in the heavens, enabled and defined its means of growth, and guaranteed its survival. As such, the hill often stands in ancient literature for Rome itself [9.1 to 9.3], especially in its capacity to endure over time.

Each of the three parts into which the hill, in accordance with its contours, is traditionally divided contributes to this picture. The hill has two summits, separated by a saddle occupied now by the Piazza designed by Michelangelo. On the southwest summit above the Tiber, the great temple of Jupiter [10.] towered over the city and ultimately over the empire: "I have given the Romans rule without limit," runs the famous promise of Virgil's Jupiter (*Imperium sine fine dedi*). Appropriately, this temple was the destination point of a Roman military triumph, with the victorious general robed and painted like the cult statue of Jupiter himself.

The other summit, topped now by St. Maria d' Aracoeli, was sometimes distinguished from the rest of the hill as the Citadel (*Arx*) proper of the hill, although the fortifications of the hill circled the entire Capitoline Hill and not just the northeast end of it. Perhaps this end,

Fig. 15 Early Republican Rome (model at Museo di Civiltà Romana)

the slightly taller of the two, retained a more fortress-like character, in contrast to the eventually crowded platform of the other summit; calling it the Arx also served to highlight this vital function of the entire hill as the most difficult part of the city to capture, on account of the Capitoline's natural escarpments in some sections and fortifications in others. Livy's account of the Gallic sack of Rome [9.9] emphasizes the emotional significance of the uncaptured Capitoline as the vital core of the city. The northeast summit also contained the Auguraculum, another important site that like the Temple of Jupiter linked weighty matters of state to the divine order.

The third major area, the saddle between the two crests, contained the sacred area called the Asylum [15.]. Tradition had it that Romulus, in need of a larger population to fill his city, designated this area as the point of arrival for newcomers to Rome who wished to start over—a strategy, Livy comments, that was crucial to Rome's advancement and eventual greatness. The Asylum-legend is a parable for Rome's subsequent policy of enfranchisement, and this part of the Capitoline, which apparently remained a distinct and designated open space even in Imperial times, represented Rome's ability to grow—not, as was guaranteed by the great Temple of Jupiter, by expanding geographically under Jupiter's all-seeing eyes through the agency of Rome's generals, but by incorporating peoples of diverse origins in the protective grove of the Roman state.

As the scene of executions, the Capitoline also provided stark visual reminders of the community's ultimate power over citizens and conquered leaders, whether the condemned were pushed off the Tarpeian cliffs [12.], or strangled in the Prison [20.] at the foot of the hill, after which the corpse might be exposed to public view on the Gemonian Steps that led up to the Capitoline from the Forum.

Even in imperial times, crowded buildings around the Capitoline's base would have diminished the hill's earlier acropolis-like profile, and several millennia of subsequent erosion along with a compost of building-rubble many yards deep around its base have done the same. Institutional changes in imperial Rome also diminished the symbolic profile of the hill. With his new Forum, Augustus stole some of Jupiter's thunder, and he moved the Sibylline Books to the Palatine [63.], where the imperial palaces eventually established that hill as a rival to the Capitoline in locating the nucleus of Rome's power.

Even so, the Capitoline retained into modern times its special role in expressing civic power. It was here that the noble families in the Middle Ages established a city government and built a town hall as a response to Pope's power, and here Cola di Rienzo (whose statue stands on the grass between the Cordonata and Ara Coeli stairways) self-consciously invoked ancient Rome in his charismatic foundation of a short-lived republic in the 1300s. Here too beginning in the 1920s Mussolini would give speeches at elaborate ceremonies that celebrated with renewed fervor the birthday of ancient Rome on April 21. And here, in circumstances richly ironic in the context of ancient praises of the hill, was the setting of Gibbon's epiphany: "It was at Rome, on the fifteenth of October, 1764, as I sat musing amidst the ruins of the Capitol, while the bare-footed fryars were singing Vespers in the temple of Jupiter, that the idea of writing the decline and fall of the city first started to my mind." (*Autobiography*, 1897, p. 302)

SOURCES

9.1   I will not wholly die: in poems, much of me
Will avoid the Reaper. With future fame
I sprout up green, so long as Pontifex
And silent Vestal climb the Capitolium.

> **Horace,** *Odes* 3.30.6–9

9.2   Before the battle of Actium, wrong to uncork   [31 BC]
The ancestral cellar's vintage wine,
While crazy Cleopatra planned the Capitolium's
Destruction, and death to Roman rule.

> **Horace,** *Odes* 1.37.5–8

9.3   Cleopatra will fall, trusting too little in her Roman mate,
And vain will be her threat to make our Capitol
Bow down to her Delta.

> **Ovid,** *Metamorphoses* 15.826–8

9.4   The Capitoline Hill gets its name from the human head [*caput*] that they say was found when the foundations for the Temple of Jupiter were being excavated. Before then the hill was called Mt. Tarpeius, after the Vestal Virgin named Tarpeia, who was killed by Sabine shields and buried on the hill. A reminder of her name endures, since the cliff here is called the Tarpeian Rock.

> **Varro,** *The Latin Language* 5.41

9.5   [Centuries before Rome was founded] Evander led Aeneas
To the Tarpeian seat and the Capitoline—
All golden now, then bristling with wild brambles.
Even then the site inspired the countryfolk
With religious dread, and they shuddered at its woods and cliff.
"This grove, this hilltop crowned in leaf," Evander said,
"A god inhabits, we know not which:
Arcadians among us think they've seen
Jupiter himself on the hill, swirling again
His black mantle to summon up the storm."

> **Virgil,** *Aeneid* 8.347–354

9.6   "Tribunes of the plebs and fellow citizens of Rome," Scipio said [in 187 BC], "today is the anniversary of the day on which I fought a pitched battle in Africa against Hannibal and the Carthaginians at Zama [in 202 BC], emerging victorious. This is no time to engage in trials and legal wrangling. And so without delay I will leave the Rostra and climb the Capitolium to pay my respects to Jupiter Optimus Maximus, Juno, Minerva, and all the other gods who watch over the Capitolium and the Citadel, and I will give them thanks that on this date and on many others the gods have granted me the will and ability to carry out our nation's business with distinction."

Livy, *History* 38.51.7–10

9.7   On the Capitolium we can find a reminder and demonstration of early building styles in the House of Romulus, and on the Citadel, in the thatched roofs of shrines there.

Vitruvius, *Architecture* 2.1.5

9.8   Climb down the family tree of anyone you wish: at the bottom you will find a humble birth. Why go into individual instances when I can prove my point by calling as a witness the entire city of Rome: these hills were once entirely devoid of buildings. In fact, amidst all of today's towering structures, nothing is more respected than the humble hut of Romulus, even though the Temple of Jupiter shines out above it, gleaming with pure gold. Can you find fault in the Romans for displaying their humble origins, which today could easily be hidden, and for believing that nothing is great unless it appears to have started small?

Seneca the Elder, *Debates* 1.6.4

9.9   [The Gauls of northern Italy descended on Rome in 390 BC] Since there was no hope of defending the city from the Gauls with the small force now left to them, the Romans resolved that the young men of military age as well as the able-bodied senators would withdraw with their wives and children to the Citadel and the Capitoline; from this fortification, after stocking it with weapons and provisions, they might defend the gods, the people, and the name of Rome. ...

While Camillus was being appointed general by Romans in nearby Veii, the Citadel of Rome and the Capitolium fell into grave danger: the Gauls had found the footprints of the messenger from Veii who had made it through their lines, or perhaps had noticed on their own that the cliffs by the shrine of Carmentis favored an attempt there [by the Tiber, above the Temple of Fortuna at S. Omobono]. On a moonless night the Gauls sent up a few unarmed men to scout out a path, and then began their climb. Handing weapons up to others at the steep spots and bracing themselves on men below or bracing others in turn, they pushed and pulled their way up the mountain as the terrain demanded. They gained the summit so quietly that they not only escaped the detection of the watchmen but of the dogs as well, a creature attuned to nocturnal noise.

They did not, however, escape the notice of the geese on the hill. Because the geese were sacred to Juno, the besieged Romans, even when running out of food, had refrained from killing them. This religious observance proved to be Rome's salvation, for the sacred geese created such an uproar by honking and flapping their wings that they woke up Marcus Manlius, an outstanding soldier who had been consul three years earlier. Manlius grabbed his weapons and dashed outside, shouting for help. While other men hesitated in fear, Manlius dislodged a Gaul, just then reaching the summit, with one blow of his shield and sent him tumbling onto the men below. Terrified, the other attackers dropped their weapons and clung to the rock with both hands while Manlius went in for the kill. Soon other defenders joined him and routed the enemy with javelins and loose rocks, and the attack collapsed in total disaster for the Gauls as they were driven headlong from the cliffs. ...

[After the Gauls withdrew from Rome, the general Camillus gave a passionate speech to dissuade the Roman people from turning their backs on the charred ruins of Rome and resettling elsewhere: "Romans, do not abandon your city.] Here, and nowhere else, stands the Capitolium; it was here that the buried human head (*capite*) was discovered and judged an omen that the Capitoline would one day be the head of the world and the summit of an empire; here is the ground that, to the joy of your ancestors, the god of Youth and the god of Borders refused to abandon when the Capitolium was being deconsecrated with augural rites to make room for Jupiter."

Livy, *History* 5.39–54, *selections*

Notes: The terminology for the Capitoline Hill is somewhat protean. The Roman names for the Capitoline include Mons Saturnius, Mons Tarpeius, Capitolium, Mons Capitolinus, Collis Capitolinus, and Arx Capitolina (see *LTUR* 1, p. 226f.; Richardson, 378). In addition, the term Capitolium can refer to three things: the southwestern crest of the hill, the whole hill, and the Temple of Jupiter Optimus Maximus. The Area Capitolina was the leveled precinct around Jupiter's temple, containing other temples as well. On the Capitoline's significance in literature, see especially C. Edwards, *Writing Rome*.

10. The Temple of Jupiter Optimus Maximus

COMMENTARY

Of the more than a dozen temples to Jupiter in Rome which singled out this or that feature of the great god's aspect and domain, the temple of Jupiter "Best and Greatest," as its name leaves no doubt, was the most central and magnificent, looming over the heart of the city as the primary home of its presiding deity. Unfortunately, no monument exhibits a greater disparity between the splendor of its ancient appearance, as attested by the written record, and the paucity of the remains today. Parts of the massive tufa podium of the temple, however, are visible inside the Palazzo dei Conservatori which at least help situate the building, as does the corner of the podium on display outside in a little pit along the Via del Tempio di Giove. In addition to the imagination's work on the following sources, perhaps the best visual impression of the temple's profusion of sculpture, painting, marble decoration, and cult-objects in ancient times can be gathered from some of the lavishly appointed churches in Rome today, one of which (S. Maria della Pace, near Piazza Navona) does indeed display statues carved from the giant Pentelic marble columns of Jupiter's vanished temple.

SOURCES

10.1 Tarquinius Priscus [ruling 616–578 BC] undertook the construction of a temple to Jupiter, Juno, and Minerva, which he had vowed to the gods during his last battle against the Sabines. The hill on which he planned to place the temple needed a great deal of preparation, being neither accessible nor level, but rather precipitous and sharply peaked. Tarquinius surrounded the hill with high retaining walls and filled in the space between these walls and the summit to create a level platform able to support temples. He died, however, before he was able to lay the foundation for the Temple of Jupiter, outliving the end of the war by only four years. Many years later, Tarquinius Superbus, the second king after him (the one who was deposed) laid the foundations and built much of the structure, though he too did not complete it. ...

The Romans finished the Temple of Jupiter [in 507 BC] in the third consulship of the Republic. Built on a high podium, the perimeter of the temple is 800 feet. Each of its sides is about 200 feet; in fact, the length of the temple does not exceed the width by a full fifteen feet. Although rebuilt a generation ago after it burnt down [in 83 BC], it rests on the same foundations and differs from the old temple only in the costliness of its materials. The front of the temple, towards the south, has three rows of columns; there is a single row of columns down each side. Inside there are three chambers, although they are under one pediment and one roof. Each of the side chambers—one for Juno, and one for Minerva—shares a wall with the center one, which is dedicated to Jupiter.

Dionysius, *Early Rome* 3.69 and 4.61

10.2 After taking control of Gabii, Tarquinius Superbus [ruling 534–510 BC] made peace with the tribe of the Aequi and renewed the truce with the Etruscans. Then he turned his attention to urban concerns, the first of which was to leave behind him, as a monument to his own reign and name, the Temple to Jupiter on the Tarpeian mount. Both of Rome's Etruscan kings, he proclaimed, were responsible for the temple: the father, because he vowed it, and the son, because he completed it. In order that the whole area might be free from competing cult-sites, reserved for Jupiter and his temple alone, Tarquinius decided to deconsecrate the existing temples and shrines there which Tatius vowed earlier at a critical moment in his battle against Romulus, and which Tatius later consecrated and inaugurated.

At the very start of this project it is reported that the gods signi-fied their will assuring the solidity of the great empire to be. For al-though the birds gave signs approving of the deconsecration of all the other religious sites, they refused it in the case of the shrine of Terminus, the god of the Border. This divine omen was taken to mean that the immovability of Terminus, alone of all the gods in not vacating the site consecrated to him, portended that the realm would be strong and stable.

After this auspice of Rome's longevity, a second portent of the empire's greatness occurred: it is said that those digging the founda-tions of the temple to Jupiter came upon a human head with its features intact. This was a clear sign that this spot would be the citadel of the empire and the head of the world, and was interpreted thus by sooth sayers, both those residing in the city and those brought in from Etruria to consider the matter. ...

In his eagerness to finish the temple, Tarquinius Superbus summoned workmen from all parts of Etruria, and not only used public funds but levied extra work from the plebs on top of their military duty.

Livy, History 1.55–56.1

10.3 The first Temple of Jupiter Capitolinus, which was built by Tarquinius Superbus but consecrated by Horatius, burned down in the civil wars [in 83 BC]. Sulla built the second temple, but Catulus got the credit for its dedication. This temple was likewise totally destroyed, this time in the rebellion of Vitellius [in AD 69], after which Vespasian began and finished the construction of a third temple. ... Shortly after Vespasian died the Capitoline burned down again [in AD 80].

The fourth and present temple was both built and dedicated by Domitian [in AD 89]. ... Even the gilding alone of this temple's roof, costing more than 12,000 talents, is beyond the means of the richest private citizen in Rome today. Its columns were cut from Pentelic marble and were originally of beautiful proportions, as I saw for myself in Athens. When they were shaped and polished in Rome, however, they didn't gain as much in smoothness as they lost in symmetry and beauty, and now appear too thin and meager.

Plutarch, Publicola 15.1–4

10.4 In all of Roman history since the founding of the city, the burn-
ing of the Capitoline in the fighting between Vitellians and Flavians
[in AD 69] was the most distressing and disgraceful event that ever be-
fell the republic of the Roman people. Not by any external enemy, but
with the gods kindly disposed (if that were possible, given our behavior!), the very seat of Jupiter Optimus Maximus, which was founded
with good omen by our ancestors as our guarantee of empire, and which
neither Porsenna, when the city had been surrendered, nor the Gauls
when it had been captured, were able to desecrate, was now destroyed
by the madness of our emperors.

The temple was first vowed by King Tarquinius Priscus during the
war against the Sabines; he too laid the foundations of it, on a scale
that accorded more with the hope of future greatness than with the
modest means available to the Roman people at that time. Soon Servius
Tullius, with the aid of allies, and then Tarquinius Superbus, with spoils
gained from the capture of Suessa Pometia, constructed the building.
The honor of the work, however, was reserved for liberty, since only
after the kings were expelled did Horatius Pulvillus dedicate the temple
in his second consulship; since that time the immense wealth of the
Roman people has ornamented the temple's magnificence more than
it has increased it. After it burnt down 415 years later in the consulship of L. Scipio and C. Norbanus, the temple was rebuilt on the same
footprint. The victorious Sulla undertook the task of reconstruction, but
did not dedicate the new temple (in this alone Fortune failed him),
and the name of Lutatius Catulus endured among all the great monuments of Caesars down to the time of Vitellius.

Vespasian assigned the work of restoring the Capitolium to Lucius
Vestinus, a man of the equestrian class but among the leading men for
his authority and prestige. The haruspices employed by him warned
that the remains of the earlier temple should be carried away to the
swamps and that the new temple should have the same dimensions as
before: the gods did not want the old plan changed.

Tacitus, *Histories* 3.72; 4.53

10.5 [After the fire had destroyed the temple,] the Emperor Vespasian
himself played an active role in the restoration of the Capitoline.
He was the first person to begin the task of clearing away the rubble,
carrying off a load of it on his own shoulders. In addition, he undertook the reproduction of three thousand bronze tablets that had also
been destroyed in the fire, after a thorough search for other copies.
These tablets were very old and precious documents of Roman rule,
containing decrees of the Senate and votes of the people concerning
alliances, treaties, and privileges granted at anytime to anyone, dating
back almost to the beginning of the city.

Suetonius, *Vespasian* 8.5

10.6 With the exception of the Temple of Jupiter, whereby mighty Rome lifts itself into eternity, there is nothing more magnificent in all the world than the Serapeum in Alexandria.

Ammianus, *History* 22.16.12

10.7 There are five kinds of temples: ... of these, the araeostyle temple has columns more widely spaced than they should be. ... In the araeostyle temple it is not possible to use stone or marble architraves to span the columns; continuous wooden beams must be used. Moreover, the look of such temples is squat, top-heavy, low, and wide, and the pediment is ornamented in the Etruscan fashion with terra-cotta or gilt bronze statues. Such are the Temple of Ceres near the Circus Maximus, Pompey's Temple of Hercules, and the Capitoline Temple of Jupiter.

Vitruvius, *Architecture* 3.3.1, 5

10.8 As heard and reported by Varro, Catulus, who was in charge of rebuilding the Temple of Jupiter [after it burned in 83 BC], said that when he wanted to lower the ground level of the large foundational platform of the Capitoline so that more steps could lead up to the temple on a taller podium that corresponded better with the size of the pediment, the existence of subterranean rooms beneath the precinct prohibited this alteration. These were underground chambers and cisterns in which the Romans were accustomed to store old statues that had fallen off the temple and other religious items that were part of consecrated offerings.

Gellius, *Attic Nights* 2.10

10.9 Tarquinius Priscus summoned the sculptor Vulca from Veii to make the cult statue of the Capitoline Jupiter. The statue was made of terra-cotta, though commonly painted red with cinnabar. The four-horse chariot on the roof of the temple was also of terra-cotta.

Pliny the Elder, *Encyclopedia* 35.157

10.10 Wealth is more important now than for early Romans.
When the people were poor and Rome was new, Jupiter
Could barely stand up straight inside his humble temple,
And the thunderbolt his right hand held was made of clay.
Garlands were his decorations then, not gems.

Ovid, *Fasti* 1.197–203

10.11 The practice of coating ceilings with gold first began in Rome with the Capitolium, after the overthrow of Carthage [in 146 BC]. ... The contemporaries of Catulus held differing opinions about him, as the one responsible for gilding the bronze tiles of the Capitolium's roof [76 BC].

Pliny the Elder, *Encyclopedia* 33.57

10.12 Times were more peaceful when we were poor; we fought our civil wars only after the Temple of Jupiter was gilded [in 146 BC].

Seneca the Elder, *Debates* 2.1.1

10.13 The eagles supporting the pediment, which were made out of old wood, spread the fire [in AD 69].

Tacitus, *Histories* 3.71.4

10.14 Marcius found Hasdrubal's shield when he captured his camp [in 207 BC]; this shield hung above the doors of the Capitoline Temple right up to the time of the first fire [in 83 BC].

Pliny the Elder, *Encyclopedia* 35.14

10.15 In his term as censor [in 179 BC] M. Aemilius Lepidus contracted to have the Capitoline Temple of Jupiter and the columns around it smoothed and whitened. He also removed statues that were inappropriately placed among these same columns, and took off the shields and all manner of military insignia that had been affixed to the columns.

Livy, *History* 40.51.3

10.16 [Quintus, Cicero's brother, argues in favor of divination:] "When the statue of the thunder god Summanus (which was still made of terra-cotta at that time) was struck by lightning on the pediment of Jupiter Optimus Maximus [in 278 BC], no one was able to find its head, until the soothsayers said it had been knocked off into the Tiber— where indeed it was found, in the exact spot the soothsayers predicted."

Cicero, *On Divination* 1.16

10.17 The books of the Sibylline oracles were kept in a stone chest beneath the Temple of Capitoline Jupiter, under the guard of ten men. When the temple burned down [in 83 BC] (whether by accident or, as some believe, by arson), the fire destroyed these books along with the other offerings consecrated to Jupiter.

Dionysius, *Early Rome* 4.62.5–6

10.18 Nicomachus painted the Rape of Persephone, which hung in the temple of Minerva on the Capitolium, above the shrine of Youth.

Pliny the Elder, *Encyclopedia* 35.108

10.19 Gaiseric, leader of the Vandals, plundered the Temple of Jupiter Capitolinus [in AD 455] and carried off half of the roof's tiles. These were not only made of the finest bronze but covered by a thick gold leaf that shone with a spectacular radiance.

Procopius, *Wars* 3.5.4

11. The Roman Triumph

COMMENTARY

Although winding through much of the city and down the Sacra Via in the Forum, the famous Roman triumphal procession is best understood in connection with the Temple of Jupiter on the Capitoline: not only did the procession end here with a sacrifice and banquet, but it was the scene of the commander's vows before he set out to war. Painted with the same red pigment as the face of Jupiter's cult statue [11.2], the triumphing general was virtually an avatar of Jupiter, as the legions were an extension of the god's power radiating out from the Capitoline along the consular roads of Rome. In this light, it is no wonder that the Romans posted a slave in the general's chariot to remind him that he was mortal [11.6].

Of the several detailed accounts we have that describe specific triumphs, I have chosen one by Josephus [11.7] because of the great historical significance of the war which this triumph concluded. This was the war of the first Jewish Revolt, which not only resulted in the devastation of Jerusalem (captured by Titus in AD 70) and the destruction of the Temple there, but put an end to the priestly and sacrificial Judaism centered on the Temple and consequently led to the rabbinical and text-centered tradition of the Jewish diaspora. This conquest also had a significant effect on Roman topography, being commemorated by the Arch of Titus [57.] and his father Vespasian's Temple (Forum) of Peace [75.]. Josephus, although a Jewish priest and one-time resister, came to terms with the Romans, and blamed the revolutionary Jewish groups rather than the Romans for the destruction of Jerusalem.

Josephus's detailed account of the triumph shows how comfortable the Romans were with the open celebration of the destruction that they visited on their enemies (witness the graphic floats) and the material gain that they derived from it. He also notes the common practice of parading the enemy's commander in the triumph. Often the triumphal procession was in effect the death march of this human trophy, since he was slain at a signal given by the Roman victor after he had climbed the Capitoline.

SOURCES

11.1 [In 167 BC, Marcus Servilius, in a speech defending a certain general's right to a triumph, explained the wider significance of the

Roman triumph:] "When a consul or praetor, accompanied by lictors in military dress, sets out to his command and to war, he declares his vows on the Capitoline. When the war is successfully completed, the victor returns to the Capitoline in his triumph, bringing well-deserved gifts to these same gods. The sacrificial animals that go before him in triumph are an important part of the triumph and make it clear that the general gives thanks to the gods for the success of his actions done in the interests of Rome's well-being."

Livy, History 45.39.11–12

11.2 The substance cinnabar is found in silver mines. Even today it is a highly treasured pigment, but formerly had an even greater and sacred significance for the Romans: trustworthy sources say that the face of the statue of Jupiter was coated with cinnabar on holidays, as were the bodies of triumphing generals.

Pliny the Elder, Encyclopedia 33.111

11.3 Those who celebrate a triumph temporarily stay the executions of the enemy's leaders so that the people of Rome can witness the beautiful spectacle and the reward of victory when these men are paraded in the triumph. But when the wagons in the procession begin their turn from the Forum to the Capitoline, they order the captive leaders to be led into the Prison [Carcer] to their death. Thus does one same day put an end to both the command of the victorious general and the life of the defeated foe.

Cicero, Against Verres 5.77

11.4 That Caesar did not refrain from adulterous affairs even in the provinces is evident from this couplet, which his soldiers shouted during his Gallic triumph:

> Townsmen, guard your wives: we bring the bald adulterer home.
> In Gaul he screwed away the gold that he borrowed here in Rome.

Suetonius, Julius Caesar 51

11.5 As Caesar proceeded through the Velabrum in his Gallic triumph [in 45 BC], he was almost thrown from his chariot when its axle broke. He ascended the Capitoline by the light of lamps that were mounted on forty elephants to his left and right. In his Pontic triumph, among the show-pieces of the procession Caesar simply displayed a placard with three words—VENI, VIDI, VICI [I came, I saw, I conquered]— commemorating not the specific events of the war, as the other displays did, but the speed with which he had achieved his victory.

Suetonius, Julius Caesar 37

11.6 When celebrating a triumph, a general rode in a chariot different from ones used in races or combat. The general's chariot in a triumph was rather fashioned to look like a round tower. ... Along with him in the chariot, however, rode a public slave. His job was to hold the gold jewel-encrusted crown over the victorious general's head, and to say to him "Look to the future!" meaning, "Consider that the future and the rest of your life are unknown, and do not let the success of the moment lead you to elevate and overrate yourself." A bell (such as are worn by those condemned to die so that others do not incur pollution by accidentally brushing up against them) and a whip are also fastened to the victor's chariot, as a reminder that terrible things could still happen to him, things for which he might be whipped and even condemned to death.

Zonaras 7.21 (from Dio, Bk 6)

11.7 [The emperor Vespasian, with his sons Titus and Domitian, celebrated a triumph in AD 71 for victory in the First Jewish War, as described by the historian and Jewish priest Josephus:] Words cannot do justice to the multitude of amazing objects on display in a Roman triumph, or to their magnificence in the quality of the craftsmanship, in the variety of the valuables, or in their natural rarity. Almost everything wonderful and costly that a wealthy people manages to gather singly over a long time from various nations is here gathered together in abundance on one day to display the greatness of the Roman empire.

In this triumph, the mass of silver, gold, and ivory, worked into every shape possible, was carried past in such profusion that it seemed to flow by like a river, along with woven cloth dyed the most precious purple or embroidered with the finest portraiture of Babylonian art. The sheer quantity of transparent gems on gold crowns and other objects brought reports of their rarity into doubt. The procession also included images of Roman gods, astounding for their size, carefully made and all of costly material. ...

Nothing, however, was more amazing than the contraptions of mobile stage-sets, many of which were so high—three or four stories—that there was some fear of their toppling over as they moved along. ... On these floats, the various episodes of the war were recreated with vivid clarity: one showed a prosperous countryside laid to waste, another, entire regiments slaughtered; here the natives fled, there they were led into captivity; towering walls demolished by siege-engines, strongholds captured, cities ringed with defenders overtaken as troops poured through the walls, the ground drenched in blood. Other floats showed the helpless raising their hands in supplication, temples set on fire, and houses pulled down on top of people still inside. ...

Such were the sufferings that awaited the Jews when they committed themselves to the war. The skill and magnificent scope of these stages rendered distant events present for those who had never been there. On each of the floats the general of a captured city was stationed in the manner he was taken. Many floats representing ships also followed.

The spoils of the war were paraded past in great heaps. The most conspicuous spoils were those taken from the temple in Jerusalem. These included a gold table of great weight, and a lamp-stand likewise made of gold, but in a different design from the lamp-stands used in everyday life. For this lamp [the Menorah], a central shaft was attached to the base; slender branches extended from this, arranged in the manner of a trident, and at the end of each branch a bronze lamp was attached—seven in all, in accordance with the importance the Jews ascribe to this number.

The last of the spoils paraded by was a copy of the Jewish law. … Then came Vespasian himself, followed by Titus and Domitian riding side-by-side. …

The procession ended at the Temple of Capitoline Jupiter. Here they halted, in accordance with the ancient custom of waiting until someone brought word that the general of the enemy had been executed. This was Simon ben Giora, who had just been paraded among the captives. With a rope around his neck, he was tormented by his captors as they dragged him to the place alongside the Forum where by Roman law those sentenced to death are executed. At the announcement of his death, all cheered, and they began the sacrifices.

Josephus, *The Jewish War* 7.132–155

12. Tarpeian Cliffs *(Rupes Tarpeia, Saxum Tarpeium)*

COMMENTARY

The radical alterations of the topography since classical times have so obliterated these once dramatic cliffs that even their general location on the Capitoline Hill is still disputed. Traditionally topographers have located them above today's Piazza di Conciliazione, on the southwest side of the hill above the Vicus Jugarius (the photo in Fig. 16 was taken near here), but others argue for a site more central to the Forum and its Prison (see Notes).

SOURCES

12.1 [This is how the name Tarpeian got attached to the Capitoline Hill and the cliffs there. In response to Romulan Rome's abduction of women from surrounding tribes, Rome's neighbors mounted a series of attacks.] The last, and the fiercest by far, came from the Sabines. … Spurius Tarpeius, the commander of the Citadel, had a daughter who was a Vestal Virgin. On one of her trips outside the walls to collect

Fig. 16 Cliffs on the Capitoline Hill today

holy water at the Camenae springs, Tatius, the Sabine king, succeeded in bribing her with gold to open up the Citadel to the Sabine soldiers. As soon as they gained entrance, however, the Sabines crushed her to death beneath their shields, whether to make it look as if they took the Citadel by force, or to make an example of her treachery by showing that a traitor could safely trust no one.

There is, however, another version of the story. In this, Tarpeia had stipulated as her reward whatever the Sabines wore on their left arms, with an eye on the massive gold armbands and the beautiful gem-studded rings they commonly wore; instead, she got their shields.

There is also a third account, in which Tarpeia is a heroine: in this version, she made the pact for "what they wore on their left arms," and then surprised them by asking for their shields instead of the gold. When the Sabines perceived the trick, they destroyed her by giving her what she demanded.

Livy, *History* 1.11.5–9

12.2 [After they found him guilty of tyrannical ambitions,] the tribunes threw Manlius, the very same hero who had repelled the Gaul's attack from the Capitoline, down from the Tarpeian Cliff [in 384 BC]. Thus did one and the same place become a monument to both the unparalleled glory [9.9] and the capital punishment of the same man. Further marks of disgrace were attached to Manlius after death, one of which had lasting public consequences: since his home had been on the Capitoline (where the temple and mint of Juno Moneta are today), the people voted that no patrician might henceforth dwell on the Citadel or the Capitolium.

Livy, *History* 6.20.12–14

12.3 [In 192 BC] a giant boulder, whether detached by the rains or by an earthquake otherwise too slight to sense, toppled off the Capitolium onto the Vicus Jugarius and crushed many people.

Livy, *History* 35.21.6

12.4 [After Marcius, a leading aristocrat, refused to confess any wrong-doing or to beg for lenience from the plebs, the tribune Sicinius] ordered them to take Marcius to the hill lying above the Forum. There is a high sheer cliff there from which the Romans customarily throw people condemned to die.

Dionysius, *Early Rome* 7.35.4

12.5 [After Spurius Cassius, suspected of planning to make himself tyrant in Rome, was tried and condemned,] the quaestors led him to the cliff that lies above the Forum and, while everybody watched, threw him off (the traditional punishment in Rome then for those condemned to death).

Dionysius, *Early Rome* 8.78.5

12.6 The supporters of Vitellius quickly marched past the Forum and the temples that preside over the Forum, and advanced their front line up the facing hill, right up to the outer gates of the Capitoline citadel. Here, on the right side of the Clivus as one ascends, there were porti-coes since ancient times. The defenders climbed out on these and hurled rocks and tiles down on the supporters of Vitellius. … Then the attack-ers made attempts from two other directions, one near the grove of the Asylum and the other where the Tarpeian Cliffs are surmounted by the Hundred Stairs. Each assault was unforeseen, though the one through the Asylum was closer and more intense.

Tacitus, *Histories* 3.71

12.7 Sextus Marius, the richest man in Spain, was falsely accused of having incest with his daughter and was thrown off the Tarpeian cliff.

Tacitus, *Annals* 6.19

12.8 [One legal judgement reads:] "Condemned of incest, she was thrown off the cliff, but lived: the punishment is repeated."

Quintilian, *Oratorical Training* 7.8.3

12.9 The hillside plunges precipitously into a pit, interrupted with jut-ting crags that either crush the body on first impact or toss it down for worse; the whole cliff-face bristles with jagged rock.

Seneca the Elder, *Debates* 1.3.3

12.10   There is an oak plank attached to the [base of the] Tarpeian rock and the Capitoline cliff; it has iron hooks, and is used to catch the bodies of people thrown off the cliff.

Notes to Lucan B 2.125

12.11   Do you really think, Favorinus, that if the penalty prescribed in the Twelve Tables for lying had not become obsolete and that today, as then, those who were convicted of perjury were tossed off the Tarpeian Cliff, we would now [c. AD 180] be witnessing so many people telling falsehoods under oath?

Gellius, *Attic Nights* 20.1.53

Notes: In the ongoing debate over the location of the cliffs, Richardson (p. 377–8) argues for their traditional location above the Piazza di Conciliazione (near the Tiber), citing Livy's observation that Manlius's moment of greatest glory (fighting the Gauls above the Shrine of Carmentis) and his punishment (thrown from the Cliffs) occurred at the same place. Others (including Wiseman in *LTUR* 4.237–8, and Coarelli) place the cliffs near the Gemonian steps, citing Dionysius's description of the cliffs as "lying above the forum," and arguing for a tighter topographical "organic" ensemble of imprisonment, execution, and display (the Prison, the cliffs, and the Gemonian stairs respectively).

Livy's report [12.3] of a loose boulder killing people on the Vicus Jugarius certainly testifies to the extreme steepness and cragginess of the Capitoline in the area where the Tarpeian cliffs are traditionally placed. As for Dionysius's description of the Cliffs as "lying above the Forum," he uses the same phrase [12.4] in reference to the entire Capitoline Hill (also in Dionysius 3.69.4, not quoted above); the phrase, that is, identifies the hill itself for his Greek audience, not a specific part of the hill. As such, the description does not conclusively place the Cliffs closer to the Forum than their traditional location closer to the river would allow.

13. Temple of Jupiter Feretrius

COMMENTARY

The temple to Jupiter Feretrius (Jupiter in some capacity as a war god) was important as the repository of the Supreme Spoils (the *spolia opima*, explained below, 13.2), the sacred flint (*silex*) used in sacrifices marking the official declaration and conclusion of wars, and a scepter that symbolized Roman victory [13.6]. No traces of this small temple have been found; it may have stood on the Area Capitolina near the Temple to Jupiter Optimus Maximus.

SOURCES

13.1   Romulus carried the spoils of the enemy's dead leader up to the Capitolium on a stretcher and deposited them there next to an oak sacred to the shepherds. At the same time, he marked off the limits of a sacred precinct in honor of Jupiter and gave him an additional title: "Jupiter Feretrius," he said, "I, Romulus, king and conqueror, bring [*fero*] these royal spoils for you, and I dedicate a sacred space, whose boundaries I have just measured off with my mind's intention, as the seat of these Supreme Spoils [the *spolia opima*]. In times to come, other Romans following my example will bring you the spoils of the enemy kings and leaders that they themselves have killed." This is the origin of the first temple consecrated in Rome.

Since that time, after so many years and so many wars, the Supreme Spoils have been won only twice: so rarely do men attain this distinction.

Livy, *History* 1.10.5–7

13.2 Properly speaking, only spoils that one commander strips from another commander are considered Supreme Spoils.

Livy, *History* 4.20.6

13.3 After the triumphal procession and the sacrifice, Romulus built a temple to Jupiter Feretrius on the summit of the Capitoline Hill. This temple was a small one, not larger than 15 feet on its long side, as shown by traces of its original dimensions. In this temple he consecrated the spoils of the Caeninian king, whom he killed with his own hands.

Dionysius, *Early Rome* 2.34.4

13.4 When the roof of the Temple of Jupiter Feretrius on the Capitolium, founded by Romulus, was caving in because of age and neglect, Augustus restored it on the advice of Atticus.

Nepos, *Atticus*, 20.3

13.5 I will now explain how the name of Jupiter Feretrius came about, and the three spoils of three leaders that are kept in his temple. …

Romulus, you were the first winner of this prize, you set the pattern for the rest when you came back weighed down with the armor of your enemy, Acron, commander of Caeninia, after he attacked the gates of Rome; his horse stumbled, and you killed Acron with a thrust of your spear.

Cossus comes second; [in 437 BC] he killed Tolumnus, chief of Veii.…

Third and last was Claudius; [in 222 BC] he drove back the enemy who crossed the Rhine, and brought back the shield of Virdomarus, the giant Belgian commander.

These three spoils are preserved in the temple; hence the name Feretrius, because, through heaven's will, leader struck [*ferit*] leader with sword; or perhaps the lofty altar of Jupiter is called Feretrian because they personally carried [*ferebant*] these conquered arms on their shoulders.

Propertius, *Elegies* 4.10

13.6 Jupiter is called *Feretrius* from *ferendo* ("bringing"), because he is considered to bring (*ferre*) peace. It is in his temple that the fetial priests involved in external affairs keep the scepter for swearing oaths and the flint for striking treaties.

Festus 81 L

13.7 [Concluding the formula for striking a treaty, one of the fetial priests spoke as follows:] "If the Roman people are the first to break this treaty with public consent and conscious deception, then may you, Jupiter, so smite the Roman people as I now strike this pig!..." So speaking, the priest slashed the sacrificial pig's neck with the flint.

Livy, *History* 1.24.8–9

14. Temple of Jupiter Tonans (Jupiter the Thunderer)

COMMENTARY

Nothing remains to be seen of this temple vowed by Augustus. Its location has been tentatively identified with a concrete foundation found during the construction of the Via di Monte Tarpeio (on a line between Jupiter's main temple and the Temple of Saturn below, closer to the former). A coin depicting the temple shows the cult statue of Jupiter holding his traditional emblems of power, a scepter in one hand, a lightning bolt in the other.

SOURCES

14.1 For his narrow escape from death Augustus dedicated the temple to Jupiter the Thunderer [in 22 BC]. When he was traveling once at night on the Cantabrican expedition [in 26 BC], a bolt of lightning grazed his litter and killed the slave who was lighting the road in front of him.

Suetonius, *Augustus* 29.3

14.2 Augustus was morbidly afraid of thunder and lightning and frequently attended the temple of Jupiter the Thunderer on the Capitolium. Once he dreamed that Jupiter Optimus Maximus complained that he was losing worshipers, to which he (Augustus) replied that the Thunderer was simply the doorman of Jupiter the Greatest. Accordingly, Augustus soon strung the gable of the Thunderer's temple with bells similar to those that frequently hang from doorways.

Suetonius, *Augustus* 90, 91

14.3 Marble was first used on walls in Rome in the stage of Marcus Scaurus, although I cannot say for certain if this marble was a veneer, or solid blocks that have been polished, such as one finds today at the temple of Jupiter the Thunderer on the Capitolium.

Pliny the Elder, Encyclopedia 36.50

14.4 The famous cult statue of Jupiter the Thunderer on the Capitolium is the unsurpassable work of the sculptor Leochares.

Pliny the Elder, Encyclopedia 34.79

14.5 Located in front of the Temple of Jupiter the Thunderer are two fine statues of Castor and Pollux carved by Hegias.

Pliny the Elder, Encyclopedia 34.78

15. The Grove of Asylum

COMMENTARY

The Asylum, apparently at one time a grove itself between two other groves on the slopes either side of it, remained a separate walled enclosure into imperial times. Ovid [16.2] suggests it was adjacent to the Temple of Veiovis (also "Vediovis"), which was at the northwest corner of the Tabularium platform that monumentalized the saddle of the Capitoline facing the Forum. This would locate the Asylum in the area around the steps of the current day Palazzo Senatorio (the seat of today's City Council).

The Asylum is one of several monuments in the city that insisted on Rome's humble beginnings. Its primary importance, however, may have been as a memorial to the Roman belief that their nation was founded not by a pure, homogeneous people "native to the land," (as Greek and other accounts commonly mythologize communal origins) but rather as a collection of diverse people. The myth of the Asylum's foundation, especially in Livy's version, has in it the experience of Rome's subsequent history of incorporating as citizens both ethnically diverse peoples and former slaves.

SOURCES

15.1 The city's defensive works kept expanding to incorporate one location after another, since they fortified the town with an eye on future population rather than the existing numbers. Then, lest large parts of the city remain empty, they had recourse to an old tactic used by city-founders for increasing population: they attract outsiders of obscure and humble origin who they then claim are native to the land. To this end, they designated a location (now an enclosure between the two groves as you ascend the Capitoline) as an asylum; a crowd of commoners, both free and enslaved, poured in from the neighboring territories, eager for new conditions. This was the first step towards the strength Romulus envisioned for Rome.

Livy, *History* 1.8.4–6

15.2 Romulus made the city large and populous in the following manner. First, he required all citizens to raise all of their male children as well as the first-born girl, and forbid them from killing any of their children under three years old, unless the children were maimed or deformed from birth, in which case the parents could expose them, provided they had shown the child to five neighbors who concurred with the parents' assessment. …

Next, knowing that many of the surrounding cities in Italy were under oppressive rule by tyrants and oligarchies, and that there were many fugitives from such rule, Romulus attempted to attract them and transfer them to his own rule, regardless of their misfortune or luck, provided they were not slaves; in this manner he hoped to increase Rome's strength while diminishing the strength of her neighbors. By consecrating an Asylum for suppliants in the area between the Capitoline and the Citadel, he accomplished his plan even as he gave it the appearance of piety.

The Romans still designate this space as "between two groves," a phrase which then did accord with the landscape, when thick woods on the flanks of each hill-top overshadowed the saddle between them. He also built a temple there (its god is not known), and to those who fled there as suppliants he guaranteed safe haven from their enemies, as well as citizenship and a share of whatever land he subsequently acquired in battle. People came running from every direction, fleeing bad conditions at home. Nor did these new-comers later resettle elsewhere after arriving in Rome, but remained there, retained by Romulus's constant care and attention.

Dionysius, *Early Rome* 2.15.1–4

16. Temple of Veiovis

COMMENTARY

Remains of the Temple of Veiovis can be seen from corridors of the Tabularium/Palazzo Senatorio that are accessible from the Capitoline museum. The unorthodox design of the temple (approached by stairs on its long side, like the Temple of Concord) belongs to a rebuilding of the original temple and can be dated to the time of the Tabularium's surrounding construction.

SOURCES

16.1 [Cypress, beyond all other woods, retains its polish in good condition.] Proof of this is the cult statue of Jupiter Veiovis on the Citadel, which has lasted [the 250 years] since the temple's dedication [in 192 BC].

Pliny the Elder, *Encyclopedia* 16.216

16.2 [On the Seventh of March, only one event: the dedication]
Of the Temple of Veiovis in front of the two groves.
Romulus, surrounding a grove with a lofty wall,
    Said, "Flee to us, whoever you are, and you will be safe."
How small the start from which the Roman people arose!
    No cause for another's envy back then in *that* population.
But, should the name Veiovis mean nothing to you,
    Learn who he is …
Veiovis is Jupiter when he was young; witness
The youthful face of his statue, then notice
    He holds no lightning in his hand yet. …
And note the goat beside him—they say a goat
    Gave milk to the infant Jove. … So why should I not conclude
That the Temple of Veiovis is the Temple of Jupiter
    Not-yet-great?

Ovid, *Fasti* 3.429–448

17. Tabularium (Archives)

COMMENTARY

The remains of the Tabularium, best seen from the Forum, form the substructure for the present Palazzo Senatorio. Two levels of the ancient building are visible as the massive wall of gray tufa closing the Forum off on its northern-most end. The lower level, pierced by windows opening into small chambers backed by the foot of the hill, formed a substructure for an arcade above that runs along the length of the building. Two of the arcade's archways remain unbricked, framed with Doric half-columns and a travertine architrave. Ruins found at the base of the wall suggest that there was at least one other arcade on top of the one remaining. Behind the remaining arcade are numerous hallways, rooms, and stairs dating to ancient times, made with concrete and faced with tufa stones.

The identification of this building as the *tabularium*, or "record office," rests on the inscription below, found near the Tabularium in the fifteenth century AD and since lost. *Tabula* are writing tablets, and many buildings had a *tabularium* to store records and archives. This Tabularium was apparently a major one with perhaps other functions as well, but we know little more about it.

SOURCES

17.1 Quintus Lutatius Catulus, son of Quintus, grandson of Quintus, when consul [in 78 BC] undertook by senatorial decree the construction of the substructure and record office (*tabularium*), and he certified the work.

ILS 35 = *CIL* 6.1314

17.2 [Living the good life in the countryside, the farmer]
Plucks the fruit that the trees and the Earth of its own accord
Bestow upon him freely, blissfully unacquainted with Rome's
Iron laws, the frenzied Forum, and the Bureau of Public Records.

Virgil, *Georgics* 2.500–2

18. Temple of Juno Moneta

COMMENTARY

Several basic questions persist concerning the Temple of Juno Moneta; its location, and the lack of vestiges, have been called "one of the great enigmas in the topography of ancient Rome"(Richardson, 215). That it stood on the summit of the Citadel rather than on the other two areas of the hill is certain, but some topographers place it under the church of S. Maria d' Aracoeli, while others place it closer to the edge of the hill in the direction of the Forum, on the ancient substructions visible in the little park there today alongside the stairway up to the back of the church.

Secondly, what is the relationship between the Temple of Juno Moneta and her earlier presence on the hill? Later tradition gave Juno a precinct on the Capitoline at least back to the time of the Gallic invasion in 390 BC, when her sacred geese honked their way into history, but tradition also has it that the temple dedicated in 344 BC was built on the site of the house of the patrician hero Manlius, not on the site of a previous temple or sanctuary.

As the ancients (incorrectly) understood the word, the epithet "Moneta" originated from Juno's role in warning (*monere*) the Romans. Subsequently, the temple also contained Rome's mint for four centuries, before it was moved to a new location near the Colosseum in Domitian's reign. *Moneta* thus came to mean "mint" in Latin, and was the origin of the English words "monetary" and "money."

SOURCES

18.1 [The Gauls climbed up the Capitoline at night without a single person noticing them,] but some of the sacred geese being raised in the sanctuary of Juno gave the alarm by honking and rushing at the intruders.

Dionysius, *Early Rome* 13.7.3

18.2 They say that on June 1st the Temple of Juno Moneta (vowed,
    Camillus, by you) was dedicated on the summit of the Citadel.
    The site was once the home of Manlius, who drove
        The armies of Gaul away from Jupiter Capitolinus.

Ovid, *Fasti* 6.183–86

18.3 Since the Aurunci had begun the hostilities and were not
shying away from battle, Lucius Furius Camillus, the appointed
dictator [in 345 BC], decided that the aid of the gods ought to be summoned for the conflict and accordingly vowed a temple to Juno Moneta.
Victorious and under the vow's obligation, he returned to Rome and
resigned from his post.

The senate appointed two commissioners to build this temple in
a style suited to the greatness of the Roman people. A site was
chosen for it on the Citadel, where the house of M. Manlius Capitolinus
had been. ... The Temple of Moneta was dedicated one year after
the vow.

Livy, *History* 7.28.4–6

18.4 [Cicero's brother Quintus argues for the validity of divination.]
"According to many accounts, one time after an earthquake occurred, a
voice was heard coming from the Temple of Juno on the Citadel, saying that an expiatory sacrifice of a pig had to be performed. This Juno
was henceforth called Moneta [the "Warner"]."

Cicero, *On Divination* 1.101

18.5 The home of Manlius was located where the temple and mint of
Moneta are located today.

Livy, *History* 6.20.13

18.6 I have written to Philotimus in Rome about getting money from
the Moneta for my journey.

Cicero, *Letters to Atticus* 8.7.3

18.7 The Books of the Magistrates are written on linen and deposited
in the Temple of Juno Moneta.

Livy, *History* 4.20.8

19. Auguraculum (Precinct for Augury)

COMMENTARY

Although the exact location of this sacred precinct for augury and
the augurs is not known, it was on the Citadel, with a view to the south
over the Caelian Hill [19.3]. A possible site is the park (Giardino dell'
Aracoeli) at the top of the stairs to the Forum, which would give the

Fig. 17 View from Auguraculum towards Alban Hills

requisite view if cleared of trees. The ruins of an old wall here (near larger substructures identified by some with the Juno Moneta temple; see Commentary on Juno Moneta) perhaps formed part of the augural station. In the distance over the Caelian Hill the Alban Hills, site of the important early sanctuary to Jupiter Latiaris on Mt. Albanus (Monte Cavo), are visible and perhaps played a role in orientation.

SOURCES

19.1 The senators of Rome unanimously voted to confer the kingship on Numa Pompilius [715 BC]. When summoned, Numa insisted that they consult the gods concerning his appointment, just as Romulus, when the city was first founded, had gained his kingship by augury.

Accordingly, Numa was led by an augur to the Citadel and seated on a rock, facing south. The augur, with his head veiled, sat down to Numa's left, holding in his right hand a staff curved at the end and free of knots (they call this a "lituus"). Then, looking out over the city and countryside, the augur prayed to the gods and demarcated the sky with a line from east to west: anything south of the line was "right," and anything north was "left." Next, having oriented himself towards a landmark as far away as sight could reach, he passed the lituus to his left hand, laid his right hand on Numa's head, and prayed as follows: "Father Jupiter: if it be your will that Numa Pompilius, whose head I now hold, become king of Rome, we ask that you send us clear signs within the boundaries I have designated." Then he specified the signs he wished to be sent. When these signs appeared, Numa was declared king and descended from the augural station.

Livy, *History* 1.18.6–10

19.2 [There are many forms of religious authority in the state,] but the highest and supreme authority is that of official augury. For what power, legally considered, is greater than the ability to dissolve assemblies and councils appointed by the highest authorities in possession of their full powers, or to rescind the decisions of those bodies? What authority carries more weight than the augur's power to dismiss any undertaking, simply by saying "Postponed to another day"? What power is greater than deciding when consuls must resign from their office? What power is more sacred than that of granting or withholding the right of assembly to the people and the plebs? Indeed, without an augur's authority, no act by a magistrate either at home or in the field has validity for anyone.

Cicero, *On Laws* 2.31

19.3 Once, when the augurs were preparing to take the auspices on the Citadel, they ordered Tiberius Claudius Centumalus, who had a home on the Caelian Hill, to pull down the higher parts of his house that impeded their observations. [Centumalus quickly sold his house to someone else, but without telling them such remodeling was necessary: was this right?]

Cicero, *On Duties* 3.66

20. The Prison *(Carcer)*/Gemonian Steps *(Gemoniae Scalae)*

COMMENTARY

Rome's only known state prison, called simply Carcer ("the Prison") or the Tullianum (its lower chamber) in antiquity, has already figured in accounts of the Roman triumph as the place of execution for captured leaders [11.3, 11.7]. Other places of detention and execution must have existed in the city, but this was *the* Prison, situated at the heart of Rome's public space and, with the Gemonian Steps where corpses were exposed, part of the Forum's political theater (see Overview of the Roman Forum below).

Today the "Mamertine" Prison (its post-classical name of unknown origin) is a popular shrine commemorating the alleged incarceration there (but not execution) of Saints Peter and Paul.

SOURCES

20.1 [Under King Ancus, c. 630 BC, many of the Latins defeated in battle were settled in Rome as citizens, especially on the Aventine.] The population grew enormously with these additions. When, as a result of this rapid growth in population, opinions grew confused over the right and the wrong way to do things, clandestine crime began to appear. In response, a prison was built overlooking the Forum in the middle of the city, countering the growth in daring with the threat of incarceration.

Livy, *History* 1.33.8

20.2 They say that the Tullianum, which refers to a specific part of the Prison, was built by Servius Tullius [c. 550 BC].

Festus 490

20.3 [On Cato's recommendation, the Senate passed the death sentence on the Catilinarian conspirators.] Cicero, as consul [in 63 BC], decided to carry it out before nightfall to forestall any further developments, and ordered the prison officials to prepare everything necessary for execution. After stationing guards around, he personally led Lentulus into the prison; praetors escorted the other conspirators.

There is a part of the prison which is called the Tullianum, where you ascend a short way on the left. The Tullianum is sunk into the earth about 12 feet and is constructed of stone walls on all sides; above this is a room with a ceiling of vaulted stone. Foul from neglect, darkness, and stench, it is an altogether terrifying sight. Into this chamber Lentulus was lowered, and the executioners of those who commit capital crimes did as they were told and strangled him. Thus did a patrician of the distinguished family of the Cornelii and former consul in Rome end his life, in a manner worthy not of his birth but of his character and his own deeds. Cathegus, Statilius, Gabinius, and Caeparius died in the same way.

Sallust, *War against Catiline* 55

20.4 C. VIBIUS C. F. RUFINUS M. COCCEIUS M. F. NERVA COS. EX S. C.

The Consuls Gaius Vibius Rufinus, Son of Gaius, and Marcus Cocceius Nerva, son of Marcus, [repaired the Prison in AD 22] by order of the Senate.

CIL 6.1539

20.5 There on the Gemonian Steps, witnessed with horror by the entire Roman Forum, lay the body of Quintus Caepio, mangled by the deadly hands of the executioner [in 103 BC].

Valerius Maximus, *Sayings* 6.9.13

20.6 [Bad omens abounded as Sejanus, the right-hand man of Emperor Tiberius, approached his end in AD 31.] When Sejanus had finished sacrificing on the Capitoline and was descending to the Forum, the crowd of people surrounding him was so dense that his bodyguards were unable to follow, and they turned down the way that leads to the Prison. As they descended the flight of stairs on which the condemned criminals are thrown, they slipped and fell.

Dio, *History* 58.5.6

20.7 [Sejanus, accused of plotting against the imperial house, was executed in AD 31.] It was decided to move against his two surviving children next. And so they were carried off to the Prison, the boy old enough to understand what lay in store for them, the girl however so innocent that she kept on asking what she had done wrong and where she was being taken; she promised she would never do it again—a spanking had always seen to that in the past. Writers of that time say that because it was unheard of to apply capital punishment to a maiden, the girl was first raped, with the rope at her side. Afterwards, she and her brother were strangled and thrown out, young as they were, on the Gemonian Steps.

Tacitus, *Annals* 6.5.9

20.8 [After the Vitellian forces took the Capitoline during the civil war of AD 69, they killed the city prefect Sabinus] and dragged his stabbed, mutilated, and headless body onto the Gemonian Steps.

Tacitus, *Histories* 3.74

Notes: For a description of the prison, and commentary on the sources, with bibliography, see Wilkins, "*Sallust's Tullianum.*"

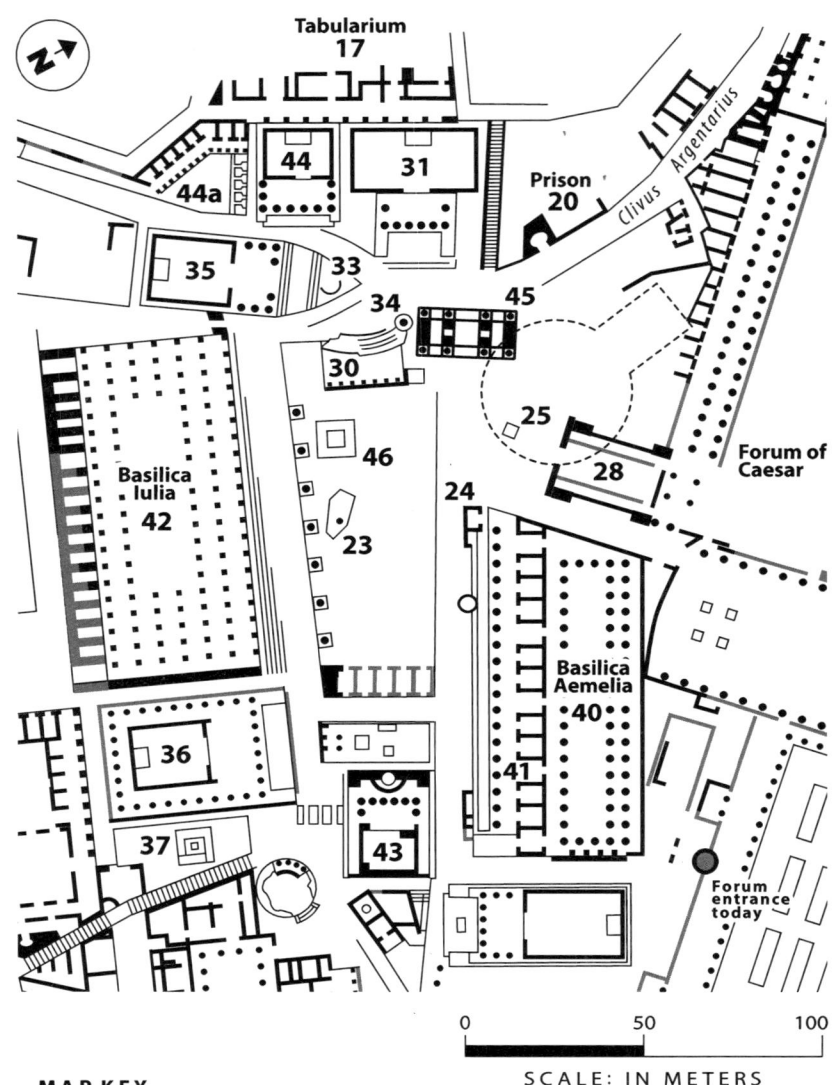

Fig. 18 Roman Forum

MAP KEY

23	Pool of Curtius
24	Shrine of Janus Geminus
25	Black Stone (*Lapis Niger*)
28	Senate House (imperial)
30	Imperial Rostra
31	Temple of Concord
33	Golden Milestone
34	Umbilicus Urbis
35	Temple of Saturn

36	Temple of Castor and Pollux
37	Shrine and Pool of Juturna
40	Basilica Aemelia (Pauli)
41	Porticus of Gaius and Lucius
42	Basilica Julia
43	Temple of Julius Caesar
44	Temple of Vespasian
44a	Portico of the Consenting Gods

45	Arch of Septimius Severus
46	Column of Phocas

IV. The Roman Forum

21. Overview of the Roman Forum

COMMENTARY

[Note: For the fairly tight and uniquely dense ruins of the Roman Forum, I have arranged the entries not by physical proximity, but by origin and function; the order of this section is loosely chronological, with some displacement for purposes of grouping some sites together because of a similarity or association in function.]

That the ancient world's most concentrated center of power was once a marshy basin with cattle-paths intrigued the ancient Romans almost as much as later centuries loved the next layer of historical irony, when the Forum reverted to pasture after the Fall of Rome. With characteristic reverance for utility, the Romans pictured the new order on dry land as beginning not with Ararat but with the Cloaca Maxima, the large central canal (eventually covered over) that dominated a network of drainage ditches. This drainage work, probably carried out in conjunction with some massive and deliberate land-fill, rendered the area suitable as a communal center. The Lacus Curtius shrine, however, long remained a testimony of the marshy area, a reminder also provided by the Tiber floods that not infrequently inundated the Forum area until the travertine embankment walls of the late 19th century effectively canalized the whole Tiber much as the Cloaca canalized the forum stream.

The later Romans envisioned burial as one of the pre-urban uses of the Forum, and the archaeological record confirms that indeed it was; the sites of just a few of the many graves found scattered beneath centuries of later pavings are indicated today by little grass plots next to the Temple of Antoninus (A in Fig. 24). Traces of huts have also been found, and there was probably at least one important road among the early paths and cattle-tracks, the old salt-route (echoed in the modern "Via *Saleria*"), which directed traffic down from the Quirinal and Pincian heights, across the subsequent forum area at the foot of the Capitoline, and down the (later) Vicus Jugarius to the Tiber ford before continuing to the salt flats north of the river mouth. In early days the topography of the area was much more defined than it is today, with deeper gullies and more visible valleys fingering their way back up to the heights of the Quirinal and Esquiline. The forum basin would have also had a more enclosed appearance, bounded by the little ridges or saddles that connected the Capitoline to the Quirinal (a ridge removed by Trajan) and the Palatine to the Esquiline (a ridge removed by Mussolini).

Burials in the forum area ceased as the hill-communities developed the area for other purposes and coalesced into the community of Rome during the 8th and 7th centuries BC. There is archaeological evidence for late 7th century paving of some of the area, and the literary tradition (corroborated in places by archaeology) records the construction of the Regia, the Temple of Vesta, the shrine to Janus, the Senate House, and the prison, even before the reigns of the two Tarquin kings, who are credited with beginning the Cloaca Maxima in the 6th century. It is significant, however, that with the exception of the shrine to Janus (which may have been a bridge over the Cloaca stream), none of these early buildings was in what became the central forum square, which was the lowest part of the basin and precisely the area bisected by the drain.

Before turning to the individual sites of the Forum and their sources, I have included several famous ancient passages as an introduction to the activities and the atmosphere of the Forum [21.1–7]. Apart from the specific information that each introductory passage contains, together they provide a sense of the Forum as a space that is intensely public and open to view, dominated by action that is in each case some species of spectacle, whether involving political oratory, public trials, aristocratic funerals, gladiatorial shows, or actual performances of plays. The triumphs and executions described in the Capitoline section [11., 12., and 20.] are also relevant here.

Polybius's description of an aristocratic funeral [21.3], one of the most evocative portraits of Rome in ancient literature, shows how difficult it can be to separate theater, ceremony, and public business from each other in ancient Rome. The passages by Plautus, Horace, and Plutarch also stress the theatrical quality of most action in the Forum. Plautus's guide to the Forum [21.2] focuses not so much on the topography as on the stock characters associated with that topography (see Notes). Horace's walk through the Forum [21.7] is a mock-tragedy that hinges on several recognition scenes and concludes with a deus ex

Fig. 19 The Roman Forum, with Colosseum in distance

machina. And Plutarch not only describes Galba's murder in the Forum [21.6] as if it were a play but assures us that the Romans who were present, instead of fleeing, quite naturally took their places on the balconies of the basilicas to watch the spectacle of an emperor's death.

The Forum's architecture of course complements this intensely public behavior, as Vitruvius notes [21.5]. The predominant style of Forum architecture might be called the architecture of the front porch, with all the visibility in both directions that this implies. In general, a good deal of important business that now is rigorously confined inside four walls and a roof—sessions of the Senate, for instance, trials, banking activity, schooling—occurred under porches and colonnades or out-of-doors in ancient Rome.

SOURCES

21.1 The "forum" is so named because it is the place where people take issues to court [*conferrent*] and where people bring [*ferrent*] their merchandise to sell it.

Varro, *The Latin Language* 5.145

21.2 I'll show you where you'll find each sort of man in town,
    To save you the trouble of tracking them down, be it men of virtue
  You seek, or men of vice, men with and without morals.
    If you need a man to perjure an oath, the Comitium's the place;
  But for liars and braggarts, go to the shrine of Venus Cloacina.
    Wealthy husbands incautious with cash haunt the Basilica—

There too the busiest hookers and the pimps who strike the deal.
Members of the dinner clubs you'll find in the Fish-market.
Gentlemen stroll at the end of the Forum, men of money;
    In the center, near the Canal, linger the pure pretenders.
Above the Lacus Curtius the slanderers gather, bold
    Malicious men who brazenly accuse the innocent
But who themselves make truer targets for their charges.
    At the Old Shops are those who lend or borrow money,
And others behind the Temple of Castor—trust them at your peril.
    On Tuscan Way, more hookers, of either sex;
On the Velabrum, bakers, butchers, and prognosticators,
    And swindlers, or those who rent the stalls for swindlers' work.

Plautus, *Curculio* 467–82

21.3 The lengths to which Roman society goes to fashion men who will endure anything to gain a reputation for bravery can be demonstrated by the following example.

Whenever a distinguished public figure dies, as part of the funeral rites his body is escorted across the Forum (most often in an upright position visible to all, or more rarely lying down) and is carried up to the Rostra. There, with the whole community gathered around, a son of the deceased (if he should have one that is grown-up and present; otherwise, someone else from the family fills in) ascends the Rostra and delivers a speech on the man's virtues and the achievements of his life. ...

After the burial and the customary rites, his family places an image of the deceased in the most conspicuous part of the house, where it is displayed in a wooden shrine. The image is a mask fashioned to resemble both the features and complexion of the person, and is extremely lifelike. ... Whenever another distinguished member of the family dies, the family brings these ancestral masks to the funeral, where they are worn by living men who most nearly resemble the physique and bearing of each ancestor. These men also dress in the appropriate togas that signify the rank each ancestor attained: purple-bordered for consuls and praetors, solid purple for a censor, and interwoven with gold for those who attained a triumph or something similar. ... When the funeral procession reaches the Rostra, all the members of this masked entourage take seats upon it in ivory chairs.

It would be hard to find a more powerful spectacle to inspire a young man eager for fame and virtue. Indeed, who would not be moved upon seeing this masked assemblage of ancestors renowned for their great deeds, seated there as if alive and breathing? What spectacle could be more inspiring than this? In addition, when the speaker is finished eulogizing the deceased, he recounts in turn the great deeds and achievements of the other ancestors represented by the masked men seated on the Rostra. In this fashion, by the constant renewal of the virtuous repu-tation of good men, both the fame of those who have accomplished something great is immortalized, and the glorious example of those who have benefited the community in the past instructs the many people present and is bequeathed to future generations.

In the end, however, the greatest effect of this ceremony is on the young men of the city, inspired to undergo any hardship for the com-munal good by the fame that follows upon the good deeds of such men.

Polybius, *History* 6.52.11–6.54.3

21.4 In honor of their father Marcus Aemilius Lepidus (who had been consul twice and an augur), his three sons held funeral games lasting three days [in 216 BC], which included twenty two gladiatorial duels in the Forum.

Livy, *History* 23.30.15

21.5 [The Greeks give their forums a square shape and enclose it in double colonnades with columns set close together.] In Italy, however, a different plan must be executed, in light of the custom established by our ancestors of holding gladiatorial displays in the forum. Because of this, the space between columns should be widened for better viewing. Place shops for bankers in the surrounding porticoes, and include view-ing balconies on the upper stories; such arrangements are both convenient and bring in public revenue.

Vitruvius, *Architecture* 5.1.1

21.6 [The struggle between the Emperor Galba and his successor Otho in AD 69 ended up as street fighting in downtown Rome. Galba, in the palace on the Palatine, hears a rumor that Otho has been murdered.] Galba climbed into his litter and sallied forth from the Palatine, in-tending to sacrifice to Jupiter on the Capitoline and show himself to the people. While he was passing through the Forum, however, a very different report arrived like a sudden change of wind: Otho, much alive, controlled the praetorian troops. … Soon Otho's horsemen appeared. Then foot-soldiers advanced through the Basilica of Paullus, shouting for all civilians to clear the area. The crowd indeed cleared out, not scattering in flight, however, but gathering on the portico balconies and other vantage points of the Forum as if to take in a show.

In the first act of the hostilities a soldier overthrew Galba's statue in the Forum. Then, after failing to hit Galba's litter with their javelins, the soldiers advanced on him with drawn swords. … In the commo-tion, Galba tumbled out of his litter onto the ground at a place called the Lacus Curtius. Soldiers ran to strike him where he lay, protected by his armored breastplate, but Galba simply offered his neck to their swords and said, "If it is better for the Roman people, do it!"

They say that when the soldiers brought Otho the head of Galba on a spear, he shouted, "This is nothing, my fellow soldiers; show me the head of Piso!" And not long afterwards the head of Galba's adopted successor also arrived, after the young man, wounded and struggling to escape, was killed outside the Temple of Vesta.

Plutarch, Galba 26.2–4, 27.1, 4

21.7 As I was walking down the Sacred Way, worrying
As usual some bit of verse into shape and lost in thought,
A man, little more to me than a name, runs up
And grabs my hand and gushes, "Horace, so *good* to see you!
How is everything?" "Not bad, considering. Good to have seen *you*."
Since the man won't leave me, I insist, "If there's anything I can do ..."
"You can get to know me" he says; "I'm a writer!"
"No shame in that," I say, desperately wanting to lose him:
I pick up speed, slow down, I talk some private business
With my slave, while the sweat rolls down to my ankles.
"My friend Bolanus wouldn't suffer fools like this!" I think
As the man drones on in praise of Rome and every little street.
Finally, not deaf to my silence, he says, "You're dying to get away,
I can see that. But it's no use, I'm sticking to you
Wherever you're headed." "No need for you," I insist,
"To go out of your way. I want to visit someone,
You wouldn't know him, quite sick in fact, in bed,
Across the Tiber, way over by Caesar's Gardens."
"No trouble at all," he says. "It'll do me good. Lead on!"
…
By the time we reach the Temple of Vesta the courts are in session,
And this man's scheduled to defend himself or lose his case.
"Please," he pleads, "I can use your support; it won't take long."
"Not a chance; I don't know the slightest thing about law."
"Well," he ponders; "which to abandon: you, or my trial?"
"Me! Choose me!" I beg. "I couldn't," he decides, and marches on.

[Eager for gossip, the man grills Horace on the literary scene; Horace bumps into an old friend, who, pretending not to know that Horace is fishing for an excuse to get away from the Boor, leaves him to his fate. But Horace is unexpectedly rescued:]

Then who should appear from out of the blue but the very man
Who was taking my barnacle to court. "There's the bastard!"
He yells, then turns to me: "Are you willing to be a witness
To this encounter?" In assent, I let him touch my ear.
Shouting breaks out and people come running as he grabs his man
And hauls him off to court. Thus did Apollo save me.

Horace, Satires 1.9.1–19, 35–42, 74–78

Notes: 21.2 Plautus's passage takes the spectator on a tour of the Forum in his day, in a winding path that starts at the Comitium and heads down the northeast side of the Forum past the shrine to Venus Cloacina and the unnamed basilica that was a forerunner of the Basilica Aemilia, past the fish market (near the later Temple of Antoninus?) to what Plautus calls the lower forum, perhaps near the Regia. He then takes us back, now in the middle of the Forum, towards the canal of the Cloaca Maxima and on to the Lacus Curtius (near which one of the praetors heard law cases, hence the reference to slanderers), before doubling back, now on the southwest side of the forum, along the Old Shops (Veteres Tabernae) and the Temple of Castor, before heading off towards the Tiber through the Velabrum on the Vicus Tuscus. See T. Moore, *The Theater of Plautus*, 131–139.

22. Cloaca Maxima ("The Main Drain")

COMMENTARY

The literary sources credit the Tarquin kings of the 6th century with the first major work of changing the Forum's landscape from a marshy basin to solid building ground, and the drainage system they developed, centered on the Main Drain, does have much in common with the drainage canals (*cuniculi*) that were prevalent in the Etruscan countryside north of Rome. Much of the channel (as reconstructed by Agrippa and later builders) remains in service as part of Rome's drainage system today, its contents diverted however into the sewage system rather than flowing directly into the River. Plautus's description of the Forum [c. 200 BC, see 21.2] refers to the Cloaca as still an open canal; it was perhaps covered over in connection with the building projects of following decades.

The mouth of the drain can still be seen in the travertine embankments of the Tiber, just downstream of the Ponte Palatino. The opening gives some idea of the channel's dimensions (varying, but averaging about 3 m. square—large enough for Pliny and Strabo's hay wagon). In the 19th century, when easier of access, the Cloaca Maxima was popular with tourists, providing the young Henry James in 1869 with "the deepest and grimmest impression of antiquity I have ever received."

SOURCES

22.1 The land where the forums of Rome now spread was once a swamp
And ditches were dank with the waters that flooded back from the river.

Ovid, *Fasti* 6.401–2

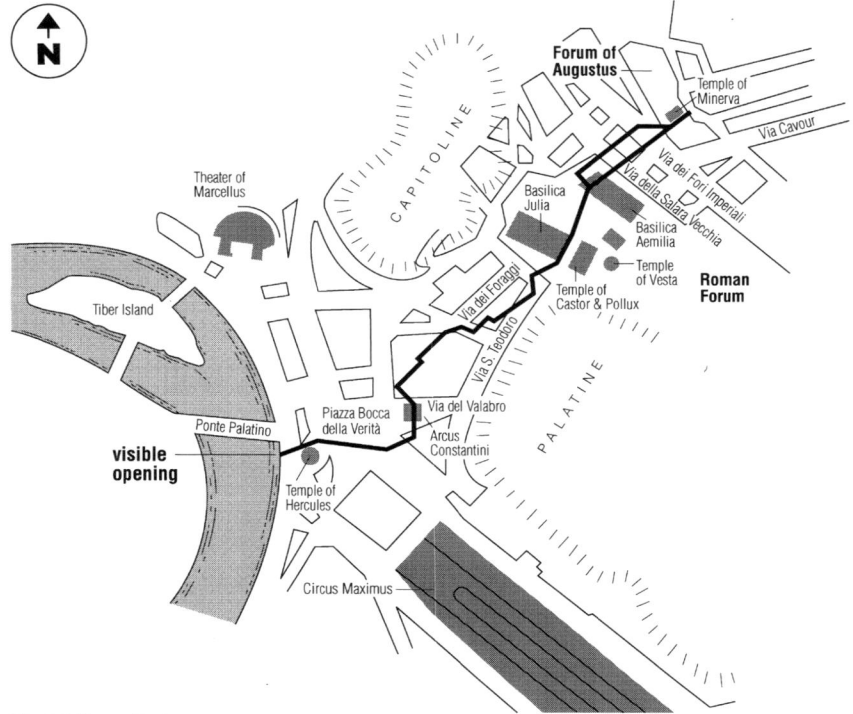

Fig. 20 Cloaca Maxima

22.2 By means of sewers sloping into the Tiber, the king Tarquinius Priscus [616–578 BC] dried out the low and flat areas of difficult drainage both around the Forum and in between the hills.

Livy, *History* 1.38.6

22.3 Under Tarquinius Superbus [534–510 BC], the work of the plebeians was directed to two other projects, the construction of the seating for the Circus, and the building of the subterranean Cloaca Maxima as a receptacle for all the city's waste—two works that even the most recent marvels of construction [in the late first century BC] have scarcely been able to match.

Livy, *History* 1.56.2

22.4 [No wonders of the world equal the splendor and wealth of Rome, although by the late Republic the excesses had become obvious.] Even then, however, the older people still marveled at the huge expanse of the Rampart and the substructures on the Capitoline, as well as the project deserving the greatest praise of all, the drainage channels, tunneled through the hills, laid beneath a suspended city, and even navigated by Agrippa when aedile [in 33 BC].

Seven streams, collected into one channel, traverse the city, rushing like a mountain torrent and sweeping off everything in their path. When further swollen by a mass of rainwater, the currents pound the sides and bed of the channels, and when the Tiber on occasion floods and backs up into them, the waters inside clash from opposite directions; still the structures hold firm against the pressure. Floods might sweep away massive material above them, buildings collapse upon them, and earthquakes shake the earth around them, but the channels have endured 700 years since the time of Tarquinius Priscus and are almost indestructible. It is said that Tarquinius had the channels made large enough to accommodate the passage of a wagon loaded with hay.

Pliny the Elder, *Encyclopedia* 36.104–106,108

22.5 As aedile, Agrippa carried out all his repairs on public building and streets in Rome without using any public money. He also had the drainage channels cleared and then inspected them by boat, floating underground to the Tiber.

Dio, *History* 49.43.1

23. The Pool of Curtius (*Lacus Curtius*) and Forum Fig Trees

COMMENTARY

The location of the Pool of Curtius is, as Livy puts it, "almost in the middle of the Forum," where the remnants of an altar and stone border can be seen (presently covered by a plastic canopy). Even in Ovid's time there was no trace of water there, but both legend and ritual preserved its connection to the underworld and to the Roman practice known as *devotio*. In this ritual (attested but not routine) an individual—typically a general, as in the second passage by Livy included here to illuminate the more pertinent story about Curtius—saved the imperiled community by consecrating his own life to the gods of the underworld. The most prominent legend regarding the name of the Pool has all the essential features of this practice, down to the proper vesture of the victim. Both Livy and Varro, however, refer to a different legend as well.

Perhaps the altar and its ritual came to replace the literal practice of *devotio*. It is tempting to regard the ceremony connected to the Pool in Augustus's day as procuring the communal well-being by providing gold coins to the Underworld, in place of offering a leader (suggesting that if death cannot be cheated, he can at least be temporarily bought off).

Some of the important landmarks in ancient Rome were not buildings, but plants. There were at least two important "monumental" fig trees in the Forum—these are alluded to by the fig growing near the Pool of Curtius today—and another by the Lupercal cave.

SOURCES

23.1 In his histories, Piso recounts how during the Sabine War between Romulus and Tatius [in the late C8 BC], a brave Sabine named Mettius Curtius, forced to retreat in the face of a charge that Romulus and his men made from the heights of the Palatine, escaped into the marshy area that occupied the Forum area before the drains were constructed. Making his way out again, he rejoined his troops on the Capitolium. Such is Piso's account of how the Pool of Curtius got its name.

Varro, *The Latin Language* 5.149

23.2 It is said that [in 362 BC] the ground, whether from an earthquake or some other agency, caved in almost in the middle of the Forum, creating a gaping chasm of unknown depths; no amount of dirt that everyone brought and tossed into the pit was able to fill it. Then they learned from an oracle of the gods that if they wanted the Republic of Rome to endure, they would have to sacrifice, on that spot, that which above all else made them strong.

They then say that Marcus Curtius, an exceptional young soldier, criticized the others for doubting that Rome's strength could reside in anything other than the weapons and bravery of her citizens. Silence fell. Curtius, gazing up at the Capitolium and the temples that rise around the Forum, stretching his hands first to the heavens and then to the pit and the gods below, consecrated himself to the Underworld. Then, armed for battle and mounted on his horse in full caparison, Curtius leapt into the chasm, and the crowd of men and women threw gifts and fruits of the field in after him. Accordingly, the Pool of Curtius is, they say, named for this Marcus Curtius, and not for the ancient Curtius Mettius, the Sabine soldier serving under Titus Tatius. In truth, the more recent event recounted here is the more prevalent story for the origin of the pool's name.

Livy, *History* 7.6.1–6

23.3 [When he saw that the Roman troops under his command were losing a battle against the Latins south of Rome in 340 BC,] the consul Decius cried out to the pontifex: "Marcus Valerius, we need the help of the gods! As public pontiff of the Roman people, come and administer the oath with which I may devote myself to the Underworld in place of the legions." The pontiff told him to put on the purple-bordered toga, to extend a hand from under the toga to touch his own chin, and to repeat the following words while standing upon a spear that lay upon the ground: "Janus, Jupiter, Father Mars, Quirinus, Bellona, Lares, gods both local and foreign, to whose power both we and our enemies are subject, and you gods below, I beseech you with prayer and seek your favor with supplication: may you promote the might and victory of the Roman people and afflict the enemies of the Roman people with terror, panic, and death. In speaking these words, on behalf of the Republic of the Roman people, the army, its legions and its allies I hereby devote the legions and allies of the enemy, along with my own self, to the gods of the underworld and to Earth."

Then Decius, with his toga draped in Gabine manner, jumped fully armed onto his horse and galloped off into the enemy's midst. To men on both sides he appeared to take on a more than human majesty, as if he were sent from heaven to expiate in full the anger of the gods and to turn destruction away from his own people and bring it upon the enemy. …

The praise for victory in the battle went to the consuls, one of whom diverted towards himself alone all the menace and danger of the gods both above and below.

Livy, History 8.9–10

23.4 The Pool of Curtius, which now supports dry altars
On solid ground, was once a pool in fact.

Ovid, Fasti 6.403–4

23.5 [There is evidence that Augustus was widely popular during his reign.] Each year men from every class would throw a small coin in the Pool of Curtius, in fulfillment of a vow for his health.

Suetonius, Augustus 57.1

23.6 There is a fig tree worshipped in the Forum itself, in the Comitium. It is considered sacred, first, because it is planted where objects struck by lightning have been buried, and even more so as a memorial of the Ruminal fig under which the wolf who nursed Romulus and Remus had originally sheltered these founders of the empire. …The withering away of this fig is always a portent, and priests are responsible for planting a new one. … There is another tree of the same species, sown there by chance, in the middle of the Forum, at the spot where Curtius, using his most precious possessions—that is to say, his courage, his commitment, and his glorious death—shored up the foundations of Roman power that were slipping away in a portent of disaster.

Pliny the Elder, Encyclopedia 15.77

23.7 A statue of the augur Attus Navius still stands in the Forum today [c. 10 BC] in front of the Senate House near the Sacred Fig.

Dionysius, Early Rome 3.71.5

Notes: (For conflicting analyses of the evidence concerning fig-trees in the ancient Forum, see Richardson, 150–1, and *LTUR* 2.248–9).

24. The Shrine of Janus Geminus

COMMENTARY

Although the precise location of this little temple is not known, Livy's passage locates it in the "lower Argiletum," a street which entered the Forum between the Senate House and the Basilica Aemilia/ Paulli. This was the most important of the several cult sites to Janus in Rome, an important and very Roman god who still makes his mark on the modern imagination. Janus was the god of gates (*ianua*) and passages, whether such passages are conceived spatially as crossing some important boundary, temporally as connecting past and future (hence "January"), or as a connector of differing states and conditions (from peace to war, or from the human to the divine). As such, Janus was commonly represented as a two-faced god, and his shrines seem to have been in the form of a covered passage-way, fitted with a gate at each end. It is possible that the shrine here was also originally a bridge over the open canal of the Cloaca Maxima.

SOURCES

24.1 Numa Pompilius [715–673 BC], invested by the augurs with kingship over a city founded by the force of arms, prepared to found Rome anew on justice, laws, and morality. Perceiving that such reforms could not be successfully promoted during wars, which rather promote ferocity, Numa thought to tame his fierce people by weaning them from their weapons. To this end, he built the Janus shrine at the bottom of the Argiletum to signify whether Rome was at peace or at war: its doors stood open when the city was in arms, and were closed when all Rome's neighbors had been pacified. Since Numa's reign, the shrine has been shut twice: once after the First Punic War in the consulship of Titus Manlius [in 235 BC], and again, as granted by the gods in our own day, when peace was established on land and sea by the emperor Caesar Augustus after the battle of Actium [in 31 BC].

Livy, *History* 1.19.1–3

24.2 The shrine of Janus Quirinus, which in all of recorded memory since the founding of Rome was only closed twice before my birth (in accordance with our ancestors' wishes that it be closed only when peace through victory reigned throughout the entire empire on land and sea) was ordered by the Senate to be closed three times during my rule.

Augustus, *Achievements* 13

24.3 The great antiquity of the art of sculpture in Italy is demonstrated by the statue of Janus Geminus dedicated by the king Numa. Janus is worshipped as the signifier of peace and war; the fingers on the statue are arranged to indicate the number 365, showing that he is also the god of passages of time.

Pliny the Elder, *Encyclopedia* 34. 33

24.4 But how do I describe you, Janus of the double face?
    For Greece has no divinity with the same domain.
    …
Janus, holding a staff in his right hand, a key in the other,
    [Revealed himself, and answered all my questions.]
"Why," I wondered, "whenever I appease the other gods,
    Do I first bring an offering of wine and incense to you?"
"So that through me you gain the passage," Janus answered,
    "To whatever gods you wish, whose thresholds I control."

"And why, when so many passage-ways [*jani*] exist, do you stand
    Worshipped only in one, at your temple next to two forums?"
["Because I stopped the Sabines here with a gush of noxious water]
    An altar was consecrated to me in a little shrine,
Where the flames consume your offerings of sacrificial cake."
    "But why do you hide during times of peace, and open in war?"
Without a moment's delay, Janus gave me the reason:
    "So the way of return lies open to the men who go out in armies
My doorways open wide in war, with the bolts drawn back.
    But I close my doors on Peace, to prevent her from leaving;
Long will I be shut, through the godly will of Augustus.

Ovid, *Fasti* 1.89–282, selections

Notes: In Pliny's passage [24.3], how did the god's fingers represent the number 365? Perhaps three were extended on the one hand, and all five on the other to represent the Roman numerals III, VI, and V.

25. The Black Stone (*Niger Lapis*)

COMMENTARY

    One of the more curious remains in the Roman Forum is a small area, surrounded now by a metal railing, of grayish limestone slabs visible in the pavement of the Forum near the Arch of Severus today and originally alongside the Republican Rostra. The level of this pavement can be dated to the C1 BC, and was originally surrounded by a *pluteus*, an enclosure formed by waist-high stones. These darker slabs of limestone pavers are probably the Niger Lapis, or "Black Stone," referred to by Festus in the passage below.

The real puzzle involves a much older stone lying *beneath* the Black Stone pavers and which the Black Stone simply serves to locate on the level of later pavement. This hidden stone, a tufa post set on an earlier pavement level of the Forum and adjacent to a small altar and column base (likewise covered over), contains one of the oldest Latin inscriptions in existence. Because the inscription is fragmentary—the top of the stone was cropped in antiquity to fit beneath the later pavement—and in very archaic Latin, both the meaning of the text and the function of the stone and site are unknown to us and probably to the imperial Romans as well. As excerpted in the sample below, the inscription seems to begin with words of a common malediction against anyone who would violate a sacred spot; elsewhere it probably refers to a king, perhaps in his capacity as a guardian of sacred spots. Since the paving of this tufa stele can be dated to the first half of the C6 BC, this may indeed refer to one of Rome's early kings.

Festus is definite in his belief that this inscribed stone was a burial marker. Archaeologists, however, have found no signs of burial in this little complex of monuments beneath the Black Stone, and some wonder if the inscribed stone originally commemorated a sacred event or deity and only later came to be understood as a funeral monument for a burial site important enough to prohibit traffic from the pavement above it (hence the Black Stone and bordering wall). Richardson suggests the possibility that it was originally a boundary stone.

SOURCES

25.1 The Black Stone in the Comitium marks off a place of burial. Some say it was destined to be the burial spot of Romulus, before he disappeared and made his burial impossible. Others say his foster-father Faustulus was buried here, still others, that it was Hostilius, grandfather of the Roman king Tullius Hostilius.

Festus 184L

25.2 Whosoever desecrates this site, let him be consecrated to the spirits below … .

ILS 4913 = *CIL* 6.36840

26. The Senate House (*Curia*), Assembly (*Comitium*) and Rostra

COMMENTARY

The Senate House and Rostra that exist today in the Forum are imperial structures which, while located close to their Republican predecessors, suggest nothing of the earlier topographical and political unity that joined these two sites to each other and to the assembly grounds between them called the Comitium. Though the Senate could and often did convene elsewhere, as could official assemblies of the People, these three sites were Republican Rome's political core. Their unity is evident in Varro's convenient summary of their functions; he groups the three sites together (and locates the Graecostasis as well, a waiting area for foreign ambassadors):

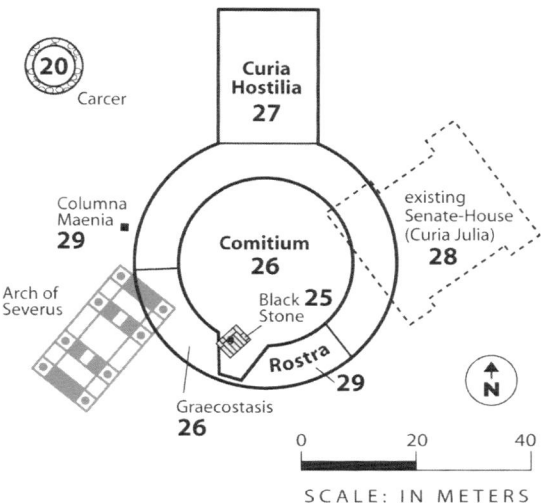

Fig. 21 Republican Senate House, Comitium, and Rostra (after Coarelli)

26.1 The Comitium is so-called because the Romans came [*coibant*] here for meetings of the Comitia Centuriata and to hold trials. As for Curia ("Senate House"), there are two kinds: one, such as the Curiae Veteres, is where priests take care [*curarent*] of divine matters; the other is where senators take care of human affairs, such as the Curia Hostilia, which the king Tullus Hostilius first built. In front of this stands the speaker's platform, called the Rostra because of the beaks [*rostra*] of captured ships that are fastened to it. To the right of this (looking from the Comitium) is a lower platform where the foreign ambassadors to the Senate wait (although the ambassadors can be from any nation, this platform is called the *Graeco*stasis—part for the whole, as is so often the case in our names for things).

Varro, *The Latin Language* 5.155

Further unifying this political ensemble of Republican times, the Senate House and Comitium were oriented by the cardinal points of the compass (Fig. 21), which may have marked them out as specially augurated space and at any rate set them off obliquely from the Forum rectangle that formed over the centuries.

Perhaps the best way to situate these vanished Republican structures in today's landscape is by using the Black Stone [25.]; the Rostra and Graecostasis stood to either side of it near the southernmost part of the Comitium. The Republican Senate House, the Curia Hostilia, would have been north of here, about where the church of S.S. Luca e Martina is located today, outside the excavated area of the Forum.

Fig. 22 Imperial Senate House (upper right). Note the unexcavated level of the Forum between the Senate House and the Arch of Septimius Severus

The Senate House of Republican Rome goes under the single name of the Curia Hostilia, although, like most buildings in Rome, it underwent significant reconstructions and enlargements, one by Sulla in 80 BC, and another by his son Faustus after a fire in 52 BC. The Comitium was an augurally defined space in front of the Senate; it too changed in appearance and level over the centuries, and was probably ringed by steps at some point, perhaps descending into a sort of cavea. The first speaker's platform to be called the Rostra was the one on the southern rim of the Comitium fitted with the ships' beaks after a naval victory in 338 BC. Presumably the speakers could mount the platform by stairs from the Comitium, or from its sides; the beaks would have faced the open Forum area, as the speaker also had the option of doing.

The imperial Senate House, the Curia Julia, is by far the best preserved ancient building in the Forum because of its conversion into a church in AD 630. The surviving structure, deconsecrated in the 1930s, is Diocletian's restoration of the Senate House after a fire in AD 283. The original, dedicated by Augustus in 29 BC, goes back to the plans of Julius Caesar that reoriented the building on more "rational" lines, squaring it up with the rectangular lines of the Forum and even more closely with his new forum [73.], to which the new Senate House formed an architectural appendage more in keeping with the Senate's increasing subordination.

After the magistrates and Senators, the most important fixture of the Senate House was the Altar of Victory, established by Augustus to commemorate his victory over Egypt and, by synecdoche, all Roman victories. Later its presence became a powerful symbol in the fourth century struggle between Christian and pagan religions. The excerpts below of letters written to the emperor by the pagan senator Symmachus [28.5] and the bishop Ambrose [28.6] encapsulate much that was essential in this struggle, the one side citing the proven efficacy of their religion throughout the ages, and the other recoiling almost viscerally from the ritual of pagan sacrifice.

When the new Senate House was built, the Comitium area was paved smooth and the Rostra dismantled. Caesar began a new Rostra facing the Forum next to the Arch of Severus. This Rostra was apparently stepped on the Capitoline side, which, with its curve, preserved something of the look of the Republican rostra that followed the contours and the stepped seating around the Comitium. It was probably on this Rostra that Caesar refused the crown offered by Antony, and where Antony, in retribution for Cicero's scathing orations against him (the *Philippics*), displayed the orator's severed head and hand [30.3].

Augustus subsequently extended the new Rostra towards the Forum, creating a larger area for displays such as statues (which were always a feature of Rome's Rostra) and the imperial family's funerals.

SOURCES
27. Republican Senate House *(Curia Hostilia)*

27.1 Romulus appointed one hundred men as senators. [After Rome defeated the nearby city of Alba, c. 650 BC,] the king Tullus Hostilius selected the leading men of Alba for enrollment in the Roman Senate in order that this component of the republic might also grow. In addition to enlarging the senatorial order, he made the Senate House a ritually consecrated space; as a result, it was called the Curia Hostilia even into the times of today's senators.

Livy, *History* 1.30.2

27.2 Varro has written of the locations in which the Senate may legally pass a decree, and he demonstrates that if a decree is passed at a site which is not designated with augury as a "templum," then the decree is not valid. For this reason, the Curia Hostilia, the Pompeia, and the Julia—all of them profane sites—were designated "templa" by the augurs, so that the Senate's business could proceed properly there in the tradition of our ancestors.

Gellius, *Attic Nights* 14.7.7

27.3 [In a philosophical dialogue set in 79 BC, Cicero has Marcus Piso comment on the powerful effect that the haunts of famous men have on later generations:] "Whenever I looked upon the Senate House

(I mean the Hostilia, not the new one, which now seems to me smaller since its enlargement) I could almost see before me the great Scipio, Cato, Laelius, and my own grandfather Piso himself."

Cicero, *On Ends* 5.2

27.4 [After his murder in 52 BC,] the people carried the body of Publius Clodius into the Senate House where, after piling up benches, platforms, tables, and books, they cremated him. With Clodius the Senate House itself went up in flames; the Basilica Porcia, which adjoined the Senate House, also burned down.

Asconius, on Cicero's *Milo* 29

27.5 [Rome, amid factional fighting, descended into chaos.] Milo, for instance, a candidate for the consulship, happened upon Clodius, his old enemy and opposing gang leader, on the Appian Way. In the confrontation, Milo first wounded Clodius and then, fearing retribution, killed him. ... The tribunes carried the corpse of Clodius into the Forum at dawn, placed it on the Rostra so that all might see him, and gave voice to their grief. The people, stirred by the spectacle, ... lifted up the body of Clodius and bore it into the Senate House, where they laid it out properly. Then, after heaping benches up into a pyre, they burned the body and with it the Senate building. ...

The Senate soon met under Pompey's guard outside the pomerium near his theater and resolved to collect the bones of Clodius. They also charged Faustus, the son of Sulla, with the rebuilding of the Senate House, the Curia Hostilia, which Sulla had remodeled.

Dio, *History* 40.48–50

28. The Imperial Senate House *(Curia Julia)*

28.1 [The Senate itself heaped excessive honors and commissions on Caesar before his assassination.] They assigned him the construction of a new Senate House, since the Curia Hostilia, although rebuilt since the fire, had been torn down.

Dio, *History* 44.5.2

28.2 [As part of their policy of linking themselves to the deified Julius Caesar,] the triumvirs Octavian, Antony, and Lepidus, following an earlier vote [in 43 BC], built the new Senate House (called now the Curia Julia in Caesar's honor) next to the Comitium [in 42 BC].

Dio, *History* 47.19.1

28.3 I built the Senate House and the Chalcidicum adjoining it [in 29 BC]. During my sixth and seventh consulships [28–27 BC], with the power of the state entirely in my hands by universal consent, I extinguished the flames of civil wars, and then relinquished my control, transferring the Republic back to the authority of the Senate and the Roman people. For this service I was named Augustus by a decree of the Senate, … and a golden shield was placed on display in the Curia Julia. An inscription on this shield states that the Senate and the Roman People gave me the shield because of my courage, mercy, justice, and devotion.

Augustus, *Achievements* 19, 34

28.4 After the triumphal procession celebrating Egypt's subjugation, Octavian dedicated the [portico of] Minerva (also called the Chalcidicum) and the Curia Julia, built in honor of his father, Caesar. Inside the Senate House he set up the statue of Victory that stands there today [c. AD 200], no doubt intending to signify that he owed his rule to her. Bringing it to Rome from Tarentum, he had it placed in the senate chamber and decorated with Egyptian spoils.

Dio, *History* 51.22.1–2

28.5 From the Senator Symmachus to Emperor Theodosius: [AD 384] [The Altar of Victory was unjustly removed from the Senate House in deference to Christianity.] Let us restore the state of religion which proved so advantageous to our country for so long. Certainly emperors may be found of both religions, of both beliefs; the earlier ones worshipped in the same ceremonies as the Senators, and the more recent ones did not prohibit these ceremonies. If the piety of the former does not provide you with a model, let the tolerance of the latter do so.

Who is so far from civilization that he does not expect to find the Altar of Victory in the Senate House? … Your eternal glory owes much to Victory, and will depend on her greatly in the future; let them scorn her power, who have not benefited so greatly from it. Do not reject the support of a divinity so conducive to triumphs. All of us are in debt to her efficacy; no one would deny that that which must be sought after must also be worshipped. But however unjust the refusal to worship this spirit, it is at least proper that the ornaments of the Senate House remain intact. We beseech you: allow us as elders to pass down to our descendants that which we received in our youth.

Symmachus, *Relationes* 3.3–4

28.6 The Bishop Ambrose to the Emperor Valentinianus [AD 384]: … These senators seek to have the Altar of Victory erected again in the Senate House in Rome, that is to say, where many Christians convene. … Must it be tolerated, that a pagan sacrifices in the presence of a Christian?

St. Ambrose, *Letters* 18.31

29. The Republican Rostra

29.1 The consuls [in 442 BC] engraved the legislation on twelve bronze tablets and affixed these to the Rostra that was then in front of the Senate House.

Diodorus Siculus, *Library* 12.26.1

29.2 [After the Romans defeated the people of Antium (modern Anzio) in 338 BC, they captured all their ships, made the people citizens, and forbid them all use of the sea.] Some of the ships were transferred to the dockways in Rome and some were burnt. A motion was approved to use the ships' beaks [*rostra*] to adorn a raised platform that was constructed in the Forum. Accordingly, they called this platform, which was also inaugurated as a templum, the Rostra.

Livy, *History* 8.14.12

29.3 The Rostra [in 52 BC] was not where it stands today [c. AD 55], but nearly adjoined the Senate House.

Asconius, on Cicero's *Milo* 37

29.4 In measuring the hours of the day in Rome only the rising and setting of the sun are distinguished in the laws of the Twelve Tables [from the fifth century BC]. Years later, noon was also officially announced. This was done by an assistant of the consuls, who declared it noon when looking [south over the Comitia] from the Senate House he saw the sun positioned between the Rostra and the Graecostasis. When the sun passed to the Carcer side of the Column of Maenius, the assistant announced the final hour. Such reckoning (which was possible only on clear days) lasted down to the time of the First Punic War [264–241 BC].

Varro reports that the first public sun-dial was erected during this war, and that it was located on a column next to the Rostra. Quintus Marcius Philippus, when censor [in 164 BC], later located a more accurate dial next to it. Even then, however, cloudy weather obscured the hours, until in the next census when Scipio Nasica was the first to reckon Rome's official time with a water clock that divided the days and night into equal hours. He dedicated this time-piece, lodged under a protective roof [in the Basilica Aemilia, according to Varro, *LL* 6.4], 595 years after the founding of Rome [159 BC]: for so many years did the Roman people live in unmeasured light.

Pliny the Elder, *Encyclopedia* 7.212–5

29.5 When Lars Tolumnius, the king of Veii, murdered four ambassadors of the Roman people, statues of these men were placed on the Rostra, where they stood down to my own memory. And rightly so: for in such manner did our ancestors distinguish those who died in the service of their country, granting them lasting fame in exchange for their shortened lives.

Cicero, *Philippics* 9.4

Notes: Coarelli (in *LTUR* 4, 212–4) and Richardson (334–5) envision different histories for the Republican Rostra. Richardson argues, especially on the evidence of Asconius, for a speaker's platform between the Senate House and Comitia pre-dating the one (the first to be called the "Rostra") that faced the Forum at the southern end of the Comitium. Coarelli acknowledges only the latter, explaining Asconius by reference to the enlarged Senate House of Sulla, which Coarelli envisions as expanding south and encroaching over half the Comitia. The wording of Diodorus's passage [29.1] supports Richardson's arrangement.

30. The Imperial Rostra

30.1 When Caesar was appointed dictator for the fifth time [in 44 BC], … the Rostra was moved from the middle of the Forum back to the position it now occupies [c. AD 220], and statues of Sulla and Pompey were restored to it. Caesar received praise for this, as well as for allowing Antony to take the credit in the inscription on the Rostra.

Dio, *History* 43.49.1

30.2 [Shortly before his assassination, Caesar and Mark Antony contrived the following test of public opinion during the festival of the Lupercalia.] Dressed in triumphal attire, Caesar observed the Lupercalia festival from a golden chair placed upon the Rostra. When Antony, who was consul at the time and accordingly one of the runners in the Lupercal rites, raced into the Forum, the crowd gave way as he approached Caesar to offer him a golden crown entwined with laurel. There was some applause, but it was more scattered and contrived than enthusiastic. As Caesar pushed the crown away, however, the entire crowd burst into applause. Antony offered it once more with the same result: offered, it drew faint clapping; rejected, loud applause. Seeing that their experiment had failed, Caesar stood and ordered that the crown be carried up to the Capitoline.

Plutarch, *Caesar* 61.3–4

30.3 Seeing that Cicero clung to the cause of liberty, Octavian no longer allied himself with him, and approached Antony through some friends to settle their differences. So the three of them—Octavian, Antony, and Lepidus—met on a small island in the middle of a river and spent three days in close conference. They agreed on most matters quite easily, quickly dividing up the entire empire as if divvying up ancestral property, but the issue of which men to put to death was a major source of contention. At first the desire of each man both to kill his enemies and save his relations led to conflicts between them, but in the end their anger against those they hated won out over concern for family and friends, and Octavian let Antony have Cicero. ...When the three of them reached an agreement, three hundred men were marked for death, and killed. After Cicero was murdered, Antony ordered his head to be cut off, along with the right hand—the one guilty of writing those speeches [the Philippics] against him.

When the head and hands of Cicero were brought to Rome ... Antony ordered them to be fastened over the ships' beaks on the Rostra. It was a sight that caused the Romans to shudder, thinking that what they saw was not so much the face of Cicero as the image of Antony's soul.

Plutarch, *Antony* 19–20; *Cicero* 49

30.4 For Augustus's funeral, a couch of ivory and gold was constructed, decorated with purple coverings embroidered in gold, while a coffin-like compartment below this concealed his body. In full view on the couch, however, was a wax effigy of the late emperor in triumphal garb. ... Following in procession behind the bier came the images of his ancestors (excepting Julius Caesar, who had been enrolled in the ranks of the demigods) and images of Romans who had distinguished themselves over the centuries, beginning with Romulus himself. ... The couch was then laid for display on the Rostra of the orators, where Drusus delivered the family's eulogy for Caesar; from the other Rostra (called the Julian Rostra), Augustus's successor Tiberius delivered the public eulogy.

Dio, *History* 56.34.1–4

Notes: 30.4 The Rostra of the orators is the Augustan Rostra; the Julian Rostra is another one extending out from the front of the Temple of Julius Caesar.

31. Temple of Concord

COMMENTARY

The Temple of Concord is not the earliest of the large temples in the Forum, but it is the closest to the Senate and Assembly area not only in distance (it sits nearby, slightly higher on the lower Capitoline slope), but in political significance, having been vowed and dedicated in political struggles between the Senate and the People. Even after Tiberius rebuilt it and emphasized the imperial family's role in establishing harmony and peace in the state, the building continued to be used to signify critical moments in the safety of the state. The Senate often met in its cella, which, after Tiberius's rebuilding, was quite large and unusually oriented with respect to the porch. It was magnificently decorated, as can be judged both by the remains of the entablature on display in the gallery of the Tabularium (accessible through the Capitoline museums), and by the sources (represented by the sampling from Pliny, 31.5), which locate enough works of art in the Temple of Concordia to make it resemble, even more than most temples, an art museum.

Though vowed in 367 BC, it seems that the Temple of Concord was not built until 131 BC.

SOURCES

31.1 [While Camillus held the post of dictator, conflict arose between the Plebs and the Senate in 367 BC when the former group agitated for the creation of a plebeian consulship. Emotions on both sides grew heated, leading to a near-riot in the Forum.] Not sure what to do in this crisis, Camillus did not renounce his dictatorship but gathered the senators together and proceeded to the Senate House. Before going in, however, he turned to the Capitoline and prayed, calling on the gods to steer the present events toward some happy conclusion and vowing to build a temple to Concord if the conflict subsided.

Inside, the Senate hotly debated the issue, but the moderates prevailed and they conceded to the Plebs the right to elect one of the two consuls from their own number. When the dictator went out and announced this as the will of the Senate, the people expressed their approval immediately, as might be expected, happy to be reconciled with the Senate, and they escorted Camillus home to cheering and applause.

On the next day the people met in assembly and voted to build the Temple to Concord that Camillus had vowed, oriented to face the Forum and the Comitium.

Plutarch, *Camillus* 42.2–4

31.2 [After his supporters in Rome grew increasingly violent, Gaius Gracchus, a populist reformer, was killed along with thousands of his followers in 121 BC after Opimius, the consul, gave orders to suppress the populist faction.] What angered the people more than anything else, however, was the building of the Temple of Concord by Opimius; it seemed that he was glorifying himself and taking pride in murdering so many citizens, almost as if he were celebrating a triumph. As a result, under the temple's inscription, some people inscribed the line: "The Temple of Concord, built by Discord."

Plutarch, *Gaius Gracchus* 17.6

31.3 [Calendar entry for January 16:]
Radiant goddess, today you moved to your snow-white temple
   Where lofty Juno lifts her steps high up the hill.
Here you can oversee, Concordia, the Latin crowds
   Now that sacred hands have performed your dedication.
Camillus, famed for his Etruscan conquests, vowed
   The original temple, and carried out the vow he'd sworn
When the People revolted and took up arms against the Senate
   And Rome had cause to fear the force of its own aggression.
The recent temple's cause is better; the Germans bowed
   Their shaggy heads beneath your rule, Tiberius,
And with the booty of this conquest that earned you a triumph
   You built a temple to honor a goddess special to you.

Ovid, *Fasti* 1.637–648

31.4 [After Sejanus, Tiberius's trusted vice-regent and commander of the Praetorian Guards, was suspected of treason and arrested] he was thrown into the Prison. [AD 31] Later that same day, however, the Senate, after seeing that the people also hated Sejanus and that his Praetorian Guards were nowhere in sight, gathered in the Temple of Concord and condemned him to death.

Dio, *History* 58.11.4

31.5 Baton made the statues of Apollo and Juno that are in the Temple of Concord. ... A painting of Marsyas Bound is likewise there, ... as are four elephants carved out of solid obsidian, which Augustus himself dedicated as objects of wonder.

Pliny the Elder, *Encyclopedia* 34.73, 35.66, 36.196

32. Mundus ("The Vault")

COMMENTARY
   Sources refer to three monuments in the upper Forum (Capitoline side) that commemorated in one way or another the center of Rome, whether conceived as a community or as a geographical center of the empire: the Mundus, the Milliarium Aureum ("The Golden Milestone"), and the Umbilicus Romae ("The Navel of Rome"). The disputes over whether all three actually existed and over their remains are discussed in the Notes below. Traditionally, the Umbilicus has been identified as the round brick ruin about 3 m. tall between the Rostra and the Arch of Severus, and the Golden Milestone is located by a pile of cut stones in front of the Temple of Saturn.

SOURCES

32.1 When founding Rome, Romulus summoned men from Etruria who guided him in all matters in accordance with their sacred customs and writings, teaching him these things as religious rites. A trench was dug around the Comitium in the form of a circle, and the first fruits of everything, whether deemed good by custom or necessary by nature, were deposited in this trench. Finally, all of the newcomers, having carried a small portion of their home soil with them, cast it over the first fruits, mixing the soils together. The Romans call this trench the Mundus, the same word they use for the heavens.

Plutarch, *Romulus* 11

32.2 The Mundus that is said to be Ceres' is customarily opened three days in the year: on August 24, October 5, and November 8.

Festus 126L

32.3 When the Mundus is opened, it is as if the door to the grim gods below were opened.

Macrobius, *Saturnalia* 1.16.18

32.4 The Mundus gets its name from that heavenly vault [*mundus*] which is above us, for its form is similar, as I have learned from those who have entered it. Our ancestors determined that the lower part of the Mundus, being consecrated to the Spirits of the Dead, must be closed at all times except for those days mentioned above.

Cato (in **Festus** 144L)

33. The Golden Milestone *(Milliarium Aureum)*

33.1 Augustus, when appointed Commissioner of Roads [in 20 BC], set up the monument called the Golden Milestone.

Dio, *History* 54.8.4

33.2 If you measured the sum total of the distance from the mile-post that stands at the head of the Roman Forum to each of the city gates [and then to the limit of Rome's buildings, you would begin to get an idea of how big Rome is].

Pliny the Elder, *Encyclopedia* 3.66

33.3 Otho, preparing his coup against the Emperor Galba [in AD 69], told his confederates to wait for him in the Forum at the Golden Milestone by the Temple of Saturn, and went up to the Palace in the morning to greet Galba.

Suetonius, *Otho* 6.2

33.4 Otho descended through the Palace of Tiberius into the Forum and approached the golden pillar erected where all the roads that cut across Italy terminate.

Plutarch, *Galba* 24.4

34. The Navel of Rome *(Umbilicus Romae)*

SOURCE
34.1 *Notitia*, Sites in Region VIII:
> The Roman Forum (sometimes called the "Great" Forum),
> contains the following:
> ... the Temple of Concord;
> the Umbilicus of Rome;
> the Temple of Saturn;
> the Temple of Vespasian and Titus;
> the Capitolium;
> the Golden Milestone,
> the Basilica Julia;
> the Temple of the Castors ...

Notes: The existence in ancient Rome of three sites—the Mundus, Milestone, and Umbilicus—all dedicated to a ritualistic centering of the community and all located at the head of the Forum, seems redundant, and there is some confusion over the identity, terminology, and location of these three sites. The trouble begins with Plutarch's description of the Mundus as the trench drawn around the Comitium; he calls the Mundus the center of the wider boundary ploughed around the city by Romulus, whereas other accounts of the Romulean foundation place the Palatine Hill at its center, and do not even include the Comitium area of the Forum as part of Romulean Rome. Perhaps some anachronisms are at play in Plutarch's account. Richardson, moreover, believes that Festus and Macrobius [32.2–32.4] all refer to another Mundus, separate from the one described by Plutarch and dedicated to the spirits of the underworld, perhaps related in form and origin to archaic underground granaries on the Palatine. Coarelli (in *LTUR* 3.288–9), again favoring the organic whole (as with his location of the Tarpeian Cliffs), considers not only that the sources refer to one Mundus, but that this unified Mundus can be further identified with the Umbilicus Romae. Richardson addresses the redundancy by equating the Umbilicus and the Milestone (discounting the division of the two terms in the *Notitia*).

That a ceremonial milestone, decorated in some way with gold and therefore often called the Golden Milestone, stood at the head of the Forum near the Temple of Saturn, and that Augustus first set this up, seems fairly certain from the sources. Whether this monument was the same as the Umbilicus Urbis ("Navel of the City") or existed separately nearby is disputed. There is no evidence that either such monument recorded distances to other cities.

The first reference to an Umbilicus Urbis is found in the *Notitia* [c. AD 300] as part of a list which places it after the Temple of Concord and before the Temple of Saturn. This list also contains a reference to the Milliarium Aureum as a separate item. There are three mentions of the Umbilicus in the Einsiedeln Itinerary for pilgrims [c. AD 800] that place it in the same area. None of the sources tells us anything about the monument, except that it was selected for the list and therefore considered more worthy of mention than many other monuments.

One thing that does emerge from the references to the Mundus, the Milestone, and the Umbilicus is the importance for the Romans of a symbolic center of the city, its center considered not as a talismanic or essential power (the Capitoline temple and the Temple of Vesta rather embody that) but as an earthbound geographical center, perhaps of a small agrarian community at first (Plutarch's Mundus), and then of an urban empire with distant reaches measured out in every direction by milestones on the major roads.

The notion of a Mundus, however hazy its nature and despite the lack of physical remains, has had a life of its own and appears—creatively interpreted as a global fountain and basin—in newly founded towns of Fascist Italy such as Littoria near Rome, where it was placed at the crossing of the two chief roads in the city center. The Foro Italico in Rome has another such Mundus-fountain across the plaza from Mussolini's Obelisk.

35. Temple of Saturn

COMMENTARY

The worship of Saturn played an important part in both the mythology and calendar of Rome. His origins, which go further back than Livy's comment might suggest, are obscure, although very early his divine powers and domain included liberation. Later he became identified with the Greek god Kronos (since Dionysus, the wilder god of liberation in the Greek pantheon, was not an option for the Forum), and was subsequently styled in myth as the deity who was ousted from the gods' throne by Jupiter and ruled for a time over an agrarian Golden Age Italy, before Jupiter went on to occupy the Capitoline as well. His worship thus allowed the Romans to honor a simpler past even as they extended Jupiter's iron dominion in every direction, and his connection with myths of the Golden Age provided the poets the means to explore complex attitudes towards urban society and Roman rule.

The sources included below on the Saturnalia, the festival in honor of Saturn, fills out Saturn's role as a god of liberation. Held on December 17 and eventually lasting several days, it was a time in which the strict hierarchical social world of Rome was held in abeyance, or in many cases inverted. This inversion was symbolically represented in a ceremony on that day that apparently unwrapped the woolen bonds kept around the cult statue of Saturn for the rest of the year. Statius's description of the Saturnalia (an excerpt of a longer poem praising an especially lavish Saturnalia in Rome put on by the Emperor Domitian) indicates some of the terms of the inversion, in a Mardi Gras-like atmosphere [35.9]. Horace simply invites his slave to speak what is on his mind [35.10].

In light of this Saturnian spirit, it may seem odd that his temple was also the site of the public treasury of the Roman Republic. Macrobius offers two attractive explanations for this; perhaps the temple's solid vault within a large podium also had something to do with it.

The gloomy remains of the Temple of Saturn are from a late C4 restoration, perhaps carried out as part of the final spirited resistance mounted by pagan Senators to the advance of regulations favoring Christianity in these years. The restoration is second-rate, and involved the reuse of damaged components from various ages.

SOURCES

35.1 Sources have it that the Capitoline Hill was originally called Mt. Saturnius, and from this Latium got the name "Land of Saturn," as the poet Ennius in fact calls it. It is also written that an ancient town named Saturnia once existed on this hill.

Varro, *The Latin Language* 5.42

35.2 When Sempronius and Minucius were consuls [in 497 BC], the Temple of Saturn was dedicated and the festival day of the Saturnalia [on December 17th] was established.

Livy, *History* 2.21.2

35.3 The founders of the Temple of Saturn wanted the building to be Rome's treasury as well, because it was said that under the reign of Saturn no robberies took place within Italy's borders, or because under his rule private property did not exist. "It was forbidden to own the earth and to divide up fields with borders; everyone strove for the common good," as Virgil describes that time [in *Georgics* 1.126–7]. Therefore, the public funds of the people were lodged in the temple of the god under whose rule the wealth of the community was held in common. ...Apollodorus says that the statue of Saturn is bound in wool fetters throughout the year, and is freed of them only on the day of the festival in his honor.

Macrobius, *Saturnalia* 1.8.3–5

35.4 [Caesar's men advanced on the Temple of Saturn.]
The tribune protecting the Treasury was thrown aside,
And the building was opened; the Tarpeian Cliff
Echoed the great groan of the doors swung back.

With that, the wealth of the Roman people vanished,
A treasure amassed since the temple's founding—
Booty from the Punic Wars, from Philip in defeat,
Whatever our frugal ancestors saved
And the rich lands of the East sent in tribute.
Grim the spoils that come from a Roman temple.
Then for the first time was Rome poorer than a Caesar.

Lucan, *The Civil War* 3.153–8; 161–2; 167–8

35.5 Julius Caesar, entering Rome for the first time after the beginning of his civil war, took from the Treasury 15,000 gold ingots, 30,000 silver ingots, and 30,000,000 sesterces in coin.

Pliny the Elder, *Encyclopedia* 33.56

35.6 Old olive-oil is considered useful in preventing ivory from rotting: at any rate, the statue of Saturn in Rome is filled inside with the oil.

Pliny the Elder, *Encyclopedia* 15.32

35.7 Munatius Plancus rebuilt the Temple of Saturn [in 42 BC] using the spoils of the war [against alpine Raetia].

ILS 886 = *CIL* 10.6087

35.8 [Inscription on the pediment of the Temple of Saturn from late C4 AD]

SENATUS POPULUSQUE ROMANUS INCENDIO CONSUMPTUM RESTITUIT.

The Senate and People of Rome restored this temple after it was destroyed by fire.

ILS 3326 = *CIL* 6.937

35.9 Father Apollo and stern Minerva:
Take holiday with the polished Muses:
We will call you all back on the first of the year.
Now Saturn, slip your shackles and reign
With drunken December, insolent Wit
And the smiling god of Mockery.
Let Jupiter wrap the world in cloud
And threaten to flood the fields
With winter rain, so long as Saturn
Showers us with abundant gifts.
Today one table feasts us all
In common, mixing young and old,
Men and women, high and low:
Here Liberty puts Rank in its place.

Statius, *Occasional Poems* 1.6.1–7; 25–7; 43–45

35.10 [Horace to his slave:]
Come now, speak up!
Take advantage of the freedoms December allows,
As our ancestors intended.

Horace, *Satires* 2.7.4–5

36. The Temple of Castor and Pollux

COMMENTARY

As its three landmark columns testify, the Temple of Castor was one of the most imposing monuments in the Forum, looming over it on a large podium that was itself twenty feet tall. Built shortly after Rome became a Republic, the temple's origins reflect a spreading of the Dioscuri cult up the Italian peninsula (a cult in which the semi-divine twins were worshipped as sudden saviors of men in peril, as befits their epiphany at Lake Regillus). It also reflects Rome's increasing dominance among other Latin communities in the Roman Campagna. The battle against the Latin coalition at Lake Regillus (near Frascati, but now dried up) in 496 BC was an important stage in the expansion of Rome's control. Since the Dioscuri are often associated with horses, it is natural that in Rome their cult at this temple became especially associated with the Equites, the cavalry-class of Roman citizens.

The podium (long spoiled of its cut-stone walls) provided not only the foundation for the temple architecture, but formed a large raised platform out in front of the columns, ascended originally by stairs on each side rather than in the front. This platform fronting the Forum provided another speaker's rostra and increased the space available for meetings of Senate and juries. In addition, the podium below was divided into numerous chambers for various activities and offices, especially those needing the protection of its thick walls. Some of the chambers served as money vaults, regarded as more secure than the Temple of Mars the Avenger, according to Juvenal [36.11]. Here too were kept the weights that formed the standard not only for the intense trading and banking business of the Roman Forum, but as the central standard for the weights of other cities as well; the inscriptions below were found on a set of weights in Aquileia.

Both the written and the archaeological record testify to the major restorations of the temple. Even the work under Verres may not have been as insignificant as Cicero's hostile speech suggests, since there are signs that the building was subject to settling in this low area near springs. The standing columns in Luna marble are from the rebuilding by Tiberius, perhaps hoping to style himself and his late brother Drusus (both of them victorious in border-wars) as imperial brothers with a divine ancestry (Ovid's "two brothers" in 36.8), analogous to the Dioscuri.

SOURCES

36.1 [After turning the tide of battle against the Latins, the Roman army was victorious.] During this battle, it is said, two horsemen appeared to the Roman commander Postumius and the men fighting around him. In beauty and size far outstripping the mortal norm and just beginning to grow a beard, the two led a charge of the Roman cavalry. Using their spears, they drove all the Latins they met into flight.

After the Latins retreated and the Romans sacked their camp (which occurred in the late afternoon), they say that there appeared in the Roman Forum, at just about the same time, two young men, striking in their size and beauty and likewise in early manhood, dressed in battle gear and with the look of battle still fresh in their faces, leading horses that were drenched in sweat. After they watered and washed down their horses at the spring which wells up into a small but deep pool next to the Temple of Vesta, they told the crowd, which had gathered around them and were eager for news of the battle, how the battle had gone and that the Romans had won. Then the two left the Forum and were not seen again, despite an intensive search by the official left in charge of the city. The next day, when the officials in town received letters from the field describing the battle and in particular the epiphany of the heavenly spirits, they concluded that they had seen a vision of the same gods at the spring, identifying them (as seems reasonable) as apparitions of the Dioscuri twins, Castor and Pollux.

There are many memorials in Rome to this strange and marvelous epiphany. They include the Temple to Castor and Pollux that the city built in the Roman Forum on the site where the apparitions appeared, and the fountain next to it likewise named after the two deities and considered sacred to this day … . But the most spectacular observance occurs after the sacrifice at this temple, when all those who own a horse for military service ride in procession, grouped in rows by tribe and century … . The horsemen, as many as five thousand of them, ride through the Forum and past the Temple of Castor and Pollux, wearing whatever insignia their commanders have awarded them for bravery in battle. This parade is a stunning expression of the power of Roman rule.

Dionysius, *Early Rome* 6.13.1–4

36.2 [In 499 BC the Roman army at Lake Regillus began to bend the battle line of the Latins.] Then the dictator Postumius, neglecting neither divine nor human help, is said to have vowed a temple to Castor … .

Livy, *History* 2.20.12

36.3 The Temple of Castor was dedicated on July 15, in the consulship of C. Fabius and L. Aemilius [in 484 BC]. The temple had been vowed during the Latin War by Postumius when he was serving as dictator, but his son dedicated it after he was appointed to a Board of Two to see to the temple's completion [after his father's death].

Livy, *History* 2.42.5

36.4 [When Verres, one of the most corrupt politicians ever produced by Rome, was praetor,] he wanted the Temple of Castor and Pollux to be the most famous memorial of his corruption, something we would not just hear about occasionally but be able to see on a daily basis. He asked who was responsible for turning over the Temple of Castor in a state of good repair, and learned that it was the son of the late Junius, who was still a minor. He was also told that the statuary and gifts to the temple were all accounted for, and that the temple itself was in fine condition all around. For someone such as Verres, it seemed a shame if such a large and magnificent temple should go unused to make himself richer, especially at the expense of a minor.

So Verres personally goes to inspect the temple. He sees that the ceiling is beautifully paneled everywhere and that everything else was maintained in good order. Verres turns and asks one of the dogs in his pack of followers what he could possibly do with the place, and is told: "Verres, there's nothing here for you to work on, unless you want to put the columns on the perpendicular." "'On the perpendicular?'" this most incompetent of humans asks; "What does that mean?" They tell him that no column can be set exactly on the perpendicular. "By Hercules, that's what we'll do then: these columns must be realigned on the perpendicular!"

All those columns that we see there, freshly whitened, were taken down with a scaffold-prop in their place, and then put back up using the very same stone as before. For this work, Verres, you accepted a bid of 560,000 sesterces. Furthermore, your contractor never even touched some of the columns, but simply scraped and re-coated them!

Cicero, *Against Verres* 2.1.130–133, 145

36.5 Metellus rebuilt the Temple of Castor and Pollux [in 117 BC]

Asconius, on Cicero's *Scaurus* 24

36.6 It came about that Caesar alone got credit for the works he and Bibulus financed together as aediles [in 65 BC]. Bibulus in fact stated openly that he suffered the same fate as Pollux: just as the temple in the Forum was built in honor of both of the twins but called simply the Temple of Castor, so were his and Caesar's good works called by Caesar's name alone.

Suetonius, *Julius Caesar* 10.1

36.7 With spoils [from the war in Germany] Tiberius rebuilt the Temple of Concord as well as the Temple of Castor and Pollux,

and dedicated them in his own and his late brother Drusus's name
[in AD 6].

Suetonius, Tiberius 20

36.8 January the twenty-seventh is the dedication date
    Of the temple built in honor of Leda's immortal twins:
    Close by the Pond of Juturna two brothers built this temple,
    Brothers from a house divine in honor of brothers divine.

Ovid, Fasti 1.705–8

36.9 Up until now I have been discussing Caligula [AD 37–41] in his
capacity as an emperor; we must now consider him in his capacity as
a monster. …

    Eventually Caligula began to claim for himself a divine majesty;
…He extended a part of the Palatine palace all the way out to the
Forum, transforming the Temple of Castor and Pollux into an entrance
hall for the Palace. There in the temple he would often take his
seat between the twin gods, presenting himself for worship to those
who approached.

Suetonius, Caligula 22.1–2

36.10 Caligula went so far as to divide in two the Temple of the
Dioscuri in the Roman Forum, making a passageway to the Palatine
that went right between the two cult statues. As a result, he was fond of
saying that he regarded the Dioscuri as his gate-keepers.

Dio, History 59.28.5

36.11 [I could show you entertainment superior to any stage]
    If you could watch the mortal dangers people risked
    To increase their holdings, stuff metal safes with money,
    And put more cash under Castor's watchful eye
    (preferred to Mars the Avenger's since he lost his own helmet
    And couldn't keep the thieves away from the deposits in his care).

Juvenal, Satires 14.258–62

36.12 [Inscriptions found on a set of weights in Milan (ancient
Aquileia); each is a bronze circular vessel, shaped such that the smaller
size fits inside the larger.]
    Weighed to the 10 lb. standard at the Temple of Castor
    Weighed to the 5 lb. standard at the Temple of Castor
    Weighed to the 3 lb. standard at the Temple of Castor
    Weighed to the 2 lb. standard at the Temple of Castor
    Weighed to the 1 lb. standard at the Temple of Castor
    Weighed to the 6 oz. standard at the Temple of Castor

Weighed to the 4 oz. standard at the Temple of Castor
Weighed to the 3 oz. standard at the Temple of Castor

ILS 8636 = *CIL* 5.8119.4

37. The Spring and Pool of Juturna

COMMENTARY

The spring (*fons*) and pool (*lacus*) of Juturna (a water-nymph with a varied mythological background) are further urbanized links to Rome's marshy past, and are indications of the Roman reverence for pure spring water, which surfaced (now below ground level) beside the Temple of Castor at the base of the Palatine. The compact area between this temple and the Temple of Vesta was a water-center of sorts, including at least one shrine to Juturna, represented now by the attractive little late third century AD restoration with the inscription to Juturna on its architrave [37.1]. Immediately in front of this shrine there is a little altar found nearby, and there are the remains of a marble well-head overtop a well to the springs. This spring is not to be confused with the larger pool, the Lacus Juturnae, closer to the Forum and oriented to the Temple of Castor, to which it was connected by the legend of the battle at Lake Regillus. It is not clear just how the curative powers of Juturna were effected: by drinking her pure spring water, or by immersion in the basin built around the pool?

A further topographical puzzle is represented by Lollianus's inscription [37.4], found nearby on the base of a statue to the emperor Constantine. This inscription, with several others also found nearby, have led most topographers to conclude that the water administration in Rome moved its headquarters (the *statio aquarum*) here from the Campus Martius in or before AD 328, and was housed in the brick-faced buildings behind the pool of Juturna. Others find grounds for doubt, disputing among other things that *statio* refers to a central office.

SOURCES

37.1 [Inscription at shrine] JUTURNA[i] S[acrum]

37.2 The water-nymph Juturna got her name because she helps (*juvaret*) people. On account of this reputation, many sick people seek water from her spring.

Varro, *Latin Language* 5.71

37.3 For 441 years after the Founding of the City [until 312 BC] the Romans were content to use the water they might draw from the Tiber,

from wells, or from springs. The reverence for old springs exists to this
day, since they are believed to restore health to ailing bodies, such as
the springs of the Camenae … and of Juturna.

Frontinus, Aqueducts 4

37.4 To the Emperor Constantine … Lollianus, Secretary of Water and
Grain, dedicates this statue with the headquarters [in AD 328].

ILS 8943 = CIL 6.36951

Note: The debate over the existence and location of the water department's
headquarters, which hinges in part on the translation of Lollianus's inscription [37.4], is laid out in detail (and in English) by P. Burgers under "Statio
Aquarum" in LTUR 4.346–9.

38. Overview of Forum Basilicas

COMMENTARY

Each of the long sides of the Roman Forum came to be dominated by the long colonnaded structure of a basilica: the Basilica Aemelia
(= Basilica Paulli) on the east side, between the Temple of Antoninus
and the Senate House, and the Basilica Julia, between the Temple of
Castor and Pollux and the Temple of Saturn. Little remains of the
magnificent structures of these basilicas, both of them famous for the
beauty of their materials and decoration, but their ground plans and
some of the stone that remains give a good indication of their size and
some idea of their splendor. The literary sources refer as well to several
earlier basilicas that occupied these and other spaces in the republican
Forum, including an unnamed basilica (later replaced by the Basilica
of Aemelia and Fulvia), Cato's Basilica Porcia in 184 BC, and the Basilica of Aemelia and Fulvia in 179 BC.

The origin of the Roman basilica has been variously traced back
to Greek stoas (covered colonnades) and Hellenistic audience halls.
The word itself is Greek and means "royal," but the form came into
its own in Roman towns, where it became the main center of business
(especially banking transactions) as well as the venue for certain
types of trials, such as the one Pliny describes. The open floor plan
allowed for audiences of shifting sizes, depending on the notoriety of
the case and the fame of the speakers, who had to compete not only
against opposing lawyers but against the orators of other trials being
held simultaneously.

The distinguishing architectural features of the Roman basilica
were a multitude of columns supporting a truss roof, and a floor plan
that includes a central aisle, or nave, flanked on each long side by a
narrower aisle, sometimes double. Not only was the interior space an

open design, due to the columns rather than walls as load bearers, but in many instances several sides of the whole building were open to the outdoors as well (in which case the structure was like an elaborately roofed pavilion without walls). A clerestory (a central story, or upper part of the nave, that rises into the clear above the roofs of the side aisles, allowing for windows down the length of the nave walls where they rise above the aisles) was not uncommon, and there was frequently a raised platform, the tribunal, where an official might preside over trials.

Starting with Constantine, when the Church acquired the liberty and wealth to construct large and prominent worship halls, the term basilica was applied to churches, for which the basilica architecture, with its capacious, open design was more suitable than the Roman temple, which was architecturally polluted by its pagan associations and was at any rate designed to house a deity in its most enclosed section, not to hold a congregation under roof (pagan assembly taking place around the sacrificial altar in front of the temple, in open air). Even the tribunal seat of the basilica was reconfigured as the seat of the bishop. That the church basilica was typically entered under a colonnade at its short side (a narthex) and had solid walls rather than columns for its outer perimeter, also had precedents in earlier basilica architecture (Vitruvius's "Chalcidian" vestibule, for example, 38.1), especially in its modifications as an audience hall for the emperor.

SOURCES

38.1 The basilicas ought to be placed in the warmest part of forums so that the businessmen can meet for business there throughout the winter without being disturbed by bad weather. The width of a basilica should be no less than a third and no more than a half of its length, unless difficulties of the site demand some other proportion. If the site does require a length of greater proportion than twice the width, put vestibules [*chalcidica*] at the ends, as at the Basilica of Julia Aquiliana.

Vitruvius, *Architecture* 5.1.4

38.2 My speech [c. 100 AD], which was in defense of one Attia Viriola, was remarkable for the rank of the woman, the rarity of the case, and the number of jurors. This woman, of noble parentage and married to a praetorian senator, was disinherited by her octogenarian father eleven days after the lovesick old man married and brought my client's new stepmother home. Her suit to regain her patrimony was being tried before a quadruple panel: all 180 jurors from the four courts combined. There was a host of lawyers on each side, benches filled with supporters, and a ring of standing spectators several rows deep around the entire court. Add to this crowd the jurors packed together up on the tribunal and still more spectators, women as well as men, leaning from the balconies above in their eagerness to see the proceedings (easily done) and hear (almost impossible).

The outcome of the trial was awaited with great suspense by fathers and daughters, not to mention stepmothers. … The stepmother, who was herself in line to get one sixth of the estate, lost.

Pliny the Younger, *Letters* 6.33.2–4, 6

39. Early Basilicas

39.1 At this time [in 210 BC] the seven shops (which were later the five) and the bankers' offices that are now called the "the New Shops" [*Tabernae Novae*] burned down; next to catch fire (since at that time there were no basilicas) were the private houses, and then the quarter of the Quarries [*Lautumiae*], the Fish Forum [*Forum Piscatorium*], and the Hall of Kings [*Atrium Regium*].

Livy, *History* 26.27.2–3

39.2 Marcus Porcius Cato was the first to build a basilica named after its builder.

Illustrious Romans 47.5

39.3 [In 184 BC] Cato bought up two halls (the Maenius and the Titius, in the area of the Lautumnian quarries) and four shops, and, after donating the land to the state, built in their place the basilica which is called the Porcia.

Livy, *History* 39.44.7

39.4 [In 179 BC] an election was held for the censors. Marcus Aemilius Lepidus (who was also the Pontifex Maximus) and Marcus Fulvius Nobilior were elected—both men of noble families but bitter opponents of each other. …[Although both men undertook building projects in Rome,] Marcus Fulvius's projects were more numerous and of greater use. They included…the basilica behind the New Shops of the bankers, and the Fish Forum, which he surrounded with shops that he sold to private owners.

Livy, *History* 40.45.6–7; 51.5

40. Basilica Aemilia (Basilica Paulli)

40.1 Among Rome's marvels, how could we not mention the Basilica of Paullus and its columns of Phrygian marble, one of the most beautiful works that the world has ever seen?

Pliny the Elder, *Encyclopedia* 36.102

40.2 [While in Gaul, Caesar worked tirelessly to build support in Rome to counter those working against him in the city.] In the year after his enemy Marcellus was consul, Caesar put large quantities of the wealth he acquired in Gaul at the disposal of those engaged in public affairs in Rome, … including 1,500 talents to the consul [Lucius Aemilius] Paullus, who used it to build his famous basilica in his family's honor, in the Forum where the Basilica of Fulvius used to be.

Plutarch, *Caesar* 29.3

40.3 Cicero sends greetings to Atticus: [54 BC]
Paullus has almost roofed over the basilica in the middle of the Forum, reusing the columns from the older one. The other basilica, however, the one that he has contracted out, he builds in magnificent style. In truth, no other monument equals it for popularity and prestige.

Cicero, *Letters to Atticus* 4.16.8

40.4 Aemilius Lepidus Paullus finished the Basilica [*stoa*] of Paullus, as it is called, out of his own funds, and dedicated it in the year he was consul [in 34 BC].

Dio, *History* 49.42.2

40.5 The Basilica of Paullus burned down [in 14 BC] … . It was rebuilt in Aemilius's name (a descendant of the man who had built the earlier one), but in truth the work was carried out by Augustus and the friends of Paullus.

Dio, *History* 54.24.1–3

40.6 At this time [in AD 22] Lepidus [probably a grandson of the L. Aemilius Paullus in Cicero's letter] sought permission from the Senate to restore and embellish with his own funds the Basilica of Paullus, the Aemilian family's public monument. … Though of modest fortune, Lepidus carried out this restoration of his family's honor.

Tacitus, *Annals* 3.72

41. Porticus of Gaius and Lucius

41.1 Augustus also constructed buildings in the name of others, including his grandsons, his wife, and his sister, such as the portico and the basilica of his grandsons Gaius and Lucius.

Suetonius, *Augustus* 29.4

41.2 To Lucius Caesar, son of Augustus, grandson of the deified [Julius Caesar], Prince of the Youth, Consul Designate at the age of 14, Augur. Dedicated by the Senate [in 3 BC].

CIL 6.36908

42. Basilica Julia

42.1 I completed two works that Caesar had begun and nearly finished: the Forum of Caesar and the basilica located between the Temple of Castor and the Temple of Saturn. When this basilica burned down, I began its reconstruction after enlarging its site, now giving it the names of my sons, Gaius and Lucius.

Augustus, *Achievements* 20

42.2 The Basilica [*Stoa*] Julia, as it is called, was built in honor of Gaius and Lucius Caesar and dedicated at this time [in AD 12].

Dio, *History* 56.27.5

42.3 In our own days [c. AD 80] the orator Trachalus seemed to tower above his contemporaries, possessing an imposing physique, intense eyes, a commanding brow, and highly expressive gestures. His voice, moreover, rather than equaling a tragic actor's, as Cicero desired, surpassed any actor's that I have ever heard. In fact, Trachalus was speaking once in the Basilica Julia before the court of the First Tribunal, when all four courts were in session at once, as is usual, and I remember that in spite of the crowd that had gathered and filled the whole building with noise, he could not only be heard and understood above the din, but to the chagrin of the other speakers he was even applauded by spectators of the other three trials.

Quintilian, *Oratorical Training* 12.5.5–6

42.4 For squandering fortunes in prodigality, the Emperor Caligula [AD 37–41] had no equal. … On one occasion he even went out on the roof of the Basilica Julia for several days running and scattered large sums in coins onto the commoners below.

Suetonius, *Caligula* 37.1

Notes: There are several puzzles that the sources raise over the identity and location of the various basilicas. First, Cicero's seeming reference [40.3] to two basilicas under construction by Paullus is confusing; is he referring to one location in which a simpler basilica was abandoned in favor of the more elaborate one (Richardson, 55), to the Basilica Julia, or to a third site (Steinby in *LTUR* 1.167)? Another confusion exists over the location and appearance of the Porticus of Gaius and Lucius, identified by many as the long portico of shops in front of the entire length of the Basilica Aemelia, and by others as a double monumental archway between this basilica and Temple of Julius Caesar. Shifting nomenclature does not help matters (e.g., the Basilica Julia was also called the Basilica of Gaius and Lucius, and the Greek word "stoa" can refer to both "basilica" and "porticus").

On origins of the basilica and a topography of early basilicas in the Forum, see K. Welch, "A New View of the Origins of the Basilica."

43. The Temple of the Divine Julius Caesar (Aedes Divi Julii)

COMMENTARY

The unsightly concrete core of the Temple of the Divine Julius Caesar contrasts with the vivid literary accounts of the dramatic events which determined the temple's location, as well as with the clear picture of the political implications of the site, which owes its origins both to a spontaneous outburst and calculated image-building.

In the confusion immediately following the assassination of Caesar in 44 BC, the Senators fled from the scene of the murder in Pompey's Theater [87.11]. The conspirators among them repaired to the security of the Capitoline Hill with an armed body of gladiators. On the following days, meetings of the Senate were held. In a compromise eventually fatal to the assassins, the Senate granted amnesty to the conspirators but also declared that Caesar's acts and decrees would have the force of law, and allowed the slain dictator a public funeral (and therefore all the elaborately staged drama and political interaction involved in such funerals). In the meantime, Brutus and Cassius had made various overtures to the people, including a visit to the Forum, where Brutus spoke without much effect. The funeral took place on March 20, with Mark Antony delivering the funeral oration. Ancient accounts of Antony's eulogy vary as to the length and emotional intensity of the speech, but they agree on its results. Although the cremation of Caesar had been scheduled to be carried out on a pyre in the Campus Martius, the crowd rioted and ended up cremating the corpse on the Forum-side of the Regia (the headquarters of the Pontifex Maximus, a post held by Caesar at the time of his death). Cicero, politically opposed to Caesar, harps in his passage on the wild, anarchic quality of his cremation, which apparently did not finish the job. Nevertheless, it was sufficient to sanctify the ground and subsequently, after the Caesarians won the day and Caesar was officially deified, to occasion a temple here.

Like the Temple of Castor nearby, the podium of Caesar's temple left ample room for a speaker's podium in front of the porch's foremost columns and level with their base. Still visible at the front of this rostra is a niche with the base of an altar, which was probably meant to designate the precise location of Caesar's cremation. Fortunately for Augustus, whose filial devotion to his now divine father was an important part of his political program, this spot was nicely aligned on an axis down the middle of the Forum, which intersected, in the middle of the opposite end, with Caesar's Rostra.

That a historical figure could be deified and worshipped with a temple and cult in the heart of the city was a momentous occasion in Roman history, even if the ancients worked with categories and gradations of divinity that have since atrophied under monotheisms (Caesar himself, after all, had just built a temple to Venus as his ancestor, and for over a century Roman generals active in the East were increasingly attracted to and experimenting with middle-eastern and Hellenistic practices of ruler-worship). The deification of emperors became standard practice; the sensible ones waited for death to receive this official and "political" honor, and it was not extended to reviled emperors such as Caligula, Nero, and Domitian. Augustus was careful, at least in Rome, to avoid living equation with a god. When he received a temple after his death, it was apparently located in the busy but relatively inconspicuous area behind the Basilica Julia, but its remains, if such exist, have not yet been identified.

SOURCES

43.1 Caesar's last will was displayed to the people assembled in the Forum, and they demanded that it be read immediately. In the will Caesar declared Octavius, the grandson of Caesar's sister, to be his adopted son. He also bequeathed his private garden to the people, and gave 75 drachmas to every Roman citizen living in the city. This began to stir some anger in the crowd against the conspirators. …

Then Piso brought the corpse of Caesar into the Forum. A crowd swarmed around the body, giving it an armed escort to the Rostra with loud cries and a lavish procession. … Sensing the mood of the crowd, … Antony spoke as follows:

"Citizens, it would not be proper for me, a single individual, to deliver the eulogy for this great man; that is rather the duty of the entire country. I will therefore read to you all the decrees that the Senate and people, united in admiration, voted in praise of Caesar while he was alive, thereby giving voice not to Antony's sentiments, but to your own."

With a sullen, gloomy expression on his face, Antony read aloud the decrees, giving special emphasis to those which voted Caesar into the ranks of gods by declaring him sacred and sacrosanct, or which pronounced him to be the father of his country, a great benefactor, a leader without equal. With each honor, Antony turned and gestured to the corpse. … Then he recited the oaths that the senators took to defend Caesar and his person with all their strength, and to avenge any conspiracy against him, or be damned. …

At the end of his speech, carried away by his emotions, Antony uncovered the body of Caesar and lifted the dead man's toga aloft, swaying it on the end of a spear so that all might see the gashes made by the daggers and the stains of the dictator's blood. Seeing this, the crowd keened like a chorus in a Greek tragedy, loudly joining Antony's expressions of grief. Once again, the emotions of lamentation aroused anger in them. …

While the crowd was in this state and on the edge of violence, someone raised a wax image of Caesar above the bier (the body itself, being supine on the bier, could not be seen). This image, which a mechanical device continuously rotated, showed each of the 23 stab-wounds that had been savagely delivered to all parts of Caesar's body as well as his face. At the sight of this the crowd could no longer endure their grief. ... [After rioting around the city against the conspirators] the people returned to the body of Caesar and carried it up the Capitoline to bury it in the Temple of Jupiter and place him among the gods. Forbidden to do this by the priest, they returned to the Forum with the body and placed it next to the Regia, the old palace of the kings. Then gathering benches and other pieces of wood that the Forum is filled with, along with anything else they could lay their hands on, they heaped it around him in a pile ... and set it on fire. A great crowd stayed and watched it burn through the night.

The site of the pyre was first marked with an altar, but then the present temple was erected when Caesar was deemed worthy of divine honors. These were accorded him by Octavius, his son by adoption, who changed his name to Caesar and followed in his father's footsteps politically, greatly strengthening the rule which Julius Caesar founded and which continues to this day [c. AD 150]. Ever since this first divination, the Romans, who formerly could not tolerate that any living man should bear the title of king, continue to accord divine honors to each of the emperors upon his death, unless he has ruled in a cruel or tyrannical fashion.

Appian, *Civil Wars* 2.143–148

43.2 Mark Antony, you were the one who shamelessly presided over the funeral rites of Caesar—if you can call chaos a ritual. You delivered the eloquent funeral oration, the moving lament, you provided the incitement to riot: in a real sense, *you* lit the flames by which the great Caesar was half-burnt.

Cicero, *Philippics* 2.90–1

43.3 [The people] set up an altar at the site of the pyre after the remains of Caesar where taken up by his freedmen and deposited in the family tomb [probably the tomb of his daughter Julia, in the Campus Martius], but when some attempted to worship him as a god with animal sacrifice, the consuls overthrew the altar.

Dio, *History* 44.51.1

43.4 At the height of the public mourning, bands of foreigners had gathered, lamenting Caesar's death in their various fashions, none more so than the Jews, however, who assembled around his pyre the whole night through. ... Afterwards the people erected a solid column of

Numidian marble in the Forum nearly 20 feet high, with the inscription "To the Father of his Country."

Suetonius, *Julius Caesar* 84.5, 85

43.5 When that limitless evil of affection for the late Caesar was snaking through the city and spreading daily, and the same people who had carried out that half-baked travesty of a cremation were now responsible for setting up a funeral altar in the Forum … the punishment inflicted against them by the consul Dolabella and his overturning of that vile column were so decisive that the change struck me as miraculous… .

Cicero, *Philippics* 1.5

43.6 Among the honors the triumvirs gave the late Caesar, they laid the foundations [in 42 BC] for a shrine to him on the spot where he was cremated.

Dio, *History* 47.18.4

43.7 [After celebrating his triumph over Egypt and other lands,] Augustus dedicated the shrine to Julius Caesar and decorated it with numerous spoils of Egypt [in 29 BC].

Dio, *History* 51.22.3

43.8 I built the Temple of the Divine Julius … and from the spoils of war I consecrated precious gifts to the temple.

Augustus, *Achievements* 19, 21

43.9 [In 30 BC] the Romans decreed that the podium of the shrine of Julius should be decorated with the beaks of ships captured at Actium.

Dio, *History* 51.19.2

43.10 [To enumerate the penalties for damaging an aqueduct] I provide the text of the law: "The consul Titus Quintius Crispinus duly put the matter to vote before the people, and the people, assembled in the Forum in front of the rostra of the Temple of the Divine Julius, passed the law [in 9 BC]… ."

Frontinus, *Aqueducts* 129

43.11 The only place in the world where a comet is worshipped is at a temple in Rome. The Divine Augustus judged the comet to be propitious to himself, since it appeared at the beginning of his rule during the games that he was putting on for Venus Genetrix… . Augustus declared his pleasure publicly: "During the very days of my games a comet appeared for seven days… . The people believed the comet signified that the spirit of Caesar had been received among the immortal gods; because of this, we added an emblem of this comet to the bust of Caesar that we consecrated in the Forum a short time later."

Pliny the Elder, *Encyclopedia* 2.93–94

43.12 [Jupiter consoles Venus after the death of Caesar:]
"Meanwhile make his soul, torn from his butchered body,
A radiance; then from his lofty temple he can gaze
Forever on my temple and the Forum, divine."

Ovid, *Metamorphoses* 15.840–42

43.13 It is not easy to say which of Apelles' paintings are his best. His painting of Venus emerging from the ocean (called Venus Anadyomene) was dedicated by the Divine Augustus to the temple of his father Caesar. This painting however decayed with age, and Nero replaced it with a painting by a different artist.

Pliny the Elder, *Encyclopedia* 35.91

44. The Temple of the Divine Vespasian (Fig. 23)

COMMENTARY

As the down-to-earth emperor Vespasian was dying in AD 79, he was heard to quip, "Alas, I think I'm becoming a god" (*Vae: puto deus fio*). Indeed he was; Vespasian became the first emperor to attain divine status since Claudius a quarter-century earlier. After succeeding his father to the throne, Titus began construction on the temple during his short reign, and Domitian completed it before AD 90.

The Temple of Vespasian is almost on an axis across the forum square from the Temple of Julius Caesar, but is displaced off to the side by the presence of the Temple of Concord, and views of the structure would have been partially obscured from much of the square by the Temple of Saturn. From its high podium part way up the slope of the Capitoline, one could see two other Flavian structures built in the same years, the Arch of Titus on the crest of the ridge opposite, and the Colosseum towering behind it in the distance.

The two sources below provide grounds for a dispute over whether the temple was dedicated to Vespasian alone or to Titus as well. The architrave of the temple originally contained only the first line of the inscription in source 44.1 (if we can trust an eighth-century manuscript that records it; only the ESTITUER of the second line remains, referring to a restoration in the early C3 AD) and argues for a solo attribution, although some manuscripts of the *Curiosum* and other post-classical references pair Vespasian with Titus.

Three Corinthian columns of the temple, white Italian marble from the original structure, remain standing on the temple's degraded

Fig. 23 Entablature of Temple of Vespasian, on display in Tabularium

podium and support a section of the architrave containing relief carvings of sacrificial implements and priestly symbols. A reconstructed section of the entablature (a fine piece of architectural decoration that managed to avoid the lime-kilns) is on display in the halls of the Tabularium nearby.

The construction of this temple on the scarce forum real estate apparently usurped some of the land previously occupied by the building next to it towards the river. This is the Portico (or Temple) of the Dei Consentes (the "Harmonious Gods"), who represented the dozen chief deities of the Roman/Greek pantheon. Their cult arose, like the worship of the more exotic Magna Mater, during the crisis of the Second Punic War. Virgil's *Aeneid* may provide the key to the significance of the epithet "harmonious," since it was divine disharmony and Juno's support of Carthage that caused so much suffering for the Trojans and later Romans. At any rate, a portico containing all their statues would have provided a visual boundary to this corner of the forum, especially before the Tabularium was built. The current ground plan contains remnants of a Flavian restoration required by the portico's reduction in size.

SOURCES
44.1 DIVO VESPASIANO AUGUSTO S.P.Q.R. / IMPP. CAESS. SEVERUS ET ANTONINUS PII FELIC. AUGG. RESTITUER(UNT)

ILS 255 = *CIL* 6.938

The Senate and the People of Rome dedicate this temple to the Deified Emperor Vespasian. The Emperors Severus and Caracalla restored it.

44.2 *Curiosum*, Region VIII:
The Temple of Vespasian and Titus

45. Arch of Septimius Severus

COMMENTARY

The Arch of Septimius Severus, one of the best preserved structures in the Forum, was awarded by the Senate in AD 203 to commemorate the Parthian victories of the emperor Severus and his sons Caracalla and Geta. The wars of this campaign, including the capture of Ctesiphon, the Parthian capital on the Tigris, are chronicled by the four massive relief panels above the side arches, and winged Victories blowing trumpets decorate the spandrels of the central archway. The Arch was the first major commission in the Forum since Hadrian's Temple to Venus and Rome eighty years earlier, and besides glorifying the Emperor's military deeds it staked Severus's claim to a dynasty with the prominent inclusion of the Emperor's sons, Caracalla and Geta, in the inscription.

One of the most interesting features of this monument is the obliteration of Geta's name from the inscription that fills the attic. Severus had first chosen Caracalla, his elder son, as heir to the throne but later named Geta to be a co-ruler with Caracalla. Upon his father's death in AD 211, Caracalla put an end to the long-standing feud between the two brothers by murdering Geta. He then subjected his brother's name to a *damnatio memoriae*, the "erasure of memory (or record)," involving the destruction of the person's statues and images, and the erasure of his name from inscriptions. Going back to republican times, the practice was also applied to emperors, including Domitian (hence the inclusion of Suetonius's passage on Domitian in this section, 45.3).

The "son of Marcus" as part of Severus's title and the name "Marcus Aurelius" as part of Caracalla's are the result of Severus's self-proclaimed "posthumous" adoption by the long-dead Marcus Aurelius.

SOURCES

45.1 IMP (eratori) CAES(ari) LUCIO SEPTIMIO M(arci) FIL(io) SEVERO PIO PERTINACI AUG(usto) PATRI PATRIAE PARTHICO ARABICO ET / PARTHICO ADIABENICO PONTIFIC(i) MAXIMO TRIBUNIC(ia) POTEST(ate) XI IMP(eratori) XI CO(n)S(uli) III

PROCO(n)S(uli) ET / IMP(eratori) CAES(ari) M(arco) AURELIO
L(ucii) FIL(io) ANTONINO AUG(usto) PIO FELICI TRIBUNIC(ia)
POTEST(ate) VI CO(n)S(uli) PROCO(n)S(uli) [P(atri) P(atriae) /
OPTIMIS FORTISSIMISQUE PRINCIPIBUS / OB REM PUBLICAM
RESTITUTAM IMPERIUMQUE POPULI ROMANI PROPAGATUM
/ INSIGNIBUS VIRTUTIBUS EORUM DOMI FORISQUE S(enatus)
P(opulus)Q(ue) R(omanus)

To the Imperator Caesar Lucius Septimius, son of Marcus, Severus
Pius Pertinax Augustus [=**Septimius Severus**], father of his country,
conqueror of the Parthians in Arabia and Assyria, Pontifex Maximus,
with Tribunician powers 11 times, triumphing general 11 times, consul
3 times, and proconsul; and to the Imperator Caesar Marcus Aurelius, son of Lucius, Antoninus Augustus Pius Felix [=**Caracalla**], with
tribunician powers 6 times, consul, proconsul, father of his country—
the best and bravest of princes—on account of the republic
restored and the empire of the Roman people increased by their
outstanding virtues at home and abroad, the Senate and the Roman
people dedicate this arch.

** This phrase was substituted for one that probably read: P(ublio)
SEPTIMIO L(ucii) F(ilio) GETAE NOB(ilissimo) CAES(ari), preceded
by ET at the end of the third line: "and to Publius Septimius, son of
Lucius, Geta, most noble Caesar [=Geta]..."

ILS 425 = *CIL* 6.1033

45.2 When the senators granted Severus a triumph for the victory over
Parthia, he had to refuse because he suffered from arthritis and was
unable to stand up in the chariot for the procession.

Imperial Lives, *Severus* 16.6

45.3 [In AD 96, when hearing that the Emperor Domitian had been
murdered], the Senate was so overjoyed that they jostled one another
to get into the Senate House, where they gave themselves over to a
verbal mutilation of the dead man's reputation, venting their hatred in
the most insulting and bitter language imaginable. They even had ladders brought in to tear down objects adorned with Domitian's likeness.
They watched as these were shattered on the ground, and then decreed
that all of his inscriptions should be erased and all record of the
man expunged.

Suetonius, *Domitian* 23

46. Column of Phocas

COMMENTARY

This 15-meter column standing on a large stepped base between the Pool of Curtius and the Augustan Rostra once supported a gilded statue dedicated by Smaradgus, governor of central Italy, to the emperor Phocas. It was this statue that the inscription at the base of the column commemorated; the fluted column and its Corinthian capital stem from earlier times and other locations, reassembled by Smaradgus on a base with steps of recycled marble veneer. These scattered origins reflect the time of the dedication in AD 608. Phocas (who never set foot in Rome) ruled in Constantinople when the imperial power in Italy was much reduced by the Germanic Lombard rulers and "the expiring dignity of Rome was only marked by the freedom and energy of her complaints," as Gibbon puts it [p. 1496]. Both money and protection from the East were increasingly tenuous.

The marble words of the inscription are belied by Phocas's sordid career. Originally a centurion who first usurped the throne and then murdered the deposed emperor and his five sons in a scenario reminiscent of Czar Nicholas's final days, Phocas was a tyrant on the order of Caligula and Domitian, and like them was assassinated. He is significant, however, for a first and a last in Rome's topographical history: he was the last public figure in antiquity to receive an honorary monument in the Forum, and his donation of the Pantheon to the Church was responsible for the first conversion of a pagan temple in Rome into a Christian church.

SOURCE

46.1 OPTIMO CLEMENTISS[IMO PIISSI]MOQUE / PRINCIPI DOMINO N(ostro) / F[OCAE IMPERAT]ORI / PERPETUO A D[E]O CORONATO [T]RIUMPHATORI / SEMPER AUGUSTO / SMARADGUS EX PRAEPOS(ito) SACRI PALATII / AC PATRICIUS ET EXARCHUS ITALIAE / DEVOTUS EIUS CLEMENTIAE / PRO INNUMERABILIBUS PIETATIS EIUS BENEFICIIS ET PRO QUIETE / PROCURATA ITAL(iae) AC CONSERVATA LIBERTATE / HANC STA[TUAM MAIESTA]TIS EIUS AURI SPLEND[ORE FULGEN]TEM HUIC / SUBLIMI COLU[M]NA[E AD] PERENNEM IPSIUS GLORIAM IMPOSUIT AC DEDICAVIT / DIE PRIMA MENSIS AUGUSTI, INDICT(ione) UND(ecima) / P(ost) C(onsulatum) PIETATIS EIUS ANNO QUINTO.

To the peerless, the most clement, and most pious Emperor, Our Lord Phocas, crowned by God for perpetual dominion, victorious and always Augustus: Smaragdus, appointed to the sacred palace, Patrician, Exarch of Italy, devoted to the Emperor's kindness for the innumerable gifts of his piety, for the peace he brought to Italy, and for the preservation of our liberty, hereby erects in his lasting honor a statue of his majesty gleaming with the splendor of gold upon this lofty column, and dedicates it on the first day of August, in the eleventh indiction, in the fifth year after the consulship of his Piety [AD 608].

ILS 837 = *CIL* 6.1200

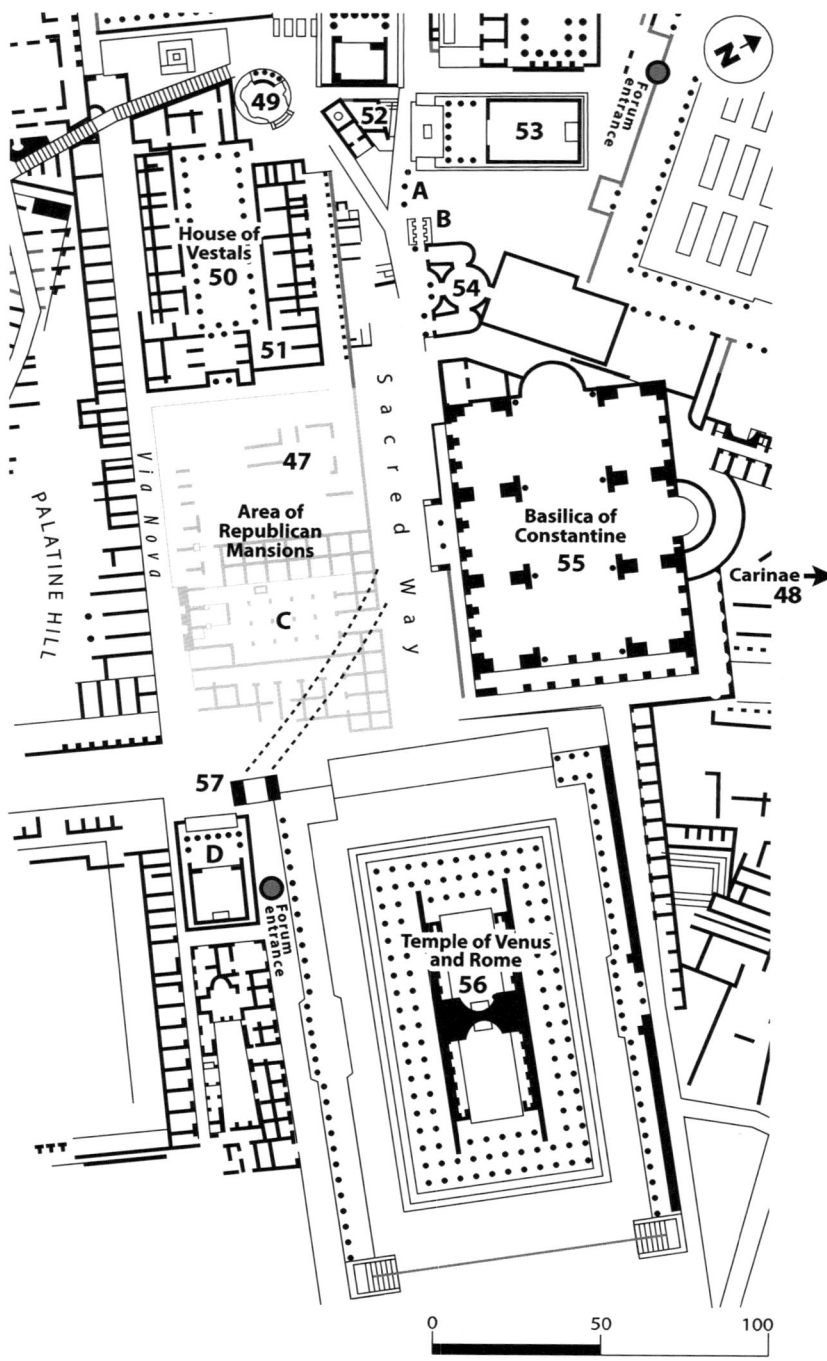

Fig. 24 Upper Sacred Way (*map key on next page*)

V. The Upper Sacra Via

Overview

By convention that has more to do with the arbitrary limits of the present archaeological park than with ancient terminology, the long slope between the Regia and the Arch of Titus is commonly considered part of the Forum. The presence of the Sacred Way certainly ties the two areas together, but this region, even after its relatively late regularization with Hadrian's Temple of Venus and Constantine's Basilica, lacked the architectural unity of the Forum Romanum proper, and it was never as intensely focused on public business. Even into the early Empire, this was an area of prestigious private homes, intermixed with shrines and temples, and especially as one proceeds uphill on the Sacred Way to the ridge connecting the Palatine and largely vanished Velia, it could be said to overlook the Forum rather than to belong to it. Such an arrangement, however, gave a high-profile visibility to such private residences, thereby using, as so often in ancient Rome, natural topography as an agent and display of social and political life. Homes (often more like mansions) here and on the adjoining slope of the Palatine kept

MAP KEY

47	Republican mansions
48	Carinae neighborhood
49	Temple of Vesta
50	House of the Vestals
51	Residence of Pontifex Maximus?
52	Regia
53	Temple of Antoninus and Faustina
54	"Temple of Romulus"
55	Basilica of Constantine
56	Temple of Venus and Rome
57	Arch of Titus
A	Archaic grave sites
B	Basement of Republican house?
C	imperial shops (Horrea Vespasiani?)
D	unidentified building (Temple of Jupiter Stator?)

Fig. 25 The Sacred Way

their owners in the public eye and allowed them and their entourages to stage dramatic entrances down into the Forum, in an ancient version of a VIP motorcade.

Because the homes of the elite on the Forum-side slope of the Palatine were so closely connected to the life of the Forum, I have included them here. That there is nothing to be seen of this aristocratic housing is due to another characteristic and defining feature of the Roman experience, the imperial family's eradication of aristocratic "pluralism" and its competing displays of power, here in the form of conspicuous real estate. Accordingly, there is little sense, among the predominantly imperial ruins, of the Palatine's long residential phase, with its network of streets that included the Sacred Way, the Nova Via (the "New Way," actually very ancient) part way up the Palatine, and connecting roads between them. Topographers generally place Cicero's house, with its address "on the Palatine" [47.3–7], higher up the hill, on what we consider the Palatine today, but Coarelli may be right in arguing that anything built on the Palatine side of the Sacred Way could have been given the address "on the Palatine" (*LTUR* 5.109–112). Excavations have demonstrated the existence of sumptuous aristocratic houses beneath the now largely vacant area between the Arch of Titus and the Hall of the Vestals. These homes were destroyed in the fire of AD 64, after which Nero and Vespasian had other uses for the area.

One might imagine this area as the side of a bowl (in place of the current park's rectangle) with the Forum proper at the lowest level and the Sacra Via rising from it to a low point on the rim near the Arch of Titus, dividing the Palatine neighborhood on its right from the Velia neighborhood on its left. Further back on the left, in the direction of the St. Peter in Vincoli church, lay another fashionable neighborhood, the Carinae [48.], whose most famous resident had been Pompey the Great, before his property was taken over by Mark Antony [48.3].

The platform and hulk of the Basilica of Constantine, as well as the trench cut in the 1920s for the Via dei Fori Imperiali on the other side of it, obscure what must in some way have been a more continuous and unified zone with primarily upper-class residences that took advantage of the terrain placing them in close physical and visual proximity to the Forum below.

Excerpts from the electioneering handbook (attributed to Cicero's brother Quintus but perhaps of later authorship) give Cicero advice on how to run his campaign for consulship, and provide graphic evidence of the importance and value placed on the high visibility of these homes and their owners [47.9]. Cicero's home also became the focal point of an intense political battle, in which his enemies, led by Clodius, had the statesman exiled, his house burned, and its ground rendered sacred so that no residence could henceforth be built there. But Cicero and his allies fought through these problems to bring about both his return to Rome and the construction of a new home on the old site.

47. Republican Mansions

SOURCES

47.1 [Sensitive to public sentiment against displays with associations of monarchical power, in 509 BC] Publius Valerius ordered the lictors who accompanied him to lower the fasces before he gave a speech to the people. He also moved his house lower down on the slope of the Velia when he noticed that his earlier choice of a site, high up on the Velia in the same spot where king Tullus had lived, was raising alarm among the people.

Cicero, *On the Republic* 2.53

47.2 The architect of private residences must concern himself with a plan for designing and arranging private space that is reserved for the master and his household, on the one hand, and public space that is shared with visitors. The public space—those areas of the home that any Roman, even uninvited, has the right to enter—are rooms such as the entrance hall, the courtyard, and peristyles… . The homes of high-ranking politicians who are holding office and need space for public duties must therefore be designed with lofty, regal entrances, spacious atriums, peristyles, and gardens with broad walkways suitably landscaped for the dignity of their high office.

Vitruvius, *Architecture* 6.5.1–2

47.3 [In 91 BC] Marcus Livius Drusus turned his efforts…towards granting citizenship to the Italians. While he was working on this problem and was returning home one day to the Palatine surrounded by the large and unruly crowd that accompanied him wherever he went, he was stabbed in front of his house with a knife that the assassin left behind in Drusus's side. Within a few hours he was dead.

I should not omit to mention one instance that reveals Drusus's character. When he was building his house on the Palatine (on the same site where Cicero later built his house, subsequently owned by Censorinus and presently [c. AD 30] by Statilius Sisenna), his architect promised that he would build Drusus a house with total privacy, shielded from the view of all prying eyes. Drusus responded, "I want you, insofar as it is in your powers, to build me a house in which everything I do will be visible to everyone."

Velleius, *History* 2.14.1–3

47.4 My house is on view to practically the entire city.

Cicero, *On his House* 100

47.5 Cicero sends greetings to Sestius in Macedonia: [62 BC]

Encouraged by your congratulations—you'll remember you wrote to me a while back, hoping things had gone well in my purchase of the house of Crassus—I went ahead and bought the property (sometime *after* your letter, actually!). I paid 3,500,000 sesterces. As a result, I'm so deep in debt now that, instead of uncovering a conspiracy, I want to *join* one (if anyone would have me). … At any rate, plenty of money is currently available at six percent.

Cicero, *Letters to Friends* 5.6.2

47.6 [Clodius, Cicero's bitterest political and personal foe, outmaneuvered him and had the orator exiled in 58 BC.] Cicero's property was confiscated, his house razed to the ground as though it belonged to a foreign enemy, and the site was dedicated for a temple to Liberty. Cicero himself received the penalty of exile, which he was forbidden to spend in Sicily, since he was banished 500 miles from Rome, with the further provision that if he should ever be seen inside this distance, both he and those who harbored him could be killed with impunity.

Dio, *History* 38.17.6–7

47.7 The violence with which Cicero's home was destroyed by Clodius [in 57 BC] was matched by the splendor to which the Senate restored it.

Velleius, *History* 2.45.3

47.8 [In court, Cicero defends a young ambitious politician against charges of political violence, arguing that the charges were trumped up by his ex-lover Clodia.] The prosecution finds it reprehensible that my client Caelius moved out of his father's house. … But that was at an age when he was old enough to run for public office, and since his father's house was far from the Forum, Caelius moved not only with his father's permission, but with his encouragement. He rented a house—at a modest rate—on the Palatine so that he would have readier access both to my and Crassus's homes and to his own supporters.

[Would, though, that he had never moved to the Palatine!] For you will find, judges, that the young man's move to the Palatine, and the Palatine Medea [his lover Clodia] whom he met there, were the cause of all his troubles, or rather the slander that caused his troubles.

Cicero, *In Defense of Caelius* 18 [65 BC]

47.9 Quintus sends greetings to his brother Marcus Tullius Cicero:

Because of our closeness I do not consider it out of place to share with you some thoughts that have come to me concerning your campaign for the consulship [of 63 BC].

As concerns your entourage of supporters, see to it that you always have a crowd around you, of all ages, backgrounds, and walks of life. From such an abundance of supporters, others can conclude how much strength you will have at the polling place itself. … And if you can manage it, descend into the Forum with your followers at the same time each day. Such a crowd of supporters at a daily appearance boosts your reputation and confers great prestige on you.

Candidates who never leave the city are at a great advantage. This benefit of your continual presence, however, derives not simply from making appearances in Rome and the Forum, but from actively canvassing support, soliciting the same people many times.

Finally, see to it that your entire campaign is an entertaining spectacle that is dazzling, showy, and popular, and that it has high visibility and prestige. Also arrange, if at all possible, that moral scandals should arise concerning the crimes, briberies, and sex life of your opponents.

Handbook on Electioneering, 1, 34, 36, 43, 52

48. The Carinae ("The Keels")

SOURCES

48.1 Evander and Aeneas resumed their walk from the river
    to the lowly home of Evander, and saw the cattle at pasture
    filling the Roman Forum and fashionable Keels with mooing.

Virgil, *Aeneid* 8.359–61

48.2 The district of the Carinae gets its name from buildings near the Temple of Tellus made in the manner of keels [*carinae*].

Servius, on *Aeneid* 8.361

48.3 [After the defeat and death of Pompey in their civil war, in 47 BC] Caesar returned to Rome from Alexandria and consigned the property of Pompey the Great to the piercing calls of an auctioneer. Only one Roman was shameless enough to make a bid: Mark Antony. As soon as he found himself surrounded by that man's wealth, he practically jumped for joy, like a clown on stage imitating a poor man who has just struck it rich. Along with the house came well-stocked wine-cellars, pound after pound of the finest silver, costly wardrobes, and an abundance of elegant and magnificent furnishings—not indeed on the scale of someone with luxurious habits, but entirely appropriate to Pompey's considerable wealth. A few days after Antony took possession, nothing was left. Entire wine-cellars were given to low-lifes as presents. Actors looted some things, actresses others; the whole house, room after room, was filled with people gambling and drinking. It wasn't long before you could find purple tapestries from the house of the great Pompey covering cots in the cubicles of slaves.

You even had the nerve, Antony, to take up residence in that man's house, to cross over that sacred threshold and show your polluted face to the household gods of his home. But tell me: when you saw the ship-beaks in the entryway of his house, could you possibly think you were entering a house that belonged to you? Surely, even to a raving drunkard like yourself, apparitions of that great man must appear at night to terrify you from your sleep, they must torment you even in waking hours. For my own part, I pity the poor walls, the very ceilings of that house, which, until you moved in, had never looked on such filth.

Cicero, *Philippics* 2.64–69

48.4 When Sextus, son of the late Pompey the Great, received the triumvirs Octavian and Mark Antony on board his ship for dinner [in 39 BC], his wit was not without point when he welcomed them to his own Keels, referring to the name of the area in Rome where his ancestral home was located, and which was occupied by Antony at that time.

Velleius, *History* 2.77.1

48.5 When Tiberius returned to Rome [in AD 2], as soon as he had accompanied his son Drusus into the Forum for his formal initiation into public life, he moved out of the Pompeian mansion on the Carinae and up to the Gardens of Maecenas on the Esquiline, where he quietly spent his time on private affairs, keeping out of the public eye.

Suetonius, *Tiberius* 15.1

49. The Vestals and the Regia

Overview

Although the ruins of the Temple of Vesta and especially the Regia give little sense of their former importance, this group of buildings has some very rich history as preserved in the sources. These sites, along with the Hall of the Vestals and the Domus Publica ("Public Residence"), are also connected to each other by more than just physical proximity, and may even be another sort of bridge, this one historical, between the public and the private spheres, as characterized in the previous section on residences.

The clearest connection between these sites is the figure of the Pontifex Maximus, who was not only the head of the priestly order in Rome, which had its central offices and important religious observances in the Regia, but oversaw the Vestals as well (indeed, Horace, reaching for an image to express how long his poetry will last, says, in what turns out to be a conservative estimate, "as long as the Pontifex Maximus and the silent Vestal climb the Capitolium together" [9.1]). His residence, moreover, called the Domus Publica, was adjacent to the Hall of the Vestals (and eventually attached to it, probably at the upper end), at least until Augustus, elected Pontifex in 12 BC after Lepidus's death, moved the residence to his own quarters on the Palatine, uniting the post of chief priest with the position of princeps.

It has been suggested, however, that these sites were even more closely connected originally, as functions of the palace of Rome's kings, an original Regia, or "Royal Palace," more extensive than the portion now known as the Regia. After the fall of the monarchy, the complex was split and rendered public, but still retained its religious functions, transformed, however, into *public* rituals and posts. Some of the king's original religious duties split off, perhaps originally to a "rex sacrorum" but eventually to the post of Pontifex Maximus. The Vestals occupied part of the old palace, now called the Atrium Vestae, and the chief pontiff another part that, no longer the residence of the ousted king, was appropriately called the Domus Publica.

Although there are many references to the Vestals in ancient literature, giving us a glimpse into their elaborately circumscribed life that in some areas also allowed them freedoms no other women in Rome enjoyed, and although there are significant remains of their residence, we cannot be sure what activities were relegated to what part of their Hall. Its size, which was considerable at least by the time of its last major rebuilding under Trajan, following an earlier enlargement after Nero's Fire, suggests that not only did the Vestals have spacious personal quarters, but were part of a busy bureaucracy that helped them prepare and perform both the duties immediately associated with the vestal cults and other responsibilities. Apparently it was felt that wills

Fig. 26 Temple of Vesta

were safe here (as money was thought to be safe in vaults below temples), perhaps because the Vestals were free of the attachments that might lead to the falsification of a will.

On the long northeast side of the courtyard in the Hall of the Vestals there are several rows of statues set upon inscribed bases. The inscriptions in each case honor a head Vestal Virgin, the Vestalis Maxima, but both the location of the statues and their pairing with their particular bases are modern conjectures. On the base of one statue is an inscription [50.10] to a head vestal whose name has been scratched out but who may be the Claudia referred to in Prudentius's poem as a convert to Christianity [50.11].

Of the Regia's structure, little more than the foundations remain, and even these are a confusing palimpsest of several pre-Republican designs and later re-buildings such as the opulent marble structure financed by Calvinus in 39 BC. Like the Temple of Vesta with its Palladium [49.4], the Regia housed a sacred object bound up with the well-being of Rome, in this case the Ancile, a sacred shield with an archaic figure-8 design. This shield and its replicas meant as decoys were used in the ritual dances of the Salii, priests of the war-god. The Regia was thus an important site in the military-religious life of Rome, sharing this concern with the Shrine of Janus Geminus [24.], the Capitoline temples to Jupiter [10., 13., 14.], and (in imperial times) the Temple of Mars Ultor [74.]. In addition to the talismanic shield, the sources tell us that the Regia also housed spears involved in the declaration of war [52.5], and, in another rite connected with Mars, was sometimes (depending on the winning team) the destination of the decapitated head of the "October Horse" and its dripping tail [52.6].

49. The Temple of Vesta

SOURCES

49.1 The current temple's shape preserves the shape of old.
　　There is solid reason for its roundness: the Earth,
　You see, and Vesta are one; for each, an undying fire,
　　And Earth, like hearth-place, signifies the Center.
　The Earth, also, is round like a ball … .
　Foolishly I used to think that Vesta had a statue,
　　Until I learned her curving dome held none.
　A perpetual flame burns hidden in that temple,
　　But neither Vesta nor the flame have sculptured form.

　　　　　　　　　　　Ovid, *Fasti* 6.265–269; 295–298

49.2 Varro also wrote that not all sacred buildings [*aedes*] are temples proper [*templa*]; not even the shrine of Vesta is an augurated temple.

　　　　　　　　　　　Gellius, *Attic Nights* 14.7.7

49.3 [After the hostile Capuans had started a fire in the Forum in 210 BC, the Roman general said that the enemy] was attempting to destroy the Temple of Vesta, with its eternal fire and the divine guarantee of Roman rule hidden in its inner shrine.

　　　　　　　　　　　Livy, *History* 26.27.14

49.4 People believe that the image of Minerva clad in armor,
　…　The Palladium, sprang down from heaven to the hills of Troy.

　Whoever it was who took it from Troy, it is Roman now,
　　And Vesta guards it here with her always watchful light.
　Imagine the fear the senators felt, the time that Vesta
　…　Caught on fire!

　The pontifex Metellus ran to the scene and shouted,
　　"Vestals, run to the rescue! It will not help to weep!
　Lift up the pledges of Rome's power in your virgin palms:
　…　Their rescue calls for human hands, not prayer."

　Metellus scooped up water, then lifting his hands he prayed:
　　"Forgive me, sacred ones! I go, a man, where a man should not.
　If this be a crime, let the punishment fall on me, not Rome:
　　Let the city be redeemed by the price of my own life."
　So saying, into the temple he burst; and the goddess, saved
　　By the actions of her pontiff, approved the deed.

　　　　　　　　　　　Ovid, *Fasti* 6.421–54 (selections)

49.5 Metellus lived his old age in blindness caused by the fire [in 241 BC] from which he rescued the Palladium in the Temple of Vesta—a deed with an admirable motive but disastrous results. Because of this, you cannot call him unfortunate, but neither can you call him blessed; the People of Rome gave him the singular honor, accorded to no one else in history, of being taken to meetings of the Senate in a chariot, but he paid for this high and mighty honor with his eyes.

Pliny the Elder, *Encyclopedia* 7.141

50. House of the Vestals

50.1 [Numa, king of Rome after Romulus, founded many religious institutions.] He appointed virgins to the cult of Vesta, to be supported by payments from the public treasury so that they could remain constant attendants at her temple. To confer sanctity and awe upon these priestesses, he set them apart with virginity and a variety of ceremonies.

Livy, *History* 1.20.3

50.2 There is a particular vase with a wide mouth and narrow base that is used in the rites of Vesta, since water which had been gathered for her rites cannot be set on the ground without sacrilege. Therefore this vase was designed so that it could not be set upright on the ground, but had to be poured before it was put down.

Servius on *Aeneid* 11.339

50.3 Originally there were four virgins serving the goddess Vesta, chosen by the kings according to regulations laid down by Numa. Their number later grew to six, however, due to an increase in their religious duties, and this remains their number today [c. 10 BC] ... .

The Vestals are required to remain celibate and single for the 30 years in which they perform their sacrifices and other religious observances. Of this 30-year period they spend ten years learning their responsibilities, ten years in the performance of the rites, and the final ten years teaching their duties to others. When the priestesses have finished their term of service, nothing forbids them from getting married, provided they have laid down their garlands and the other insignia of the priesthood. Some very few of them have done this, but they came to such pitiable ends that the others consider these misfortunes an omen and remain in the service of the goddess until death, at which time the priests appoint another virgin to fill the vacancy.

The Vestals receive many distinguished honors from the Romans and as a result have no yearning for children or marriage. Stiff penalties are visited on those who fail in their duties. By law, the priests are responsible to investigate and punish the infractions of the Vestals. For a minor infraction the priests beat the Vestal with sticks, but if one has been unchaste, she is put to a shameful and gruesome death. While still alive, she is carried out on a bier in a funeral procession proper for the dead, accompanied by a keening procession of family and friends. When she has been brought to the Colline Gate, she is entombed in an underground chamber prepared for her inside the walls, dressed in funeral clothes but given no monument or libations or any other customary funeral rites.

There are many indications if a Vestal is not performing the holy rituals with the proper purity, but chief among them is the extinction of the flame. Whatever the cause of its going out, the Romans fear this above all other signs as portending the destruction of the city, and they bring a new flame into the temple with many rites of atonement.

Dionysius, *Early Rome* 2.67

50.4 [In 206 BC, the war against Hannibal dragged on.] In a country worn by the stress of a perilous war, people attributed the causes of all events, favorable and unfavorable alike, to the gods, and numerous prodigies were reported. North of the city in Caere, a two-headed pig was borne, as well as a lamb that was both male and female; in Alba, they say two suns were seen. But more terrifying than any of the portents, whether reported from other towns or seen in Rome, the fire in the Temple of Vesta went out, and the Vestal in charge of the fire that night was whipped, by the order of the Pontifex Maximus, Publius Licinus.

Livy, *History* 28.11.1, 3, 6

50.5 During the same year [420 BC], the Vestal Virgin Postumia was put on trial for the charge of unchastity. She was innocent, but had come under suspicion because she dressed too attractively and showed too free a spirit for a Vestal. After the trial was postponed, she was acquitted, but the Pontifex Maximus, speaking officially for the priesthood, ordered her to restrain her wit and to dress in a fashion more prim than prom-like.

Livy, *History* 4.44.11–12

50.6 In that year [337 BC] the Vestal Minucia, having first come under suspicion because she dressed more stylishly than was proper for a Vestal, was then accused of unchastity by one of her servants. The pontiffs who heard the charge ordered her to abstain from her sacred duties, and to retain her servants (so that, as slaves, they might be tortured for further evidence). She was convicted and buried alive near the Colline Gate, to the right of the paved road in the Accursed Field—named, I believe, as a result of her unchastity

Livy, *History* 8.15.7–8

50.7 The Senate prohibits by law the burial of anyone within the boundaries of Rome. The Vestal Virgins, however, are not bound by Rome's legal system, and have their tombs within the city. ... Even the Vestal Virgins who have broken their vow of chastity are not bound by the burial laws, since they too are interred (admittedly while alive) within the city, in the Accursed Field.

Servius on *Aeneid* 11.206

50.8 [When the Vestal Cornelia, falsely accused of unchastity by the tyrant Domitian,] was taken down into the subterranean chamber for burial, her robe caught on something. She stopped and turned to free it, and when the executioner reached out a hand to help her, she flinched back to avoid his polluting touch—the last act of piety, it seems clear, to protect a pure and undefiled body.

Pliny the Younger, *Letters* 4.11.9

50.9 Pliny sends greetings to Priscus:

I am worried about Fannia's health. She came down with her sickness when she was nursing the Vestal Junia, which she was doing originally on her own (the two women are related) and then by the authority of the pontiffs, since Vestals forced by an illness to leave their compound are entrusted to the care and oversight of a married woman. It was during her performance of this duty that Fannia herself fell sick.

Pliny the Younger, *Letters* 7.19.1–2

50.10 OB MERITUM CASTITATIS PUDICITIAE ADQ(ue) IN SACRIS RELIGIONIBUSQUE DOCTRINAE MIRABILIS C / / / / / / E V(irgini) V(estali) MAX(imae) PONTIFICES V(iri) C(larissimi) PROMAG(istro) MACRINIO SOSSIANO V(iro) C(larissimo) P(ontifice) M(aximo)

In recognition of her chastity, purity, and her outstanding knowledge in ritual and religious matters, the pontiffs, under the illustrious Pontifex Maximus, Macrinius Sossianus, (dedicate this) to C[——]a, head priestess of the Vestal Virgins.

ILS 4938 = *CIL* 6.32422

50.11 [From the day that St. Lawrence was martyred, pagan worship dwindled.]
> A pontiff whose cult wore a head-band
> Now nods to the sign of the cross,
> And the Vestal Virgin Claudia
> Now enters, Lawrence, your shrine.

Prudentius, *Crowns of Martyrdom* 2.525–28

51. Domus Publica (House of the Pontifex Maximus)

SOURCES

51.1 Caesar first lived in a modest dwelling in the Subura, but then moved to the Domus Publica when he became Pontifex Maximus.

Suetonius, *Julius Caesar* 46

51.2 When holding games while dictator, Caesar once used linen cloth to canopy the entire Forum as well as the stretch of the Sacred Way between his residence and the top of the Capitoline Hill. Indeed, these awnings were a more amazing spectacle than his gladiatorial games themselves.

Pliny the Elder, *Encyclopedia* 19.23

52. Regia

SOURCES

52.1 King Numa lived first on the Quirinal Hill, and then in what is still called the Regia, next to the Temple of Vesta.

Solinus, *Handbook of Geography* 1.21

52.2 Numa built what is called the Regia, or "royal house," next to the Temple of Vesta. He spent much of his time here, performing religious duties, training priests, or simply spending time in solitary meditation upon the divine. He had another house on the Quirinal Hill, which the Romans still point out today [c. AD 100].

Plutarch, *Numa* 14.1

52.3 [Numa tells the people of a prophecy he heard from Jupiter himself:]
"When the disc of tomorrow's sun first clears the horizon
    Jupiter will send us a guarantee of Roman rule."
...
In the cloudless dawn, Jupiter flashed and thundered thrice.
    Behold: a shield, twisting lightly in a gentle breeze,
Fell from heaven. Mindful that the fate of Rome
    Was bound to this shield, the king contrived an ingenious plan:
He ordered identical copies made of the shield from heaven,
    To fool the eyes of any enemy plotting its theft.

Ovid, *Fasti* 3.353–82, selections

52.4 After fighting in Spain, the general Calvinus was allowed a triumph by Octavian [in 39 BC]. He only used gold from Spanish cities to pay for the triumph, and even then only part of the gold; the majority of it went towards the Regia, which had been destroyed in a fire. Calvinus rebuilt the Regia and dedicated it, providing it with impressive decorations, especially statues.

Dio, *History* 48.42.4

52.5 At the start of any war, the one responsible for its conduct entered the shrine of Mars [in the Regia] and would first shake the divine shields and then the spear of the god's statue itself, saying, "Mars, awaken!"

Servius on *Aeneid* 8.3

52.6 The October Horse is the name given to the horse (specifically, the right-hand horse of the winning chariot) sacrificed to Mars each year after the race in the Campus Martius. The head of this horse becomes an object of fierce contention between two neighborhoods: those from the Sacred Way hope to mount it on the wall of the Regia, and those from the Subura want to attach it to the Tower of Mamilius.

The tail of the October Horse, however, is quickly transported to the Regia so that some of its blood can trickle onto the sacrificial hearth and make a link to Mars. Some people say that this is offered to the War-god in place of a sacrificial victim (not, as the story commonly goes, as a punishment visited upon this creature because the Trojans, ancestors of the Romans, were defeated by the Wooden Horse).

Festus 190

Notes: On the origins of the Regia, see T.J. Cornell, *The Beginnings of Rome*, 239–241. Cornell summarizes and revises Coarelli's hypothesis that the Regia and Vestal buildings originally had an organic unity as parts of the palace of the kings.

53. Temple of Antoninus and Faustina

COMMENTARY

Protected in some measure by its early status as a Christian church, the Temple of Antoninus and Faustina offers more to see than to read about in sources. Although its original roof and much of its decorative elements are gone, its columns, the walls of the cella, and its attractive marble frieze remain standing, with portions here and there of the elaborate cornice. In addition, numerous architects of the Renaissance, including Pirro Ligorio and Andrea Palladio, sketched it, attracted by its proportions and design. Over the centuries as a property of the Church, its porch was enclosed for a period of time with chapels. A building was also attached to the front of the columns over the (since reconstructed) front steps of the temple. The notches in the upper part of some of these columns probably mark where the sloping tile roof of this building was fitted into the ancient structure, not (as one can sometimes hear on Forum tours) because the columns were grooved to give purchase to the ropes of Christians eager to pull the columns down. Certainly much good stone from the temple was reused elsewhere, including the Lateran.

"If a man were called to fix the period in history of the world during which the condition of the human race was most happy and prosperous," Gibbon boldly wrote, "he would without hesitation name that which elapsed from the death of Domitian to the accession of Commodus." Of the "five good emperors" who ruled Rome in these eighty-odd years—Nerva, Trajan, Hadrian, Antoninus Pius, and Marcus Aurelius—Antoninus was the only one to receive a temple in the Forum. In truth, it was to Antoninus's wife Faustina that the temple was first built: originally only the second line of the prominent inscription appeared on the temple, on its architrave. Space for Antoninus's name was cleared on the frieze upon his death twenty years later. It is possible that Antoninus never envisioned sharing the temple with his mismatched wife [53.2], but he more probably assumed with the Senate that this would be his temple as well. If so, another passage from the *Imperial Lives* [53.4] gives some indication of how the temple's location helped to style the emperor's image in line with the epithet "Pius" that was accorded to him. The temple stands directly across the Sacred Way from the Regia, which was founded by King Numa, Rome's paradigm of piety.

SOURCES

53.1 DIVO ANTONINO ET / DIVAE FAUSTINAE EX S(enatus) C(onsulto)

> To the deified Antoninus and the deified Faustina, by decree of the Senate.
>
> ILS 348 = CIL 6.1005

53.2 Much was said about the wildness and loose living of Faustina. Antoninus tried to suppress these reports, which caused him much grief.

Imperial Lives, *Antoninus* 3.7

53.3 In the third year of his reign [AD 141] Antoninus Pius lost his wife Faustina. She was deified by the Senate, who also voted her games, a temple, priestesses, and statues of gold and silver.

Imperial Lives, *Antoninus* 6.7

Fig. 27 Temple of Antoninus and Faustina

53.4 Upon his death [in AD 161] Antoninus was pronounced divine by the Senate. Everyone competed to praise his piety, clemency, intelligence, and upright life. He was voted all of the honors which were ever bestowed on the best emperors before him, and was awarded a flamen-priest, games, a temple, and a priesthood to serve the temple.

Practically alone of all the emperors Antoninus lived his personal life without shedding the blood of either countryman or foreign foe, and he is deservedly compared to Numa, whose prosperity, piety, tranquillity, and religious rites he always maintained.

Imperial Lives, *Antoninus* 13.3–4

53.5 The emperor Antoninus took away the salaries of many people who got money for doing nothing; he said that there was no one lower, no one more cruel, even, than the person who nibbled away at the state without contributing anything to it with their work. On these grounds he also lowered the salary of the lyric poet Mesomedes.

Imperial Lives, *Antoninus* 7.7–8

54. "The Temple of Romulus" (Temple of Jupiter Stator?)

COMMENTARY

The building that still stands between the Temple of Antoninus and the Basilica of Constantine is interesting not only for its peculiar design, but as an example of how gaps in the evidence, both written and archaeological, can leave the identity of even a centrally located building such as this a mystery. Its identification as the Temple of Romulus (the deified son of the emperor Maxentius, not Rome's founder) rests chiefly on coins struck in the early C4 AD that show a building in honor of Romulus and other family members that bears some resemblance to this once-domed structure along the Sacred Way. Many topographers, however, reject this identification, either maintaining an agnostic reserve called for by the uncertainty of the evidence, or arguing for various alternate identifications with other buildings that are mentioned in the written sources but have no established location. In addition to whatever other function it may have had, this building seems to have served as a connector between the differently oriented axes of the Sacred Way and the Forum of Peace.

The most interesting of the other candidates for this building's identity is the Temple of Jupiter Stator, which was clearly an important monument in this area of the upper Sacred Way. As the sources show, the Temple of Jupiter Stator had strong associations with the city's foundation by Romulus, and Cicero, perhaps to play on these old associations with the city's salvation during a crisis, called a meeting of the Senate at the Temple of Jupiter Stator to deliver the first of his famous speeches that exposed the conspiracy of Catiline to overthrow the government.

The sources locate the Temple of Jupiter Stator close to the Palatine, the Sacred Way, and the old Romulean (Palatine) city's Porta Mugonia. Most topographers place the nexus of these three locations close to the Arch of Titus and have tentatively identified ruins of a building near the arch as the remains of the Jupiter Stator temple (the site of the medieval Turris Cartularia, also since demolished). Coarelli, however, in part by relying on his extension of the Palatine zone, as noted at the beginning of this section, and questioning as well traditional locations of the Porta Mugonia and the course of the Sacred

Way, interprets all the evidence for this temple as pointing to a site closer to the Forum, and argues that this site was none other than the erroneously named "Temple of Romulus."

SOURCES

54.1 [Aided by the treachery of the Tarpeian girl] the Sabines now held the Capitoline citadel. On the following day the Roman troops were stationed throughout the field that lay between the Palatine and the Capitoline. ... When their champion Hostius was killed, the Roman line gave way at once and the soldiers retreated to the old gate of the Palatine. Romulus, also driven back by the crowd of those fleeing, raised his arms to the sky and prayed: "Jupiter, here on the Palatine in obedience to your birds I laid the foundations for this city: ... take away the terror here and stay this shameful flight. I vow to build a temple here to you as Jupiter the Stayer, as a monument to posterity that the city was saved by a manifestation of your power." When he finished his prayers, as if perceiving that they had been granted, he called to the troops, "Fellow Romans, here is the place where Jupiter Optimus Maximus commands us to take our stand and renew the fighting." And the Romans stood, as if receiving a command straight from heaven.

Livy, History 1.12.1–7

54.2 The 27th of June is the day of the temple of Stator,
  Which Romulus founded once at the base of the Palatine ridge.

Ovid, Fasti 6.793–4

54.3 [In battle against the Sabines,] Romulus vowed a temple to Jupiter the Stayer near the Mugonian Gate, which leads to the Palatine from the Sacred Way.

Dionysius, Early Rome 2.50.3

54.4 The consul [in 294 BC] Marcus Atilius Regulus raised his hands to the sky and in a clear voice that all might hear vowed a temple to Jupiter the Stayer if he should stay the retreating Roman troops, and by renewing the battle, cut down and defeat the legions of the Samnites. ... Earlier, Romulus had also vowed a temple to Jupiter the Stayer, but only set aside a *fanum*, that is, a place reserved for a temple.

Livy, History 10.36.11; 37.15

54.5 Yesterday, after learning that I had barely escaped assassination in my own home, I convened a meeting of the Senate in the Temple of Jupiter Stator and laid the matter before them [in my first speech against Catiline]. When Catiline arrived,...the leaders of the Senate even

Fig. 28 Statue of Constantine (courtyard of Palazzo dei Conservatori)

abandoned the area of the benches where he took his seat, leaving them bare and deserted.

Cicero, *Against Catiline* 2.12

Notes: Coarelli defends his position in *LTUR* 2.155–158, where he quotes or notes numerous other relevant sources. Of those quoted here, the one by Dionysius seems most at odds with Coarelli's theory, even allowing Coarelli's extension of the Palatine as a geographical locater, as I am inclined to do in the case of Palatine residences. Dionysius says that the temple was near a road that led to the Palatine away from the Sacred Way, a phrase that better suits the Arch of Titus area or higher as a location for the temple. In Livy's account [54.1], Romulus's reference to the augural birds "here on the Palatine" also demands something loftier than Coarelli's location.

55. Basilica of Constantine (or Basilica Nova)

COMMENTARY

One of ancient Rome's most impressive buildings, and also one of its last, the Basilica of Constantine is scarcely mentioned in the literature. By Roman standards, its design may have been overreaching—its massive central nave may have fallen in an earthquake only (!) five hundred years after it was built—but the remains impressed and influenced the leading architects of the Renaissance, including Bramante's design of St. Peter's basilica. The design of the Basilica of Constantine, in turn, was influenced more by the central halls of the great imperial baths than by the post-and-beam architecture of the famous basilicas in the Forum. Some idea of the construction and effect of the central hall of the Basilica can be had from the nave of St. Maria degli Angeli (Piazza della Reppublica), formerly the central hall of the Baths of Diocletian, as refurbished by Michelangelo and others. One marble column remains from the nave of the Basilica of Constantine, now standing in front of St. Maria Maggiore.

The Basilica of Constantine was actually begun by Maxentius after he ascended the throne in AD 306. Maxentius then lost to Constantine both his life and the perpetuation of his name through this building. After Constantine defeated Maxentius in the famous battle at the Milvian Bridge in AD 312, he altered the design of the basilica, giving it a grand entrance in the middle of the long side facing the Sacred Way, adding a large niche (still standing) on the opposite side, thereby giving the building another axis in addition to the longer one down the center of the nave. This long axis (parallel to the Sacred Way, and entered by a narthex-like porch on the end towards the Colosseum) also ended at a semi-circular niche, which is probably where the giant statue of the seated Constantine was located, parts of which can now be found in the courtyard of the Palazzo dei Conservatori museum on the Capitoline (Fig. 28).

SOURCES

55.1 Each of the magnificent works which Maxentius constructed— the Shrine of the City and the Basilica—was credited by the Senators to Constantine.

Aurelius Victor, *On the Emperors* 40.26

Note: The "Shrine of the City" (Urbis Fanum) was perhaps the Temple of Venus and Rome, which Maxentius restored after a fire. Others have identified it with the "Temple of Romulus" discussed above [53.], which, at least in its present form, was built in the time of Maxentius and Constantine, and had (Renaissance drawings show) an inscription that identified it as the work of Constantine.

56. Temple of Rome and Venus

COMMENTARY

As with Hadrian's other masterpiece in Rome, the Pantheon, the Temple of Rome and Venus puts a traditional face on a unique interior. Here the traditional element is a classic Greek design of a temple on a low podium accessible from all sides, with the cella surrounded by columns on all sides. The unusual element is the arrangement of the cella's interior: rather than having an inner and an outer chamber, this temple had what was really two cellas back-to-back, one for each of the deities housed here. Although less dramatically than the Pantheon's dome, this design makes the spatial center of the temple a focal point, which nicely expresses the idea of Rome as the center of the universe. It is also an architectural arrangement—the cult statues of Roma and the goddess of Love (*Amor*) would have been seated back-to-back in the middle of the temple, facing opposite directions and separated by a common wall—which embodies in visual form the palindrome of Roma-Amor. Such a whimsical application of a literary trope to an architectural form is all the more plausible given Hadrian's avid participation in both literary and architectural arts, and in light of the imaginative designs of his villa near Tivoli, which included the multi-sectioned "pumpkin" domes ridiculed by Apollodorus.

In his chronology St. Jerome provides the date of AD 121 for the beginning of the building's construction, and a reference in Cassiodorus gives AD 135 as its dedication date, although archaeological evidence suggests completion under Antoninus Pius after Hadrian's death in AD 138. Dio, steering clear of such details, gives us, along with some background and judgement concerning the temple, a disturbingly believable picture of what an envious artist, given the power and impunity of an emperor, would do to rival artists. It is not clear whether Apollodorus's judgment (that Hadrian's cult statues were over-sized for their surroundings) was accurate; as for his other complaint concerning the elevation of platform area, it seems there would have been room even in Hadrian's "flawed" design" to store equipment below the Colosseum-end of the platform, since large vaults can still be seen there.

This was, at any rate, a splendid temple built on a massive scale. The whole platform on which it was built, which included the two long colonnades down each of the sides at some distance from the temple, was as large as the Forum of Augustus, although there is no evidence that it was as busy. Each of these colonnades ended in a flight of stairs above the Colosseum and would have provided an attractive, airy, and shaded way from the Forum to the arena. The number of solid granite and marble columns used in the colonnades and temple respectively is staggering, and nothing again in Rome, including Diocletian's and Caracalla's giant concrete baths with their veneers and strategic columns, can match this prodigal use of imported stone.

The passage by Prudentius analyzing the idolatry of Rome's topography can be seen as part of the concerted "consciousness-raising" efforts of Christian critics to expose, delineate, and then eliminate the ways in which pagan practices, from the cradle to grave, permeated society and surrounded the five senses in daily life.

SOURCES

56.1 Hadrian's ambitions were all-encompassing. Along with his literary pursuits he tried his hand at numerous other endeavors, including some of the most insignificant, such as sculpture and painting. And his envy of others who excelled in anything was fearsome, ending the careers of some and the lives of many others.

One target of his anger was the architect Apollodorus, who had been Trajan's builder in Rome, designing the Forum of Trajan [78.], the Concert Hall (*Odeon*), and Stadium [89.]; Hadrian first banished and then killed him. Some charge was drawn up, but the real reason goes back to an earlier incident. Apollodorus was consulting with Trajan on one of their projects, when Hadrian, also present, chimed in with some remark that prompted the architect to turn to him and say "Go design some of your pumpkin-domes. You wouldn't understand these matters." This occurred at a time when Hadrian was priding himself on designing a dome of such a description.

Then Hadrian became emperor [in AD 117] and neither forgot Apollodorus's slight nor tolerated his outspokenness. On one occasion Hadrian sent Apollodorus the plans of the Temple of Venus and Rome, intending to prove to the architect that a great building could arise without him: did he not think this building a masterpiece? Apollodorus responded that, first, the temple should be set higher, while the ground around it should be excavated away; this way, standing aloft, it would not only be more visible from the Sacred Way but would have more room below to store the Amphitheater's staging equipment, which could then be assembled out of sight and moved to the Amphitheater without drawing notice. Secondly, Apollodorus went on, the two statues of the temple's gods were too large for the height of their homes: "If they wanted to stand up to take a walk outside, they'd bump their heads!" Apollodorus remarked. Hadrian, angered by the bluntness of this critique and plagued by the awareness that he had made a mistake that could not be fixed, allowed his anger and grief to steer him, and he put Apollodorus to death.

Dio, *History* 69.3.2–3; 4.1–6

56.2 The Senate [in AD 176, after the death of Faustina] decreed that silver statues of Marcus Aurelius and his wife Faustina should be set up in the Temple of Venus and Rome, as well as an altar on which all newly-wed couples in the city were to make a sacrifice.

Dio, *History* 72.31.1

56.3 [In pagan families, a child absorbs idolatry from the cradle on.]
Later, leaving the house during festivals and games,
He stands in awe, gaping as the priests in laurel wreathes
Tend the temples of pagan gods on the lofty Capitol,
And the Sacred Way resounds with the lowing of cattle consigned
To sacrifice on the altar of Rome (she too gets blood
Like a goddess—even the name of a city has godhead here,
Where the temples of Rome and Venus rise to equal height,
And the incense meant for one is shared with its goddess twin);
Impressed, and thinking whatever the noble Senate has sanctioned
Must be true, he entrusts his faith to idols … .

Prudentius, *Against Symmachus* 1.215–224

57. Arch of Titus (Fig. 23)

COMMENTARY

Of the three triumphal arches remaining in Rome—Severus's, Titus's, and Constantine's—the one in honor of the deified Titus (on the center coffer inside his arch, see him carried aloft by an eagle) is by far the most elegant, even as the surviving literary record provides, in Josephus's history of the Jewish Wars, the fullest and most harrowing account of Rome's destruction of an enemy's capital [11.7].

The relief-sculpture carved inside the arch on the Palatine-side depicts a scene from Titus's triumph, and includes two of the holiest objects from the Temple of Jerusalem, as described by Josephus below before they became the booty of Rome. In the center is the seven-branched menorah, and to its right the heavy table for the Shew-Bread (the Bread of Presence). The passage by Procopius helps to trace the whereabouts of these objects some five centuries later.

The inscription on the attic of the Colosseum-side refers to the restoration that Pius VII carried out beginning in 1822. Giuseppe Valadier, the leading Italian architect of his day who also designed one of the buttresses to shore up the Colosseum, directed this restoration, which involved a complete rebuilding of the arch (with the Arch of Trajan in Beneventum as a model). By substituting travertine stone for missing sections of the original Pentelic marble, Valadier pioneered a technique of restoration that readily distinguishes the original portion of a monument from the reconstructed portion.

Fig. 29 Arch of Titus

SOURCES

57.1 SENATUS / POPULUSQUE ROMANUS / DIVO TITO DIVI VESPASIANI F(ilio) / VESPASIANO AUGUSTO

The Senate and People of Rome dedicate this arch to the deified Titus Vespasian Augustus [d. AD 81], son of the deified Vespasian.

ILS 265 = *CIL* 6.945

57.2 [An inscription recorded on another arch to Titus, since destroyed, near the Circus Maximus:] The Senate and People of Rome dedicate this arch to the Emperor Titus... because, with the Senate's advice and counsel and with the auguries, he conquered the nation of the Jews [in AD 70] and destroyed Jerusalem, which all of the generals, kings, and nations before Titus had either failed to do or even to attempt.

ILS 264 = *CIL* 6.944

57.3 [The temple in Jerusalem was a splendid edifice with numerous parts.] After you passed through the monumental gates you entered the ground floor of the sanctuary. This structure was ninety feet high, ninety feet long, and thirty feet wide. Its length, however, was divided into two parts. The first hall was sixty feet long, and contained three of the world's most incredible and famous works of art: the lampstand, the table, and the incense altar. The lampstand, which branched into seven lamps, symbolized the seven planets; the twelve loaves of bread [the "Shew-Bread," or "Bread of Presence"] on the table represented the circle of the Zodiac and the year; the altar of incense is kept replenished with thirteen aromatic incenses collected from both land and sea, and from places both inhabited and deserted, thus symbolizing that all creation is of God and for God.

Josephus, *The Jewish War* 5.215–18

57.4 [Belisarius, the emperor Justinian's famous general, defeated the Vandals in Africa in AD 534, and returned to Constantinople, now the capital of the Roman empire.] When he reached Constantinople with his captive Vandals and their king Gelimer, he was awarded honors given to the greatest Roman generals of old—honors which for nearly six hundred years had not been granted to anyone except emperors, such as Titus and Trajan and other victorious emperors who warred against the barbarian peoples. Belisarius displayed both the booty and the enslaved captives of the war in a procession that the Romans call a triumph. … Many thousands of pounds of silver were paraded, as well as the entire imperial treasury of Rome which the Vandals under Gaiseric had plundered [in AD 455] from the Palatine when they sacked the city, as I mentioned earlier [in Book 3.5.3]. Among the booty were the treasures of the Jews, which Titus, the son of Vespasian, and others had brought to Rome after the sack of Jerusalem.

As the triumphal procession went by, one of the Jews standing alongside an imperial official said to him, "The Romans, I predict, will come to regret taking this plunder of Jerusalem into the palace in Constantinople: these objects belong in one place only, where Solomon placed them long ago when he was king of the Jews. That is why Gaiseric was able to sack the palace of Rome, and why the army of the Romans has now captured the Vandals." When his words were relayed to the emperor, Justinian quickly had the Jewish treasure delivered to Christian sanctuaries in Jerusalem.

Procopius, *Wars* 4.9.1–3, 5–9

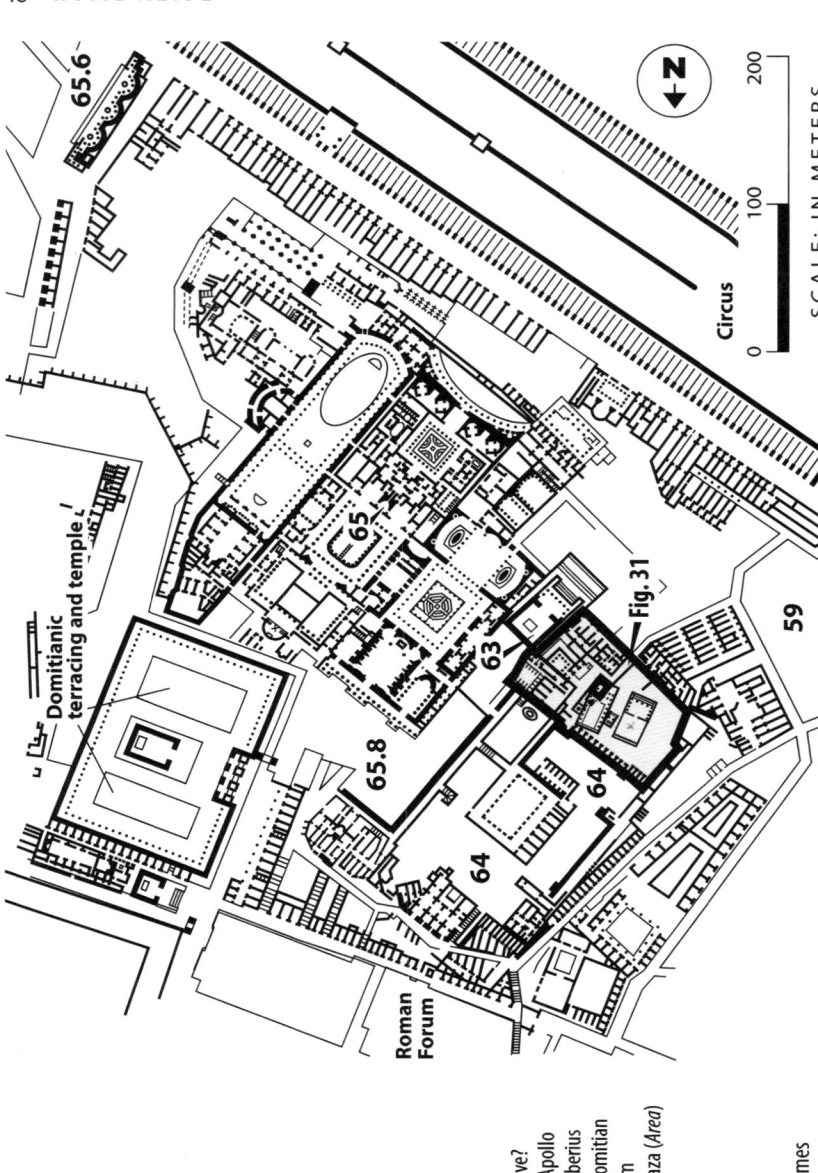

MAP KEY

59 Lupercal cave?
63 Temple of Apollo
64 Palace of Tiberius
65 Palace of Domitian
65.6 Septizodium
65.8 Palatine plaza (*Area*)

Fig. 30 Palatine Hill in Imperial Times

VI. The Palatine Hill

58. Overview of the Palatine Hill

COMMENTARY

The pre-urban topography of the Palatine, like the Capitoline's, is lost to us, having undergone a far greater transformation than even Propertius could envision when, although writing before the imperial palaces took over the entire hill, he marveled at Rome's urbanity:

> **58.1** Visitor to mighty Rome: wherever you look
>   Was simply grass and hill before Aeneas came;
>   Along the Palatine's crest where Apollo's temple stands
>   Evander's cattle roamed and ruminated at will.
>
> **Propertius**, *Elegies* 4.1.1–4

Although most of the hill looks today as if it has reverted to the conditions of Evander's day (with herds of a different species), the greenery is deceptive, rooted on platforms and debris several stories above the natural bedrock in some places.

Much of the Palatine has remained unexcavated, but there is one part of the Palatine—the corner of the hill closest to the Tiber, overlooked by the southern balcony of the Farnese Gardens—that not only has been plundered and excavated down to very early levels, but which contains the core sites that determined the hill's later imperial makeover. Here in close proximity to each other are the houses of Augustus's compound [62.], with the Temple of Apollo [63.] on one side of them and the older temples of Victory [60.] and the Great Mother Goddess [61.]

on the other. In meaningful proximity to Augustus's residence was the Hut of Romulus [62.], and further down the slope of the hill here was the Lupercal cave [59.]. Admittedly none of these remains is impressive. Some attractive frescoes are preserved in the House of Augustus; the temples have mostly disappeared, and the exact locations of the Hut of Romulus and the Lupercal cave are not known. But if the ruins of this zone are surpassed by both the ruins and the lurid stories of the subsequent palaces, it is the richest section of the Palatine for the intersection of archaeology, legend, and history.

59. The Lupercal Cave

COMMENTARY

The Lupercal Cave remains something of a mystery, both in its location and in the meaning of its ritual, which combines a purificatory circling of communal boundaries with fertility magic, while involving in some capacity wolf (legend), goat, and dog (sacrifice). The rites of the Lupercalia were at any rate important for the Romans. In the last years of the fifth century AD some prominent Roman senators, at least nominally Christian, sought to revive the February 15 rites of the Lupercalia, worried that the city's health and well-being depended on their performance—a flare-up of idolatry that was swiftly doused by Pope Gelasius.

The *general* location of the cave is clear: between the Circus Maximus and the Temple of the Great Mother. Legend puts it above the flood-plain, but perhaps not far above; there was a grove around it, and eventually a theater between it and the Temple of the Great Mother [59.4, 5]. Augustus rebuilt it, perhaps as part of his attempt to style himself as a founder of a new Rome à la Romulus. But that one could "build" a cave suggests that it was by then a largely artificial grotto, perhaps more building than cave. If so, when such a structure was dismantled and destroyed in later centuries, it is understandable that the location of the cave would have vanished with it.

SOURCES

59.1 [The wolf suckled the abandoned infants where she found them near the Tiber. When some shepherds approached, she calmly left the twins and walked away.] Not far off there was a holy place, thickly shaded by trees surrounding a cave with springs. It was said that this was the grove of Pan, and there was an altar here to that god. This is where the wolf went and hid herself. Today [c. 20 BC] the grove is gone, but the cave and spring are still pointed out, built into the side of the Palatine along the road that leads from the hill to the Circus, and there is a sacred precinct nearby which contains a bronze statue of ancient workmanship commemorating the event, depicting the wolf suckling the two boys.

Dionysius, *Early Rome* 1.79.8

59.2 [Romulus and the other young men living near the Palatine prepared to celebrate the festival of the Lupercalia on February 15.] After offering sacrifice to Pan, the young men ran a course around the city, naked except for loin-cloths fashioned from the animals just sacrificed. This was—and still is [c. 20 BC]—performed as a traditional rite of purification for the community.

Dionysius, *Early Rome* 1.80.1

59.3 [The festival called the Lupercalia derives its name from the she-wolf (*lupa*) story.] We see that the course that the Luperci run around the city begins where Romulus was left to die as an infant. The rites of the Lupercalia, however, rather obscure this connection, since the priests sacrifice not wolves but goats, after which some of them touch the bloodied sacrificial knives to the foreheads of two young men of noble birth, who are required to laugh when others wipe the blood away with wool soaked in milk. After this ceremony, they cut the goat-skins into strips, and clad in nothing but these they run through the city using the swags of goat-skin to lash people along the course. Women of child-bearing age make no effort to avoid the contact, believing it promotes fertility and an easy delivery. In another peculiarity of the ritual, the Luperci sacrifice a dog.

Plutarch, *Romulus* 21.4–5

59.4 [In 154 BC] the censor Cassius built a theater behind the Lupercal towards the Palatine.

Velleius, *History* 1.15.3

59.5 Our ancestors wanted the Megalesian games to be performed and celebrated in front of the Temple of Magna Mater, under the very gaze of the goddess.

Cicero, *Response of the Soothsayers* 24

59.6 [Among my many works in Rome] I built the Lupercal.

Augustus, *Achievements* 19

60. The Temple of Victory

60.1 Before joining his soldiers in Sora for battle against the Samnites, [in 294 BC] the consul Lucius Postumius dedicated the Temple of

Victory, which he had built using money from fines he collected earlier as aedile.

Livy, *History* 10.33.9

61. The Temple of the Great Mother Goddess (*Magna Mater*)

COMMENTARY

The origins of the worship of the Great Mother in Rome are, as with so many temples in Rome, ascribed to a crisis in war time. Having trouble defeating Hannibal, on the advice of the Sibylline Books the Romans imported the goddess from Asia Minor, where she was worshipped under the names of both Cybele and the Great Mother (the Greek word for "great" is *Megale*; hence the "*Megale*sian" games in her honor). The goddess's connection with victory in war (as the motivation for importing her) is strengthened by the location of her temple beside the Temple of Victory, which was in fact her home until her temple was finished.

This much sounds very Roman, but there were at least two unusual features about the worship of the Great Mother. First, her cult-image was not a statue but simply a black stone [61.2], which was set onto an enthroned statue of the goddess in the place of a representational head. (A headless statue, flanked by two lions, was found near her temple and is on display in the Palatine Antiquarium).

Secondly, her yearly rites in Rome were led by non-Roman priests who continued to come from Phrygia and who, in becoming devotees of the goddess, had castrated themselves, after the pattern of Attis, a mythological prototype of the devotees of Cybele. Catullus responded to the strangeness of her worship with one of the more imaginative poems in Latin literature [61.12], which attempts to get inside the head of young Attis "the morning after" his ecstatic initiation; perhaps, after his affair with Lesbia, Catullus himself could identify. At any rate, the excerpt is interesting for its dichotomy of urban and wilderness landscapes, which parallels the careful ritual divisions between Roman and foreign participants, as described by Dionysius of Halicarnassus [61.11].

SOURCES

61.1 At that time [in 205 BC] a sudden religious fear overtook the Romans when, after the frequent volcanic showers of stone that year, they consulted the Sibylline books and found an oracle stating that any foreign enemy who attacked Italy could be driven out of Italy and defeated only if the Mother of Mt. Ida was brought to Rome from Pessinus. ... The Roman ambassadors went to King Attalus of Pergamum, who received them kindly and led them to Pessinus in

Phrygia [central Turkey]. There he presented them with the sacred stone that the natives say is the Mother of the Gods, and he invited the Romans to take it back to Rome.

When the ship carrying the Mother of Mt. Ida approached the mouth of the Tiber [in 204 BC], Publius Cornelius Scipio sailed out, as required, to the offshore waters to receive the goddess from her priests, and he brought her in to the shore where the leading matrons of Rome were waiting to receive the goddess. (Among these women the name of the Vestal Quinta Claudia is conspicuous, since her help in bringing the goddess to Rome caused her reputation for purity, until then apparently under some suspicion, to shine into posterity.) Passing the stone hand to hand in unbroken succession, the women sent the sacred stone on its way to Rome. The entire city poured out to watch. Incense-burners were placed at the doorways of homes all along the route, and when the stone passed, they lit incense and prayed that the goddess would enter Rome willingly and look upon them favorably. The matrons brought her to the Temple of Victory on the Palatine on April 12, her holy day, and a crowd of people brought the goddess gifts; a banquet for the gods was held, as well as games called the Megalesia.

Livy, *History* 29.10.4–5; 11.7; 14.11–14

61.2 They say that nothing else was transported from Phrygia by King Attalus besides a stone, and a smallish one at that, able to be carried by a single man without any strain. Its color is a deep black, and it has tiny irregularities in its shape. As we can all see today [c. AD 300] where it sits in place of a head on the statue itself of the Great Mother, it bears only the crudest resemblance to a face.

Arnobius, *Against the Pagans* 7.49

61.3 Not far downstream of Rome, the smoothly flowing Almo
    Meets the Tiber and loses it name to the larger river.
Here in his purple robe the ancient priest of the goddess
    Washed her stone and sacred tools in the Almo's stream.

Ovid, *Fasti* 4.337–340

61.4 Down by the Almo, where they wash
    The eastern ore of the Mother …

Martial, *Epigrams* 3.47.2

61.5 They say that the summer harvest of the year in which the Mother of the Gods was brought to Rome was the biggest in ten years.

Pliny the Elder, *Encyclopedia* 18.16

61.6 The censors M. Livius and C. Claudius [in 204 BC] contracted the building of the Temple of the Great Mother on the Palatine.

Livy, *History* 29.37.3

61.7 At about the same time [in 191 BC] the Temple of the Great Mother of Mt. Ida was dedicated,...thirteen years after the temple was commissioned. Marcus Junius Brutus dedicated it, and games, called the Megalesia, were also established with the dedication. Valerius Antias says these games were the first to include dramatic performances.

Livy, *History* 36.36.3–4

61.8 The statue of Quinta Claudia that stood at the entrance to the Temple of the Mother of the Gods twice remained untouched by flames when that temple was destroyed by fire, once [in 111 BC] in the consulship of Scipio and Bestia and again [in AD 3] in the consulship of Servilius and Lamia.

Valerius Maximus, *Sayings* 1.8.11

61.9 I rebuilt the Temple of Magna Mater on the Palatine.

Augustus, *Achievements* 19

61.10   I wondered why the Megalesian games were the first
To be held each year in Rome. But the Muse had sensed my query
And answered: "The other gods, because she gave them birth,
Yield and give the games of the Mother Goddess this pride of place."

Ovid, *Fasti* 4.357–360

61.11 If on rare occasions Rome does introduce foreign religious rites into the city, she nonetheless observes them according to her own customs, jettisoning the esoteric mythical nonsense. The worship of the Idaean Mother is a good example [of how the Romans deal with outlandish cults]. Every year the praetors perform sacrifices and hold games in her honor, in accordance with Roman customs, but both the priest and priestess of the goddess are Phrygians, and they are the ones who parade her image through the city, begging alms in the Mother's name as is their custom, wearing images around their chests, beating on drums and accompanied by the ritual flute music of their followers. By custom and a decree of the Senate, no native Roman begs alms for Cybele or parades to flute music in multi-colored robes or worships the goddess with ecstatic Phrygian rites.

Dionysius, *Early Rome* 2.19.3–5

61.12   [Attis, in a frenzy of worship, castrated himself
And led a band of devotees to Cybele's wild mountain]
But when the clear-eyed sun rose up with his golden face

Illuminating sky, firm earth, and wild sea,
Attis, unpossessed, saw where he was and what
He wasn't, and spoke in torment to his homeland:
"Is this really me in the forest, so far away from home,
Away from forum, stadium, wrestling-ring and gym?
I, who was once the star of the schoolyard and the pride of the ring,
A serving-girl of the gods, Cybele's slave-girl?
Now I can see and suffer, only now regret my loss!"
But Cybele heard; unleashing the lions yoked to her cart,
She lashed the one on the left, the foe of flocks, and said:
"Be off! Attack that man! I want him wild again.
See that the whip of fury drives him back to the woods,
for thinking that he is free, for wanting to slip my rule."
O Great Goddess, Cybele, Mistress God of the Mountain,
May the fury you inspire be distant from my home:
Arouse your frenzy in others, drive others, not me, insane.

Catullus, *Poem 63* (selected lines)

62. The House of Augustus (*Casa di Livia*) (Fig. 31)

COMMENTARY

Between Domitian's palace and the Temple of Victory the remains of two residences can be seen today. The one to the north, abutting the Farnese Gardens, is traditionally ascribed to Augustus's wife Livia and called the Casa di Livia, and the other was traditionally assigned to Augustus himself. Although the division between separate spousal quarters is no longer accepted, together they formed part of the imperial compound Augustus gradually assembled on the Palatine, and the "Casa di Livia" may indeed have been the refurbished home of Hortensius that Augustus bought before he became sole ruler [62.1].

Although this whole area was a nice neighborhood in any event, there were some features of this part of the hill that, if they didn't determine Augustus's purchase, were nonetheless significant for his developing image. Nearly contiguous with the back of the house was the Temple of Victory, a goddess much esteemed by Caesar's heir [28.4]. Also somewhere nearby was the Hut of Romulus, held to be a facsimile of his simple hut on its original site. Directly in front of the temples of Victory and the Great Mother, in fact, archaeologists have discovered post-hole traces of Iron Age huts, and a small enclosure there may have contained the dwelling that the Romans preserved and honored as their founder's (oddly, another was preserved on the Capitoline; see 9.7]. At any rate, we gather elsewhere from Suetonius that Augustus, as a sort of second founder of Rome after the chaos of the civil wars, cultivated a connection with Romulus, and was even close to receiving

"Romulus" as a title instead of "Augustus" (Suetonius, *Augustus* 7.2, 95.2). As so often in Rome but rarely with a finesse equal to Augustus's, topography came to the aid of topology, and did the same work as an overt title, with much more subtlety.

With Victory and Romulus behind the house, that left the front for an even bigger message, and it was here, in the space between his house and the later Palace of Domitian, that Augustus built the famous Temple of Apollo on land that he had personally owned but then made over to the public (thereby both allowing for a temple, which could be built on private land, and yet closely tying it to his person). It is not clear how this temple precinct included a large portico as well as two libraries—possibly on a platform in the direction of the Circus Maximus; the portico may also have surrounded the temple on three sides.

Ancient accounts refer to the splendor of this temple. Augustus's own private residence, remaining simple, allowed him to project a character of frugal Republican virtue, while the precinct in front, separate and yet part of his compound, could be lavish to a remarkable degree, justified as an expense for the god even as it projected in no uncertain terms Augustus's own economic and political power.

The temple was vowed five years before the sea-battle at Actium in 31 BC, in which Augustus defeated Antony and Cleopatra, but it was finished afterwards, and the passage by Virgil shows that the presence of a temple to Apollo on the heights at Actium was a serendipity that didn't go to waste. The sculptural program described by Propertius may also be significant reminders of Rome's (Augustus's) victory over the wild forces of Antony and Cleopatra in the East: the daughters of Danaus murdered their aggressive cousins from Egypt, and Apollo himself had a hand in punishing the recklessness of the Gauls and Niobe.

Another side of Augustus's character and of his power to suppress is dramatically displayed in the passage by Ovid [63.7], who had been exiled to distant borders by Augustus in AD 8 because of a "poem and a mistake" offensive to the emperor (certainly the puritanical moral reformer must have been galled by Ovid's *Art of Love*). Later in his career, writing in exile, Ovid imagines one of his books as a visitor who has made it back to Rome. Displaying his creator's characteristic combination of humor with pathos and cheek with flattery, the walking, talking book goes around the Augustan city looking for lodging in one of its libraries, only to find out he has been banned from all of them, including the one at the Temple of Apollo.

SOURCES

62.1 At first Augustus lived near the Roman Forum above the Stairs of the Ringmakers [in the region of the upper Sacra Via], in a house

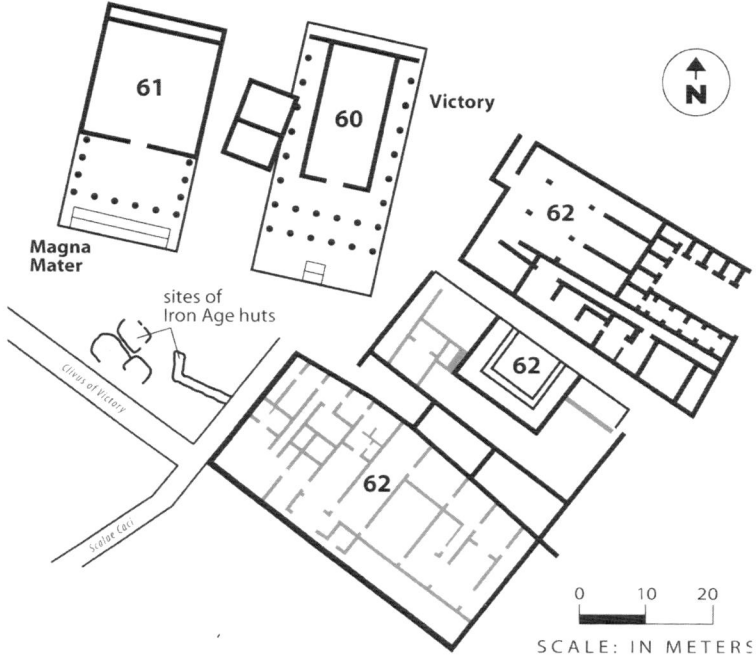

Fig. 31 Palatine Detail: Residence of Augustus

which had belonged to the orator Calvus. After that he moved to the Palatine, but to the no less modest house of Hortensius, which was conspicuous for neither its size nor elegance, having short colonnades with columns of Alban tufa and rooms without marble or fancy flooring. Here he remained for more than forty years, sleeping in the same room both winters and summers, even though winters in Rome did not agree with his health and were hard on him. If he felt the need for doing business in secrecy or without interruption, he could withdraw to a special room elevated above the rest of the house, which he called either his "Syracuse" or "the Shop," or would take refuge in a nearby villa that belonged to one or another of his freedmen. If he was sick, however, he would convalesce at the home of Maecenas. During longer retreats, he frequented the coast and islands of the Bay of Naples or towns nearer Rome such as Lanuvium and Praeneste, as well as Tivoli, where he frequently held court under the colonnades of the Temple of Hercules.

Suetonius, *Augustus* 72.1–2

62.2 The emperor's residence is called the Palatium, not because of any official designation, but because Caesar Augustus lived on the Palatine Hill and had his military headquarters there. Augustus's house, however, gained a degree of fame from the hill itself, as the place where Romulus had built his house.

Dio, History 53.16.5

62.3 Romulus and Remus lived the life of herdsmen and earned their living with their hands. They lived for the most part on the hills, building huts entirely out of wooden poles and reeds. One of these huts survives even to my own day, preserved on the slope of the Palatine facing the Circus and called the Hut of Romulus. Those in charge of its care preserve its sanctity and resist improvements that would make it more stately. When the hut gets damaged by storm or routine wear, they replicate its earlier appearance as closely as possible.

Dionysius, Early Rome 1.79.11

62.4 The Hut of Romulus also burnt down [in 12 BC] when crows dropped flaming sacrificial meat they had taken from an altar somewhere.

Dio, History 54.29.8

62.5 During my sixth and seventh consulships [in 28–27 BC], with the power of the state entirely in my hands by universal consent, I extinguished the flames of civil wars, and then ceded control, transferring the Republic back to the authority of the Senate and the Roman people. For this service I was named Augustus by a decree of the Senate, the doorposts of my house were wreathed with laurel, and the Civic Crown [of Oak-Leaves] was fastened above my door … .

When serving my thirteenth consulship [in 2 BC], the Senate, the equestrian order, and the entire Roman people named me Father of the Country, and decreed the title to be inscribed in the reception hall of my house, in the Senate House, and in the Forum of Augustus below the chariot statue awarded to me by the Senate.

Augustus, Achievements 34–5

62.6 [On January 13, 27 BC] the Senate decreed that the Crown of Oak-Leaves be fastened above the doorway of the house of Emperor Caesar Augustus, because he restored the Republic to the Roman people.

Calendar Inscription (Fasti Praenestini)

62.7 Calendar for April 28:

> Vesta, accept your day of honor! Vesta has been received
>   in the home of her kinsman Augustus: justly has the Senate decreed.
> Apollo has his portion, another portion is Vesta's,
>   And what remains, a third one claims for himself.
> Palatine laurels, may you prosper; long prosper the home
>   wreathed with oak leaves: one house for three immortal gods.

Ovid, Fasti 4.949–54

63. The Temple of Apollo

[For commentary, see preceding entry.]

SOURCES

63.1 [After the war against Sextus Pompeius in Sicily, in 36 BC]
Augustus returned to the city and announced that he was dedicating
to public use those homes which he had purchased earlier through his
agents to expand his own home. He also promised to build a temple
to Apollo with a portico around it, a project he carried out with
exceptional magnificence.

Velleius, *History* 2.81.3

63.2 Augustus built the Temple of Apollo on that part of his compound
that, after lightning struck it, the soothsayers said was wanted by the
god. He included colonnades with Greek and Latin libraries and when
he was old often convened the senate here and reviewed the senatorial
panels of jurors.

Suetonius, *Augustus* 29.3

63.3 [In 28 BC] Augustus finished and dedicated the Temple of Apollo
on the Palatine, along with the precinct around the temple and the
libraries there.

Dio, *History* 53.1.13

63.4 [The poet contrasts Cynthia's wild ways with his own upstanding
use of time:]
> You wonder why I'm late, my love? The mighty Augustus
>> Just opened Apollo's golden portico.
> Columns of African marble border the temple grounds,
>> And the fifty daughters of Danaus stand between them.
> A marble Apollo seems to outshine the god himself,
>> Lips parted to sing along with his silent lyre,
> And spaced around the altar, looking almost alive,
>> Four bulls from the famous hand of Myron stand.
> Then, in the middle, a temple of radiant marble rises,
>> A home more dear to the god than Delos itself.
> The chariot of the Sun is upon its pediment.
>> The doors are Libyan ivory, finely wrought,
> One door lamenting the Gauls tossed from the peak of Parnassus,
>> The other mourning the death of Niobe's children.
> Next, the god himself, between his mother and sister,
>> The Pythian Apollo sings in a lengthy robe.
> I wish that you, in your free time, would stroll such grounds!

Propertius, *Elegies* 2.31; 32.7–8

63.5 Looking down from his temple above the battle of Actium,
Apollo bent his bow, and all our eastern enemies
from Arabia, Egypt, and India turned and fled in terror.
...
The shield portrayed Augustus sitting on the snow-white threshold
Of radiant Apollo, receiving the gifts of foreign peoples
On the god's behalf and attaching them to the lofty door-posts.

Virgil, *Aeneid* 8.704-6, 720-2

63.6 After Augustus assumed the office of Pontifex Maximus [in 12 BC], he collected all the Greek and Latin prophetic writings in circulation that were anonymous or attributed to unqualified authors, and burned more than two thousand of them. He preserved only the Sibylline verses (though editing even these) and deposited them in two gilded cases beneath the pedestal of the Palatine Apollo.

Suetonius, *Augustus* 31.1

63.7 [Ovid, exiled by Augustus, sends a book (or scroll) of poems to the reader in Rome; the book itself is addressing the reader:]

"Sent to Rome by my author in exile, I come with misgivings.
    Lend a kindly hand, dear reader, to a weary book,
And have no fear that in welcoming me you may be disgraced:
    Not a couplet in this poem on the art of making love.
Reader, if it isn't much trouble, could you show me the way?
    Where can a book from the borders find some lodging in Rome?"

[Ovid's book manages, after difficulties, to find a reader to be his guide, and they walk together to the Palatine and its new library. Ovid continues the conceit of his talking book:]

Marveling at each of the sights in turn, I spot a dwelling
    Fit for a god, its doorposts gleaming with weapons.
"Is this the home of Jupiter?" I ask, my mind
    Divining as much from the crown of oak-leaves dear to the god.
When I learn the mansion's master, "Ah, then I did not err;
    This truly is the home of mighty Jupiter.
But why is the doorway adorned with a screen of sacred laurel,
    Why does the dusky laurel frame this august entry?
Because that house has earned for itself perpetual triumph?
    Or perhaps the house is always loved by the god Apollo?
...
An inscription explains the wreath of oak that crowns the door,
    a witness to citizens protected by the power of the man within."
...
Then with an even pace I am led up the lofty steps
    To the bright and towering temple of the young and beardless god,

Where statues alternate with columns of foreign marble,
    The Danaid brides with their savage father, his sword unsheathed.
Here whatever ancient or modern authors have captured
    With a writer's craft and insight awaits the public's perusal.
I look for my brothers there (except of course for those books
    That even my father Ovid now wishes he never begot),
But while I search for them in vain, the head librarian
    Approaches and says he must ask me to leave this sacred ground.

Ovid, *Tristia* 3.1, selections

64. The Palace of Tiberius (*Domus Tiberiana*)

COMMENTARY

After Augustus, the building of palaces began. His successor Tiberius must have built something grander than Augustus's collection of homes, since the large area now taken up by the Farnese Gardens became known as the Palace of Tiberius (the Latin word for this and Domitian's palace continued to be *domus*). The earliest palace foundation here, however, appears to go back only to Nero, who no doubt had to rebuild the palace after the Fire, and perhaps took the opportunity to make it larger. The Palace of Tiberius, whatever transformations and expansions it underwent, would have been the principal Roman imperial residence for Tiberius, Caligula, Claudius, and Nero in the early part of his reign. Nero made several attempts at a wholesale expansion via independent structures, first with his Domus Transitoria and then after the fire of AD 64, with the Domus Aurea, and there are significant though mostly subterranean Palatine remains from his reign. The colorful marble floor exposed in the western courtyard of Domitian's banquet hall, a consummate example of ancient Roman stonecraft, goes back to the Domus Aurea phase of Nero's reign.

After Nero's death, Vespasian, perhaps as part of a general attempt to dissociate himself from the excesses of Nero, seems to have avoided the palace. His son Domitian was responsible for the next, and grandest, expansion of palace buildings, and in the process built over much of what was distinctive from Nero's reign. The Palace of Tiberius, however, continued to be used under its own name at least into the reigns of the Antonines and perhaps much longer.

There is little in the sources on the construction and appearance of the Palace of Tiberius in any of its phases, with the exceptions of Caligula's extension of the Palace of Tiberius out over the Forum and the bridge he built to connect the Palatine to the Capitoline. Although in the first instance Caligula's architecture, in the service of his intimacy with Castor and Jupiter, is illustrative of a notoriously unbalanced megalomaniac, it is also part of the ongoing and evolving imperial attempt to increase and express the power of the imperial office. It is as if what the other emperors (above all, Augustus) were able to manipulate symbolically, Caligula tried to embrace all too literally, a not uncommon dysfunction.

SOURCES

64.1 Up until now I have been discussing Caligula in his capacity as an emperor. We must now consider him in his capacity as a monster. ...

When Caligula was on the verge of assuming a royal crown, converting the appearance of the Principate into the institution of monarchy, and someone pointed out to him that he already rose above both emperors and kings, Caligula began to claim for himself divine status. He gave out orders that the exceptionally revered and beautiful statues of deities, such as the Jupiter at Olympia, were to be brought to Rome from Greece, decapitated, and supplied with a head of his own likeness. He also extended a part of the Palatine palace all the way out to the Forum, transforming the Temple of Castor and Pollux into an entrance hall for the Palace. There in the temple he would often take his seat between the twin gods, presenting himself for worship to those who approached. Some even greeted him as Jupiter Latiaris, [a form of Jupiter worshipped on Mt. Albanus].

On clear nights when the Moon was full, he would welcome the lunar deity into his bed with passionate embraces, but by day he had private words with Jupiter Capitolinus, and would whisper in the god's ear or put his own ear to Jupiter's lips. At times he would raise his voice and even quarrel with the god: once he was heard to quote Homer in threatening tones, "Either you move me, or I move you...!" Finally Caligula announced that he had been won over by Jupiter's entreaties to live together. He then built a bridge above the Temple of the Deified Augustus to connect the Palatine and the Capitoline, and soon laid the foundations of a new house near the Temple of Jupiter.

Suetonius, *Caligula* 22.1–4

64.2 [The praetorian conspirators assassinated Caligula.] Even when the emperor fell dead they did not hold back, but kept stabbing him savagely, some of them even tasting his flesh. ... Thus did Caligula learn that he was not in fact a god.

Dio, *History* 59.29.7

64.3 [Claudius, the uncle of Caligula, was long the object of jokes and humiliation. But when Caligula was assassinated in a conspiracy of centurions and tribunes,] Claudius, at the age of fifty, became emperor in the strangest manner imaginable.

When the conspirators had killed Caligula and were dispersing the crowd by pretending that the emperor was still alive and just wanted to be alone, Claudius, excluded along with the others, withdrew into a summer room called the Hermaeum. A short time later he heard a report that Caligula had been murdered. In terror, Claudius slipped outside to a balcony off the Hermaeum, concealing himself behind the curtains that hung across the doorway. By chance, one of the rank-and-file wandering around the Palace saw his feet sticking out from under the curtain. Checking to see who it was, the soldier recognized Claudius and pulled him inside. As Claudius fell to his knees in fear, the soldier hailed him emperor.

The soldier led Claudius back to his fellow soldiers, who were still raging and roaming about without a plan. They placed Claudius on a litter, and since his own litter-bearers had run off, they took turns carrying him back to the [Praetorian] Camp. … But on the following day, while the Senate delayed out of weariness and disagreement over what should be done next, and while the crowd that had gathered outside demanded a single ruler and shouted for Claudius by name, Claudius allowed the soldiers to assemble in arms to swear an oath of allegiance to him. Claudius also paid them 15,000 sesterces each (becoming the first of the Caesars to secure the loyalty of troops with a cash payment).

Suetonius, *Claudius* 10.1–4

64.4 You're shocked by the vices of an ordinary woman?
Regard the ones who rival gods, and hear what Claudius
Endured in Messalina. No sooner was he snoring
Than our hooker for a Highness donned a hooded cloak,
Willing to trade her Palatine sheets for a tattered blanket
And leave the Hill behind with a single servant in tow.
No longer brunette but blonde, thanks to a wig, and wrapped
In a ragged quilt, she'd sneak inside a hopping whorehouse
To the room reserved for the Empress under the name of "Wolf-girl."
Then stripping down to her gilded nipples she went to work,
Offering up the loins that bore the prince Britannicus,
Absorbing the impact of man after man without a break,
And when the boss dismissed his girls, it was too soon
for Messalina; reluctantly she'd close up shop
and sadly limp her way back up the Palatine.

Juvenal, *Satires* 6.115–130

64.5 The emperor Vespasian resided infrequently on the Palatine, spending most of his time at the estate called the Gardens of Sallust, where he would receive anyone who wished to see him, not just the senators. … He was considered an autocrat only in his care of the public welfare; in all other respects he lived a common life on the level of others.

Dio, *History* 65.10.4, 11.1

64.6 At the beginning of his reign [c. AD 81], Domitian customarily spent hours in seclusion each day, doing nothing other than catching flies and stabbing them with a finely-pointed stylus. When someone once asked if anyone was inside with Caesar, Vibius Crispus aptly quipped: "No one … not even a fly."

Suetonius, *Domitian* 3.1

64.7 [There are many examples of Antoninus Pius's (AD 138-161) peaceful and generous character.] There was a Greek philosopher from Chalcis named Apollonius who had been summoned to Rome by the emperor. When Antoninus sent word for him to come to the Domus Tiberiana (where the emperor was then living) to tutor Marcus Aurelius, Apollonius said, "The teacher should not come to the pupil, but the pupil to the teacher." Antoninus only smiled, saying "It was easier for Apollonius to get from Greece to Rome than from his own house to the Palatine."

Imperial Lives, *Antoninus Pius* 10.4

64.8 [A tomb inscription:] Julia Gemella, wife of Isidorus, died at age 25. Albanus, slave of Caesar, assigned to the furnishings at the Domus Tiberiana, died at age 45.

ILS 1773 = *CIL* 6.8654

65. The Palace of Domitian (*Domus Augustiana*) (Fig. 32)

COMMENTARY

The bulk of the visible ruins on the Palatine today belong to the Palace of Domitian. Extensive as these ruins are, the work under Domitian transformed even more of the hill than is apparent today. By the time Domitian's builders were done, the imperial residences spread in a broad horseshoe around the Palatine—the Palace of Tiberius taking up much of the west side, ending at the compound of Augustus and associated temples above the Circus, continuing along the south side with the various sections of the Palace of Domitian, and then extending back towards the Forum again along the east side on a large platform, first built under Domitian for gardens and a temple. Much of the remaining space in the center of this horseshoe was itself given over to the main approach to the temple from the Forum, and included a Domitianic temple (perhaps a rebuilding of Jupiter Stator) and a public gathering space [65.8] in front of Domitian's towering audience hall.

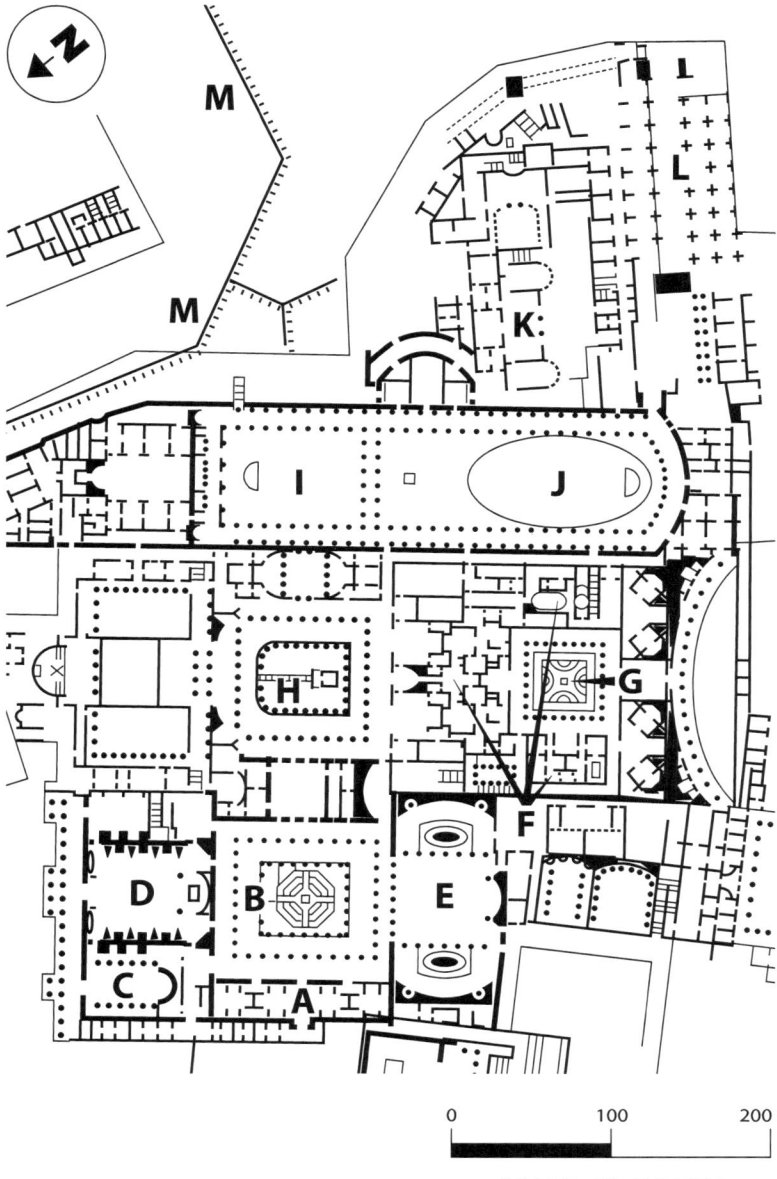

Fig. 32 Palace of Domitian

Although confusing in detail, the overall layout of the Palace of
Domitian is clear enough if one approaches it from one of its public
entrances, across the way from the House of Augustus, behind the
Temple of Apollo. Approached from this entrance (as guests invited to
a banquet probably did) the space makes sense as an aristocratic house
writ large. (See Fig. 32.)

First there is the space devoted to the public, a section of the palace sometimes separately named the Domus Flavia, although this designation is modern; the customary ancient name for the whole palace was the Domus August(i)ana. After the entrance hall connected to the street (A in Fig. 32), one comes upon a large courtyard (B) with a pool (schematically, like an atrium with the impluvium in a traditional *domus*). On the left, towards the Forum, the emperor and his officials conducted business in three rooms; the room in the corner (C) is sometimes called the "basilica" because of its architecture. Plutarch refers to a splendid "basilica" in the palace (65.1), but that may refer instead to the huge central audience hall next to it (D), which would have formed another prominent and more official component to the complex, with its own entrance towards the Forum. On the opposite side of the courtyard, towards the Circus, the emperor held public if still exclusive dinners, such as the one in AD 94 that elicited Statius's description [65.4] of the great banquet-hall (E).

Past this layer of public space are the more private quarters of the palace, a multi-layered warren of rooms (F) between and around two further courtyards (G, H). Beyond this more residential zone (partially excavated, and partially reconstructed in the 1930s), in place of the traditional peristyle, a long two-storied peristyle garden (I) stretches across the "back" of the house. Although it looks like a race-track (much like the one Domitian built in Piazza Navona area), it probably was not used for sports, although in late antiquity someone had a small amphitheater installed at the Circus-end of it (J). The palace continued beyond this garden with services such as baths and perhaps some of the quarters for servants, concubines, etc. (K). Subsequent emperors greatly expanded the palace in this direction (towards the Caelian Hill), especially Septimius Severus, who built the towering substructions (L) that artificially extended the hill towards the Septizonium, and apparently contemplated another monumental entrance to the palace from this direction [65.6]. Also on the southeastern side of the hill is a large section of an aqueduct extension by Domitian (M), which supplied the new palace with the copious supply of water that the ponds, fountains, baths, and staffing demanded.

SOURCES

65.1 Anyone who is amazed at the expense of Domitian's restoration of the Temple of Jupiter should see just one colonnade in the Palace of Domitian, or its basilica, its bath, or the quarters there for the concubines. ... Then he would be moved to tell Domitian, "You are not pious, or even ambitious: this obsession to build is a sickness. Like King Midas, you want everything you touch to turn to gold or marble."

Plutarch, *Publicola* 15.5

Fig. 33 Entablature Carving at the Palace of Domitian

65.2 Rabirius: you piously brought the stars and heaven to earth
When your genius built Domitian's palace on Evander's turf.
Martial, *Epigrams* 7.56.1–2

65.3 The ceilings of the palace rest on columns that cannot be counted
And the cross-beams glitter brightly, coated in Dalmatian gold.
Coolness drops from the shade where ancient trees arrest
The heat, and sparkling fountains jump in marble ponds.
Here Nature obeys no seasons; the Dog-Star chills,
Winter warms, and the house conforms the year to its wishes.
Statius, *Occasional Poems* 1.2.152–157

65.4 [Virgil and Homer have each described great banquets of heroes,]
But how shall I, whom Caesar has granted the novel delights
Of dining with divinity at the imperial table,   [AD 94]
Tune my lyre to match my sense of debt and tender
Adequate gratitude?

The hall is sublime and vast: no hundred columns merely,
But enough to hold the gods and heaven above the earth,
Should Atlas retire. Jupiter in his temple gapes
At your home in awe, Domitian, and the gods rejoice
In your equal footing. No need for you to hasten to heaven;

Fig. 34 Severan Substructions of Palace, seen across Circus Maximus

That structure spreads immense, and the reach of its giant hall,
More open than a field and holding in its embrace
More space than the sky, is only outdone by its lord: he fills
The happy home with his mighty spirit. Here stone competes
With stone, Numidian yellow rivaled by Phrygian purple,
Granite from Egypt, blushing marbles, and sea-green stone;
White slabs of Luna are relegated to the bases of columns.
The ceiling is a distant view, and the eyes must strain to reach
Its summit, to glimpse, it seems, the gilded panels of heaven.
Such was the setting where Caesar commanded the senators
Of Rome to sup together with knights at a thousand tables

Statius, *Occasional Poems* 4.2.5–8;18–33

65.5 Feared and hated by all, Domitian was finally overthrown [in AD 96] by a conspiracy composed of his friends, intimate freedmen, and even his wife. For a long time he had had a premonition of the year and final day of his life … . As the time of suspected danger approached, he grew more anxious by the day and had the walls of the colonnades where he like to stroll covered with a veneer of moonstone, so that he could see in its polish the reflections of whatever was happening behind his back.

On the day of his death, when Domitian asked the time, one of the conspirators told him it was the sixth hour, knowing that Domitian feared the fifth. Thinking the danger past, Domitian happily hurried off to exercise and bathe, but was stopped along the way by his chamberlain Parthenius, who said someone had to see him about some weighty matter or other that couldn't be put off. And so Domitian, having dismissed his attendants, entered his bedroom, where he was killed.

Suetonius, *Domitian* 14.1, 4; 16.2

65.6 When Septimius Severus constructed the Septizonium [in AD 203], he simply intended it as a monument to greet travelers arriving from Africa by the Appian Way. He is said, however, to have wanted an entrance to the Palatine (the imperial residence) from that quarter of the hill, but was thwarted when a Prefect of Rome put up a statue of Severus in the middle of the monument when Severus was out of town. Alexander Severus was planning to create an approach to the palace from there as well, but was prohibited by the soothsayers.

Imperial Lives, *Severus* 24.3

65.7 In honor of the spirits of the dead, Tiberius Claudius Thallus, in charge of the awnings of the Domus Augustiana, made this tomb for himself and his children.

ILS 1775 = *CIL* 6.8649

65.8 While we were waiting in the Palatine Square [*area*] to pay our respects to Caesar, the philosopher Favorinus spotted Caecilius, the great law-scholar, and approached him.

Gellius, *Attic Nights* 20.1.2

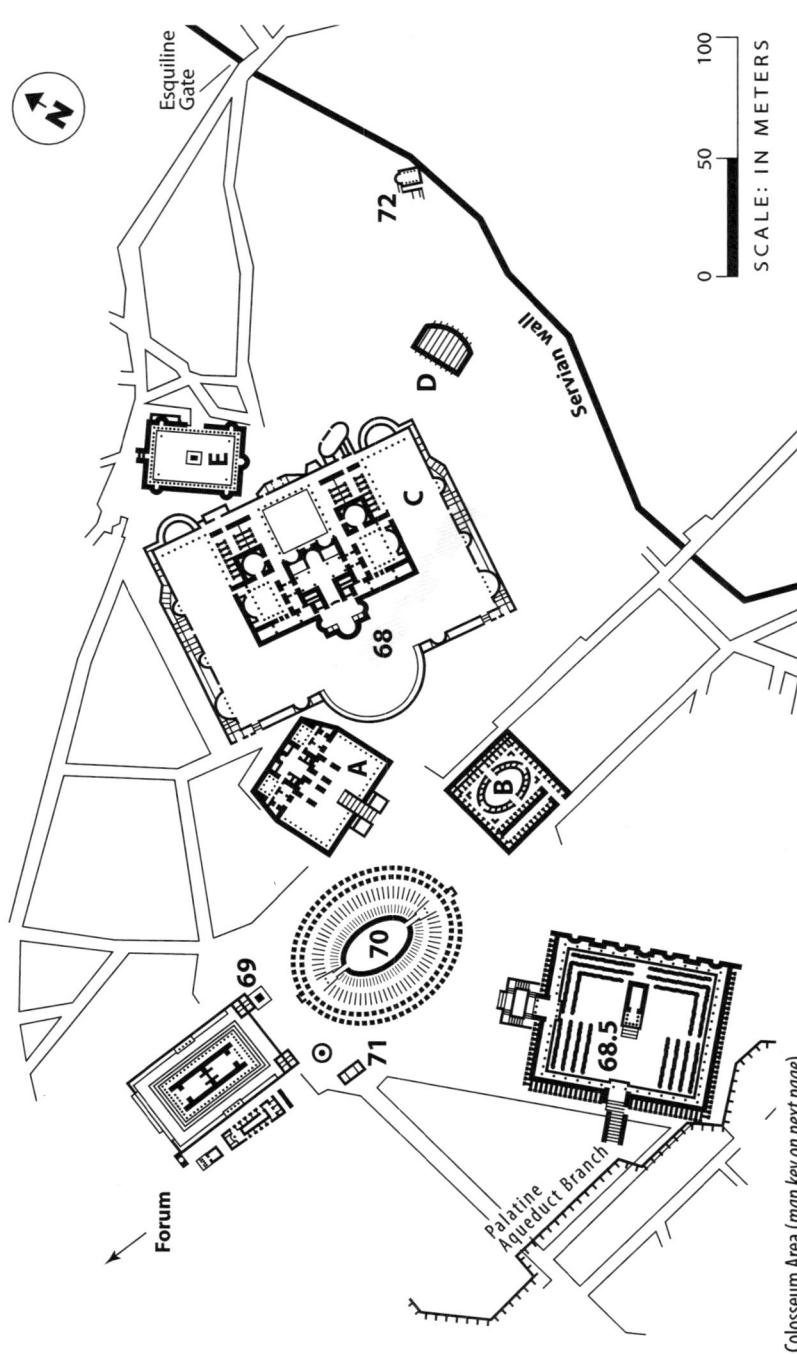

Fig. 35 Colosseum Area (*map key on next page*)

VII. The Golden House, Colosseum, and Esquiline Hill

66. The Fire of AD 64

COMMENTARY

Although Nero's famous fire started in the Campus Martius and spread over most of downtown Rome, the Colosseum-basin is a fitting place to include ancient descriptions of it, not only because Nero's signature work in Rome, the famous Golden House (the Domus Aurea) was built around the basin, but because the fire gave Nero greater liberty in its creation.

MAP KEY

68	Golden House
68.5	Temple of Claudius
69	Colossus of the Sun-god
70	Flavian Amphitheater (Colosseum)
71	Arch of Constantine
72	Gardens of Maecenas
A	Baths of Titus
B	Gladiatorial school (*Ludus Magnus*)
C	Baths of Trajan
D	Cistern for Baths
E	Porticus of Livia

In addition to a famous passage about Crassus's profiteering that testifies to the frequency of fires in Rome [66.1], I have also included here a few sources that indicate the possible impact that Nero's fire may have had on the Christian topography of Rome. The first known persecution of Christians in Rome was a result of the fire. Tacitus reports that Nero blamed the fire on the Christians to deflect the suspicion that he started it, and he had many of them executed, some of them used as torches in mockery of the crime they were charged with, others by crucifixion. Tacitus further tells us that some of the executions took place in Nero's circus in the Vatican fields, a racetrack (apparently begun by Gaius Caligula;

see 94.2] that stretched all along the left side of the present Basilica of St. Peter. Alongside this racetrack was a street lined by tombs, and it is possible that Simon Peter was not only one of the Christians killed in this persecution, but that he was killed in Nero's circus and buried in this cemetery. Early Christians, at any rate, believed his bones rested here [67.3] and built a shrine above them in the C2, followed, under Constantine, by the large basilica that was the forerunner of the current St. Peter's.

The ruins of Nero's circus are no longer visible, but the obelisk located at its center still stands, transported by Pope Sixtus V in 1586 a short distance to the piazza in front of the new St. Peter's Basilica (See Fig. 1). The ancient cemetery, complete with street and mausoleums that are preserved deep underground among the massive foundations of the present basilica, is one of the more astounding sites in Rome and can be visited with advance reservations.

SOURCES

66.1 The best indication of Crassus's love of wealth is the size of his fortune and the means he used to acquire it [c. 60s BC]. … Perceiving that deadly fires and building collapses were a common and predictable occurrence in Rome because structures were built too high and too close together, Crassus began to purchase slaves trained in architecture and construction. When he had amassed a crew of 500, he would buy up properties on fire or those next to a fire, which their owners, out of fear and uncertainty, sold for bargain prices. In this manner Crassus came to own the greater part of Rome.

Plutarch, *Crassus* 2.5

66.2 At this time [AD 64] a disastrous fire occurred. Whether it was an accident or due to the treachery of Nero is not known (since writers have handed down both accounts), but it was clearly the most serious and destructive fire ever to ravage Rome. It began in the part of the Circus that borders on the Palatine and Caelian Hills. Feeding on the highly flammable merchandise there, the fire grew rapidly. Whipped by the winds, it raced down the length of the Circus, encountering here none of the obstructions, such as walls that surround mansions and temple precincts, that might have delayed the flames. Spreading quickly, it charged across the level areas, then up the hills and back down again to destroy the lower spots, outstripping all preventive measures by its speed. The city was all the more vulnerable because of the narrow alleyways and the irregular, twisting blocks of buildings that characterized old Rome. … In addition, no one dared to fight the fire, since anyone making an attempt was subjected to repeated threats by many people; others were even openly throwing torches about, claiming they had the authority to do so (whether to plunder more freely, or because they were indeed under orders).

When the fire started, Nero was in Antium and did not return to the city until the fire was nearing the palace he built to connect the Palatine Hill to the Gardens of Maecenas. The fire, however, could not be stopped before it consumed the Palatine, the palace, and everything around it. By way of relief for the people made homeless by the fire, Nero opened up to them the Campus Martius, the monuments of Agrippa, and even his own gardens [on the Vatican Hill], and erected temporary structures to house the large numbers of homeless. Food supplies were brought upstream from Ostia and neighboring towns, and the price of grain was lowered to three sesterces a peck. But all of these efforts, although popular in nature, won Nero no favor with the people, since the rumor had surfaced that while the city was still on fire he got up on his private stage and sang his poem "The Fall of Troy," noting the correspondences between the present calamities and that ancient catastrophe.

Finally on the sixth day the fire died out at the lower slopes of the Esquiline Hill, where a wide swath of buildings had been purposefully demolished so the advancing inferno would come up against open field and empty sky. But before there was time for either fear to subside or hope to return, the fire broke out again and this time ravaged the more open quarters of the city, where the loss of life was smaller than in the first fire, but the destruction to temples and porticoed parks was even greater. This second blaze aroused more suspicion because it originated in the Aemilian estates [probably located in the Campus Martius just north of the Capitoline] of Nero's associate, Tigellinus, and because it seemed that Nero wanted to be famous for founding a new Rome named after himself.

Of the fourteen regions into which Rome is divided, four of them remained untouched by the flames and three were completely leveled; in the remaining seven regions, scattered remnants of buildings still stood in burnt ruin.

It would not be easy to list all the fine homes, apartment buildings, and temples which were destroyed by this fire. Among the losses were the some of the oldest sacred sites in Rome, including Servius Tullius's Temple of the Moon-Goddess, the large altar and shrine that Arcadian Evander consecrated to Hercules for his help, the Temple of Jupiter Stator vowed by Romulus, Numa's Regia, and the Temple of Vesta along with the Penates of the Roman people. Also lost were treasures gained in numerous victories, masterpieces of Greek art, and the old, original manuscripts of great writers. As a result, even though the city rose again in such great splendor, the older people remembered many losses which could never be made good.

Some people noted that the fire began on July 19, the same date of the fire the Gauls once started when they sacked the city [in 390 BC].

Others went to the trouble of calculating that the interval between the two fires can be divided up into the same number of years, months, and days [454 years equaling 418 years, 418 months, and 418 days].

Tacitus, *Annals* 15.38–41

66.3 [Nero blatantly started the fire.]
Viewing it from the tower of Maecenas and inspired, as he said, "by the beauty of the flames," Nero sang his "Sack of Troy" from beginning to end, dressed in his customary stage costume.

Suetonius, *Nero* 38.2

66.4 Those parts of Rome left over from Nero's new palace were not rebuilt in the random and disorderly fashion that characterized reconstruction after the Gauls burned the city, but rather in rows of measured streets, wide thoroughfares, and open spaces. Building heights were regulated and porticoes protected the fronts of apartment buildings. Nero promised that he would build the colonnades at his own expense, and that he would hand properties back over to their owners when he finished clearing away the rubble. In addition, he offered a reward, varying according to each person's station and the size of his property, for rebuilding homes and apartment buildings within a certain time. He also designated the marshes of Ostia as a land-fill for the rubble, which was taken down the Tiber on boats that had unloaded their shipment of grain.

As for the new buildings themselves, Nero stipulated that a certain portion of them must be built without wooden beams, using either Gabine or Alban stone [= peperino tufas], since this type of stone stands up to fire.

To increase the volume of the water-supply and deliver it to more places in public, guards were assigned to stop the illegal tapping of the aqueducts, and each building (which could no longer share a wall with another building) had to have fire-fighting equipment on the premises.

Such regulations adopted for utility led to a more beautiful city as well. There were some, however, who believed that the old look of the city was more conducive to the well-being of the inhabitants, arguing that the narrower streets and taller buildings had helped to break the heat of the sun that baked the open and shadeless spaces of the new Rome.

Tacitus, *Annals* 15.43

66.5 Nero devised a new arrangement for buildings in the city, and provided his own money to construct porticoes in front of apartment buildings and homes so that fires could be fought from the roofs of these porches. He also planned to extend the walls all the way to Ostia, and to bring the sea into the city center with a canal.

Suetonius, *Nero* 16.1

67. The Circus of Gaius and Nero and Christian Persecutions

(See Fig. 1 for location)

67.1 Nero had a space in the Vatican valley enclosed where he might practice his chariot-racing. At first he raced in private, but soon he was inviting the public in to cheer him on.

Tacitus, *Annals* 14.14.4

67.2 [After the fire, various rituals were performed to appease the gods.] But neither the emperor's expense and generosity nor the appeasement of the gods could avert the suspicion that Nero ordered the fire. To quell this rumor Nero falsely accused others—"Christians," as they were commonly called, already hated for their scandalous conduct—and he subjected them to the most elaborate tortures. (Their founder was a man named Christ, who was executed in Tiberius's reign by the orders of the Roman governor Pontius Pilate. The deadly cult was thus suppressed for the moment, but then burst forth anew, not only in Judaea, the source of this evil, but throughout Rome as well, where all things shocking and disgraceful gravitate and thrive.)

First some Christians were arrested who confessed to the crime, and by their evidence a host of others were convicted, not so much for the crime of arson as for their hatred of humankind. Mockery attended their death: dressed in the hides of animals they were torn apart by dogs, nailed on crosses, or were themselves set on fire after dark and used as torches. Nero opened his gardens to this spectacle and made a show of their executions in his circus, dressed as a charioteer and mingling with the people, or riding on a chariot. As a result of his behavior, people felt pity for these Christians, not because they didn't think them guilty and deserving of novel punishments, but because it seemed that they were being slaughtered not for the public welfare but to satisfy the savagery of one man.

Tacitus, *Annals* 15.44

67.3 It is recorded that the Apostles Paul and Peter were killed under Nero in Rome itself, the former by decapitation and the latter by crucifixion. That this occurred in Rome is corroborated by the existence of cemeteries there in their names, and by no less an authority than Caius, a church historian who wrote when Zephyrinus was Bishop of Rome [c. AD 210]. ...

Discussing the location of the relics of the apostles in question, Caius reports: "I am able to point out the burial monuments of these apostles: if you care to go out to the Vatican field or the road to Ostia, you will find the monuments of the founders of our Church."

Eusebius, *Ecclesiastical History* 2.25.5–7

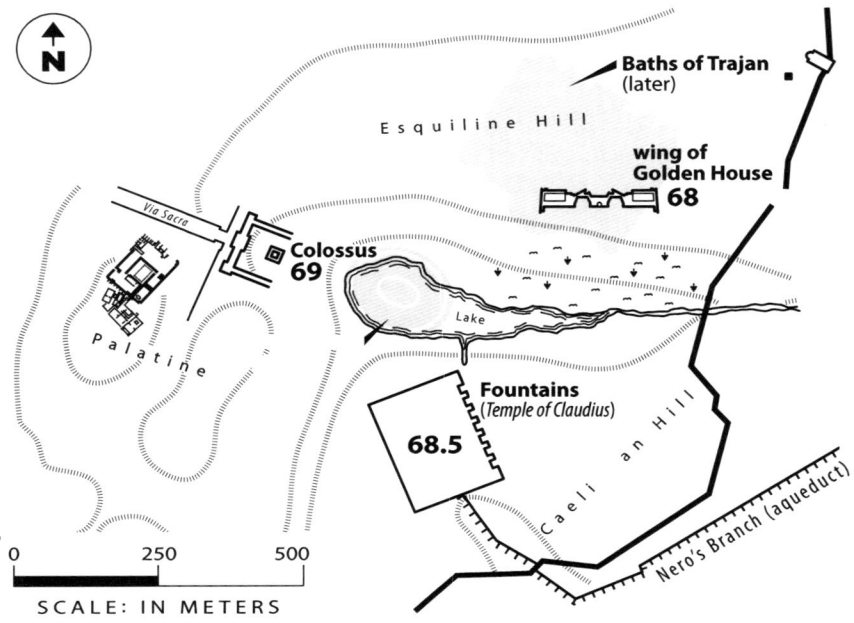

Fig. 36 Nero's Golden House

68. Nero's Golden House (*Domus Aurea*)

COMMENTARY

Although Julius Caesar and Nero differed so greatly from one another in character and temperament, they shared a fatal independence and lack of tact with regard to some of Rome's sacred institutions and time-honored ways that got them both killed by aristocratic conspiracies. Their approach to Roman topography is symptomatic of this offensive independence: the one, had he lived, might have moved the Tiber [2.4], and the other actually did create, practically in the heart of the city, a rural estate centered on a man-made lake.

The lake, located where the Colosseum stands today, was the geographical centerpiece of the Domus Aurea, Nero's new imperial estate stretching from the Palatine to the Gardens of Maecenas on the Esquiline. The most famous and well-preserved part of the estate, an architecturally innovative wing on the lower Esquiline, goes by the name Domus Aurea today, but Suetonius uses the term to refer to the whole property, which comprised numerous buildings, long colonnades, and faux-countryside with farms and vineyards on the slopes around the lake. Although the Colosseum-basin is still fed by springs, perhaps with enough volume to form a pond when dammed, Nero's extension of the Aqua Claudia down the Caelian could have been used to feed the lake after supplying fountains and gardens with water (perhaps even powering the machinery that rotated the domed ceiling of his dining room).

Several of the sources show how deeply offended the Romans were at this cavalier use of Roman space for private enjoyment, and subsequent emperors reaped the benefits of returning this land to the people's use, most dramatically in the form of the Colosseum.

SOURCES

68.1 After the fire, Nero took personal advantage of his country's calamity and built himself a downtown residence. The cause for amazement was not so much its profusion of gems and gold (luxuries common enough by then) as its fields and ponds, with woods resembling a wilderness on one side and open spaces with vistas on the other. This was all designed and directed by Severus and Celer, who possessed both the talent and the audacity that were needed to create by art what nature herself refused, and to beguile away the resources at an emperor's disposal.

Tacitus, *Annals* 15.42.1

68.2 For all Nero's extravagance elsewhere, nothing matched his wastefulness in building. He built a palace that stretched from the Palatine to the Esquiline, which he at first called the Passage House [*Domus Transitoria*] and then, after this was soon destroyed in the fire and rebuilt, renamed the Golden House [*Domus Aurea*]. The following details will suffice to give an idea of its size and luxury.

In the forecourt of the Golden House stood a statue in the likeness of Nero 120 feet tall. The palace was so extensive that it had a triple colonnade a mile long. A pond, in imitation of the sea, was bordered with buildings to look like cities. In addition there were various types of countryside, with cropland, vineyards, pastures and woods, plentifully stocked with all manner of wild and domestic creatures.

In the rest of the palace, everything was overlaid with gold and adorned with gems and mother-of-pearl. The dining rooms had ceilings with ivory panels that swiveled aside so that pipes might shower petals and perfume on banqueters below, and the main dining room had a dome that revolved day and night like the heavens. The baths flowed with waters from the sea and the Albulan sulfur springs [near Tivoli]. When Nero dedicated the palace constructed in such a fashion, he simply expressed his approval by saying, "Finally a home fit for a human being."

Suetonius, *Nero* 31.1–2

68.3 Nero proved surprisingly tolerant towards those who made him the target of their witticisms and verse-lampoons. There were many of these in circulation, in Greek as well as in Latin. The following about the Golden House is one example:

> Rome is now a private home,
> It's time to emigrate—
> Assuming other lands exist
> When they finish this estate.

Suetonius, *Nero* 39.2

68.4 [In 65 BC a conspiracy (betrayed before it was carried out) formed against Nero, with the aim of replacing him with Calpurnius Piso.] The conspirators wanted to rush the assassination along and do it while Nero was still staying at Piso's villa near Naples. But Piso refused, saying it was better for them to kill him in Rome, either in the hated home that Nero had built on land plundered from Roman citizens, or out in the open, to finish *in* public what they had undertaken for the *Re*public.

Tacitus, *Annals* 15.52

68.5 Vespasian built the Temple of the Deified Claudius on the Caelian Hill. The temple had actually been begun by Claudius's widow Agrippina, but Nero demolished it nearly down to its foundations.

Suetonius, *Vespasian* 9.1

68.6 Where now the Sun's Colossus has its closer view of the stars
> And towering scaffolds loom above the street,
> The hated entrance halls of that wild king once gleamed
> And a single dwelling stood in all the city.
> Where now the venerable mass of the Amphitheater rises
> High above Rome, the pond of Nero spread.
> Where now we gaze in wonder on the sudden Baths of Titus,
> A haughty estate deprived the people of homes.
> Where now the Claudian colonnade unfolds its spreading shade
> The furthest part of the palace came to an end.
> Rome has been restored to Rome, Titus, with you as her defender,
> And pleasures grabbed by a tyrant return to the people.

Martial, *On Spectacles* 2

69. Colossus of Nero

SOURCES
69.1 In the entry area of Nero's Golden House stood a statue in the likeness of Nero 120 feet tall.

Suetonius, *Nero* 31

69.2 There exists a giant class of bronze statues called Colossi, tall as towers. The Colossus of the Sun-god in Rhodes, built by Chares, was the most famous of them. Larger than all of them, however, was a colossus made in our own time by Zenodorus. Summoned to Rome by Nero, he made a colossus 106 1/2 feet tall, intended originally to represent the emperor, but since dedicated to the Sun-god after the crimes of Nero were condemned.

Pliny the Elder, *Encyclopedia* 34.39, 41, 45

69.3 In Vespasian's sixth consulship and Titus's fourth [AD 75], ... the statue called the Colossus was set up on the Sacred Way. They say that it is one hundred feet high and has the face of Nero, according to some, or Titus, according to others.

Dio, *History* 65.15

69.4 Among his many architectural activities in Rome, Hadrian had the Colossus moved from the site of his new Temple of [Venus and] Rome. The architect Decrianus directed the work, suspending and transporting the statue in an upright position, an object so massive that it required twenty-four elephants. Hadrian then had the features of Nero removed (the statue's original dedicatee) and consecrated it instead to the Sun-god, which he planned to accompany later with a colossus of the Moon designed by Apollodorus.

Imperial Lives, *Hadrian* 19.12–13

69.5 [The emperor Commodus (ruling AD 180–192) was obsessed with the idea of being a famous gladiator.] He actually had the head of the Colossus removed and replaced with a new one in his own features. He also gave the Colossus a club and had a bronze lion placed at its feet to suggest the figure of Hercules, and then added the inscription: "Best of the Gladiators."

Dio, *History* 73.22.3

69.6 So long as the Colossus stands, Rome shall stand; when the Colossus falls, Rome too shall fall; and when Rome falls, so falls the world.

Pseudo-Bede (P.L. 94.543)

Notes: There are several basic disputes surrounding the Colossus. There are some contradictions in the sources quoted, and some topographers deny that it was built by Nero (see C. Lega in *LTUR* 1.295ff. for a survey of opinions). Another area of disagreement surrounds Bede's famous pronouncement linking the "Colisaeus" with the survival of Rome: does Bede's prediction (which actually comes from a collection of sayings falsely attributed to Bede) refer to the Colosseum, as popular opinion and some scholars hold, or to the statue that is no more?

70. Colosseum (*Amphitheatrum Flavii*)

COMMENTARY

It is not known exactly when the Colosseum got its name from the colossus next to it, although it was well into the Middle Ages; in antiquity Rome's most famous building was known as the Flavian Amphitheater, or simply as *the* Amphitheater. A recent reconstruction of an inscription found on one of the Colosseum's blocks [70.1] confirms that the monument had the standard financing, in this case booty from the Jewish War waged by the first Flavian emperor Vespasian and his sons Titus and Domitian. The Romans since time immemorial had staged gladiatorial combat at various venues, including the Forum and Pompey's Theater, and Seneca's account below, written under Nero, shows how sated and desensitized the audience had become even before the Colosseum was built, but Vespasian gave the city an installation it could be proud of, and on land reclaimed for the people from Nero's hated estate.

As an icon of ancient Rome, the Colosseum's attractive power today is generated by a strong polarity: on the one hand the structure is a marvel of engineering and design still not exhaustively documented, and on the other it stands as a symbol of depravity, decadence, and cruelty. Our condemnation itself of the arena is, like that of Alypius so famously depicted by St. Augustine, no simple matter, and popular portrayals of the arena in cinema today suggest that any investigation and condemnation of the arena, with its manic emperors and craven (but ultimately good-hearted) crowds, that didn't at the same time give us serious bloodsport would be a box-office flop; we condemn, and get in line. Even the crosses later stationed in the arena as a witness to its crimes partake of the complexity of the fascination with gruesome deaths.

In several ways, the Colosseum is also a fitting symbol for the Roman empire in its physical extent. The entertainment there was geographically coded, featuring both human combatants from distant lands trained in the characteristic fighting skills of those lands, and exotic animals from all reaches of the empire. The environmental impact was significant: ecologically as well as architecturally, the Colosseum resembles nothing so much as the mouth of a lamprey. One curious consequence of Rome's voracious consumption that emptied some lands of animal species was a proliferation of species of plant life in the Colosseum: before the overgrowth of vegetation was cleared away in 1871, over 400 species of plants grew on the ruins, a variety made possible both by the seeds attached to or ingested by animals supplied for the games, and the Colosseum's special microclimate.

Frequently damaged by lightning and earthquakes, the Colosseum was repaired up into the C6, when the last of the animal hunts was held there (gladiatorial games, gradually withering under a Christian ethos, ceased to be held there in the early fifth century). After that, although falling progressively to ruin, the amphitheater was put to use as shelter by rich and poor, and the powerful family of the Frangipani built their palace there c.1200. Rome's revival in the Renaissance was at first detrimental for the monument, which was treated as a quarry. In the C15 and C16 many of the large travertine blocks that compose the Colosseum's two outer rings, as well as miles of marble seating, went into the construction and decoration of both municipal and Church projects, including the facade of St. Peter's. When it was declared sacred ground in 1675, the pillaging stopped, and it was fitted with stations of the cross to commemorate the Christian martyrs who formed one class of the criminalized who met their end here. The massive structural buttresses that terminate the outer rings, retarding further dilapidation, are papal projects of the early 1800s.

SOURCES

70.1 The Emperor Vespasian ordered a new amphitheater to be built from the booty [of the Jewish War in AD 70].
                                                    Inscription (see Claridge, p. 278)

70.2 Vespasian built an amphitheater in the middle of Rome, a building he knew Augustus had also been planning.
                                                    Suetonius, *Vespasian* 9.1

70.3 The emperor Titus was second to none of his predecessors in his provision of public entertainment. When the Amphitheater was dedicated [in AD 80] along with the baths hastily constructed next to it, Titus gave phenomenally lavish and expensive games. He also put on a mock naval battle in the old Naumachia [a stadium designed to be flooded], and then held gladiatorial combats in the same place, which on one day alone included 5,000 wild animals of all kinds.
                                                    Suetonius, *Titus* 7.3

70.4 During his reign [AD 79–81] Titus did little that was exceptional, apart from the incredible shows he gave for the dedication ceremonies of the hunting theater [the Colosseum] and the baths that are named after him. One contest pitted whooping cranes against each other; in another four elephants fought. Animals both tame and wild were slaughtered, to the number of 9,000. Women (though none of any standing) took part in the killing; many men fought in single combat, but many others fought in squads, on both foot and in boats, since Titus had this same theater quickly flooded … Others also fought on boats in the basin in the Gardens of Gaius and Lucius [the Naumachia], which Augustus had excavated for just such battles. … Such spectacles lasted for one hundred days. Titus supplemented them with some more useful entertainment: he threw little wooden balls down on the audience of the amphitheater, each inscribed with a little picture of the prize that those who caught the balls could pick up from the appropriate officials: the prizes included food, clothing, vessels of silver and gold, horses, mules, cattle, and slaves.

On the last day of his games, Titus was seen to weep. When they were over, he accomplished nothing great, dying the following year.

Dio, *History* 66.25

70.5 The Emperor Commodus [AD 180–192], initially an avid spectator of the gladiatorial shows, then participated in them is well. In the arena, he would drape his bare shoulders in a purple cloth. … Although the audience would cheer his frequent appearances in the arena as they would a god's, he suspected it was all in mockery and had the naval crew (stationed at the Colosseum to work the awnings) execute spectators.

Imperial Lives, *Commodus* 15.3,6

70.6 [Bad omens abounded in the short reign of Macrinus, Caracalla's successor. In AD 217] the hunting theater was struck by lightning on the very day of the Vulcanalia which started such a serious fire that the entire upper ring and the arena at the bottom were consumed by flame, and the rest of the structure in between was cracked and weakened by the fire. … For several years, gladiatorial combats had to be put on in [Domitian's] Stadium.

Dio, *History* 79.25.2, 3

70.7 The Emperor Alexander Severus [c. AD 230] placed a tax on pimps and both male and female prostitutes, with the stipulation that the income thus raised go not into the public treasury but towards the cost of restoring the Theater, the Circus, the Amphitheater, and the Stadium.

Imperial Lives, *Severus Alexander* 24.3

70.8 [Visiting Rome for the first time in AD 357] the emperor Constantius II gazed over the regions of the city and suburban estates that ringed it, thinking, as each object met his view in turn, that it excelled everything else in height: the Temple of Jupiter, rising above its surroundings the way divine things rise over earthly; the imperial baths, piled high to the volume of a province; the sturdy mass of the Amphitheater encased in its frame of travertine, soaring to heights difficult to reach with the human eye.

Ammianus, *History* 16.10.14

70.9 [In AD 508] the consul Venantius Basilius repaired at his own expense the arena and the podium around the arena after they were destroyed by a terrible earthquake.

ILS 5635 = *CIL* 6.32094

70.10 Seneca to Lucilius: [Note: Seneca's account was written before the Colosseum was built.]

You ask me what, above all else, we should avoid in life? The crowd, I say. You are not yet ready to expose yourself to it unscathed. In fact, I'll confess my own weakness in this regard: I never bring back home the same morals I had before I entered a crowd.

Nothing, however, compares with the damage done to a good character by spending time in the crowd at the games. … The other day I happened to attend the midday intermission of a gladiatorial show, expecting to catch something amusing and refreshing, something to give the eye a break from all the human gore. I couldn't have been more mistaken. The midday show made the earlier fighting look like compassion; this was pure homicide, without any of the former frills. … There were no helmets and no shields. Why involve armor, or skill? Such things would just get in the way of death. In the morning, men are thrown to lions and bears; at midday they are thrown to the spectators. Those who are victorious and kill their opponent are forced to face others who will kill them; the victor must always fight again, until he dies; there is no way out but death. To make sure the fights continue, the criminals are prodded with spears and branded by fire. This is what happens when the arena is empty, *between* shows.

"But the man in the arena is a robber, he killed someone!" you might respond. But why should *you* have to sit through such a spectacle because *he* killed someone? What did you do wrong, that you deserve to witness this? "Kill! Strike! He hangs back: burn him! … Why doesn't he die with more enthusiasm? Whip him back into the fight." And if there is a break in the action: "Boring! Let's have some throats slit!"

Seneca the Younger, *Letters* 7, selections

70.11 My friend Alypius had come to Rome before me [c. AD 380] with the intent of learning law, and was swept away by a violent and extraordinary passion for gladiatorial shows. Until then he detested and avoided such entertainment, but one day some of his friends and schoolmates ran into him on their way back from lunch, and although he resisted and spoke strongly against joining them, they dragged him off with friendly force into the amphitheater on a day that featured cruel and mortal combat. "Maybe you can drag my body into the stadium," Alypius said, "but can you force my mind and eyes to attend such entertainment? I will be present, and yet absent, and so defeat both you and the games."

When his friends heard this, they pulled him along with no less enthusiasm, perhaps eager to find out if he was able to make good on his boast. By the time they were able to find seats, the crowd was in a state of brutal rapture. Alypius shut tight the doors of his eyes, forbidding his mind from paying attention to such evils. If only he could have sealed his ears! For when, in response to some knock-down in the arena, the giant roar of the entire crowd pounded on him, Alypius, overcome by curiosity but still confident that he could condemn and be the master of whatever he looked on, opened his eyes. Struck with a wound more deadly for his soul than for the body of the man who was the object of his sight, he fell, and fell more pitifully than that man whose fall occasioned the uproar. … For as soon as he saw the blood, he drank up the savagery, and did not then look away, but stared and swallowed the fury without knowing that he drank, thrilled by the crime of the combat and intoxicated by the bloodlust. No longer was he the person who had entered, but one of the crowd he had joined; he was now the true companion of those who had led him in.

St. Augustine, *Confessions* 6.8

71. Arch of Constantine

COMMENTARY

The Arch of Constantine, as proclaimed in the inscription on its attic, celebrates his victory over Maxentius, the reigning emperor (styled "the tyrant" in the inscription) whom Constantine deposed. The friezes immediately below the round reliefs were specifically sculpted for this occasion. The one over the right-side archway, on the Circus-side of the arch, portrays the battle at the Milvian Bridge, where Constantine defeated Maxentius in AD 312. Most of the decoration of the arch, however, was taken from other monuments built under Trajan, Hadrian, and Marcus Aurelius, a sign (soon to be confirmed in Constantine's foundation in 324 of the New Rome of Constantinople) that the city was in decline.

Constantine, though famous for promoting Christianity in the empire, proceeded carefully in the capital, locating his most impressive donations to the Church—the basilicas of St. Peter and St. John of the Lateran—on the periphery of the city. The Senate who awarded the arch was still composed primarily of pagans; hence also the vagueness of the phrase *instinctu divinitatis* in the inscription, "by divine inspiration," which is probably a reference to Constantine's vision of a cross in the sky before he defeated Maxentius.

SOURCES

71.1 IMP(eratori) CAES(ari) FL(avio) CONSTANTINO MAXIMO / P(io) F(elici) AUGUSTO S(enatus) P(opulus)Q(ue) R(omanus) / QUOD INSTINCTU DIVINITATIS MENTIS / MAGNITUDINE CUM EXERCITU SUO / TAM DE TYRANNO QUAM DE OMNI EIUS /

Fig. 37 Arch of Constantine

FACTIONE UNO TEMPORE IUSTIS / REM PUBLICAM ULTUS EST
ARMIS / ARCUM TRIUMPHIS INSIGNEM DICAVIT

To the Emperor Caesar Flavius Constantinus Maximus Pius Felix
Augustus the Senate and the Roman People dedicate this arch [in AD
315] as a memorial to his military triumphs, who by the inspiration of
divinity and his own genius avenged, with righteous arms in one instant, the Republic against the tyrant [Maxentius] and his faction.

ILS 694 = *CIL* 6.1139

71.2 [In AD 312 Constantine and his armies descended from Gaul
into Italy to fight Maxentius, who had usurped the throne.] Realizing
that he was in need of assistance more powerful than an army, on account of the deadly and demonic magic assiduously employed by the
tyrant Maxentius, Constantine looked for divine aid. … As he weighed
the evidence, he reflected that his foes who trusted in numerous gods
had all met with various forms of destruction, leaving behind them
neither family, sons, lineage, name, nor monuments among men,
whereas the God worshipped by his father Constantius had given many
clear signs of his power. … He therefore called on this deity in prayer,
beseeching him to reveal who he was and to offer his right hand to
Constantine in his present difficulties.

As he was praying for this with intense fervor, a most
marvelous sign from heaven appeared to him. … About noon, with
the sun just beginning its descent, he said that he saw with his own
eyes the victorious sign of the cross, formed out of light in the sky

above the sun. This image was accompanied by the inscription "In this Sign Conquer" (τούτῳ νίκα).

Constantine said that he continued to ponder and reason out the meaning of this vision as night came on, and that in his sleep, Christ the Son of God appeared to him along with the same sign he had seen in the sky, urging him to fashion a likeness of this heavenly sign and to use it as a protection in all his battles against his enemies. … Afterwards, the emperor made use of this sign of salvation as a safeguard in every battle against enemy forces, and ordered that similar emblems of the cross should be carried in front of all his armies. … Strengthened in his position by well-founded hopes in Him, Constantine advanced to quench the remaining fire of tyranny.

Eusebius, *Life of Constantine*, 1.27–32, selections

Notes: On Constantine's building activities in Rome and their religious ramifications, see R. Krautheimer, *Rome: Profile of a City, 312–1308.*

72. Gardens of Maecenas

COMMENTARY

Maecenas was for a time one of Augustus's closest advisors, and a famous patron of artists, including the poets Horace, Virgil, and Propertius. The land for his estate on the Esquiline was acquired by covering over the burial pits located just outside the Rampart of the Republican Wall on the Esquiline. Both Horace and Suetonius refer to some sort of tower on the estate that gave views of both the city and the mountains, but this has not survived. A suggestive hall, however, does remain, near the crossing of Via Merulana and Via Mecenate. Called the Auditorium of Maecenas today, it was probably a banquet and performance hall, perhaps where the artists under his patronage would debut some of their work.

Many tombs from the earlier burial ground have also been found, as well as some of the pits. Observing work on the new Via Napoleone III in 1887, the topographer Rudolf Lanciani describes the excavations of seventy-five pits, which also included the remains of animals "reduced to a uniform mass of black, unctuous matter. … The field of death served also as a dumping place for the daily refuse of the city. This hotbed of infection was suppressed by Augustus at the suggestion of his prime minister Maecenas. The district was buried under fresh earth to the depth of 24 feet, and a public park, a fifth of a mile in extent, was laid out on the newly made ground"(*The Destruction of Ancient Rome*, p. 14).

SOURCES

72.1 The word "Pitkins," referring to graveyards one finds outside the walls of cities, is formed from "pit," because human corpses were thrown into pits there; or perhaps it was formed from "putrefaction," because the bodies would rot there, in the public burial ground outside the walls on the Esquiline.

Varro, *The Latin Language* 5.25

72.2 Evicted by death from their tiny rooms, the corpses of slaves
Were commonly carried to the Esquiline Hill in a cheap box;
Here too were the burial grounds for the poorer citizens.
But today the hill is wholesome, healthy enough for homes,
And one can stroll along the sunny Rampart, where lately
One gazed across a landscape littered with bleached bones.

Horace, *Satires* 1.8.7–10,14–6

72.3 Maecenas, it is time you pay my country home
A visit; viewing the lovely Alban Hills
And the watered slopes of Tivoli from Rome,
You've gazed enough on beauty at a distance.

Tear yourself away from tiring abundance,
From your tower aloft in piles of Esquiline clouds,
Free yourself from this endless fascination
With the smoke, splendor, and noise of the city below.

Horace, *Odes* 3.29.5–12

72.4 Viewing the fire from the tower of Maecenas and inspired, as he said, "by the beauty of the flames," Nero sang his "Sack of Troy" from beginning to end, dressed in his customary stage costume.

Suetonius, *Nero* 38.2

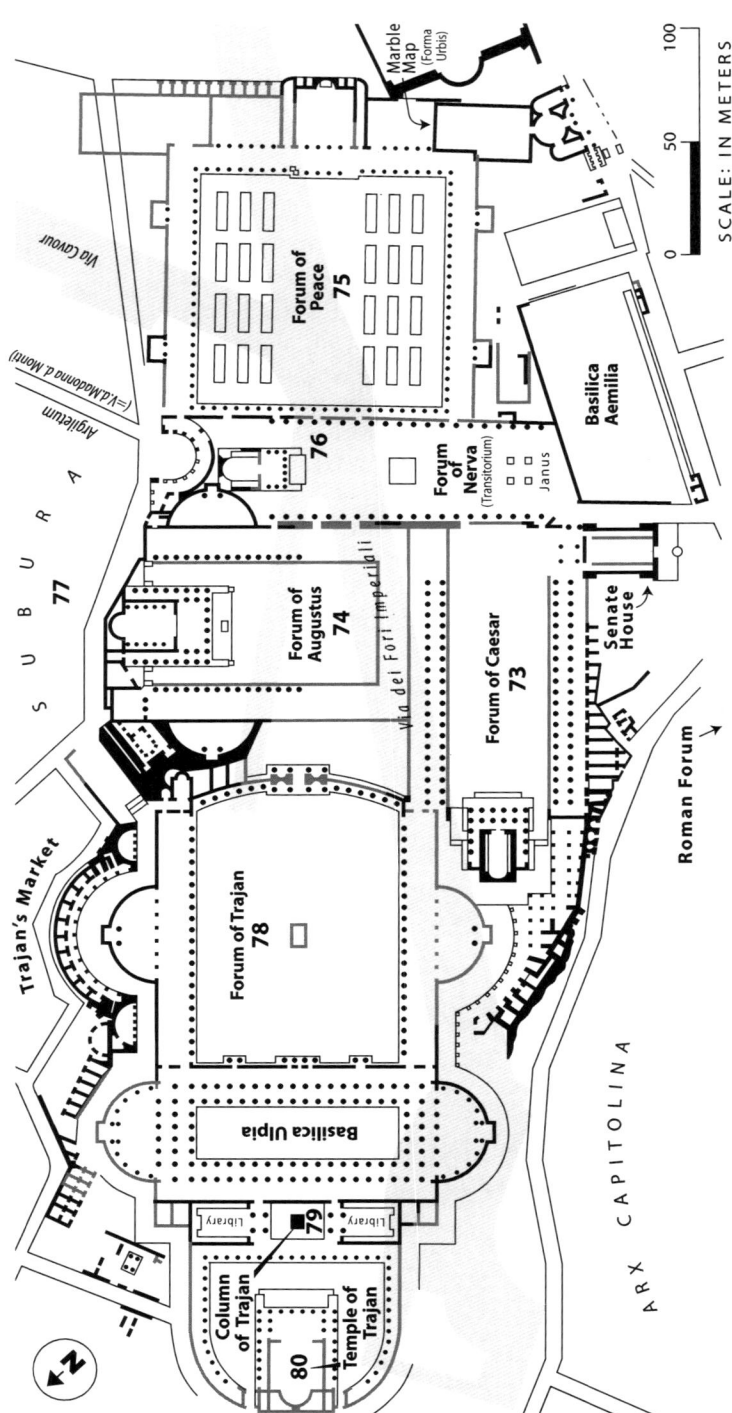

Fig. 38 Imperial Forums

VIII. The Imperial Forums

Overview

As the business of Rome expanded over the centuries, the central Forum grew with it until gradually, under pressure for space, the legal and political business took precedence over private trade and squeezed out the various markets from the central Forum. Even so, by the 50s BC, the Forum could no longer contain the political, legal, and financial business of an empire increasing by the size of France every few decades. Caesar responded to this pressure with a new forum alongside the old one. By the time the fifth and final of the imperial forums was created by Trajan in AD 112, Rome had not only increased by several fold the room available for official business but had created a magnificent and monumental center that, in conjunction with the massive building and rebuilding going on all over the city in this period, overcame the time-lag between Rome's power and its ability to project that power architecturally to both natives and visitors.

Although the space of the Roman Forum itself was increasingly "rationalized," especially by Caesar and Augustus, and although the imperial forums themselves remained active and underwent development for many centuries after their creation, it seems that the imperial forums were largely free of the archaic topographical idiosyncrasies— primitive shrines, sacred figs, pits to hell, etc.—that dotted the older forum. The imperial forums were the result not of centuries of haphazard accommodation and aristocratic competition but of five internally unified plans, with all the major lines and axes of each of them oriented by the lines of the Forum of Caesar. In part because the present Via dei Fori Imperiali cuts across the forums at their crucial intersections, we can only presume that their connections with one another were also carefully worked out.

The imperial forums show the familiar connection between practical urban necessities, political programs of Roman rulers, and the booty that not only paid for the premium real estate and construction but stocked the finished forums with foreign art works and precious gems. Vespasian's Forum of Peace and the Forum of Trajan were specifically paid for by the conquest of Jerusalem and Dacia (Romania) respectively, and were, in at least some of their decoration, monuments to these foreign victories. Although Caesar and Augustus before them were able to fill public and private coffers with their own respective victories in Gaul and Egypt, their choice of deities for the temples that dominate their forums reveal two rulers who, at this early stage of the Principate, were more overtly concerned to consolidate their still novel position among fellow Romans.

Notes: On the imperial forums in general, see J. Anderson, Jr., *The Historical Topography of the Imperial Fora.*

73. The Forum of Caesar (*Forum Caesaris, Forum Julium*)

COMMENTARY

Cicero's breezy evaluation of urban real estate and construction [73.1] shows that the need for the Forum's expansion was widely acknowledged and that Caesar's addition would be part of other projects extending the city over the saddle between the Capitoline and Quirinal, and up to the Voting Pens (*Saepta*) in the Campus Martius. The Forum of Caesar, begun by Caesar, who dedicated the temple in 46 BC, and finished by Augustus, set both the orientation and the general pattern for the subsequent imperial fora (with significant variations by Trajan): a plaza lined with a colonnade (or double colonnade) down each of its long sides, culminating in a temple on a high podium at the center of the long axis.

According to Appian [73.3], Julius Caesar first vowed a temple to Venus Victrix, Venus as a bringer of victory, but then dedicated it to Venus Genetrix—Venus in her capacity as a creative force in general (as poeticized by Lucretius) and as the mother of the Julian clan in particular, through Aeneas and his son Iulus. Perhaps this is an instance of uncharacteristic tact on Caesar's part. Caesar had vowed a temple to Venus Victrix in a civil war, and the victory she celebrated was over senatorial forces led by Pompey the Great. Pompey, in fact, had himself built a temple to Venus Victrix earlier [87.2], as part of his theater complex (where Caesar would fall at the foot of Pompey's statue). By dedicating his temple to Venus Genetrix, Caesar could steer the em-

Fig. 39 Forums of Caesar (lower right, partially obscured), Augustus, and Trajan (from plaster model of Rome)

phasis away from deadly politics and towards the Roman past, while still glorifying the family name. It was Caesar's imperial behavior at this same temple, however, that more than anything else engendered the mortal hatred in the senators against him, according to Suetonius [73.6].

The sources document some of the works of arts which Caesar displayed on a novel scale—gems, paintings, and numerous statues, including two of Caesar, standing and riding, and one of Cleopatra that remained there at least into the third century.

The tufa and concrete core of its podium lies open to view from the balconies along the Via dei Fori Imperiali, as does a portion of its travertine pavement. The three standing columns of the temple are from a restoration in the time of Trajan after a fire, carried out in conjunction with the construction of the adjacent Forum of Trajan.

The major street to the Campus around this side of the Capitoline was known in the Middle Ages, and probably in antiquity as well, as the Clivus Argentarius. Between this street and the new forum numerous vaulted rooms were built and later expanded with a second floor. These housed a variety of activities, including senatorial offices and a large latrine in a hemicycle. Graffiti nearby also testify to an elementary school located on the Capitoline side of the temple, in part of a structure there identified as the Basilica Argentaria. The graffiti include the beginning of the alphabet, the first line of Virgil's *Aeneid*, and names of people and places [73.14].

SOURCES

73.1 Cicero sends greetings to Atticus: [54 BC]

Nothing is more impressive than Paullus's new basilica, nothing more suited to advance a reputation. And so, I must confess, we "friends of Caesar" (I refer to myself and Oppius, even if that causes you to explode) have spent without any qualms sixty million sesterces towards that monumental work you used to praise so highly—the expansion of the over-crowded Forum, and its extension all the way to the Atrium of Liberty. The private owners of the land would not have sold for a lesser sum. But the results of our efforts will be magnificent, since we also have in mind to reconstruct the Voting Pens [*Saepta*] for the tribal assemblies in the Campus Martius, this one made of marble and roofed over, and we will surround it with a lofty colonnade a mile long. The Villa Publica will be attached to it as part of the same project. I know you're probably wondering what possible advantage *I* get out of these show-pieces, but let's not go into that now.

Cicero, *Letters to Atticus* 4.16.8

73.2 [To gain favor in Rome while he was still waging war in Gaul, c. 54 BC] Caesar let no opportunity pass to lavish funds and favors in all directions both publicly and privately. Using booty from his wars, he began his Forum, the property for which cost more than a hundred million sesterces.

Suetonius, *Julius Caesar* 26.2

73.3 [In 48 BC, learning that Pompey meant to face him in battle at Pharsalus the next day, Julius Caesar readied his forces.] Then in the middle of the night he performed a sacrifice, calling on the aid of Mars and his own ancestress Aphrodite (for the Julian clan considers its name, with slight changes, to be descended from Ilus, son of Aeneas). He vowed that if successful in battle, he would set up a temple in Rome as a thank-offering to Venus, Bringer of Victory [*Venus Victrix*].

Appian, *Civil Wars* 2.68

73.4 Caesar built a temple to Venus Genetrix, which he vowed just before he fought Pompey at Pharsalus. He surrounded it with a space intended as a forum for the Romans, although not for commerce, but for the exercise of civic business (as in Persia, where people come to the forum to seek justice or to study the laws). Alongside the statue of Venus he placed a beautiful statue of Cleopatra, which stands there today [c. C2 AD].

Appian, *Civil Wars* 2.102

73.5 On the last day of his triumph [September 26, 46 BC], after the banquet, Caesar entered his own Forum, wearing slippers and a garland of various flowers. … This forum, which he built and which bears his name, is far more beautiful than the Roman Forum, although it has increased the reputation of the old forum, which is now known as "the Great Forum." Having constructed his forum and the Temple of Venus (as the founder of his family), Caesar dedicated them on this same date.

Dio, *History* 43.22.1–2

73.6 It was the following incident that aroused the extreme and deadly hatred towards Caesar. When the entire body of the Senate approached Caesar with numerous resolutions of the highest honor, Caesar stayed seated as he received them in front of the Temple of Venus Genetrix. Some believe that he was on the verge of standing but was restrained by Cornelius Balbus; others, that not only did he not rise, but even glared at Gaius Trebatius when Trebatius suggested that he stand.

Suetonius, *Caesar* 78.1

73.7 I completed the Forum of Caesar.

Augustus, *Achievements* 20

73.8 Of the five types of temples, the first is called pycnostyle; that is, with crowded columns. ... In pycnostyle temples, the space between each column is only the width of one and a half columns, as in the Temple of the Divine Caesar and the Temple of Venus in the Forum of Caesar.

Vitruvius, *Architecture* 3.3.1–2

73.9 The late Cleopatra herself, although defeated and captured by Rome, has been glorified: her ornaments are now dedicated in our temples, and a gold statue of the queen herself is on view in the Temple of Venus.

Dio, *History* 51.22.3

73.10 Julius Caesar permitted a statue of himself, in breastplate, to be dedicated in his forum.

Pliny the Elder, *Encyclopedia* 34.18

73.11 It is reported that Caesar's horse allowed no one else to ride him, and that his fore feet were similar to those of a human, as is represented on the statue of the horse located in front of the Temple of Venus Genetrix.

Pliny the Elder, *Encyclopedia* 8.155

73.12 But it was Julius Caesar who by example especially encouraged the public display of art, dedicating paintings [by the great Timomachus] of Ajax and Medea in front of the Temple of Venus Genetrix.

Pliny the Elder, *Encyclopedia* 35.26

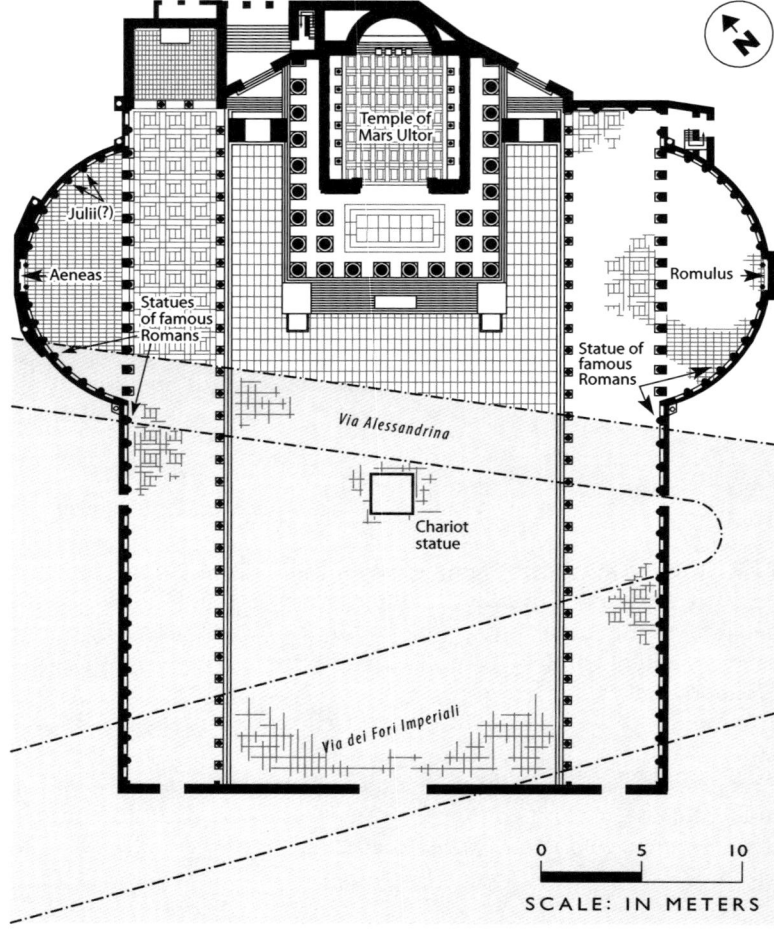

Fig. 40 Forum of Augustus (after Kockel and Zanker)

73.13 Among other gifts to Capitoline Jupiter, Pompey the Great dedicated a gem case that had belonged to King Mithridates. … Following his example, Julius Caesar consecrated six gem cases in the Temple of Venus Genetrix.

Pliny the Elder, *Encyclopedia* 37.11

73.14 ABCDEFGIL … "The town of Mantua gave me birth"…"I sing of arms and the man who first from the shores of Troy"… Mt. Soracte … Hector…Caecilius, a former student…Farewell, Smirina!

Graffiti at the Basilica Argentaria (from Dudley)

74. The Forum of Augustus (Fig. 40)

COMMENTARY

Of all Rome's ancient monuments, the Forum of Augustus provides the most satisfying collusion of archaeological and literary evidence, both of which are relatively substantial. Without the former, we would be ignorant of something so basic as the forum's signature hemicycles (exhedras); without the latter, we would miss much of the forum's meaning and function in antiquity, especially its ceremonial role in resolving the internal political difficulties confronting Augustus and the Romans as he consolidated his power.

On a utilitarian and routine level, the Forum of Augustus was a response to the crowding of the existing forum space and its inability to handle the volume of legal cases that the burgeoning city and empire were generating. That the forum was open for business before its completion testifies to the urgency of this practical matter [74.6]. Most of the legal business must have taken place under the colonnades and hemicycles on each side of the courtyard—a considerable area, since the long rectangular space of each colonnade is approximately 15m by 110m, with another 15m added by the hemicycles. (The width of the forum can be readily observed today from the street cutting across it, the Via Alessandrina; more than half of the forum's length remains buried.)

The forum had other functions in addition to the forensic. Its ceremonial functions and programmatic decoration made it an unparalleled display of Augustan propaganda. As might be expected in a forum presided over by a temple to Mars, these other elements coalesce in the act of War.

Augustus's original impulse for the forum was a vow before the battle at Philippi in 42 BC, before Octavian (as Augustus was then known) defeated Brutus and Cassius (the senators who led the conspiracy to assassinate his adoptive father). The Temple to Mars *the Avenger* stresses the reactive, rather than aggressive, nature of Augustus's violence against fellow Romans: "Thus they would have it," as Caesar famously put it before *his* civil war. The forum and its temple cast Octavian's role in civil war as an act of *pietas* toward both his family and the god who granted victory.

The special ceremonial functions which Augustus later prescribed for his forum also deal with war. Here young men assumed the toga virilis that signifies they have reached military age. Matters of military distinction were decided here by the Senate, and a commander going forth to war, or to rule a province, officially set forth from here [74.8]. Mars as the Avenger also oversees this activity, since (as the popularity of Virgil's *Aeneid* suggests) the Romans were fond of the ideal that they waged war against violators of civilized standards, as avengers of of-

Fig. 41 Forum of Augustus (model in Trajan's Markets)

fenses, not as aggressive war-mongers. Also under the category of vengeance is Augustus's pointed designation of the inner temple as the repository for the recovered standards of Crassus's expedition against the Parthians [74.13]. Although most of these aspects of war concern the state as a whole rather than its single ruler, they now take place under the sponsorship of Augustus (whose name, Ovid's verse indicates [74.10], was prominently displayed on the temple).

The decoration of the forum continues the theme (see Fig. 40). The hemicycles and colonnade walls were lined with the statues of great Romans, one of the prime qualifications for whose inclusion was their role in the expansion of Rome's territory [74.12]. The individual inscriptions of notable achievements that accompanied each statue were written, Pliny suggests [74.14], by Augustus, although we also know that statues were added after the emperor's death. The elogium of Appius Claudius Caecus [74.16] shows how central warfare was to his résumé, although his famous road and Rome's first aqueduct also receive mention.

Ovid's description of the Forum of Augustus allows us to reconstruct another component of the forum's message. The statues set up on one side of the forum had as a focal point a tableau of Aeneas with his father and son (probably located in the central niche of the hemicycle), and were all descendants of Aeneas. On the other side, Romulus was the central figure. Thus the pride of place on each side is given to the two great founders of Rome, who both figure prominently in Augustan literature, especially in Livy and Virgil. Also prominent, however, in the image-making generated by Caesar and Augustus was their family's descent from Aeneas, the son of the goddess Venus. The forum, in ranking Augustus's family as equal in distinction to the entire parade of other Roman heroes chosen from all the other Roman families, both elevates Augustus above the rest, and yet situates him as a part of the greater whole and demonstrates his respect for Roman tradition. His proclamation that this gallery of heroes was meant to provide a standard of achievement for both himself and his predecessors suits the *primus inter pares* message of the statuary. Further programmatic unity exists in connection to Mars, who is not only the consort of Venus, but also the father of Romulus (somewhat problematically, Ovid hints [74.11], since Romulus's mother was Rhea Silvia, not Venus).

Excavations of the Forum of Augustus in the 1920s brought forum inscriptions to light that help reconstruct the colonnades' galleries of famous Romans; these are supplemented by inscriptions for statues in Arretrium and Pompeii that were organized in imitation of Augustus's Forum. Of the 108 statues that Degrassi estimates lined the colonnades and hemicycles, evidence remains to identify about thirty with some certainty. This leaves much in the dark, such as how Augustus handled his personal foes in the civil wars, from Brutus to Mark Antony; certainly the latter, by military standards, deserved a place, but probably did not get one. Pompey, however, the foe of Caesar, was included (a posthumous reconciliation foreshadowed by the statues that Caesar allowed on his new Rostra; see 30.1). We also know that Marius and Sulla each had a statue—men who were mortal foes in earlier civil wars, but here harmoniously united in the Forum's parade of heroes.

The entire forum in its original condition—Pliny calls it one of the three most beautiful works in Rome, and there are many remains of its polychromatic marbles and decorations imported from distant parts of the empire—was both a visual marvel and a sophisticated piece of propaganda. Begun as the partisan vow of a young warlord engaged in the violence that had pitted Roman against Roman for generations, the forum evolved into an elaborate vision of Rome at peace with itself, safe in the embrace of the Pater Patriae and united in the forum's business of taking the war to someone else who deserved it.

SOURCES

74.1 Are not the Basilica Paulli, with its columns of Phrygian marble, the Forum of the Deified Augustus, and the Temple of Peace built by the Emperor Vespasian the most beautiful works that the world has ever seen?

> **Pliny the Elder,** *Encyclopedia* 36.102

74.2 Augustus made his forum smaller than planned, out of his reluctance to appropriate the adjoining homes from their owners.

> **Suetonius,** *Augustus* 56.2

74.3 When the Forum of Augustus was being constructed, the builder kept postponing its completion. During this period it happened that many people prosecuted by Severus Cassius were being acquitted, prompting Augustus to quip "I wish Cassius would prosecute my *forum.*"

> **Macrobius,** *Saturnalia* 2.4.9

74.4 I built with war booty the Temple of Mars the Avenger and the Forum of Augustus on my own land.

> **Augustus,** *Achievements* 21

74.5 The entire people of Rome gave me the title "Father of the Country," and had it inscribed in the vestibule of my residence, in the Senate House, and in the Forum of Augustus beneath the chariot sculpture placed there in my honor by decree of the Senate.

> **Augustus,** *Achievements* 35

74.6 Augustus constructed numerous public works, among which the following are perhaps the most outstanding: his forum with its temple of Mars the Avenger, the temple of Apollo on the Palatine, and the temple of Jupiter the Thunderer on the Capitoline.

Augustus built his forum because the two existing forums could no longer accommodate the increasing number of people and law cases, so that a third was thought necessary. Because of this need for space it was opened for business even before the temple was finished, and it was stipulated that the new forum be the venue for public trials as well as the selection of jurors by lot. He had vowed the temple to Mars during the battle at Philippi, which he fought to avenge the death of his father Julius Caesar. He decreed, therefore, that the Senate use the forum to deliberate on war and the awarding of triumphs, that those heading off to provinces with military command be officially escorted from here, and that those who returned victorious should deposit the insignia of their triumphs in his forum.

Suetonius, *Augustus* 29.1–2

74.7 In addition to conquering Spain and other countries whose plaques adorn his forum, the deified Augustus made Egypt a tributary country, thereby adding almost as much revenue to the treasury as his father Julius Caesar did by conquering Gaul.

Velleius, *History* 2.39.2

74.8 [Augustus determined that the following activities should take place in his Forum:] Those passing from the class of boys to young men of military age should all be enrolled here; those appointed to commands abroad should set out from here; the Senate should make decisions here regarding the awarding of triumphs, and those celebrating a triumph should dedicate both crown and scepter to the War God here; for anyone awarded a triumph or other military honor, a statue in bronze should be set up in the forum; any military standards captured by an enemy and then recovered should be placed in the temple.

Dio, *History* 55.10.2–4

74.9 The Emperor Claudius was eager for food and wine anywhere and anytime. Once, while trying a case in the Forum of Augustus, having detected the savor of a banquet prepared by the Salii in the nearby Temple of Mars, he deserted his tribunal seat and climbed up the stairs to join them at their table.

Suetonius, *Claudius* 33.1

74.10 Am I deceived, or did arms ring out? Indeed, arms rang,
    For Mars is coming, and signals his advent with sounds of war.
The Avenger himself descends from the sky to his place of honor,
    To his wonder of a temple in the Forum of Augustus.

The god, and so his temple, are mighty: not otherwise
    Should Mars be housed in the city of Romulus, his son.
This temple is a worthy place for trophies won from the Giants,
    And fitting for Mars to sally off from here to wage his wild wars,
Whether some unholy foe in the East should strike against us,
    Or an enemy towards the setting sun calls for subjugation.
The god of War surveys the heights of his lofty temple
    And approves that gods unconquered possess the pediment.
He surveys the various weapons that decorate the doorways
    And the arms of other lands defeated by his soldiers;
He sees Aeneas, bent by the precious weight of his father,
    And the lengthy line of descendants sprung from the noble Julus;
Across stands Romulus, shouldering the arms of a conquered leader,
    And the row of Romans above their records of famous deeds.
He sees on the front of the temple the name of Augustus
    And the work appears greater still when he reads that name.
Augustus vowed it when he was young, and dutifully took up arms:
    With great beginnings our Princeps had to begin.

                         Ovid, *Fasti* 5.549–570

74.11 [For the weak in character, suggestions for sexual license abound:]
Should a matron enter your temple of mighty Mars, Augustus,
There in armor by the door stands Venus beside the Avenger.

                         Ovid, *Tristia* 2.295–6

74.12 Next to the immortal gods, Augustus most honored the memory of those leaders who created the mighty empire of the Roman people from small beginnings. Accordingly he restored the public works of each man, retaining their original inscriptions. Furthermore, in the colonnades of his forum he dedicated statues to all of them in triumphal garb, declaring in an edict that he contrived this so that the citizens might have the example of these eminent men as a standard to which he during his own life as well as subsequent rulers must conform.

                         Suetonius, *Augustus* 31.5

74.13 After defeating enemies in Spain, Gaul, and Dalmatia, I recovered the numerous military standards lost by other generals there. I compelled the Parthians to return the spoils and standards of three Roman armies, and to seek as suppliants the friendship of the Roman people. I deposited these standards in the inner shrine of the Temple of Mars the Avenger.

                         Augustus, *Achievements* 29

74.14 [Scipio Aemelianus was awarded the "siege crown" for rescuing an army], an event which the divine Augustus recorded in his forum below the statue of Scipio.

                         Pliny the Elder, *Encyclopedia* 22.13

74.15 [Statue inscription]
Aeneas, son of Venus, king of the Latins, ruled three years.
Elogium (Degrassi, 13.3.1)

74.16 [Statue inscription]
Appius Claudius Caecus captured numerous fortified towns from the Samnites. He routed the armies of the Sabines and the Etruscans. He opposed peace with King Pyrrhus. When censor, he constructed the Appian Way and brought water to the city. He built the Temple of Bellona.
Elogium (Degrassi, 13.3.79)

74.17 Although a man of undistinguished origins, the senators granted Lucilius Longus [a friend of the Emperor Tiberius] a statue in the Forum of Augustus at public expense.
Tacitus, *Annals* 4.15

74.18 [Severus Alexander set up statues in the Forum of Nerva,] following the example of Augustus, who located marble statues of the most illustrious men in his forum and accompanied them with an inscription.
Imperial Lives, *Alexander Severus*, 28.6

74.19 Caligula consecrated the three swords intended for his assassination to Mars the Avenger, accompanied by an inscription.
Suetonius, *Caligula* 24.3

74.20 [Servius's commentary below is relevant to the following lines in Virgil's *Aeneid* 1.294-6, which represent the Augustan suppression of warfare:
Unholy Furor squats inside on savage weapons
 Arms bound behind his back with a hundred chains of bronze,
His mouth foaming with blood.]

"Unholy Furor within." A painting of War was portrayed not in the Temple of Janus, but among others in the Forum of Augustus. It was located on the left as you enter, along with Furor sitting upon weapons, bound up just as Virgil described.
Servius on *Aeneid* 1.294

74.21 Surpassing all in the public prominence he gave to paintings, Augustus displayed two paintings in the most visited part of his forum, one with figures representing War and Triumph, the other with Castor and Pollux and Victory.
Pliny the Elder, *Encyclopedia* 35.27

Notes: The major discrepancy in various recreations of the Forum's statuary centers on the short passage from Ovid's *Tristia* [73.11], which in some way or other links Venus and Mars together in the temple. Some, in accordance with Zanker's influential treatment of the Forum, interpret this to refer to the main statues of the cella, which also purportedly included, on the evidence of a statuary group found elsewhere, a statue of the Deified Caesar. Others (with Kockel in *LTUR*, 2.292) place Mars alone in the cella, and an alternative reading of Ovid's text suggests that some such tableau may have stood outside the cellar doors.

The Elogia are gathered by A. DeGrassi, *Inscriptiones Italiae*, 13.3

75. Forum of Peace (Temple of Peace)

COMMENTARY

Although grouped with the other imperial fora and called a forum at least by late antiquity, this large nearly square area was known as the Temple of Peace (with "temple" here signifying, as often for the Romans, the whole inaugurated space of which the deity's dwelling was one part). None of the sources mentions what business occurred here, and it may have been a more leisurely complex with museum and library rather than an expansion of the Roman Forum's business, which may have been compacted into the fora of Caesar and Augustus, and later Trajan. There are some designs on the Marble Plan, however, which Claridge (155) tentatively suggests may represent a long series of market-stalls in the open area of the Forum of Vespasian, noting that the area was once the sight of a Macellum, or market area. Others interpret the designs as blocks of landscaping, such as would be appropriate for a museum-like setting or park.

One of the most interesting items that was on display in this forum was the famous Marble Plan. Though not mentioned in the ancient sources, it is often called in Latin the "Forma Urbis (Romae)," and can be dated to the reign of Septimius Severus, between AD 203 and 211. This map of the city consisted of an entire wall of marble panels inscribed with the lines and often the names of city buildings, including walls, columns, and aqueduct arches. Only about ten percent of the map survives, and less than that can be securely located since many of the pieces, found in various parts of the city in various centuries, are too small to show any context, but it is a major tool in recreating the Roman city, and work on it continues, as does the hope that more will be found.

SOURCES

75.1 The emperor Vespasian's activities also included the building of public structures, among them the Temple of Peace right next to the Roman Forum.

Suetonius, *Vespasian* 9.1

75.2 The Temple of Peace was dedicated in Vespasian's sixth consulship and Titus's fourth [AD 75].

Dio, *History* 65.15

75.3 After his triumph was finished [in AD 71] and Roman rule was re-established on a firm foundation, Vespasian decided to build a Temple of Peace. This was completed very quickly, and in a style that beggars the imagination. Not only did he have enormous financial resources at his disposal, but embellished it with old masterpieces of painting and sculpture. In fact, into that one sacred precinct were gathered and stationed all the art-works that people had been willing to travel the world over to see, even when they were scattered. Vespasian also proudly kept here the works of gold taken from the Temple of the Jews, but ordered that their Law and the purple veil of the inner temple be kept safely in the palace.

Josephus, *The Jewish War* 7.158

75.4 The most famous of the art works in Rome that I have mentioned above were originally brought to Rome by Nero's looting and placed around the private rooms of the Domus Aurea, but were since dedicated by the emperor Vespasian to the Temple of Peace and his other buildings.

Pliny the Elder, *Encyclopedia* 34.84

75.5 [Near the end of Commodus's reign in AD 191] the entire precinct of the Temple of Peace, the largest and most beautiful of all the buildings in Rome, burned to the ground. It was also the richest temple in the city, since it is decorated with numerous gold and silver items that people deposited there to keep them safe—a caution which the fire rendered futile, sending many wealthy people into poverty.

Herodian, *History* 1.14.2–3

75.6 On a trip to Rome once, I heard the following story from a Roman senator. He said that it took place when the Gothic king Atalaric, grandson of Theoderic the Great, was ruling in Italy [c. AD 530]. Late in the day a herd of cattle came into Rome from the countryside and was passing through the square that the Romans call the Forum of Peace because of the Temple of Peace that is located there (now damaged by lightning). At the front of the forum there is an old fountain on which a bronze bull stands, a work of Pheidias, I believe, or perhaps Lysippus. … (This forum also contains Myron's Calf; the ancient Romans were eager collectors of the best of Greece's art and displayed it with great pride.)

One of the passing cattle—a gelded steer, the senator said—left the herd and climbing onto the fountain mounted the bronze bull. By chance, at the same time a man was passing, an Etruscan by birth, who understood the import of this scene (for even down to my day the Etruscans are skilled in the art of prophecy): one day, he prophesied, a eunuch would bring down the ruler of Rome. … [And in truth it was the general Narses, an imperial eunuch, who defeated the Gothic king Totila.]

Procopius, Wars 8.21.10–17

Notes: On the Marble Plan, see L. Richardson's entry "Forma Urbis Romae" in *An Encyclopedia of the History of Classical Archaeology*, ed. by N. de Grummond, 451–3.

76. Forum of Nerva (*Forum Transitorium*)

COMMENTARY

The Forum of Nerva is the smallest of the imperial fora, being more a long transitional space between the areas on all sides of it than a business center in its own right. Fittingly, in the late classical period it is the Forum Transitorium, the Transit Forum. Traffic (primarily foot traffic until late antiquity, when the wagon ruts still visible were worn into the stone pavement) passed through the forum not only side-to-side, into one of the larger fora of Augustus and Vespasian, but lengthwise along the course of the Argiletum. The Argiletum was the ancient street that exited the Roman Forum between the Senate House and the Basilica Aemilia and climbed up the valley to the Esquiline towards the Porta Esquilina (the lower part of this route is represented today by the Via Madonna dei Monti; in ancient times it was called the Clivus Suburanus). Further filling the space of the forum was a temple to Minerva and an elaborate new shrine to Janus near the other end, as described below by Martial [76.5].

The sources and remains indicate that the Forum was substantially a creation of Domitian's. The decorations still visible from the street today, above and between the two marble columns left standing, are related to Domitian's favorite deity Minerva, who appears in the attic relief and is represented on the frieze by Arachne, the Muses, and the implements of spinning and weaving. (Much of her temple survived into the Renaissance, when it was dismantled by Pope Paul V for its marble, some of which found its way to the Acqua Paola Fontana on the Janiculum.) That the Forum should be named after Nerva, who succeeded Domitian, is understandable in light of the *damnatio memoriae* visited upon Domitian's name after his assassination [45.3].

The area behind the Forum of Nerva, in the rising basin between the Esquiline and Viminal Hills (roughly, along today's Via Cavour) was a neighborhood called the Subura, which is portrayed in the sources as one of the most vibrant and characteristically Roman neighborhoods, with people from all walks and most stations of life. Being in a basin but rising away from the lower forum, it would have been free from most floods and yet not a conspicuous location for aristocrats engaged in public life, for whom the higher crescent extending from the Carinae over to the Palatine provided the preferable and more expensive properties on view from the Forum. Shopkeepers, writers, and artisans lived in the Subura in the company of the wealthier citizens, who would sometimes have owned the apartment buildings and lived on the more desirable ground floor. Caesar lived here in a modest home, only moving when he became Pontifex Maximus and was housed in the residence that came with the office [51.1]. Others, in the manner of Caelius [47.8], will have lived in similar "mixed" neighborhoods until they felt the need for one of the higher profile residences to match their career ambitions.

The passages excerpted from Juvenal's third satire [77.6], while not specifically set in the Subura, and describing scenes that could be found throughout much of the city, belong here to illustrate daily life (with the proviso mentioned in the Introduction). It is interesting that both Martial and Juvenal, in evoking street life, mention wagons with building materials, much of which would have been destined for the construction of the imperial fora. Moreover, Juvenal's fear of Rome's "midnight terror" (fire) is materialized architecturally in the large stone wall still standing at the back of the Forum of Augustus, which would have formed some sort of fire-break from the Subura, as would a similar wall that bordered the Forum of Trajan.

SOURCES

76.1 The emperor Domitian built the forum that is now called Nerva's.

Suetonius, *Domitian* 5

76.2 As the day of his assassination grew nearer, Domitian had a dream in which Minerva (a goddess for whom he had an especially strong and personal veneration) came forth from her temple and told him she could no longer guarantee his safety because Jupiter had disarmed her.

Suetonius, *Domitian* 15.3

76.3 The emperor Nerva Caesar ... consul for the third time, built the Temple of Minerva [in AD 97].

CIL 6.31213

76.4 In the Forum of Nerva (which is also called the Forum Transitorium) the emperor Alexander Severus set up larger than life-size statues of the deified emperors, some of them nude and on foot, others on horseback. The statues were accompanied by all the titles of each emperor and by bronze columns that contained an account of their achievements (this was done in imitation of Augustus, who had placed marble statues of leading men in his forum, accompanied by accounts of their notable deeds).

Imperial Lives, *Severus Alexander* 28.6

76.5 [To Janus:]
O glorious begetter of years and the radiant rounds of the sky,
    First to hear our prayers and public vows,
Until today you lived in a narrow passageway
    Where all of crowded Rome came trooping by.
But now your thresholds, Janus, are ringed by the gifts of Caesar
    And each of your faces beholds a separate forum.
In return for such a striking improvement, holy father,
    Keep your gateways sealed with iron bolts.

Martial, *Epigrams* 10.28

77. Argiletum and Subura

77.1 Lest you wonder, reader, where my book is sold,
    Or waste time looking, I'll be your trusty guide:
Go to the shop of Secundus, the freedman of learned Lucensis,
    Behind the Temple of Peace and the Forum of Minerva.

Martial, *Epigrams* 1.2.5–8

77.2 My poor little book of poems: why would you live in a bookshop
    On the Argiletum, when my shelves at home have room enough?

Martial, *Epigrams* 1.3.1–2

77.3 Julius Caesar originally lived in a modest house in the Subura, but moved to the Domus Publica on the Sacred Way after he became the Pontifex Maximus.

Suetonius, *Julius Caesar* 46

77.4 The other day Gellianus, the auctioneer,
    Was trying to sell a girl with a reputation
    Equal to those who work the streets of Subura.
When the bidding stalled below his hopes

He tried to convince us the girl was clean
By pulling her to him against her will
And kissing her long and hard on the lips.
Perhaps you wonder what such a kiss
Accomplished? Every bidder withdrew.

Martial, *Epigrams* 6.66

77.5 [To visit my wealthy friend who lives on the Esquiline]
   I have to climb the long incline of Subura's street
      On sloppy paving stones that never dry,
   And struggle to make my way past the long trains of mules
      And masses of marble dragged along by rope.

Martial, *Epigrams* 5.22.5–8

77.6 [Umbricius, a friend of the poet, catalogues his complaints about
Rome before leaving the city for the countryside.]

"You and I, we live in a city that's propped, for the most part,
On the sub-standard lumber the superintendent uses to keep
The place from collapsing, who tells us we can sleep in peace
As he plasters over cracks in a building poised to crumble.

I won't miss the fires here either, that midnight terror.
Downstairs, some hero is already calling for water and hauling
His things to the curb by the time the smoke has reached your apartment.
But you're oblivious: those who climb three flights of stairs
Burn last—the ones with nothing between themselves and the rain
But the tiles where the softly cooing rock-doves lay their eggs.

Even sleep is expensive in Rome; it won't be found
In apartments, that's for sure, and this sleeplessness ruins our health:
The noise of the traffic, when a cart gets stuck in a tight turn
Of the narrow street and blocks a flock of bleating sheep,
Would rouse a sunning seal, or the Emperor Claudius, from slumber.
But the wealthy have other means; called by important business,
A rich man floats through town on a litter the size of an ore-boat,
Catching up on his correspondence, his reading, and shut-eye,
Gently rocked to sleep in his little curtained world—
And he still gets there before us, however hard we wade
Against the crowd in front and are shoved by the crowd behind.
One man jabs me with elbows, another connects with an axle,
Followed by someone who knocks my head with a beam or a barrel.
My legs are smeared with muck and bruised by the crowd's collective
Kick, while the studs on a soldier's boot trace its shape on my foot.

...Down the street a giant trunk of fir
comes bobbing along on wheels; another wagon
delivers a load of pine swaying dangerously above the crowds.
And if a single axle transporting Cararra marble
snaps and spills its mountain on the commoners below,
what's left of the bodies? Who troubles to find the limbs and gather
the bones of common people? When we get crushed, our corpses
vanish with our souls.

Consider next the multitude of dangers that night brings on;
Reckon the speed a tile attains in the distance between
That roof and your head, and how many leaking and broken vases
Are tossed from windows, as dents on the paving stones at the point
Of impact attest. Only a man who is grossly negligent
And careless of his family's future would dare head out for dinner
Without a will; as many mortal dangers lie in wait
For you to pass as open windows shine above your head.
So let it be your fervent prayer, your pitiful little wish
That the ladies above are content to dump only piss from their windows.

Then there's the drunken punk who's angry from lack of action; ...
He sleeps better after assaults. But however young and stupid
And stoned he is, he'll shy from the man whom purple robes,
A long train of companions, and the slaves who light his way
With torches and bronze candelabras protect untouched.
But me, scraping along in the dark lit only by moonlight
Or the guttering flame I coax from a little homemade lamp,
He despises, and starts a quarrel designed to end in a fight—
If you can call it a fight, when one man does all the hitting.

Juvenal, *Satires 3*, selections

77.7 [Epitaph]   Quintus Gavius Primus, freedman of Gavius, a boot-maker from the Subura, lived 25 years.

ILS 7547 = *CIL* 6.9284

77.8 [Epitaph]   This stone marks the double grave-plot of Donatus, a linen-maker who lived in the Subura near the monumental fountain.

ILS 7565 = *CIL* 9526

78. Forum of Trajan

COMMENTARY

As Ammianus reports [78.2], corroborated by significant remains, the Forum of Trajan was the most splendid of them all, stretching for

310 meters by the time Hadrian finished it with a temple to Trajan at the northwest end. Some of its characteristic features and its design are visible today from the street at numerous angles and one of the hemicycles can be visited through the Markets of Trajan on the Quirinal above it.

The design of the forum recalls the Forum of Augustus, with its elaborate program of statuary and giant exhedras that open off a single colonnade on each side. Where the Temple of Mars concluded the Forum of Augustus, however, Apollodorus designed a large basilica crossing the forum from side to side, duplicating at each end the hemicycles of the colonnaded square preceding it. Beyond the Basilica Ulpia (Ulpius was the family name of Trajan), formerly framed by two libraries (one Greek and one Latin) that have since fallen, Trajan's famous column still stands after nineteen centuries. Constructed of mammoth marble drums, the column is decorated with an upward spiraling, scroll-like series of very fine low-relief carvings, which tell the story of Trajan's wars in Dacia (AD 102–6), which paid for much of the forum. Inside the drums a stairway (closed, but still functioning) led to a viewing platform on the top and a statue of Trajan, where the statue of St. Peter stands today.

One puzzle of this forum has been the nature and extent of the earth-removal carried out by the forum's builders and referred to on the inscription of Trajan's column [79.1]. It seems unlikely, both geographically and from archaeological excavations, that, before construction began to level the forum area, a ridge the height of the column connected the Capitoline and Quirinal. Explanations vary, however; perhaps the inscription meant "to the height of the *base* of the column," or perhaps the column only *generally* located the excavations, which may have been carried out up to the height of the column but over against the Quirinal Hill, where it was cut into by Trajan's Market.

SOURCES

78.1 Apollodorus was Trajan's builder in Rome, designing among other things the Forum of Trajan… .

Dio, *History* 69.4.1

78.2 [During his visit to Rome in AD 357,] when the emperor Constantius came to the Forum of Trajan, which in my opinion is the most outstanding structure anywhere on earth, a marvel even in the judgement of the gods, he stood still in amazement, gazing around him at the gigantic creations, which can neither be conveyed in words nor ever again duplicated by mortals. His hopes of equaling something of this scope dashed by this sight, Constantius said he was willing and able to create an imitation of Trajan's horse alone, a statue of which, mounted by Trajan, was located in the center of the courtyard. Standing near him and hearing this, the prince Ormisdas responded with customary Persian wit: "Emperor, order first a similar stable to be built, if you can manage it. Then the horse you propose to make can range as widely as the one we see here." When someone asked Ormisdas his impression of Rome, he said that the only thing giving him any comfort was learning that the men who lived there were mortal like himself.

Ammianus, *History* 16.10.15–16

78.3 All around the Forum of Trajan on the roof of the colonnades there are gilded statues of horses and military standards, and below them is written "From the sale of booty in war." Favorinus, walking around in the courtyard of the forum while he was waiting for his friend (a consul hearing cases from the tribunal) asked about the precise meaning of this phrase.

Gellius, *Attic Nights* 13.25.1–2

78.4 Many nobles also died in this Germanic (or rather Marcomannic) war [c. AD 170], and Marcus Aurelius had statues of them placed in the Ulpian forum.

Imperial Lives, *Marcus Aurelius* 22.7

78.5 The emperor Alexander Severus relocated statues of famous men, gathered from numerous other places, in the Forum of Trajan.

Imperial Lives, *Alexander Severus* 26.4

78.6 Lest some reader think that I am relying too heavily on some Latin or Greek writer as my source here, there is in the Ulpian Library, in Case 6, an ivory book which contains this senatorial decree, to which the emperor Tacitus himself appended his signature in his own hand.

Imperial Lives, *Tacitus* 8.1

78.7 When I was looking for something else in the library of the Temple of Trajan, the edicts of old praetors fell into my hands by chance, and I took the opportunity to read and become familiar with them.

Gellius, *Attic Nights* 11.17.1

78.8 When the emperor Marcus Aurelius had exhausted the entire treasury while waging the war against the Marcomanni, he refused to consider raising funds through an extra tax upon the provincials, but held instead an auction of imperial valuables in the Forum of the deified Trajan. The sale, which included gold, crystal, and agate goblets, the vases of kings, his wife's silk robes embroidered with gold, and even numerous jewels that he had found stored away by Hadrian in a

Fig. 42 Column of Trajan

special box, lasted for two whole months and raised enough money to
carry out the remainder of the war according to plan.

Imperial Lives, *Marcus Aurelius* 17.4–5

78.9 [Statue inscription:] In honor of Claudius Claudianus...,
tribune and notary, practitioner of various polite arts but with un-
matched glory in the art of poets. His poems alone would bring him
immortal fame, but to acknowledge the esteem they have for him,
Arcadius and Honorius, our most fortunate and learned Emperors,
ordered with the Senate's encouragement that his statue should be set
up in the Forum of Trajan [c. AD 395].

ILS 2949 = *CIL* 6.1710

78.10 [Statue inscription:] The invincible Emperors Honorius
Theodosius and Constantius, judges and rewarders of virtue, ordered
at the bidding of the full Senate and the people of Rome that a statue
be set up in the Ulpian forum to Petronius Maximus, city prefect, as a
lasting memorial of his merits.

ILS 809 = *CIL* 6.1749

79. Column of Trajan (Fig. 33)

79.1 SENATUS POPULUSQUE ROMANUS / IMP(eratori) CAESARI
DIVI NERVAE F(ilio) NERVAE / TRAIANO AUG(usto) GERM(anico)
DACICO PONTIF(ici) / MAXIMO TRIB(unicia) POT(estate)
XVII IMP(eratori) / VI CO(n)S(uli) VI P(atri) P(atriae) / AD
DECLARANDUM QUANTAE ALTITUDINIS / MONS ET LOCUS
TANTI(s ope)RIBUS SIT EGESTUS

The Senate and the People of Rome [dedicate this column] to
the emperor Caesar Nerva Trajan Augustus Germanicus Dacicus, son of
the deified emperor Nerva, Pontifex Maximus, with tribunician power
for the 17th time, hailed as Imperator for the 6th time, consul for the 6th
time [AD 113] and Father of his Country, to show the height and location of the hill removed for such great structures.

ILS 294 = *CIL* 6.960

79.2 [Among Trajan's many activities in Rome before setting out of
Parthia in AD 113,] Trajan also built libraries. In his forum he set up
a large column, both as a tomb for himself and as a memorial to his
work on the forum. For the whole area around it was formerly hilly,
and he had to excavate down the distance shown by the height of the
column to create a flat site for his forum.

Dio, *History* 68.16

79.3 The ashes of Trajan's cremated body were buried beneath his
column in the Forum of Trajan, and a statue of him was placed on the

top, arrayed like a triumphing general when he comes into the city with a senatorial and army escort.

Aurelius Victor, *On the Emperors* 13.11

79.4 Trajan was enrolled among the deified emperors, and received the singular honor of burial within the city boundaries: his bones were lodged in a golden urn under the column in the forum he built.

Eutropius 8.5.2

80. Temple of Trajan

80.1 Although he had countless public buildings constructed in all regions, Hadrian never had his own name inscribed on them, except in the case of the temple of his father Trajan.

Imperial Lives, *Hadrian* 19.9

80.2 In accordance with a decree by the Senate, the Emperor Hadrian, ... son of the deified Trajan, grandson of the deified Nerva, ... dedicated this temple to his parents, the deified Trajan and the deified Plotina.

ILS 306 = *CIL* 6.31215

Notes: For an extensive study and elaborate recreation-drawings of Trajan's forum, see J. Packer's *The Forum of Trajan*.

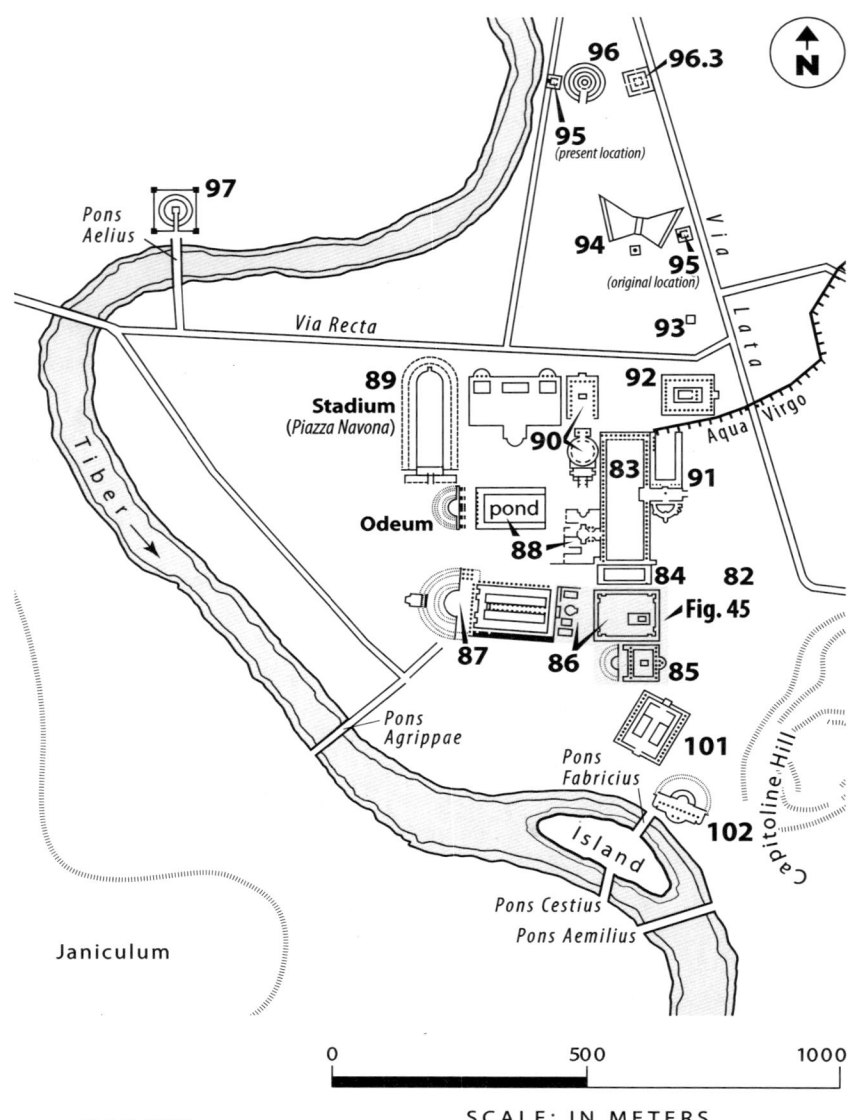

Fig. 43 Campus Martius

IX. The Campus Martius

81. Overview of the Campus Martius

As Strabo depicts the "Field of Mars," this flat expanse north of the city, even when the population of Rome approached a million in the time of Augustus, preserved an open, grassy look, studded with monuments of rulers but largely free of congestion. There were some early Republican uses for the southern part of the plain not far from the Capitoline and along the river leading up to sharp bend at today's Ponte Vittorio Emanuele, but much of it remained a blank slate for the projects of dynasts, beginning with Pompey and burgeoning under Augustus and Agrippa. The general impression from the sources is that this was an area of the city that most people *visited* rather than inhabited. Flooding may have had something to do with this, although this didn't stop the Campus from becoming the city center since the Middle Ages.

It is instructive that Strabo puts Pompey, Caesar, and Augustus in the same category as builders. Although Pompey and Caesar became mortal enemies in life and protagonists in a civil war that long continued to haunt Roman memory, they were twin products of the Roman system. Amazingly, for all the turmoil of the late Republic, Rome expanded and grew rich as never before, in part because of the competitive system that encouraged foreign aggression as a way of promoting political careers at home. The new wealth of Asia and Gaul, and then Egypt found its way to the Campus with Pompey's Theater, Caesar's voting precinct, and numerous projects under Augustus.

81.1   [After the Tarquin royal family had been expelled from Rome in 509 BC,] their land, which lay between the city and the river, was consecrated to Mars and became the Campus Martius.

Livy, *History* 2.5.2

81.2   Especially in recent times [the late C1 BC] the Romans have adorned their city with many beautiful buildings [in addition to the utilitarian works of sewers and aqueducts]. In fact, Pompey, the deified Caesar, and Augustus, along with his children, his friends, his wife Livia, and his sister Octavia, have outdone all others in the energy and funding they have devoted to construction. The Campus Martius has been the site for most of this work, thereby adding to its natural beauty the beauty of design.

The extent alone of this plain is impressive, providing so much room that chariot-racing and the other equestrian exercises can occur simultaneously with a multitude of other people exercising at ball-games, ring-toss, and wrestling. The grounds that are green with grass all year long, the monuments and works of art interspersed throughout, and the crests of the hills beetling right up to the river plain give the Campus the look of a painted backdrop for a stage.

Next to the Campus Martius is yet another plain, with numerous encircling colonnades, sacred precincts, three theaters, an amphitheater, and lavish temples, all very close together and almost giving the impression that the other part of the city downtown is an outgrowth of it.

Strabo, *Geography* 5.3.8

Notes: On the possible identity of this "other plain" next to the Campus Martius, see T.P. Wiseman, "Strabo on the Campus Martius: 5.3.8." Wiseman identifies Strabo's three theaters [81.2] as those of Marcellus, Balbus, and Pompey, and the amphitheater as Taurus's (of uncertain location, perhaps at today's Monte de' Cenci). Cicero's language in 87.7 supports this.

Villa Publica; The Voting Grounds (*Saepta Julia*) and Ballot Office (*Diribitorium*)

Overview

One of the earliest and most important functions of the Campus Martius was as a mustering ground for Roman citizens. Here they would come to be counted in a census, to be enrolled in an army, or to cast a vote in an election. Since Roman elections involved many groups of people gathering simultaneously, a large open area was needed, and since one of Rome's important assemblies (the *comitia centuriata*) was a mustering of citizens in their military units, it was also necessary that this location be beyond the pomerium, inside of which such military gatherings could not occur. The Campus Martius suited both needs.

One of the gathering areas in the Campus was the Villa Publica, an apt name but difficult to translate: Varro [82.2] stresses the communal, public quality of this "common," while "villa" suggests both an open, park-like setting as well as structures of some sort, whether simply porticos that could hold and be used to confine crowds, or buildings and offices as well [82.1].

Cicero tells us that the Villa Publica was next to the Saepta, "the Voting Pens," used for elections in which the centuriate and tribal assemblies voted. We know where the Voting Pens were: in terms of today's landscape, Bernini's elephant in front of Maria sopra Minerva stands near the middle of the Voting Pens; at the southern end of the Pens was Agrippa's Ballot Office, a corner of which touched on a corner of the area of the four Republican temples in Largo Argentina. It isn't clear, however, on which side of the Voting Pens the Villa Publica was located; east and south both have their supporters. The extent of the Villa at various periods is also vague. It is possible that the Voting Pens and Ballot Office preserved some of the original land and function of the Villa, while the remainder of the land was subsequently developed for other purposes.

Historically, perhaps the most famous event in the Villa was catalogued in communal memory under the heading of Cruelty, Excessive. It was here that the dictator Sulla, victorious in a civil war against fellow Italians but simulating clemency, lured 8,000 Samnite soldiers, perhaps on the pretence of enrolling them in the army of the lawful State. Their screaming, audible at least as far as a senate meeting in the Temple of Bellona, has been used to locate the Villa in the direction of the Circus Flaminius.

"Saepta" might be translated as "enclosure," but since this site was also called the "Ovile," the "Sheep-pen," "Pens" preserves the sense of the herding that must have gone on here to manage large numbers of men in ways that also called for precision. The colonnades bordering the area would form one large enclosure, but perhaps ropes and planks came into play for further divisions (hence the plural *saepta*?). Since gladiatorial games and strolling also took place here, it is not likely that more permanent internal divisions were built.

82. The Villa Publica

SOURCES

82.1 [In 435 BC] the censors approved the creation of the Villa Publica in the Campus Martius, and the first census of the People was held there.

Livy, *History* 4.22.7

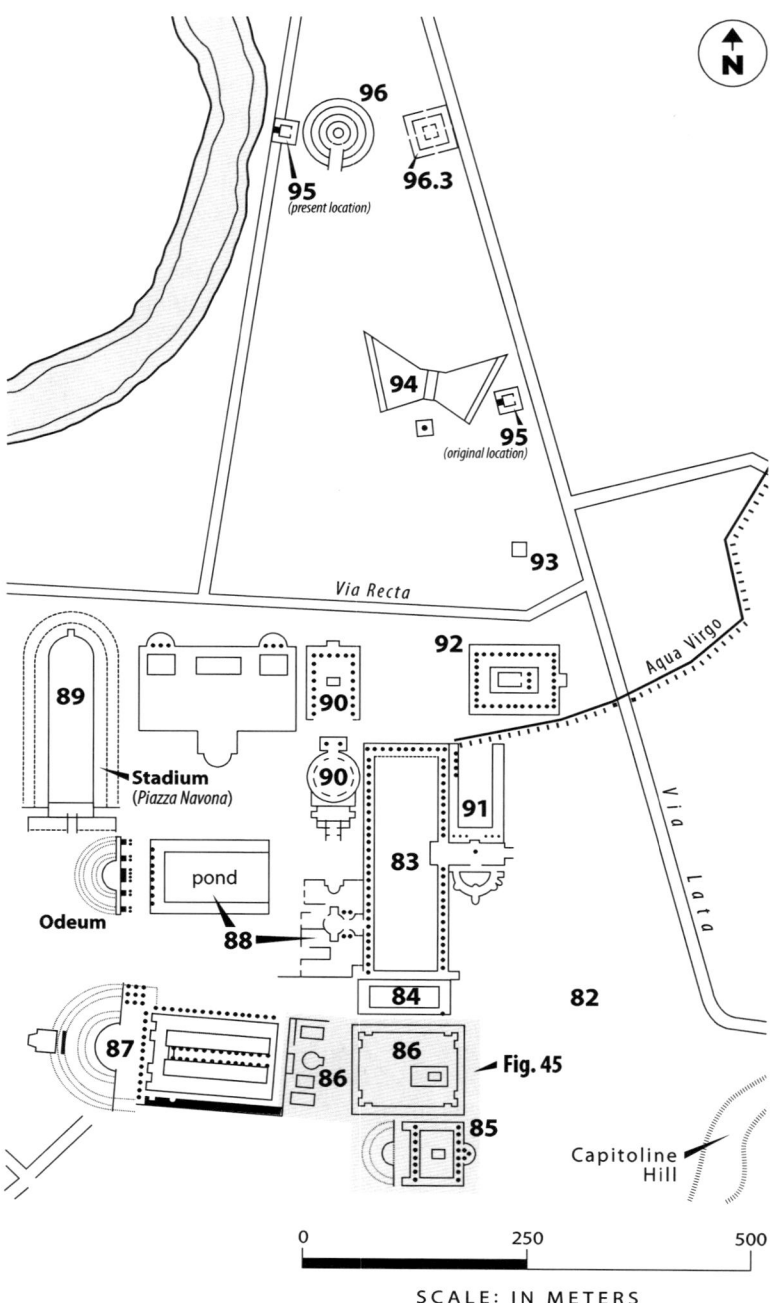

Fig. 44 Campus Martius, (detail)

82.2 The Villa Publica is the common property of the entire population. … It functions as a place to transact public business, where cohorts muster for a levy at the command of a consul, where they gather for an inspection of arms, and where the censors convene the people for a census.

Varro, *Agriculture* 3.2.4

82.3 Sulla lured four legions of the opposing army into the Villa Publica, and as they begged for mercy from his treacherous hand, he had them slaughtered.

Valerius Maximus, *Sayings* 9.2.1

83. The Voting Pens (*Saepta*)

SOURCES

83.1 Cicero sends greetings to Atticus: [54 BC]

We "friends of Caesar" also plan to reconstruct the Voting Pens for the tribal assemblies in the Campus Martius, this one made of marble and roofed over, and we will surround it with a lofty colonnade a mile long. The Villa Publica will be attached to it as part of the same project.

Cicero, *Letters to Atticus* 4.16.8

83.2 The arches of the Virgo begin below the Gardens of Lucullus and end in the Campus Martius in front of the Voting Pens.

Frontinus, *Aqueducts* 22

83.3 In his eighth consulship [26 BC], Agrippa dedicated the structure in the Campus Martius called "the Pens," which had earlier been surrounded by Lepidus with colonnades for voting by tribes. Rather than repairing one of the major roads leading out of town [projects which Augustus encouraged the Roman senators to undertake], Agrippa finished the Saepta with marble plaques and paintings, and called it the Saepta Julia in honor of Augustus.

Dio, *History* 53.23.1–2

83.4 The emperor Caligula sometimes gave gladiatorial games in the Voting Pens.

Suetonius, *Caligula* 18.1

83.5 Mamurra strolls around the Voting Pens at length,
   Where all of golden Rome consumes its goods.
He scrutinizes pretty boys on sale and eats
   Them with his eyes—not those on the blatant block

> But tucked away on viewing stands behind the scenes
>   That the common crowd and my sort never see.
> Having gazed to satiety, he asks to inspect
>   Quilt-wrapped tables and ivories high on shelves,
> And sighs that a dining couch for six in tortoise shell
>   Clashes with the citrus-wood back home.
> Lifting a cup, he consults his nose as a judge of bronze,
>   Or notes the flaws in a statue by Polyclitus.
> Finding fault with a crystal's "streak of common glass,"
>   He puts on hold ten precious agate vases.
> He weighs the antique cups for wine and any goblets
>   Made famous by the master hand of Mentor. ...
> When the day is done, weary from shopping he totes, all told,
>   Two cups he bought for a dollar back to his room.
>
> **Martial**, *Epigrams* 9.59.1–16, 21–22

84. The Ballot Office (*Diribitorium*)

84.1 Augustus finished the Ballot Office begun by Agrippa. Its roof had the largest single span of any building. The roof, however, has since been entirely destroyed, and today [c. AD 200] the building stands open, unable to be spanned again.

Dio, *History* 55.8.4

84.2 [Some exceptionally large trees have made their way to Rome as building material.] There was in my own time a huge log worthy of wonder, kept in the portico of Agrippa's Voting Grounds. This piece of timber, left over from the building of the Ballot Office, was one hundred feet long and a foot and a half in diameter

Pliny the Elder, *Encyclopedia* 16.201

84.3 Among Rome's most noteworthy structures, should not we mention the roof of the Ballot Office built by Agrippa?

Pliny the Elder, *Encyclopedia* 36.102

85. Theater of Balbus

COMMENTARY

The Theater of Balbus, the third and smallest of Rome's stone theaters (its seating for 7,000 spectators was little more than half the capacity of the Theater of Marcellus built shortly before it), was only recently assigned to the ruins that bear its name today, after a reinterpretation of several fragments of the Marble Plan sketched in Fig. 45.

On one of the fragments the word "Theatrum" is clearly visible, the remnants of "Balbi" below it less so. Today's Via delle Botteghe Oscure follows the path of an ancient colonnade adjacent to the Theater. The ruins visible from the Via delle Botteghe Oscure belong to a temple that stood at the middle of this neighboring site, the Porticus Minucia, a distribution center for grain.

Nearly across from these ruins is a museum located atop ruins of the large forecourt of the Theater of Balbus. An explicit point of the museum is to illustrate, in addition to the architecture of this theater and of the Porticus Munucia that lay just to the north of it, the various layers of activity here subsequent to the

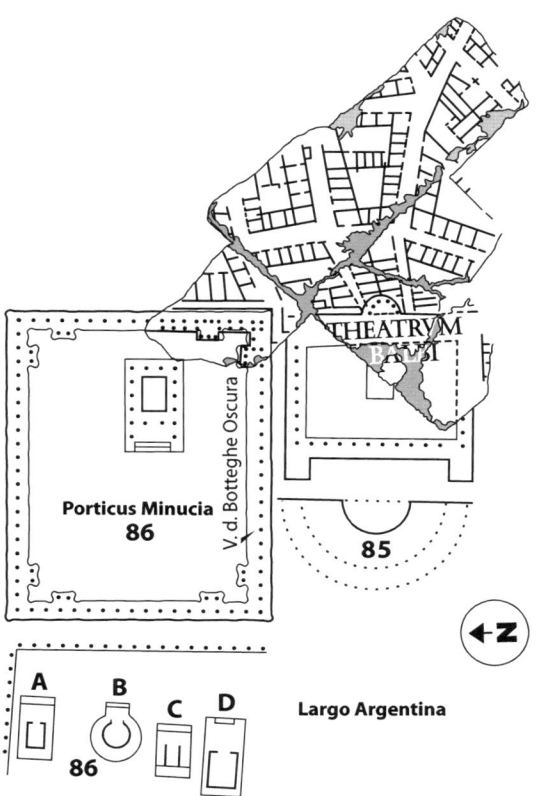

Fig. 45 Fragments of Marble Plan with Theater of Balbus

fall of ancient Rome. The exhibit combines the findings of archaeology with written sources and artistic renderings to give expression to the growing sensitivity towards post-classical ruins, which tended to be treated by earlier generations of archaeologists as so much detritus on top of the imperial past. The ban against squatters (c. AD 400) in the Campus Martius included in this section [85.3] looks ahead to the transition from imperial capital to medieval backwater.

SOURCES

85.1 During his reign Augustus often encouraged the leading men of Rome to adorn the city with new monuments or to restore and embellish old ones. Many buildings were indeed constructed then by a variety of individuals, such as…the theater by Cornelius Balbus.

Suetonius, *Augustus* 29.4–5

85.2 [In 13 BC] Cornelius Balbus happened to be celebrating the dedication of the theater still known by his name, when news came that Augustus was returning to Rome from abroad. Balbus prided himself that he was responsible for bringing Augustus back to Rome—this, when he couldn't enter his new theater except by boat because the Tiber was in flood.

Dio, *History* 54.25.2

85.3 The Emperors Arcadius and Honorius, to the People: We order that whoever tries to occupy the Campus Martius with houses or shacks is to be deprived of all of his belongings and sent into perpetual exile, on command of the illustrious Prefect of the City.

Theodosian Code 14.4

86. The Porticus Minuciae and the Four Republican Temples (*Largo Argentina*) (Figs. 45, 46)

COMMENTARY

The porticoes of Minucia were used for the distribution of the grain doled out to the public. As Juvenal's "bread and circuses" quip suggests [128.16], this makes the porticoes the scene of a primary point of contact between the Roman citizen and his government. The connection Juvenal makes between entertainment, food-supply, and politics is confirmed in the passage by Tacitus describing public protests during a grain-shortage [86.3].

In Augustus's time, 200,000 of the urban plebs received free grain, a number that is one indication that we should not think of the grain-dole as a preserve of the poorest Romans. It was in fact a sign of some status that one was on the dole (as suggested by the epitaph below, 86.2), rather than a necessity for most of the recipients, who at any rate had to buy grain from private dealers to supplement the amount they received for free from the state.

The epitaph contains other interesting details: that recipients of free grain were assigned a specific day and a specific gate for the pick-up of their grain, that such numbers evidently loomed large among a person's vital statistics, and that it could be given to dependents as well as adults.

There were apparently two porticoes called Minucia, the Minucia Vetus ("old") and the Minucia Frumentaria ("dealing in grain"), but since both sources and ruins are scanty, there is much disagreement over their location and differentiation. It is generally agreed, however, that one of them was the large colonnaded space between the Theater of Balbus and the Ballot Office, east of today's Largo Argentina and mentioned above in the commentary on the Theater of Balbus. If this

Fig. 46 Temple Area at Largo Argentina Temples

was the Minucia Vetus, then the temple ruins on the Via delle Botteghe Oscure belong to the Temple of Lares Permarini, and the Minucia Frumentaria lay elsewhere; Richardson suggests a location along the Corso, where there are subterranean remains of a giant warehouse that stretched for 400m. Coarelli and others argue, however, that this structure north of the Via delle Botteghe Oscure is the later Minucia Frumentaria, and that the original distribution center was a colonnade just west of it which surrounded the four temples on display today at Largo Argentina, one of which would then be the Temple of Lares Permarini (spirits which presided over voyages at sea, vowed during a naval battle off Syria). The warehouses along the Corso, or others found nearby just to the east of the Saepta, may have been used at any rate as a storage area for the grain before its distribution in the Porticus Minucia.

The identities of the four Republican temples are so provisional that it is customary to letter them A to D, north to south (see Fig. 45). What complicates matters is that there are references to numerous temples in the Campus Martius that have never been found, so that it is not simply a matter of lining up four ruins with a list of four possible temples. The round temple, B, has the securest identity of the four, probably being the round colonnaded temple Catulus vowed in battle to Fortuna Huiusce Diei [86.8] ("Fortune of This Very Day" literally; Fortuna especially was worshipped under many different cult titles, here apparently in her capacity to make or break one's fortune in a single day). If one of the four Republican temples is the Lares Permarini, it is probably D, since only it has the characteristics of a temple built in the early second century BC. Temple A is generally identified as that of Juturna, on the strength of Ovid's couplet (86.10; it is the closest temple of the four to the Baths of Agrippa, the major destination of the Aqua Virgo).

One thing that is clear from the four temples and their display (which owes much to Mussolini, who wanted to shoot the officials arguing that this space had better uses) is how much the current surface of Campo Marzio has risen on the ruins of antiquity. Various levels of pavement around the four temples show how the process had begun even in antiquity, culminating in the travertine pavement of Domitian's time, after the great fire of AD 80.

SOURCES

86.1 [In 2 BC] I gave 60 denarii to each member of the plebs who was at that time a recipient of the public dole of grain; the number of people was slightly more than 200,000.

Augustus, *Achievements* 15

86.2 [Epitaph:] In memory of Gaius Sergius Alcimus, son of Gaius, who lived 3 years, 3 months, and 3 days. He received grain on the 10th of each month at bay 39.

ILS 6069 = *CIL* 6.10224

86.3 [In AD 32] the price of grain almost led to rioting in Rome, and for many days unusually outspoken criticism was directed against the Emperor Claudius when he attended the theater. Disturbed by this, the emperor accused the magistrates and the Senators of failing to use the proper authority to control the populace, and he enumerated in addition all the provinces from which he was importing grain, and in much greater quantities than Augustus imported.

Tacitus, *Annals* 6.13

86.4 [In 103 BC] the Celtic tribe of the Scordisci were defeated by Minucius, who built the porticoes which are famous even today [c. AD 30].

Velleius, *History* 2.8.3

86.5 *Notitia,* Sites in Region IX:
… the Porticus of Philip;
the two Minuciae (the Vetus and the Frumentaria);
the Crypt of Balbus; …

86.6 [In 179 BC] the censor Marcus Aemilius dedicated the Temple of the Lares Permarini in the Campus. Lucius Aemilius Regillus had vowed the temple 11 years earlier, during a naval battle against the generals of the Seleucid king, Antiochus III.

Livy, *History* 40.52.4

86.7 The Temple of the Lares Permarini is in the Porticus Minucia.

Calendar Inscription (Fasti Praenestini)

86.8 [As the Cimbri advanced on the Romans in northern Italy in 101 BC,] the general Marius washed his hands and raised them towards heaven, promising to sacrifice a hecatomb to the gods. Catulus likewise raised his hands and vowed a temple to Fortune of the Moment.

Plutarch, *Marius* 26.2

86.9 "[On my property you will find] a *tholus*, a round building with a colonnade, like the temple built by Catulus."

Varro, *Agriculture* 3.5.12

86.10 The very same morning, Juturna, saw you enshrined
There where the Campus is met by the Aqua Virgo.

Ovid, *Fasti* 1.463–4

87. Theater of Pompey

COMMENTARY

Rome's first stone theater was the great theater of Pompey, erected while Caesar was making his name in Gaul. In 55 BC it would have towered over the plain of the Campus, still largely undeveloped especially to the north. The round contours of the theater are visible in a street plan of Rome today, in the curve of the Via d. Grotta Pinta. In the center, at the top of the stands (high above the eastern side of Campo dei Fiori today) stood a temple to Venus Victrix, flanked by several other shrines. The foundation walls of Pompey's theater can still be seen in several restaurants near Campo dei Fiori.

"Theater" only describes part of the complex built by Pompey. A larger part of the site was taken over by a large portico which, in addition to the practical function it had during a rain-delay of the theater, was a favorite site for strolling amidst greenery, fine stone, and art works. Attached to this courtyard at its far end, where it abutted the area of the four Republican temples in the Largo Argentina, was Pompey's Curia, which was some sort of inaugurated hall, exhedra, or chamber in which the senate could meet, as it did for the session in which Caesar was assassinated. As fatefully and famously described by Plutarch [87.11], the topographical irony of the scene is unequalled. Augustus's own designs for Pompey's statue were almost as deep.

He dismantled the Curia to deprive any neo-liberators a cult-site (the latrine [87.15] is a nice touch), but simply relocated the statue of Caesar's rival to another prominent position. As in Augustus's Forum, Pompey could be included as part of the Rome Augustus was restoring.

SOURCES

87.1   During these same days [in 55 BC] Pompey dedicated the theater in which we still take pride. At the dedication he put on shows of music and gymnastic competitions.

Dio, *History* 39.38.1

87.2   Tiro, the freedman of Cicero, once wrote: "When Pompey [in 52 BC] was about to dedicate the Temple to the Venus of Victory (the one whose steps serve as theater seats as well), and was writing the text for the inscription of his name and title, he began to consult others on whether it was proper to write 'consul tertio' or 'consul terti*um*.' ["third consul" or "thrice consul"] ... Finessing the issue, Cicero persuaded him to abbreviate it as "consul *tert*."

Gellius, *Attic Nights* 10.1.7

87.3   The emperor Claudius put on many lavish shows. ... For the dedication of the Theater of Pompey, which he restored after a fire, he presided over the entertainment from a tribunal seat erected in the orchestra, after first praying at the temples above and descending through the middle of the auditorium while everyone sat in silence.

Suetonius, *Claudius* 21

87.4   I especially wish to demonstrate for other Christians how those traditional spectacles of Roman entertainment are not compatible with the true religion and the true worship of the one true God. ...

Let us consider the true nature of theatrical entertainment, beginning with the vice inherent in its setting. The theater, rightly seen, is a shrine to Venus. Indeed, this type of building came into the world in the name of Venus. For originally, even the heathen censors were concerned to destroy theaters as quickly as they arose, foreseeing the serious moral damage that would result from the licentious spirit of the theater. ... Because of this attitude, when Pompey the Great (only his theater was greater than he!) had constructed that citadel of every vice and was afraid that because of this his memory might one day suffer from official censure, he added on to his theater a temple to Venus, and when he summoned the people to the dedication, he did not call the structure a theater, but a temple "to which we have added," he said, "some seating for shows."

Tertullian, *Pagan Entertainments* 1, 10

87.5   Catia was such a loose woman that she had sex with the tribune Valerius Siculus at the Theater of Pompey, behind a curtain in the Temple of Venus.

Porphyry on Horace, *Satires* 1.2.94

87.6   When designing a theater, you should include porticoes behind the stage to house the audience when a sudden downpour disrupts the performances, and to provide some open space for the preparation of stage sets. The Pompeian Portico is an example of this.

Vitruvius, *Architecture* 5.9.1

87.7   [A region's climate affects the character of a people, but leaves our will free to choose.] What possible influence can regional climate have, for instance, on a decision to take our walk in the Portico of Pompey rather than in the Campus?

Cicero, *On Fate* 8

87.8   [Why, Cynthia, do you flee the city for smaller towns nearby?]
I suppose the Portico of Pompey, with its columns of shade
   And tapestries of threaded gold, seems squalid to you,
With its solid rows of plane trees shaped to an even height,
   The streams of flowing water that slide off the Slumbering Satyr,
And the liquid sounds of splashing around the entire basin
   When Triton suddenly blows the water from his mouth.

Propertius, *Elegies* 2.32.11–16

87.9   Varro writes that Coponius also created the statues of the 14 nations which are placed around Pompey's complex.

Pliny the Elder, *Encyclopedia* 36.41

87.10   Polygnotus also did the painting (now in the Porticus of Pompey but formerly in his Curia) in which you cannot be sure whether the man with the shield is climbing or descending.

Pliny the Elder, *Encyclopedia* 35.59

87.11   The scene itself of Caesar's death-struggle and assassination later made it clear to all that some spirit-power [*daemon*] had taken the event in hand to bring it about. For the meeting-site of the senate that day contained a statue of Caesar's late rival Pompey, which Pompey himself had dedicated as one more ornament to his theater. …

Because Mark Antony was not only loyal to Caesar but physically powerful as well, the conspirators had arranged for Brutus Albinus to detain him outside in a lengthy conversation. Caesar himself, however, entered, and the senate rose in his honor. Some of the conspirators then moved into position behind Caesar's chair, while others, approaching him from the front as if in support of a petition being pleaded by

Tillius Cimber on behalf of his exiled brother, gathered closely around Caesar's chair to argue the case. Sitting down, Caesar tried to brush them off, but they continued to harass him with their request until Caesar was driven to show some violence of temper. It was then that Tillius gave the signal to begin the attack, jerking Caesar's toga down from both his shoulders.

Casca was the first to strike, stabbing Caesar in the neck with his dagger, but because he was understandably nervous about initiating a deed of such daring, the wound was neither deep nor deadly, and Caesar was able to turn around, grab the knife, and hold it away. ... So the attack began. Those who were ignorant of the plot stood there in shock, neither fleeing nor coming to Caesar's defense with so much as a shout. Those in the know and intent on murder, however, all drew their knives in a ring around Caesar, so that whichever way he turned he was exposed to blades aimed at his face and eyes, trapped like an animal and struck by every hand.

Since all of the conspirators had to take a part in the sacrifice, as it were, and to taste of Caesar's murder, Brutus also stabbed him once, in the groin. Some say that up until then Caesar was shouting and attempting to deflect and dodge the blows of the others but when he saw that Brutus too had drawn his sword, he pulled his toga over his head and sank down (whether by chance, or pushed there by his killers) at the base of Pompey's statue, spattering it with blood so that it seemed his former enemy in war stood over him in vengeance, with Caesar laid out at his feet quivering from his multitude of wounds. It is said he had been stabbed twenty-three times in all. Many of his assassins also received stab wounds, having struck one another by accident in their attempt to land so many blows on one body.

Plutarch, *Caesar* 66.1, 3–7

87.12 [Would we necessarily want to know our futures, assuming they were fated and inescapable?] Consider the case of Caesar. Imagine him knowing, by means of divination, that among the very Senate whose members were largely of his own choosing, in the Senate hall (*curia*) of Pompey's theater, in front of the statue of Pompey himself, with so many of his own centurions looking on, he should be murdered by Rome's finest citizens, some of whom owed their success entirely to Caesar, and knowing that when he lay there dead not even one of his servants, let alone one of his friends, would approach his corpse. Would he not have been tortured all his life, knowing this to be his fate?

Cicero, *On Divination* 2.23

87.13 Augustus moved the statue of Pompey out of the Senate Hall where Caesar was murdered and placed it on a marble arch opposite the main door of the stage.

Suetonius, *Augustus* 31.5

87.14 The Senate voted that the Senate hall where Caesar was murdered be walled up, and that the Ides of March be called the Day of Parricide, on which the Senate should never meet again.

Suetonius, *Caesar* 88

87.15 The triumvirs [Octavian, Antony, and Lepidus, in 42 BC] first closed the building where Caesar was murdered. Later they had it rebuilt as a latrine.

Dio, *History* 47.19

88. The Baths of Agrippa

COMMENTARY

Even before Augustus had consolidated his power, he and Agrippa (Augustus's trusted military partner) turned their attention to developing large stretches of the Campus Martius, continuing (as so often elsewhere in the city) work begun or envisioned by Julius Caesar and extending it with newly conceived projects. The Baths of Agrippa, the Aqua Virgo, the Pantheon [90.], the Basilica of Neptune (a portico between the baths and the Pantheon), the Sun Dial [94.], the Altar of Augustan Peace [95.], and the Mausoleum [96.] were all projects undertaken in the reign of Augustus, in addition to the completion of the Voting Pens [83.] and Ballot Office [84.].

The Baths of Agrippa, the first of Rome's great bathing complexes, evolved in several stages, beginning simply as an exercise area with a dry sweat bath (the Laconicum, or "Spartan Bath"). Agrippa's subsequent construction of the Aqua Virgo allowed for something much more elaborate. Low in elevation, this aqueduct entered Rome from the north and emerged on the river plain where the Spanish Steps are today. An arcade (visible in sections and still supplying the Trevi Fountain with water) crossed the Via Lata and extended almost to the Pantheon, from where its waters were delivered by pipe to various parts of the developing Campus as needed.

Agrippa made use of the water not only for the central part of his baths, but channeled some of it into a canal called the Euripus, which ran from the bath complex and joined the Tiber just upstream of today's Ponte Vittorio Emanuele. This canal was used for swimming, or for a cold plunge [88.4], functioning in effect as the cold swimming pool built into the later imperial baths. In between his baths and the Tiber, Agrippa also excavated a large pond (the Stagnum Agrippae), which was apparently ornamental in nature, like the ponds in city parks today, and surrounded it with grounds for strolling. Nero's inventive mind found other uses for the setting [88.6].

SOURCES

88.1 [In 25 BC] Augustus finished these wars and shut the gates of Janus, which had remained open because of the fighting. Agrippa, meanwhile, was beautifying Rome. He completed the Basilica named for Neptune in honor of their naval victories, and distinguished it with the painting of the Argonauts, and built the "Spartan Bath" as well (it was called this with reference to its own gymnasium, where patrons exercised naked and oiled, a practice associated above all with Sparta at the time).

Dio, *History* 53.27.1–3

88.2 When he died [in 12 BC], Agrippa willed over to the people his gardens and the baths named after him, and gave Augustus some estates to support the baths so that the people might bathe free of charge. Augustus then turned these estates over to the state.

Dio, *History* 54.29.4

88.3 But it was Julius Caesar who by his own example especially encouraged the public display of art, and after him, Marcus Agrippa, though he was a man more given to rustic than sophisticated pleasures. In the warmest part of his baths he placed small paintings framed in marble, which were recently [c. AD 70] removed when the baths underwent repairs.

Pliny the Elder, *Encyclopedia* 35.26

88.4 [As I age, my exercise and bathing habits have changed radically.] I, the great lover of cold water, who used to greet January 1st by plunging into the Euripus, celebrating the New Year with a jump into the Aqua Virgo's water as naturally as I might read, write, or speak, have had to alter my habits, transferring my allegiance first to the Tiber, and now to this plunge-tub warmed by the sun.

Seneca the Younger, *Letters* 83.5

88.5 My dear and distant friends, my thoughts are filled with you,
　　With my beloved wife back home and our sweet daughter.
Seeing it all in my mind, as if in Rome, I leave
　　Our house and visit again the sites of that beautiful city:
I see the forums, the temples, the theaters robed in marble,
　　And stroll down colonnades that stretch over leveled earth
To the green grass of the Campus bordering lovely gardens;
　　I see the pond, the channels, and the Aqua Virgo waters.

Ovid, *Letters from Exile* 1.8.31–38

88.6 To give the impression that he enjoyed himself in Rome more than anywhere else, Nero held banquets in public places and used the entire city as if it were his home. … One time he had a special party-boat constructed which was towed around the Pool of Agrippa by other

Fig. 47 Stadium of Domitian (Piazza Navona), with Odeum and Theater of Pompey above (from plaster model of Rome)

boats, all of them finished in gold and ivory and having for rowers male prostitutes grouped according to their age and erotic specialty. He supplied it with birds and animals imported from distant lands, and sea-creatures from as far away as the Atlantic. Brothels were constructed on the shores of the pond and stocked with well-born ladies; on the opposite shore, out in the open, naked prostitutes danced and gestured obscenely. As dusk fell, the adjoining grove and the surrounding buildings resounded with song and glowed with lamplights.

Tacitus, *Annals* 15.37

Notes: Richardson identifies the Euripus of the Aqua Virgo, mentioned by Seneca, as a channel distinct from the one which connected the Baths of Agrippa with the river (traceable by remains for a good deal of its length). Coarelli, in *LTUR* 2.237–9, argues that this latter channel and the one fed by the Virgo are one and the same.

89. Stadium of Domitian; Concert-Hall (*Odeum*)

COMMENTARY

The Stadium of Domitian is conspicuously located by the Piazza Navona, which preserves the shape of the ancient running track. The buildings lining the piazza today are also built upon the substructures of the stands, as can be seen from the street that runs tangent to the north end of the stadium.

The stadium was built as a venue for Greek-style athletic competitions. Foremost among them must have been foot-races. The Latin stadium comes from the Greek stadion, which was first a measure of distance (approximately 600 feet), and then a race-track (the most famous of them, at Olympia, being exactly one stade long). But as the sources make clear, other competitions took place here.

Less certain is what role, if any, Apollodorus and Trajan played in the Stadium's construction, which Suetonius ascribes to Domitian [89.2]. If Apollodorus had a hand in it, he may have put the finishing touches largely carried out under the direction of Domitian's architect Rabirius. But even this Domitianic stadium may have had a forerunner in the temporary wooden structure Augustus erected on the Campus to house similar competitions [89.1].

Borromini's St. Agnese in Agone, built over ancient substructure on the west side of the Stadium, commemorates the martyr's death of the 13-year old St. Agnes, which, tradition has it, occurred in a brothel located in the stadium. Prudentius [89.9] recounts one version of her death, which he locates in a brothel in an open square, but does not specify which square. The passages from the *Imperial Lives* [89.7, 89.8] locate a brothel in the Stadium, at any rate. Brothels in Rome were often called *fornices*, "archways," of which the Stadium had plenty and thus a like place for "fornication."

The Odeum was a covered auditorium. Most archaeologists identify it with ruins found between the Theater of Pompey and the Stadium of Domitian. The order of buildings in Ammianus's passage [89.3] would seem to corroborate this, but his list of the fabulous architecture that met Constantius's eyes has no overall topographical order.

SOURCES

89.1   [In 28 BC] Augustus held gymnastic competitions in a temporary wooden stadium constructed in the Campus Martius.

Dio, *History* 53.1.5

89.2   Domitian's construction projects in Rome included both the Stadium and the Odeum.

Suetonius, *Domitian* 5

89.3   [The Emperor Constantius, entering Rome for the first time in AD 357, gazed in amazement on one after another of its monuments:] … the Pantheon, which seems to vault an entire neighborhood with its beautiful, lofty dome; the columns inside of which one can climb to platforms that hold statues of former emperors; the Temple of Rome, the Forum of Peace, the Theater of Pompey, the Odeum, and the Stadium, among other marvels of the Eternal City. But when he came to the Forum of Trajan… .

Ammianus, *History* 16.10.14

89.4 The architect Apollodorus, Trajan's builder in Rome who designed his Forum, the Concert-hall, and the Stadium, was first banished and eventually killed by Hadrian.

Dio, History 69.4.1

89.5 In this period of Septimius Severus's rule [AD 200], gymnastic competitions were held. So many athletes were compelled to participate that we were amazed that the Stadium had room to hold them. Women also took part in these contests, and they competed against one another with such ferocity that the jeering remarks of spectators began to be aimed at distinguished women in the audience as well as the female athletes. As a result, women, whatever their background, were subsequently forbidden to participate in one-on-one wrestling.

Dio, History 75.16.1

89.6 [In AD 217 the Colosseum was struck by lightning and badly damaged in the resulting fire.] As a result, gladiatorial combats were held in the Stadium for many years.

Dio, History 79.25.3

89.7 The Emperor Alexander Severus [c. AD 230] placed a tax on pimps as well as on both male and female prostitutes, with the stipulation that the income thus raised go not into the public treasury but towards the cost of restoring the Theater, the Circus, the Amphitheater, and the Stadium, [all structures rich in "archways"].

Imperial Lives, Severus Alexander 24.3

89.8 The emperor Elagabalus [AD 218–22] rounded up into a public hall all the prostitutes from the Circus, the Theater, the Stadium, the baths and everywhere else they frequented. Addressing them like a general would his troops, he called them his fellow soldiers and reviewed with them the various positions and techniques of their profession.

Imperial Lives, Elagabalus 26.3

89.9 The Romulean city boasts the body
Of Agnes, courageous girl and famous martyr.
Her faith enraged a pagan judge in Rome,
Who sentenced her to serve in a public brothel
Unless the maiden kneeled at Minerva's altar
And begged forgiveness from the virgin goddess
She scorned, though proud of her own virginity.
When she refused, he ordered her exposed
Outside a brothel in the corner of a square.
But no one turned his head to look at her;
Appalled, they glumly passed. [After this failure
To defile the girl, a soldier was sent to kill her.]
When Agnes saw the savage man approach

With naked sword in hand, she gave a cry
Of happiness. "A suitor such as this—
Violent, rough, uncouth, and armed—
Is lovelier to me by far than a youth
Of smooth and pretty ways, whose soft embrace
Would kill me with the loss of chastity.
This soldier, I confess, has won my maiden heart!"
He gave his sword one swing, and she lost her head.

Prudentius, *Crowns of Martyrdom* 14, selections

90. Pantheon

COMMENTARY

Ancient Rome's best preserved building (due to its sturdy construction, as well as its conversion into a church in AD 608), one of the finest structures of antiquity, also exhibits among its relatively few sources one of the most deceptive inscriptions of antiquity [90.1]. Agrippa did indeed build the original Pantheon, but the present building was built by Hadrian from the ground up with a design radically different from the design of the original, which burnt in the fire of AD 80 and again under Trajan.

In contrast to our knowledge of the Pantheon's structure is the confusion over the building's function. Dio's speculation [90.6] is significant for most interpretations: his suggestion that the dome is meant to resemble the Heavens has given impetus to those who would see it as a temple to the cosmos with all its deities (the stunning opening in the center of the dome also encourages this), but his openly avowed uncertainty has led others to doubt this and posit more mundane functions. Dio also notes [90.7] that it was used by Hadrian as a tribunal, suggesting that the building may have functioned primarily as an imperial audience hall, for which any religious associations of the building (its statuary, and the traditional temple architecture of its porch) would have been an ambiguity welcomed by an emperor.

There is perhaps some meeting of the ways in the mathematical harmonies of the dome's design. The cupola, which is a perfect hemisphere, has the same height as the diameter of the cylindrical drum on which it sits, and the number of the rows of coffers which divide the cupola—28—was recognized in antiquity as one of the rare "perfect" numbers, equal to the sum of its divisors (1, 2, 4, 7, 14).

SOURCES

90.1 M(arcus) AGRIPPA L(ucii) F(ilius) CO(n) S(ul) TERTIUM FECIT

Marcus Agrippa, son of Lucius, made this building when consul

for the third time [in 27 BC]

ILS 129.1 = *CIL* 6.896

90.2 Diogenes of Athens adorned the Pantheon of Agrippa. The columns of the temple include some in the shape of Caryatids that are ranked with the very finest sculpture, as are the statues placed on the pediment (although these are less celebrated because of their distance from the viewer).

Pliny the Elder,
Encyclopedia 36.38

90.3 [Cleopatra made a wager with Antony that she could spend 10,000,000 sesterces on a single banquet.] As arranged by Cleopatra, her servants placed a single cup before her, filled with a vinegar strong

Fig. 48 Pantheon

enough to dissolve even pearls. As Antony watched wondering how she could possibly win the wager with one cup, she detached an earring that held one of the most precious pearls on earth. She then dropped it in the cup and drank the liquefied gem.

The story continues with the pearl in the other earring that she was wearing (the uneaten second helping, as it were): later, when Cleopatra was captured by Augustus, this pearl was cut in half to decorate the ears of Venus's statue in the Pantheon.

Pliny the Elder, *Encyclopedia* 9.120–1

90.4 On January 12th, during the same consulship [in AD 59], Calpurnius Piso, chairman of the Arval Brethren, made sacrifice at the Pantheon to the goddess Dia, in the presence of ... the Arval Brethren.

ILS 229 = *CIL* 6.2041 (selection)

90.5 In Rome, Hadrian rebuilt the Pantheon, the Saepta, the Basilica of Neptune, many temples, the Forum of Augustus, and the Baths of

Fig. 49 Pantheon and forecourt (from the plaster model of Rome)

Agrippa. He dedicated all of these buildings in the names of their original builders.

Imperial Lives, *Hadrian* 19.10

90.6   Agrippa also completed the building called the Pantheon ["All-Divine"]. Perhaps it got this name because it had the statues of many gods among the sculptures that adorned it, including those of Mars and Venus, but I personally think it is because the dome resembles the Heavens. Agrippa had intended to place a statue of Augustus there and to name the building after him, but when the emperor denied the honor, Agrippa placed a statue of Julius Caesar in it instead, while placing statues of himself and Augustus in the porch.

Dio, *History* 53.27.2–3

90.7   The emperor Hadrian always carried out the more important and urgent business with the help of the Senate, and gave his rulings in the presence of the leading men, whether in the palace, the forum, the Pantheon, or various other places—always from a tribunal seat so that the transactions were officially public.

Dio, *History* 69.7.1

90.8   The emperor Caesar Lucius **Septimius Severus** Pius Pertinax Augustus, conqueror of the Parthians in Arabia and Assyria, Pontifex Maximus, with tribunician powers 10 times, triumphing general 11 times, consul 3 times, Father of his Country, and proconsul; and the emperor Caesar Marcus Aurelius Antoninus Pius Felix Augustus [= his son **Caracalla**], with tribunician powers 5 times, consul, proconsul, rescued the Pantheon and all its ornament from the damage of old age [in AD 202].

ILS 129.2 = *CIL* 6.896

Notes: For a general discussion of both Agrippan and Hadrianic Pantheons, see A. Ziolkowski's article (in English) in *LTUR* 4.54–61. He rejects the "cosmic" interpretations of the building's function and concludes that the "safest definition of Hadrian's Pantheon is thus: a free-standing imperial aula."

91. The Temple of Isis and Serapis

COMMENTARY

On the other side of the Voting Pens from the Pantheon was a large temple-complex dedicated to the Egyptian fertility goddess Isis and her consort Serapis. The worship of both deities had a long and complex history in the Mediterranean. They were already popular in Italy and Rome in the late Republic when the triumvirs voted a temple to them, perhaps this temple on the Campus. Augustus, Tiberius, and the Senate subsequently made attempts to repress the cult as being insufficiently subordinate to official control, but later emperors, notably Vespasian (who spent the night before his official triumph in this temple of Isis) and Hadrian (whose fascination with Egypt and the Egyptian Antinous is well-known), were enthusiastic supporters and helped to fashion Serapis as a god intimately connected with Roman rulers [91.3, 91.4]. Isis was revered as a nurturing, life-giving protector, and was especially popular with women. In contrast to most traditional Roman cults, the hierarchy and status of the worshipper played a minimal role in her rituals; the girlfriend/courtesan in Catullus's Poem 10, looking for a ride to the Temple of Isis, thus reflects several aspects of Isis worship. Juvenal's passage alludes to the importance of water in the rites of Isis. For more insight into the universal range and supreme reverence according to Isis, Apuleius's *Metamorphoses*, Book 11, is invaluable, where the hero prays to Isis in all her dimensions and describes her epiphany that leads to his transformation. This explains his eagerness to worship her when he arrives in Rome, as described below [91.2].

Juvenal's passage, some archaeological ruins, sculptures found in the area, and a fragment of the Marble Plan locate the complex, which stretched much of the length of the east side of the Voting Pens, an area bounded today by the Via del Seminario on the north and the Via di S. Stefano del Cacco on the south. The northern area contained the Temple of Isis, and the southern area the Serapeum. Between the two there was apparently a public square, entered on the east and west ends by archways monumentalizing the thoroughfare (roughly along the Via

Fig. 50 Bernini's elephant with obelisk from Temple of Isis

Pie' di Marmo and the Piazza del Collegio Romano) that connected the Via Lata with the Voting Pens.

Numerous Egyptian sculptural decorations have been found in or around the temple complex, and several remain in the area. A statue of a baboon ("[ma]cacco," if it isn't the dog-headed Anubis) is reflected in the name of the church where the statue stands today, S. Stefano del Cacco. The Via Pie' di Marmo gets its name from the giant marble foot located near the same church; this was perhaps part of the cult statue of Serapis. An early C3 AD statue (popularly called "Madama Lucrezia" by Romans today) carved with the costume of Isis is located outside the Palazetto Venezia near the little park of the Piazza di S. Marco, and this may be the upper half of the cult statue of Isis. Of the half-dozen small obelisks known to have come from this temple-complex, two are nearby: one on Bernini's elephant in Piazza della Minerva and the other in front of the Pantheon.

SOURCES

91.1 [Among the follies Roman women perpetrate]
  Your superstitious wife will go on pilgrimage
All the way to blazing Egypt and the upper Nile
  Just to bring back water to sprinkle the Temple of Isis
That rises right beside our ancient Voting Pens.
Juvenal, *Satires* 6.527–9

91.2 [After Isis had transformed me back into human form, I went to Rome.] There I had no more urgent business than to pray daily to the supreme power of Queen Isis, who is worshipped with greatest devotion as Isis "Campensis" because of where her temple is located.
Apuleius, *Metamorphoses* 11.26

91.3   [In the early C3 AD] the emperor Severus Alexander embellished the temples of Isis and Serapis with fitting additions of statues, eunuch-slaves out of Delos, and all the paraphernalia for the mystic rites.

Imperial Lives, Severus Alexander 26.8

92. Temple of Hadrian

COMMENTARY

     When Hadrian died in AD 138, the practice of deifications continued, as did their commemoration by monuments built by successor-sons, in this case by Antoninus Pius, who dedicated his temple to Hadrian in AD 145. The Regionary Catalogues place this building somewhere between the Column of Marcus Aurelius and the Baths of Alexander (the earlier Baths of Nero), which were between the Stadium of Domitian and the Pantheon [92.3]. This area contains the significant ruins of an otherwise unidentified temple, and since the architectural style of this can be dated to Antonine Rome, it is generally agreed that the location of the Temple of Hadrian has been found.

     The architectural remains in question are built into the Borsa, Rome's Stock Exchange, alongside the Piazza di Pietra. Thirteen marble columns survive, with capitals and entablature (the highest section being a reconstruction), as well as much of the podium. The precinct of the temple was much larger, taking up several of the blocks around the Borsa today.

     Also in the neighborhood, the *Notitia* tells us, was the Basilica of Matidia and Marcia, the grandmother and mother of Hadrian's wife Sabina. The columns to both Antoninus Pius and Marcus Aurelius also stood nearby, as well as a temple to the latter (Antoninus Pius managed to have his temple built close to the Forum itself, next to Caesar's and the former home of the pious Numa [53.]). This entire area, then, between the Hadrianic Pantheon and the Via Lata (the Corso) was heavily cultivated by Hadrian and his Antonine successors, until Commodus's delinquency put an end to the Antonine dynasty.

SOURCES

92.1   Of the works built by Antoninus Pius, the following remain: in Rome, the Temple of Hadrian, in memory of his father … .

Imperial Lives, Antoninus Pius 8.2

92.2   Antoninus Pius dedicated the temple to his father on the day that Verus assumed the toga virilis [in AD 145] and gave a largess to the people.

Imperial Lives, Lucius Verus 3.1

92.3 *Notitia,* Sites in Region IX:
… the Pantheon;
the basilica of Matidia and Marciana;
the Temple of [Marcus Aurelius] Antoninus,
 and his helicoidal column,
175 1/2 feet tall with 203 interior steps and 56 windows;
the Temple of Hadrian;
the Baths of Alexander and Agrippa; …

93. Column of Marcus Aurelius

SOURCES
93.1 Although people were skeptical about Romulus's apotheosis, everyone assumed without debate that Marcus Aurelius had been received among the gods [when he died in AD 180], and in his honor, temples, columns, and many other monuments were decreed.
Aurelius Victor, *The Caesars* 16.14

94. The Obelisks of Rome; Sundial of Augustus

COMMENTARY
 The obelisk of pink Aswan granite that now stands in the Piazza di Montecitorio, though not the largest of Rome's ancient obelisks (that distinction belongs to the obelisk at the Lateran), is perhaps the most interesting, and the inscription on its base gives the essentials of Rome's long-standing and continuing fascination with these counters of power and axial markers:

 94.1 IMP(erator) CAESAR DIVI F(ilius)
 AUGUSTUS
 PONTIFEX MAXIMUS
 IMP(erator) XII CO(n)S(ul) XI TRIB(unicia)
  POT(estate) XIV
 AEGUPTO IN POTESTATEM
 POPULI ROMANI REDACTA
 SOLI DONUM DEDIT.

The emperor Caesar Augustus, son of the deified Caesar,
Pontifex Maximus, triumphing general 12 times, consul 11
times, with tribunician powers 14 times, gave this obelisk
as a gift to the Sun after Egypt had been brought under the
power of the Roman people. [10 BC]

ILS 91 = *CIL* 6.702

The Roman conquest of Egypt under Augustus made these monuments available for the taking, and especially under Augustus they are fresh trophies of that victory, preserving however the Egyptian association with the sun and its rays (symbolized by the taper of both the shaft and of the little pyramid that sits on top). This particular obelisk, however, also served as the pointer (gnomon) of a large open-air sundial built by Augustus. The sundial, described by Pliny [94.3] and surviving in fragments (still in place but far below the street-level of today's Via di Campo Marzio), was located, as was the obelisk originally, on the other (north) side of the Chamber of Deputies. After lying buried and broken in five pieces, the obelisk was patched back together in the late C18 century with the help of granite left over from the ruined Column of Antoninus Pius, which stood nearby.

Rome's other ancient obelisks have been similarly peripatetic. Their first journey of course was between quarry and the obelisk's ancient Egyptian site. From there, they were taken, in three separate feats of engineering, down the Nile, across the Mediterranean, and up the Tiber. Today, none of them stands in its original Roman location, having been moved (after excavation and reassembly, in most cases) by city-scaping Popes, chief among them Pope Sixtus V, who through his architect Domenico Fontana set up three of them during their intensive reshaping of the city in the 1580s, as did Pope Pius VI during his long reign two centuries later.

For maximum visibility, Augustus located his other obelisk-trophy on the spina of the Circus Maximus. It had fallen into three pieces and disappeared under rubble and sediment by the time it was found again by Sixtus V's crews and reassembled in the Piazza del Popolo in 1589. The base of this obelisk has the same inscription as the one quoted above.

The obelisk in St. Peter's Square, also a Sixtus/Fontana project, was imported under Caligula and originally stood nearby in the Circus of Gaius (Caligula) and Nero. This obelisk had remained standing in its original location until Fontana contrived a way to transport it vertically to its new position in front of Christendom's prime basilica, the then relatively new St. Peter's. The spiked globe of bronze that originally topped this obelisk is on display in the Capitoline museum (Palazzo dei Conservatori).

Of the two post-Augustan obelisks which posthumously became attached to his Mausoleum, Sixtus V moved one to the apse-end of St. Maria Maggiore. The other Mausoleum obelisk has stood in the Piazza del Quirinale since 1786. Like its counterpart at St. Maria Maggiore, it has no hieroglyphs and may have been cut specifically for the Mausoleum, although the occasion for this is not known.

The obelisk that once decorated the sumptuous Gardens of Sallust was reassembled by Pius VI above the Spanish Steps, where, in front of St. Trinità dei Monti, it was prominently visible down the long street axis from the obelisk at Maria Maggiore in one direction, and up the Via Condotti in another. (The Gardens of Sallust were the most splendid of the suburban estates that ringed Rome, covering much of area dissected by the Via Veneto today, extending from the Aurelian Walls down to Piazza Barbarini.) This obelisk, as well as the two from Augustus's Mausoleum, is of a lesser size than the first three obelisks mentioned (roughly 14m. versus 25m.). Its hieroglyphs are not an Egyptian product, but inaccurate Roman copies of the glyphs on the Augustan obelisk now in Piazza del Popolo.

The story of the Lateran obelisk is told by Ammianus and in the excerpted inscription [94.5, 94.6]. It is not only the largest obelisk known (32 m. high, 520 tons), but is the oldest in Rome, although the last to be transported there in ancient times. Pope Sixtus V had it excavated from the Circus, where it lay broken in three pieces under 6m of soil and rubble, and set up near the St. John in Lateran, at the head of the Via Merulana.

Two other major obelisks in Rome deserve mention. The obelisk so brilliantly supported by the seemingly airy base of Bernini's fountain in Piazza Navona goes back at least to the time of Domitian, as can be inferred from the hieroglyphic hymn to Domitian and the Flavian dynasty carved on the obelisk. The obelisk's original Roman location is not known, however, since it is not mentioned in any ancient source and was found miles away, decorating the race track at the giant Villa of Maxentius on the Appian Way. Perhaps it is back at its original location on the spina of the Stadium of Domitian, but the Circus of Gaius and Nero, the Temple of Isis, and the Temple of the Flavians on the Quirinal have all been argued as possible Domitianic locations.

In light of the obelisk's historical and visual associations, it should come as no surprise that Mussolini erected one. Forty meters tall and quarried from the same Cararra marble favored by Caesar and then Michaelangelo, it stands in its original location at Foro Italico, fronting the Tiber on the north side of town. Dispensing with hieroglyphs, it simply proclaims "Mussolini Dux" in block letters running its length.

SOURCES

94.2 Aswan granite is also the stone the Egyptian kings used for the monoliths they erected in a kind of rivalry with one another. They designated these obelisks as sacred to the Sun-god, and indeed their shape is a symbol of the sun's rays, which are signified by the Egyptian *word* for obelisk as well [*tekhen*, meaning both "obelisk" and "ray of sunlight"].

[The Egyptians worked out ways of transporting obelisks on the Nile.] A greater difficulty was faced by the Romans in transporting obelisks by ship to Rome, and the ships that did it were famous sights themselves. The emperor Augustus donated one such transport (the ship which carried the first of his two obelisks) for permanent display at a dock in Puteoli, but this has burnt. For several years Claudius preserved the boat which Caligula used for his obelisk, considering it the most amazing ship ever to float the oceans, but then constructed concrete piers on it (using the volcanic sand of Puteoli in the cement) and had it towed to Ostia and sunk to make part of his new harbor.

Ships to transport these obelisks up the Tiber from the coast were a whole other challenge… .

Pliny the Elder, *Encyclopedia* 36.64, 70

94.3 The obelisk that the emperor Augustus set up in the Circus Maximus was quarried by the king Psammetichus, who was ruling when Pythagoras visited Egypt. It is 85³/₄ feet tall, excluding its base, which is made from the same kind of granite. His obelisk in the Campus Martius is nine feet shorter, and was quarried by Sesoth. [Note: Pliny has his pharaohs reversed here.] The hieroglyphic inscriptions on both of them express the Egyptian philosophy of nature.

The emperor Augustus used the obelisk in the Campus to construct a marvelous sun-dial, on which the shadow cast by the obelisk indicates the length of both days and nights, as marked out on the stone pavement built to measure it. The shadow on the shortest day of winter falls at the six-hour mark, and gradually shortens by an interval each day as the days grow longer (as marked out by bronze rods set in the pavement), after which the shadow lengthens again towards winter. It is altogether an object worthy of study, a creation of the mathematician Facundus Novus. He added a gold ball to the top of the obelisk, which gathered a clear shadow around it, otherwise diffused around the obelisk's tapering point—an idea, they say, which Facundus got from observing the shadow of the human head. These measurements, however, have been inaccurate for about thirty years now [due, Pliny speculates, to either solar changes, or a settling of the obelisk after earthquakes and floods].

A third obelisk in Rome is in the Circus of Gaius and Nero. … We should mention in passing, since we speak of Egypt, the pyramids, those useless and idiotic displays of royal wealth… .

Pliny the Elder, *Encyclopedia* 36.71–73, 74, 75

94.4 The emperor Constantius was eager to visit Rome for the first time. [Entering the city, he was amazed by the concentration there of astounding buildings and monuments raised there by rulers before him.] He deliberated at length over what he might accomplish there;

in the end he decided to add something beautiful to the appearance of the city, and had an obelisk erected in the Circus Maximus [in 357 AD].

Ammianus, *History* 16.10.17

94.5   The emperor Constantius set up an obelisk in the Circus Maximus. Some people remain unaware that Augustus refrained from disturbing this obelisk when he had his other obelisks shipped to Rome: it was a gift of special significance dedicated to the sun-god, rising, as if the summit of the world, from the sacred precinct of the sun-god's temple, not to be profaned by movement. Constantine, however, put no great stock in this association and uprooted the gigantic mass from its seat, rightly judging that it would be no offense against religion if he took this marvel from one temple and consecrated it in Rome, which is to say, in the temple of the entire world. For a long time Constantine allowed it to lie there in Egypt while the means to convey it were readied. After the stone was transported down the channel of the Nile and unloaded in Alexandria, a ship of unheard of size needing three hundred rowers was constructed for the voyage by sea.

When things had progressed this far, Constantine died, and the project languished. Finally, however, under Constantius the obelisk was loaded on the ship, and floated across the sea and up the Tiber…it was unloaded three miles south of the city in the Vicus of Alexander. There it was placed on sleds, dragged slowly through the Ostian Gate, between the two Aventines, and on into the Circus Maximus. …

Other obelisks were brought to Rome after Augustus's day; of these, one stands on the Vatican, another in the Gardens of Sallust, and two in front of the mausoleum of Augustus.

As for Constantius's obelisk that stands today in the Circus, I give below a Greek translation of the hieroglyphs cut long ago in its stone, found in a book by Hermapion: …

[first line, south side:]

"Helios, the sun-god, speaks to Ramestes. I have granted you joyful dominion over the inhabited earth, you whom Helios loves. …"

Ammianus, *History* 17.4.1, 12–18

94.6   The emperor Constantius, regaining the world entire,
Dedicates this work and gift of his father [Constantine the Great],
    Rome, to you,
And founds a marvel your earth never carried and your past never saw,
A gift to match the emperor's glorious victories.
His father, intending for this monument to grace
Constantinople, removed it from Thebes, where it was quarried …

ILS 736, lines 1–6 = *CIL* 6.1163

Fig. 51 Altar of Augustan Peace

95. Altar of Augustan Peace ("Ara Pacis Augustae")

COMMENTARY

The Altar of Augustan Peace originally stood between the Sundial of Augustus and the Via Lata, the main road by which Augustus had returned to Rome in 13 BC after a three-year absence in Spain and Gaul. In some respects the altar was a companion to the Altar of Fortuna Redux (of "Prosperity Restored") decreed for the Via Appia when Augustus returned to Rome from that direction in 19 BC, but as its name and Ovid's poem [95.5] bring out, Augustus's return in this instance is treated as a synecdoche for the return of peace in general after the civil wars. In subsequent generations the Pax worshipped here in a minor cult grows still wider into the concept of the Pax Romana and receives a major temple in Vespasian's Forum of Peace.

The altar itself was surrounded by a precinct wall covered with sculptured reliefs that are among ancient Rome's finest public art, portraying not only a religious procession of the imperial family and other Romans, but the world of nature, both vegetative and allegorical, prospering as if in response to the right rule of Augustus.

Much of the Altar of Peace remains today, parts of it having been painstakingly excavated from among the foundations of buildings in 1937–1938. It was reassembled, however, not in its original location but next to the Mausoleum of Augustus at the northern reaches of the Campus, housed first in a glass and concrete pavilion from the Fascist era that has since been demolished in favor of a more elaborate installment for the Altar designed by Robert Meier (to the dismay of those who wish to see the Porta Ripetta restored instead. This was Rome's upstream port and a major point of contact between the city and its river before the Tiber embankments and their roads were constructed).

SOURCES

95.1   In the consulships of Tiberius Nero and Publius Quintilius [13 BC], when I returned to Rome after my successful conduct of affairs in Spain and Gaul, the Senate resolved that an altar to Augustan Peace, consecrated to my return, should be set up in the Campus Martius, and ordered that the magistrates, priests, and Vestal Virgins should perform an annual sacrifice.

Augustus, *Achievements* 12

95.2   In honor of my return, the Senate consecrated the Altar of Fortuna Redux next to the temples of Honor and Virtue at the Porta Capena, and ordered that the pontiffs and Vestal Virgins should make an annual sacrifice there on the anniversary of my return to the city from Syria [on Oct. 12th, 19 BC]; the Senate also named this day the Augustalia, after my cognomen.

Augustus, *Achievements* 11

95.3   [Under July 4 in a list of Roman holidays:] Holiday by decree of the Senate because on this day in the consulship of Nero and Varo [in 13 BC] the Altar of Augustan Peace in the Campus Martius was decreed.

Calendar Inscription (Fasti Amiterni)= *CIL* 1².244

95.4   [Under January 30 in a list of Roman holidays:]
Holiday by decree of the Senate because on this day in the consulship of Drusus and Crispinus [9 BC] the Altar of Augustan Peace in the Campus Martius was dedicated.

Fasti Praenestini

95.5   The day has come, the second to last of January,
    To celebrate the dedication of the Altar of Peace:
Goddess of Peace, be present, your tresses wreathed in the laurels
    Of Actium, and gently make the entire world your home.
As long as Rome lacks enemies (and chances for a triumph),
    Peace, not War, will give our leaders greatest glory.
Let soldiers wield their arms only against the aggressor,
    And reserve the horn's harsh tunes for civic celebrations.
Let all the lands, from first to last, fear to fight us,
    And if some lands lack fear of Rome, then let them love us.
Priests, now add the incense to the altar's flames of peace:
    Let the sacred victim, white and wine-splashed, fall,

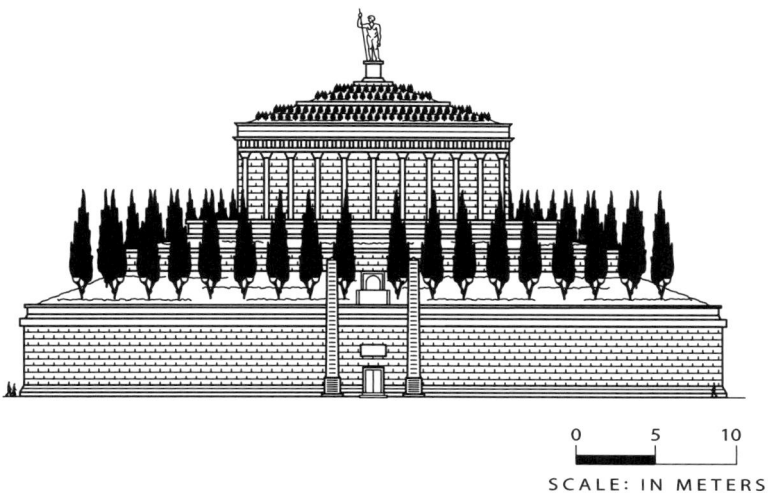

0   5   10

SCALE: IN METERS

Fig. 52 Mausoleum of Augustus (after Gatti)

And ask the gods to lend an ear to your pious prayers
That the House which brought us peace, in peace will long endure.
Ovid, *Fasti* 1.709–722

96. Mausoleum of Augustus (Fig. 52)

COMMENTARY

It may seem odd that one of Augustus's first major building projects was a giant tomb for himself and his family, but it was probably attractive for several reasons. Politically, it may have been motivated by the discovery (made when Augustus illegally opened Antony's will) that his opponent wished to be buried alongside Cleopatra in Alexandria [96.1], where it was also reported he planned to move the capital of Rome (thus anticipating by over three centuries Constantine's move to the East). Octavian's tomb—for he perhaps began it even before Actium and at any rate before he consolidated his power and received the title of Augustus—would have declared his allegiance to Italian soil, in contrast to his besotted rival in Egypt.

The size of the Mausoleum (40–45 m. high, 300 m. in diameter) makes it, at least in size, comparable to the eponymous Tomb of Mausolos in Halicarnassus, one of the Seven Wonders of the ancient world. Augustus's tomb never attained such a ranking, but it must have been a towering presence advertising the new ruler's power, wealth, and preeminence, whether visible up-close during a stroll in the park that surrounded it, or spotted afar by those approaching the city from the north and by those doing business elsewhere in the Campus Martius.

Because Augustus built his tomb relatively early in life, and because many in his family circle died untimely deaths, his tomb had received the ashes of several family members before his own were placed in its inner recesses in AD 14. The pre-deceased include Marcellus, his nephew, whose death in 23 BC Virgil movingly memorialized in Aeneas's trip to the Underworld. Then there were, among others, his sister Octavia, the trusted Agrippa, and the young Lucius and Gaius, his adopted heirs. Tacitus [96.10] calls the Mausoleum the "Tomb of the Julians," and that holds true not only of the Julio-Claudian emperors who died in good standing after Augustus (Tiberius and Claudius), but of Nerva, whose interment in AD 98 was probably the last burial to open its doors. Urns with the ashes of Vespasian, Domitian, and Titus were deposited in their own temple on the Quirinal, while Nerva's successor Trajan had his own special chamber at the base of the column at the head of his forum. After that, Hadrian's tomb functioned as the imperial mausoleum.

Augustus's implacable streak, exercised on the exiled Ovid and his books, was especially noted in his treatment of the two Julias, his daughter and granddaughter, whose indiscretions, particularly embarrassing in light of the patriarch's moral reforms, were a source of life-long bitterness to him, and he forbid their burial in the family tomb.

In addition to a statue of Augustus on the pinnacle of the tomb, two bronze columns or tablets were located at its entrance containing the long inscription known as the "Res Gestae," which was Augustus's own summation of his achievements for the Roman state. This inscription has survived not in its bronze version but carved on a temple to Augustus in Turkey. I have included here the sections of the inscription [96.13] that focus on Augustus's building activities in Rome, as partial illustration for Suetonius's famous exaggeration that Augustus transformed the capitol from brick (and an inferior sun-baked brick at that) to marble [96.14].

SOURCES

96.1 [In his will, illegally opened by Octavian and read to the Senate and in Assembly,] Antony ordered that he be buried in Alexandria at Cleopatra's side. In their outrage over this, the people were inclined to believe as true the rumor that Antony, if he should defeat Augustus, would give Rome as a gift to Cleopatra, and transfer the seat of power to Egypt.

Dio, History 50.3.5–4.1

96.2 Because the Romans regard with a religious reverance the grounds of the Campus Martius, they have built here the tombs of their most illustrious men and women. The most remarkable of these is the so-called Mausoleum, a great mound near the river ringed by a tall base of white stone and shaded by evergreens up to its crown. On the very top stands a bronze statue of Augustus Caesar. Beneath the mound are buried the remains of Augustus himself, his family, and his household. Behind the Mausoleum stretches a sacred grove with wonderful promenades.

In the middle of the Campus another wall of white marble encloses the place of Augustus's cremation. A circular iron fence surrounds the wall, inside of which black poplars have been planted.

Strabo, *Geography* 5.3.8

96.3   Although limits were placed on the extent of his funeral honors, Augustus was eulogized twice: once by Tiberius in front of the Temple of Julius Caesar, and again by Tiberius's son Drusus on the old rostra. After this, he was carried to the Campus Martius on the shoulders of senators, and cremated there; nor was an ex-praetor lacking to swear he saw his image ascend from the funeral pyre into the sky. The leading men of the equestrian order, in bare feet and unbelted tunics, gathered up his bones and deposited them in the Mausoleum. Augustus built this monument between the Via Flaminia and bank of the Tiber in his sixth consulship [28 BC], and opened up the surrounding groves and walkways to the public.

Suetonius, *Augustus* 100.3–4

96.4   How many cries of sorrow keened in the Campus will reach
Our mighty city of Mars! And you, Father Tiber,
What funerals you'll see, as you glide on past the fresh tomb!

Virgil, *Aeneid* 6.872–4

96.5   After Augustus buried Agrippa within your tomb, Marcellus,
      The same confines contained both of his sons-in-law,
And scarcely had its doors closed tightly on Agrippa
      When the emperor's sister herself received the funeral rites.
And now on top of these offerings three times given, a fourth
      In Drusus claims the imperial tears of the great Augustus.
Seal the doors now, Fates, of a sepulcher too often opened,
      Seal the doors: that dwelling has opened more than is just.

Consolation to Livia 67–74

96.6   [In his will,] Augustus forbade that either his daughter Julia or his granddaughter Julia should be interred in his tomb upon their deaths.

Suetonius, *Augustus* 101.3

96.7   [Here lies] Marcellus, son of Gaius, son-in-law of Caesar Augustus. [d. 23 BC]

[Here lies] Octavia, daughter of Gaius, sister of Caesar Augustus. [died AD 11]

L'Année Epigraphique 1928.2

96.8   [Herein lie the] bones of the emperor Tiberius, son of Augustus, Pontifex Maximus, with tribunician power 38 times, hailed Imperator eight times, consul five times. [died AD 37]

ILS 164 = *CIL* 6.887

96.9   [Herein lie the] bones of Agrippina, daughter of Marcus Agrippa, granddaughter of Augustus, wife of Germanicus, mother of the emperor Caligula. [died AD 33]

ILS 180 = *CIL* 6.886

96.10 [Nero's second wife] Poppaea died after Nero, in a flash of anger, kicked her when she was pregnant. … Her body was not cremated in the Roman custom, but was embalmed with spices in the manner of foreign kings and laid to rest in the tumulus of the Julians. [died AD 65]

Tacitus, *Annals* 16.6

96.11 When Nerva died, his body received an official escort of the Senate—as had Augustus's—to his burial place in the tomb of Augustus. [died AD 98]

Aurelius Victor, *On the Emperors* 12.12

96.12 Of the three scrolls that Augustus left behind him, one contained directions for his funeral, another contained an account of his achievements which he wished inscribed on bronze plaques and set up in front of his Mausoleum, and a third summarized the condition of the entire empire… .

Suetonius, *Augustus* 101.4

96.13 I, Augustus, built the following:
  the Senate House and [its annex] the Chalcidicum [28 BC];
  the Temple of Apollo on the Palatine, with porticoes [28 BC];
  the Temple of the Divine Julius [28 BC];
  the [shrine or grotto] of the Lupercal;
  the portico at the Circus Flaminius (which I let be named the
    Octavia, after Octavius, the builder of the earlier portico [167
    BC] on the same site) [33 BC];
  the box-seat for the gods [*pulvinar*] at the Circus Maximus;
  the temples of Jupiter Feretrius and Jupiter the Thunderer [22
    BC] on the Capitoline Hill;
  the Temple of Quirinus [16 BC];

the temples of Minerva [16 BC], Juno Regina, and Jupiter of Liberty on
the Aventine Hill;
the Temple of the Lares at the high point on the Sacred Way;
the Temple of the Divine Penates on the Velia;
the Temple of Youth;
the Temple of the Great Mother on the Palatine.

I restored the Capitoline Temple of Jupiter and the Theater of Pompey,
both at great expense and without any inscriptional credits to myself on
either building.

I restored the aqueduct channels that were collapsing from age in many
places, and doubled the volume of the water called the Marcia by adding a new
spring to its channel.

I finished two works begun and nearly completed by my father: the Forum
of Julius Caesar and the basilica [Julia] between the Temple of Castor and the
Temple of Saturn. When the basilica burned down, I enlarged its site and began [in
12 AD] to rebuild it in the name of my sons [Gaius and Lucius Caesar]; I ordered
that the work be completed by my heirs, should I die first.

I restored eighty two temples of the gods in Rome, by authority of
the Senate in my sixth consulship [28 BC], overlooking none that needed to
be restored.

In my seventh consulship [27 BC] I restored the Via Flaminia from Rome to
Rimini, and all of its bridges except the Milvian and Minucian.

I built with war booty the Temple of Mars the Avenger and the Forum of
Augustus [completed in 2 BC] on my own land.

I built the Theater [11 BC] beside the Temple of Apollo, for the most part
on ground that I purchased from private owners, and had it named after Marcus
Marcellus, my son-in-law.

I dedictated gifts from war booty to the Capitolium, to the Temple of the
Divine Caesar, to the Temple of Apollo, to the Temple of Vesta, and to the Temple
of Mars Ultor; their sum total was approximately 100,000,000 sesterces.

Augustus, *Achievements* 19–21

96.14 Finding Rome's architecture both lacking in imperial dignity and
prone to floods and fires, Augustus improved the city so greatly that he
could rightly boast to have found it sun-baked brick and left it marble.

Suetonius, *Augustus* 28.3

97. Mausoleum of Hadrian

COMMENTARY
 As with the Pantheon, Hadrian's other famous surviving structure in Rome, the Mausoleum of Hadrian recalls Augustan rule, and
once again, while preserving the overall dimensions of his predecessor's
monument, the result is a different order of splendor and complexity.

Fig. 53 Mausoleum of Hadrian (Castel S. Angelo), as seen from the Pons Aelius

In the case of his tomb, he didn't replace the Augustan structure, but built a new one across the river, though closely connecting it to the Campus Martius with a new bridge called the Pons Aelius after Hadrian's family name. Brick stamps show construction on the mausoleum began in AD 134, four years before Hadrian's death, but it was only finished under his successor Antoninus Pius, whose dedicatory inscription [97.4] dated to AD 139 once stood over the entrance.

Though some of the tomb's interior complexity can still be experienced, not only the tomb's lavish decoration of statuary and marble but its upper reaches have been stripped or destroyed. Its basic structure was a tall square podium (87 m.) surmounted in the middle by a solid cylinder, the concrete core of which is visible today. An entrance corridor, aligned with the bridge, led straight into a ground-floor chamber with a large niche (probably for a statue of Hadrian). From this chamber, a helicoidal staircase led up through the mass of the cylinder to reach in one spiral the level of the burial chamber, reached by a radial corridor that led to the center of the tomb. (Today's corridor, built in 1492, still leads into this chamber, but on a ramp that crosses the burial chamber high above its floor). Further ancient ramps or stairs led to higher chambers, but the configuration of the top of the tomb is not known. Presumably then, as today, one could walk to the top to enjoy panoramic views of the river and the city beyond.

The central burial chamber had three arched niches to display the funerary urns. Inscriptions and the sources tell us that the Mausoleum of Hadrian was in use from his death in AD 138 at least until the death of Caracalla in AD 217, the sixth emperor to be buried in the tomb and the last recorded deposition of imperial remains in it.

Even in antiquity, however, the tomb began to function as the fortress for which it was so well suited, being not only tall, sheer, and sturdy but perfectly situated as a bridgehead that preserved access to the right bank of the Tiber via the Pons Aelius. Sometime after the Aurelian Wall was built and before the Ostrogoths besieged the city in the sixth century, the tomb had been incorporated into Rome's defenses. Later it became a papal fortress, accessible from the Vatican in times of trouble by means of an elevated walkway built in 1277. The common name for the fortress/tomb, Castel S. Angelo, derives from a vision Pope Gregory the Great had in AD 590, when, shortly before a terrible plague was lifted from the city, he saw the archangel Michael sheath his sword, as depicted by the statue on top of the fortress today.

SOURCES

97.1   Hadrian built the bridge named for his family [the Pons Aelius] and the tomb alongside the Tiber.

Imperial Lives, *Hadrian* 19.11

97.2   Hadrian lived for 62 years, 5 months, and 19 days, having ruled for 20 years and 11 months. He was buried right by the river, in front of the Aelian bridge. It was here that he had prepared his tomb, since the Mausoleum of Augustus was full and from this time forward received no more remains.

Dio, *History* 69.23.1

97.3   Among the projects of Antoninus Pius that remain today … is the Tomb of Hadrian, which he completed.

Imperial Lives, *Antoninus Pius* 8.2

97.4   Antoninus Pius…set this up [in AD 139] in honor of his parents, the late emperor Hadrian (son of the deified Trajan, grandson of the deified Nerva)…and the deified Sabina.

ILS 322 = *CIL* 6.984

97.5   [Epitaph]   In memory of the empress Faustina, wife of Antoninus Pius… .

ILS 349 = *CIL* 6.987

97.6   [Epitaph]   In memory of emperor Caesar Titus Aelius Hadrianus Antoninus Augustus Pius [died AD 161], Pontifex Maximus, with tribunician power 23 times, hailed as imperator twice, consul four times, Father of his Country.

ILS 346 = *CIL* 6.986

97.7   Spurred on by the emperor Commodus's cruelty, which they had endured too long, Laetus, prefect of the guard, and Marcia, Commodus's concubine, formed a conspiracy to assassinate the emperor. First they tried to poison him. When that didn't work, they had his athletic trainer strangle him.

The people and Senate demanded that Commodus's corpse be dragged by hook and thrown in the Tiber, but the new emperor Pertinax ordered it taken to the Tomb of Hadrian.

Imperial Lives, *Commodus* 17.1–4

97.8   [Epitaph]   In memory of the emperor Commodus, son of the deified Marcus Aurelius, grandson of the deified Antoninus Pius, great-grandson of the deified Hadrian, great-great-grandson of the deified Trajan, and great-great-great-grandson of the deified Nerva … .

ILS 401 = *CIL* 6.992

97.9   [When the emperor Septimius Severus died in Britain] his sons Caracalla and Geta each got an equal share in the rule of the empire. They decided to sail from Britain, and arrived in Rome escorting the remains of their father, which had been placed in an alabaster urn after his cremation. This they intended to place in the sacred imperial mausoleum. …

When they arrived in Rome … the brothers, dressed in the imperial purple, led a procession, followed by the consuls carrying the urn with the remains of Severus. Those who approached the new emperors in greeting also bowed before the urn. … They escorted the urn to the shrine that displays the sacred tombs of Marcus Aurelius and his imperial predecessors [=Hadrian's Mausoleum].

Herodian, *History* 3.15.7 and 4.1.3–4

97.10   The remains of Severus were interred in the tomb of Marcus Aurelius, who was Severus's favorite of all the emperors.

Imperial Lives, *Severus* 19.3

97.11   The body of Caracalla was cremated and his bones placed in the tomb of the Antonines. They had to be smuggled in secretly, since everyone—senators and commoners, men and women alike—bore him a passionate hatred.

Dio, *History* 79.9.1

97.12   [The Goths, under Vittigis, subjected Rome to a lengthy siege and fought several battles with the Romans, who were led by the famous general Belisarius.] One of the Gothic assaults [in AD 537] occurred in the following manner at the Porta Cornelia, just in front of the Aelian Bridge.

Across the bridge, not more than a stone's throw outside this gate, stands the spectacular tomb of the Emperor Hadrian, made out of white marble from Paros that is fit together with such precision that no mortar was needed. It has four sides of equal length, again about the distance of a stone's throw; their height exceeds that of the city's defensive walls. On top of the tomb's outer walls, statues of men and horses are mounted, beautifully carved from the same white marble as the walls. Since it occurred to earlier inhabitants that the tomb might serve as an enemy fortress against the city (it does indeed look like a high tower built opposite the gate), they made it part of the city's defenses by extending two walls to it from the circuit walls [running from the sides of the tomb to the right bank?].... .

When the Goths made their assault, they mounted an attack at both this tomb and the Porta Cornelia. They had no siege engines, but carried numerous ladders and thought they could easily overwhelm the defenders with showers of arrows and then take the fortress without much trouble because it was undermanned. Equipped with long shields, the Goths advanced under the cover of the colonnade extending from the Aelian bridge to St. Peter's, thereby escaping the notice of the Romans until they were quite close to the tomb, where they sprung out and immediately began fighting. Their proximity took the Roman ballistae out of play (since these machines can only shoot horizontally) and the long shields of the Goths protected them from the defender's arrows. The Goths kept up their assault, sending out volley after volley, and were on the point of setting up their ladders. ...

For a short time the Romans were at a loss, unable to find a way to defend themselves. Then by mutual agreement they shattered most of the huge marble statues into hundreds of rocks, and began to hurl them down on the heads of the enemy. The Goths gave way under this barrage [and soon were routed].

Procopius, *Wars* 5.19, 5.22.12–22

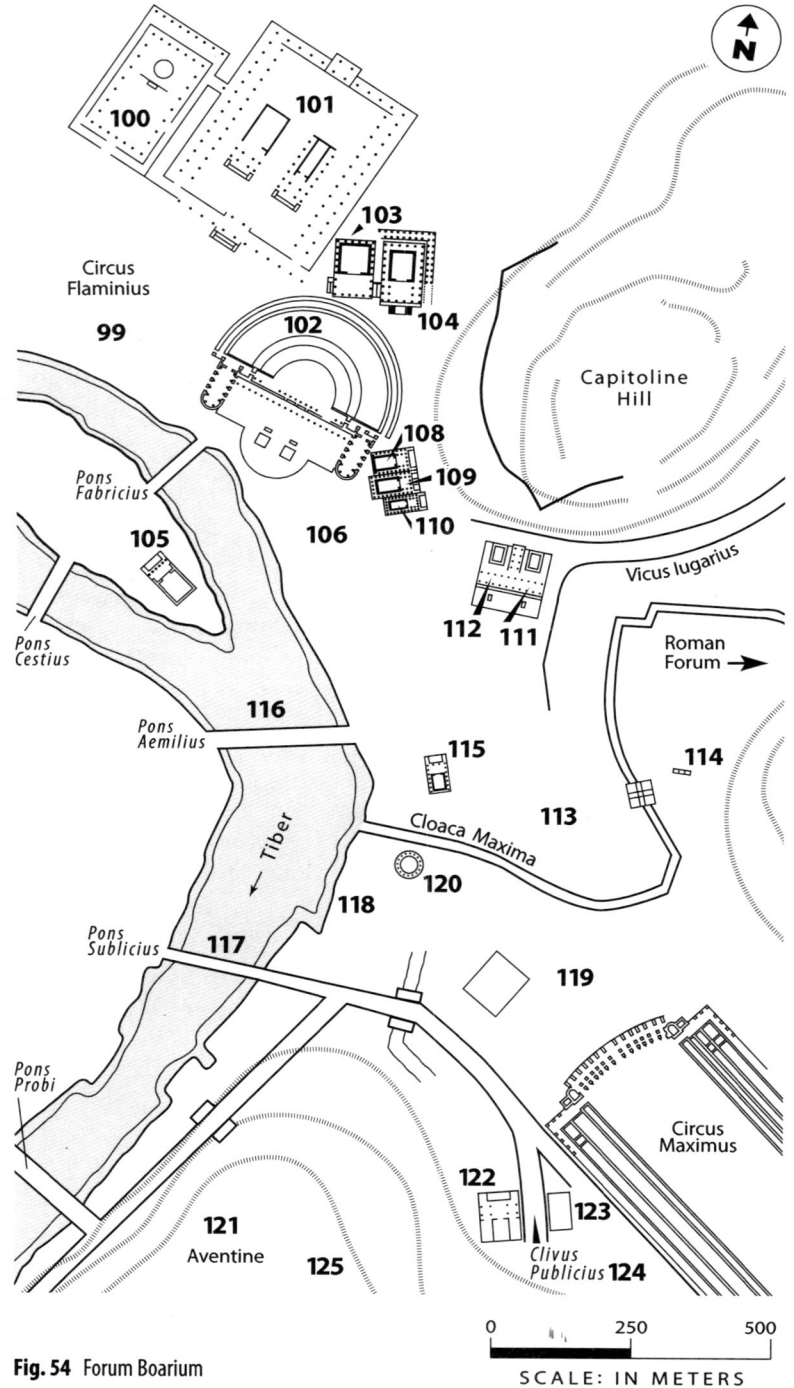

Fig. 54 Forum Boarium

SCALE: IN METERS

X. Forum Boarium and Aventine Hill

98. Overview of Forum Boarium

Although the various quarters of the city covered in this section had no special administrative or topographical unity, and the first part of it, treating the area around the Circus Flaminius, is often included in modern discussions of the Campus Martius, there is one element that the entire area, from the Circus Flaminius to the south side of the Aventine Hill, shares in addition to their proximity to the Tiber on its lower course through the city: each section has strong connections to plebeian and/or mercantile interests. These interests are most dramatically asserted on the Aventine Hill, where the temples and even the real estate were conceived as being in distinct opposition to the political and economic interests of the patricians, but the lower zones along the river were precisely the areas dominated by the utilitarian activities engaged in by the lower social orders. That this was a topographical characteristic recognized in antiquity is best suggested in the following passage by Valerius Maximus, when in a discussion of filial piety, (which, significantly for the importance of Roman topography in Roman thought, proceeds by means of exempla attached to specific monuments in the city), Valerius moves from the elite precincts of the Temple of Vesta in the Forum to the Temple of Pietas in the vegetable market along the river:

> **98.1** Please forgive us, O venerable hearths of Vesta, if in our discussion of Pietas we turn from your holiest of temples and proceed to a section of the city that is more commercial than beautiful: for the worth of Pietas is not cheapened by the harshness of circumstance or any squalor, which serve rather to confirm its worth.
>
> **Valerius Maximus**, *Sayings* 5.4.7

Under Augustus, the social distinction between the characteristic activities of these two areas even took on a stark visual expression:

> **98.2** Augustus gave the aediles the task of making sure that no one was allowed in the Forum or the Circus unless they wore a toga without a cloak.
>
> **Suetonius**, *Augustus* 40.5

Since the bright, expensive whiteness of togas formed such a contrast to the common darker clothing, infractions would have been easy to detect; if enforced, such a dress-code would have formed an effective barrier between the work of the riverside and the business of the Forum.

In an earlier chapter, "The Site of Rome," I included sources describing, from a vantage point privileged by hindsight, how Rome was ideally located for greatness, accounts in which the Tiber was given a major role [1., 2.]. The sources in this section give a more detailed picture of this particular area where, from the privileged vantage point of most ancient writers, hands were sullied by labor and souls corrupted by commerce.

In terms of natural topography, the area was distinguished by the river-crossing below the Tiber island. There is archaeological evidence from as far back as the fourteenth century BC that the salt road from the Apennines crossed the Tiber here by ford or ferry (heading for the salt flats north of the Tiber mouth), and that there was significant north-south traffic along routes that were later developed as the Via Aurelia north and the Via Appia south. There is also ample archaeological evidence of Greek trade in this area as early as the eighth century BC.

99. Circus Flaminius

COMMENTARY

The Circus Flaminius was not a built-up stadium with permanent seating in the manner of the Circus Maximus but part of an open area (the Campus Flaminius) that could be used for the Taurian horse races every five years, assemblies, markets, and as a staging ground for the triumphal processions that set out from here. The zone of the Circus Flaminius extended lengthwise along the river, over much of the area that later became the Jewish ghetto; today, Rome's primary synagogue stands roughly in the middle of the former circus area, on its southern side. The area was eventually reduced, and became bordered with architectural distinction on the north side by the Temple of Hercules of the Muses [100.] and the Porticus of Metellus/Octavia [101.], and terminated on the east by the Theater of Marcellus [102.] when that monument was built under Caesar and Augustus. Nothing of this Circus remains to be seen, although the ruins of the Porticus of Octavia help to locate the circus's northeastern corner.

Confusing the sources' picture of the circus's history, it seems that the area, for one reason or another, was early on connected with the name Flaminius, long before Gaius Flaminius carried out his significant development of the area. Gaius Flaminius, it should be noted, was a supporter of plebeian interests who was opposed by most members of the Roman Senate. His reputation suffered further damage when he and 15,000 soldiers, ambushed in the morning fog, were killed by Hannibal's forces at Lake Trasimene in 217 BC.

SOURCES

99.1 [In 449 BC the tribunes of the plebs called the people to vote.] These matters were transacted by the Assembly of the Plebs in the Flaminian Fields, which are now called the Circus Flaminius.

Livy, *History* 3.54.15

99.2 Gaius Flaminius, when he was censor, paved the Via Flaminia and built the Circus Flaminius [in 221 BC].

Livy, *Summary*, Bk. 20

99.3 The Circus Flaminius got its name because it is built around [*circum*] the Campus Flaminius, and because during the Taurian Games, which are held here, the horses run around [*circum*] the turning posts.

Varro, *The Latin Language* 5.154

99.4 The fickle tribune Fufius called upon Pompey to address the Assembly. This was being held in the Circus Flaminius, where, on the same day, a festive market-day crowd had gathered.

Cicero, *Letters to Atticus* 1.14.1

100. Temple of Hercules, Defender of the Muses
(*Aedes Hercules Musarum*)

COMMENTARY

Nothing remains of this temple to Hercules, but fragments of the Marble Plan locate it on the west side of the Porticus of Octavia, surrounded by a portico of its own, and an image on an ancient coin suggests that the temple was round. The sources, however, provide us with a glimpse into the temple's significance for the Romans as an architectural and public expression of the link between military power and the arts, and more personally, between commanders and poets. The symbiotic relationship described in the panegyric [100.2] reflects the particular circumstances of the temple's founder, Fulvius Nobilior, who in league with the great Roman poet Ennius forged a new, more Hellenistic model of poetic patronage, conveniently patterned by Hercules as patron of the Muses. Ennius was not only on Nobilior's staff to Ambracia but wrote a poem celebrating the campaign. This relationship, however, persisted as the paradigm into Cicero's time, who devoted a good portion of his speech defending the poet Archias to a description of the services that a poet can provide his Roman Hercules. Cicero's mention [100.1] of the temple in support of his defense of poetry is an excellent example of how the topography of Rome and its monuments were repositories of communal memory that could be exploited to give expression and authority to ideas and arguments.

SOURCES

100.1 [Gentlemen of the jury: great generals from Rome's past knew the importance of poetry.] Even the famous Fulvius Nobilior, who waged war in northern Greece [in 189 BC] with the poet Ennius on his staff, did not hesitate to consecrate the spoils of the war to the Muses. Therefore it is fitting that, in a city where generals of Rome, while still practically in battle gear, saw fit to honor the names of poets and temples of the Muses, Roman jurors today [in 62 BC] should not shrink from offering respect to the Muses and protection to their poets.

Cicero, *In Defense of Archias* 27

100.2 The famous Fulvius Nobilior built the Temple of Hercules, Friend of the Muses, in the Circus Flaminius, using funds at his disposal as censor. He did this not only because he was fond of literature and was a friend of Rome's greatest poet, Ennius, but because when campaigning in Greece he had learned of Hercules "Musagetes," that is, of Hercules as a companion and leader of the Muses. As a result, he was the first Roman to consecrate nine statues of the Muses, brought to Rome from Ambracia in western Greece, under the guardianship of

Hercules's powerful spirit—as is in reality the case, since the two do-mains ought to be mutually supportive of one another with the characteristic virtue of each: the tranquility of the Muses is safeguarded by the protection of Hercules, and the deeds of Hercules are given fame by the Muses.

Latin Panegyrics 9.7.3

101. The Porticus of Octavia (and earlier, the Porticus of Metellus)

COMMENTARY

The Porticus of Octavia was built by Augustus but in the name of his sister, as Suetonius stresses in a passage that shows how active Augustus's building program was in this part of the city. The Augustan colonnades replaced the earlier Porticus of Metellus, which may have been the first colonnade in Rome to wrap around a square. Like the Porticus of Octavia, the Porticus of Metellus was built to surround the temples of Juno Regina and Jupiter Stator (not to be confused with the Temple to Jupiter Stator near the Sacra Via), which were also rebuilt in Augustus's time. Pliny's explanation [101.4] for the gender reversal of the cult art in each of these temples (a mistake by the movers) is perhaps to be connected with Velleius's identification [101.2] of these temples as the ones "lacking inscriptions."

Both porticoes were well-known for the famous works of art displayed in their precincts. The Porticus of Octavia housed a major library as well, which, like the library in the precinct of Apollo on the Palatine, refused to admit the poetry of Ovid into its holdings.

A significant section of the monumental gateway leading into the Porticus survives behind the Theater of Marcellus and contains the inscription of the Severan restoration in AD 203 after a fire [101.5]. The stone of the pediment was recycled, as can clearly be seen from the irregularities of the back-side surface; most probably this view was origi-nally obscured, since it would be some time before such open displays of cost-cutting were common.

SOURCES

101.1 During the final pitched battle in his conquest of the Ligurians, Marcus Aemilius Lepidus vowed a temple to Juno Regina [in 187 BC].

Livy, *History* 39.2.11

101.2 Metellus Macedonicus was the original builder of the colon-nades (*porticus*) around the two temples lacking inscriptions that are now surrounded by the Porticus of Octavia. He also brought back from Macedonia the squadron of equestrian statues that face the front of these temples and are still the outstanding ornament of the site. It is said that Alexander the Great had these statues cast by Lysippus, the greatest bronze sculptor of his day, requesting that the horsemen resemble companions Alexander lost in the cavalry battle at the river Granicus; one of the riders is said to look like Alexander himself.

Metellus was the very first person in Rome to construct a temple out of marble, which was located among the monuments just mentioned. He can thus be called the originator of this sort of grandeur (or rather luxury).

Velleius, *History* 1.11.3–5

101.3 Augustus even constructed some buildings under the names of others in his family, … such as the Porticus of Octavia and the Theater of Marcellus. In addition, he often encouraged other leading men, each according to his means, to improve the city's appearance by financing new monuments or rebuilding and ornamenting old ones. And many monuments were indeed built by many patrons: the Temple of Hercules, Defender of the Muses, was rebuilt by Marcius Philippus, Augustus's stepfather; … a theater was built by Cornelius Balbus, an amphitheater by Statilius Taurus, and numerous outstanding works by Marcus Agrippa.

Suetonius, *Augustus* 29.4–5

101.4 Nor should we forget the artists Saurus and Batrachus, who [in Augustus's time] rebuilt the two temples that are enclosed in the Porticus of Octavia. … Curiously, in the one to Jupiter, the paintings and all the other decorations have themes concerning women. It is said that this temple was intended for Juno but that the movers switched the cult-statues by mistake. This alteration was subsequently preserved by religious scruple, as if the gods themselves had thereby chosen their seat. For the same reason, the ornamentation originally designed for Jupiter is found in the neighboring temple to Juno.

Pliny the Elder, *Encyclopedia* 36.42–43

101.5 Inscription on the Porticus of Octavia:

[IMP. CAES. L. SEPTIMIU]S SEVERUS PIUS PERTINAX AUG. ARABIC. AD[IABENIC. PAR]THIC. MAXIMUS / TRIB. POTEST. XI IMP. XI COS. III P. P. ET / [IMP. CAES. M. AURELIU]S ANTONINUS PIUS FELIX AUG. [TRIB. POTEST. VI] COS PROCOS / INCENDIO CORRUPTAM REST[ITUERUNT]

[In AD 203] the emperor Caesar Lucius Septimius Severus Pius Pertinax Augustus Arabicus Adiabenicus Maximus, with tribunician power for the 11ᵗʰ time, hailed as Imperator 11 times, consul for the third time, father of his country, and the emperor Caesar Marcus

Aurelius Antoninus Pius Felix Augustus [= Caracalla], with tribunician power for the sixth time, consul and proconsul, restored this portico ruined by fire.

CIL 6.1034

101.6 Appointed by Augustus, the freedman Gaius Melissus assumed responsibility for arranging the libraries in the Porticus of Octavia.

Suetonius, *On Grammarians* 21

101.7 [Epitaph:] In memory of Philoxenus Julianus, a slave posted at the Greek library in the Porticus of Octavia.

ILS 1972 = *CIL* 6.2348

101.8 [Ovid's book continues its journey looking for a home in Rome; see 63.7]

Rejected, I head for the temples adjoining a nearby theater,
Only to find that these are barred to my entrance as well.

Ovid, *Tristia* 3.1.69–70

102. Theater of Marcellus

COMMENTARY

The Theater of Marcellus was the largest of Rome's three theaters in seating capacity. It lacked the large portico-annex of the theaters of Balbus and Pompey nearby, although the Porticus of Octavia, rebuilt about the same time as the Theater of Marcellus, in effect served as a portico-annex nearly as large as Pompey's and would have protected the crowds in a downpour. Richardson speculates that the stage-area for this theater was more provisional and adaptable than in traditional theaters, allowing a greater variety of spectacles (such as gladiatorial shows and animal hunts) to be produced here that took advantage of an area included in the theater behind the stage.

The Theater of Marcellus can be seen in relation not only to the Porticus of Octavia, but to the Temple of Apollo as well. Livy refers to an earlier theater located close to the Temple of Apollo [102.1]. Little else is known about this theater, but as with the theater built against the Palatine for the dramatic performances in honor of the Great Mother, this earlier theater was probably connected with dramatic performances (*ludi scaenici*) in honor of Apollo, who had his own important festival (the Ludi Apollinares) in various venues. It is perhaps significant that Augustus [102.3] also identifies the Theater of Marcellus as the theater "beside the Temple of Apollo," suggesting that this former connection with Apollo and dramatic performances at the adjacent theater was still perceived. If so, the ensemble of temple, theater, porticus, and senate chamber found unified in Pompey's theater complex had an earlier, looser connection here, all parts of which were upgraded in Augustus's day.

Several Corinthian columns of Luna marble and some of the entablature that belonged to the Temple of Apollo Medicus ("The Healer") have survived to suggest something of the temple's beauty. They belong to a restoration carried out in Augustus's early reign, probably by Gaius Sosius (hence Pliny's epithet [103.5] for the temple, Sosianus), a consul in 32 BC and a one-time opponent of Augustus who later fell in line. The sources reveal that the Temple of Apollo Medicus, like the Porticus of Octavia next to it, was a repository of famous art.

SOURCES

102.1   When censor [in 179 BC] Lepidus financed the building of a theater and stage at the Temple of Apollo.

Livy, *History* 40.51.3

102.2   Caesar was eager to build a theater to match Pompey's, and laid the foundations for one before his death [in 44 BC], but Augustus had to finish it and named it after his nephew Marcus Marcellus. Caesar, however, got blamed for the demolition of the houses and temples on the site, and also because he burned their cult statues (almost all of which were wooden) and appropriated the large sums of money housed in the temples.

Dio, *History* 43.49.3

102.3   I built the theater that stands beside the Temple of Apollo, for the most part on land that I purchased from private owners; I named this theater after Marcus Marcellus, my son-in-law.

Augustus, *Achievements* 21

102.4   [As part of the Secular Games in 17 BC] we gave shows…at the theater located in the Circus Flaminius.

ILS 5050.156–8 = *CIL* 6.32323

102.5   Augustus was the first person to exhibit a tiger in Rome; tamed and caged, it was displayed at the dedication of the Theater of Marcellus on May 7 [11 BC], in the consulships of Quintus Tubero and Paullus Fabius.

Pliny the Elder, *Encyclopedia* 8.65

102.6   When the emperor Vespasian dedicated the new stage at the Theater of Marcellus, in addition to plays he brought back the old entertainment of talent shows. He awarded 400,000 sesterces to the tragic actor Apelles, 200,000 each to two lyre-players, numerous awards of 100,000 and 40,000, and many gold crowns.

Suetonius, *Vespasian* 19.1

103. Temple of Apollo Medicus

SOURCES

103.1 An epidemic that year [433 BC] forced other problems into the background. The Temple of Apollo was vowed for the people's health. … The losses in both city and countryside were nonetheless severe, striking humans and livestock alike.

Livy, *History* 4.25.3

103.2 Gaius Julius, consul [in 431 BC], dedicated the Temple of Apollo when his fellow consul Quinctius Cincinnatus was away at war, without drawing lots. When Quinctius learned of this after he had disbanded his troops and returned to the city, he took offense but complained to the Senate in vain.

Livy, *History* 4.29.7

103.3 Lest you think that Cicero in his speech is referring to the beautiful temple of Apollo *on the Palatine*, you should remember that he could only have meant the one which lies outside the Porta Carmentalis, between the Forum Holitorium and the Circus Flaminius, since that was the only one existing in Rome in Cicero's time.

Asconius, on Cicero's *Toga* 80–81

103.4 Marcus Fulvius Nobilior returned from Aetolia [in 187 BC]. In a meeting of the Senate convened in the Temple of Apollo, he recounted his military achievements abroad, and petitioned the senators to grant him a triumph. … After the tribune who objected left the temple to much criticism, the praetor put the matter to a vote, and a triumph was decreed.

Livy, *History* 39.4.1–2, 5.6

103.5 There is some doubt as to whether the statues of Niobe's dying children in the Temple of Apollo Sosianus are the work of Scopas or Praxiteles.

Pliny the Elder, *Encyclopedia* 36.28

104. Temple of Bellona

COMMENTARY

Bellona was another ancient Italic deity of warfare. As the passage by Livy [104.2] may suggest by locating the temple's inceptive vow in the thick of ferocious fighting, Bellona was warfare in its most frenzied dimension, recognized and worshipped as the necessary but transgressive brutality of the battlefield. The temple was a common place for meetings of the Senate, especially when they deliberated over the awarding of triumphs and the declaration of war.

In the demolitions of the 1930s that opened up the Forum Boarium area for Mussolini's "Road to the Sea," the drab remains of a temple podium were uncovered on the east side of the Temple of Apollo, and this is now considered the best candidate for the Temple of Bellona. A location here accords well with the detail by Ovid [104.3] that there was a narrow line of sight from the temple to the end of the Circus— presumably the Circus Flaminius, which would in Ovid's day have been just visible between the Theater of Marcellus and the corner of the Porticus of Octavia.

SOURCES

104.1 The goddess of battle is called Bellona. A short column stands in front of her temple called the Columna Bellica, and it is customary to throw a spear over this column whenever the Romans declare war.

Festus 30

104.2 It is reported that during a critical part of battle against the Samnites [in 296 BC], the general Appius Claudius was seen in the front lines raising his hands as he uttered this prayer: "Bellona, if you grant us victory today, I vow to build you a temple." ... The Samnite camp was captured and plundered, and the massive amount of booty there was given over to the soldiers. 7,800 of the enemy were slain in this battle.

Livy, *History* 10.19.17, 22

104.3   From the temple, one small place gives a view of the Circus,
        And here there stands a little column of no little fame:
    From here, when war is declared, by custom a spear is hurled
        Against the king and people that Rome has decided to fight.

Ovid, *Fasti* 6.205–208

104.4 No tyrant was ever more thirsty for human blood than Sulla, who ordered 7,000 Roman citizens to be killed [for backing the opposing faction in a civil war], a deed which took place while he was presiding over the Senate in session nearby at the Temple of Bellona. When Sulla heard the screams of the men being butchered with swords, he said to the terrified senators: "Let us continue our business, Senators; a few traitors are being executed by my orders."

Seneca the Younger, *On Clemency* 1.12.2

105. Tiber Island and the Temple of Aesculapius

COMMENTARY

Although nothing of the Temple of Aesculapius remains to be seen, the Tiber Island preserves several interesting reminders of its ancient past. The hospital that dominates the island today is a reminder that this was the ancient city's center for healing and home to the healing god Aesculapius (a more approachable divinity, or hero, than Olympian Apollo). Sanctuaries to Aesculapius (the Greek Asklepios) were typically located on the edges of a city, for both hygienic and symbolic reasons; here, the Tiber's only island provides a similarly marginal area close to town. There are also remains of some travertine embankment walls that gave the downstream end of the island the shape of a ship, reflecting the origins of the snake-god's arrival in Rome by boat, as described by Livy [105.2] (a longer poetic account of this arrival can be found in Book 15 of Ovid's *Metamorphoses*). These ruins, on the north side of the island's "stern," can be seen from the bridge downstream of the island, where one can also make out the image, carved in a travertine medallion, of a snake coiled around a staff, the icon of the god and a fore-runner of the medical profession's icon today.

The Pons Fabricius leading to the island from the left bank is the best preserved of Rome's ancient bridges. The Pons Cestius, connecting the island to the Transtiber, has been largely rebuilt in modern times.

SOURCES

105.1 [After the Tarquin royal family had been expelled from Rome in 509 BC,] their land, which lay between the city and the river, was consecrated to Mars and became the Campus Martius. It is said that the Campus happened to be covered at that time with a crop of wheat ready for harvest, but since it was now consecrated and could not be consumed, a large crew of men was sent in together to cut it down, stalk and all, and carry it in baskets to the Tiber, where it was to be dumped. Since it was midsummer and the river was low, as is usual at that time of year, heaps of grain piled up in the shallows and became coated with sediment. Gradually an island arose, enlarged by the various materials that the current accumulated here. Later, I presume, man-made embankments were added and improvements carried out to create a platform suitably high above the water and firm enough to sustain even temples and colonnades.

Livy, *History* 2.5.2–4

105.2   When Rome was suffering from a plague, ambassadors traveled to Epidaurus [in 293 BC] to transfer the cult statue of Aesculapius to Rome. They came back instead with the snake that the divine power of the god himself was said to inhabit. In Rome, the snake left the ship and went ashore at the island in the Tiber, where the Romans then founded the temple to Aesculapius.

Livy, *Summary* Book 11

105.3   Marcus Ulpius Honoratus ... set this memorial up to Aesculapius and Hygieia, in return for his own health, his family's, and his doctor's, Lucius Julius Helix, who, alongside these gods, has taken expert care of me.

ILS 2194 = *CIL* 6.19

105.4   Since some people were abandoning slaves weakened by illness on the island of Aesclepius instead of troubling to care for them, the Emperor Claudius decreed that such slaves were to be set free if they recovered.

Suetonius, *Claudius* 25.2

105.5   Inscription on the Pons Fabricius:
L(ucius) FABRICIUS, C(ai) F(ilius), CUR(ator) VIAR(um), FACIUNDUM (pontem) COERAVIT.
[Note: coeravit = curavit]

Lucius Fabricius, son of Gaius and Curator of Roads, under-took the construction of this bridge [in 62 BC].

ILS 5892 = *CIL* 1305

106. The Forum Holitorium and four temples

Overview

The Forum Holitorium was, as its name and Varro [106.1] tell us, a vegetable market between the Capitoline and the Tiber just downstream of the Theater of Marcellus. The ruins of three temples partially preserved within and alongside the S. Nicola in Carcere, a small church next to the theater, locate the market in general, perhaps designated the edge of a more or less open square that occupied the available space between the temples and the base of the Capitoline Hill and included some of the ground eventually taken up by the theater.

The identity of the three temples at S. Nicola in Carcere is disputed. The sources refer to four temples in the area of the Forum Holitorium: oldest to youngest, these were Janus, Spes ("Hope"), Juno Sospita, and Pietas, all built in the third and second centuries BC. The temple to Pietas is generally located north of the three S. Nicola temples (although Richardson, 290, identifies it as the southern-most of these three temples). Coarelli reasons that since the fire of 213 BC burned the Temple of Hope but not the Janus, an open space existed between them that was later filled by the temple to Juno, thus identifying hers as the middle of the three temples. At any rate, all four temples, which were located on the triumphal route, were built in fulfillment of a vow made before a battle: Janus and Hope in the first war against Carthage, Juno in the campaign against the Insubrians (one of the more powerful peoples settled between the Po and the Alps), and Pietas in a battle against the Seleucid king Antiochus. The density of temples in this area (which included not only these four, but the five cited previously around the Circus Flaminius) is understandable as prime location along the triumphal parades that began in the circus. In front of S. Nicola in Carcere are remnants of arcades belonging to covered colonnades that lined the triumphal route here.

SOURCES

106.1 [Varro on the etymology of the market-place names:] Merchandise of the same product can provide the distinguishing name to a part of the city, as in the case of the Forum Bovarium, for its cattle [*boves*], and the Forum Holitorium, for its vegetable-growers [*holitor*]; this was the ancient Market Grounds, with an abundance of vegetables for sale. … The area along the Tiber near the Temple of Portunus they call the Forum Piscarium, for its fish [*pisces*].

Varro, *The Latin Language* 5.146

107. Temple of Pietas

COMMENTARY

Although the Roman concept of *pietas* expressed the proper devotion and duty rendered to family, community, and the gods, the piety worshipped at this temple seems to be the piety of a child for a parent. The initial circumstances of the vow [107.1], it is true, mention no occasion other than the standard promise of a temple in return for success, but both the son's extraordinary statue of his father [107.2] and the legend that became attached to the temple stress the devotion of a child to parent. The legend is interesting as well in connection with the

"Milking Column" (*lactaria columna*) in the Forum Holitorium, known only from Festus's statement below [107.3]. Richardson hypothesizes that milk was doled out at this location to the children of the poor, an attractive idea in light of the legend, the quarter's humble character, and the proximity of a cattle market where milk might be had.

SOURCES

107.1 Two temples were dedicated that year [181 BC]. One was the Temple of Pietas in the Forum Holitorium, dedicated by Manius Acilius Glabrius as duumvir. He also placed here the first gilded statue in all of Italy, a statue of his father, who had earlier both vowed the temple prior to his defeat of King Antiochus in a decisive battle [191 BC] and had contracted out its construction by the authority of the Senate.

Livy, *History* 40.34.4–6

107.2 There are numerous examples of family loyalty (*pietas*) all over the world, but none can compare to an instance in Rome. A poorer and undistinguished member of the plebeian class who had just given birth was given permission to visit her mother in prison. The guard always searched the woman before she was allowed to enter the cell of her mother (who was not permitted any food) but eventually caught the woman giving her mother nourishment from her own breasts. The mother was pardoned on account of her daughter's exceptional act of piety and both were granted life-long support by the state. The location was consecrated to the goddess of such acts, and in the consulship of Gaius Quinctius and Manius Acilius a temple to Pietas was built on the site of the prison where the Theater of Marcellus stands today.

Pliny the Elder, *Encyclopedia* 7.121

107.3 The Milking Column in the Forum Holitorium is so named because babies are brought there to be nourished by milk.

Festus 105

108. Temple of Janus

108.1 At this time [c. AD 17] Tiberius dedicated some temples which had been ruined by age or fire and which Augustus had begun to repair. These included the Temple of Janus that Gaius Duilius had constructed in the Forum Holitorium after becoming the first Roman to wage a successful naval campaign (a victory, against the Carthaginians [in 260 BC], which earned him a naval triumph).

Tacitus, *Annals* 2.49

109. Temple of Juno Sospita

COMMENTARY
Juno Sospita is Juno in her capacity as a savior of warriors in their hour of need. As Livy describes it [109.1], the vowing of a temple by the commander in battle had the power to rally the troops, as did Constantine's cross.

SOURCES
109.1 At the beginning of the battle against the Insubrians [in 197 BC], the consul Gaius Cornelius Cethegus vowed a temple to Juno the Savior if the enemy should be routed. The soldiers shouted out that they would bring his prayer to fulfillment.
Livy, *History* 32.30.10

109.2 [Among the temples dedicated in 194 BC] was the temple of Juno Matuta in the Forum Holitorium, which had been vowed and contracted out four years earlier by Gaius Cornelius in the Gallic war against the Insubrians.
Livy, *History* 34.53.3

109.3 [Events in 90 BC:] Metella Caecilia said that she learned in a dream that Juno the Savior had fled from her temple because it had been polluted by filth, and that only with the greatest difficulty was the goddess persuaded by Metella's prayers to return: women had desecrated Juno's temple with an obscene and sordid business, and a dog with a litter of pups had even made her home at the base of Juno's statue. Metella restored the temple to its original splendor after it was purified with prayers of adoration.
Julius Obsequens 55 *(summarizer of Livy)*

110. Temple of Hope

110.1 The Temple of Hope, vowed by Aulus Atilius in the First Punic War [c. 250 BC], was rebuilt and consecrated by Germanicus [in AD 17].
Tacitus, *Annals* 2.49

110.2 Since the spirit is strengthened by the anticipation of good things, Aulus Atilius Calatinus rightly consecrated a temple to Hope.
Cicero, *Laws* 2.28

110.3 [Among the many prodigies reported in the winter of 218 BC,] the Temple of Hope in the Forum Holitorium was struck by lightning.
Livy, *History* 21.62.4

110.4 Triumvirs were elected [in 212 BC] to rebuild the Temple of Hope outside the Porta Carmentalis; the temple had burned down in the fire of the preceding year.

Livy, *History* 25.7.5–6

Temples at S. Omobono (to the goddesses Mater Matuta and Fortuna)

COMMENTARY

Twin temples were found in the 1930s during construction in the area of S. Omobono. Though analysis of the complex ruins continues, these have been identified by most scholars as the temples to the goddesses Fortuna and Mater Matuta ("Prosperity" and "Mother Dawn"). The sources attribute the original construction of both temples to Servius Tullius, the sixth king of Rome, who had a special fondness for Fortuna, a fertility deity with myriad temples in Rome. Mater Matuta, as a goddess of dawn and the beginnings of young life in general, is appropriately twinned with Fortuna, although she has some functions of her own distinct from agrarian fertility, including her tie to the sea, as expressed in the myth of Ino/Leucothoe and her son, identified as Portunus, the god of the port, who had his own temple nearby [115.].

The church of S. Omobono (St. Homobonus, patron saint of tailors) stands on the site of one of the temples, and the ruins of the other lie open to view beside it. These are perhaps the arrangement of the temples after Camillus's rebuilding in 396 BC. Six meters below, at a level that must have been frequently flooded, are the remains of an archaic temple that goes back to the sixth century BC—the time of Servius, whose traditional dates of rule are 578–534 BC.

111. Temple of Mater Matuta

SOURCES

111.1 They say that the sceptered hands of Servius consecrated
　　The temple to Mater Matuta in the Forum Boarium.
...

"You will be called Leucothea by Greeks, but Matuta by Romans,
　　And total control of the port will belong to your son,
Whose name in Latin will be Portunus, Palaemon in Greek."

Ovid, *Fasti* 6.479–80, 545–7

111.2 [In 396 BC] Camillus vowed that if he captured Veii he would repair and dedicate the Temple of Matuta Mater, which had been originally dedicated by Servius Tullius.

Livy, *History* 5.19.6

111.3 The ancients called the goddess of Dawn "Mother" on account of her generosity.

Festus, p.122M

111.4 [The personal whims of gods cannot steer nature's course:]
The hour when Morning unfurls the rosy dawn across
The shores of heaven and spreads her light is quite predictable.

Lucretius, *On the Nature of Things* 5.656–7

111.5 [In 174 BC] a painted panel was placed in the Temple of Mater Matuta with this inscription: "Under the command and auspices of the consul Tiberius Sempronius Gracchus, the legion and army of the Roman people conquered Sardinia. In that province more than 80,000 of the enemy were killed or taken captive. After achieving success for the state and liberating its allies, with yearly payments reimposed, he led his army home safe, sound, and rich with the spoils of war. He returned to the city of Rome where he celebrated his second triumph. He gave this panel commemorating the event as an offering to Jupiter." On the panel was a map of Sardinia, painted with pictures of the battles there.

Livy, *History* 41.28.8–10

112. Temple of Fortuna

112.1 Fortuna, you share with Matuta the 11th of June as your day
Of dedication; you share the same founder, same site as well.
But the statue inside – who is that concealed beneath the togas?
It is Servius, all agree, but the cause for concealment varies.

Ovid, *Fasti* 6.569–72

112.2 [Pliny discusses properties of wool:] Varro informs us that Tanaquil wove the billowing royal toga in the Temple of Fortuna that her son Servius Tullius used to wear. … Remarkably, this toga veiling the statue of Fortune lasted up to the death of Sejanus [in AD 18], neither decaying nor suffering any damage from moths for a period of 560 years.

Pliny the Elder, *Encyclopedia* 8.194,197

112.3 When the Temple of Fortuna burned down [in 213 BC], the statue of Servius Tullius remained unharmed.

Valerius Maximus, *Sayings* 1.8.11

112.4 In Rome a terrible fire [in 213 BC] lasted for two nights and a day. Everything between the Salinae and the Porta Carmentalis burned to the ground, including the Aequimaelium, the Vicus Jugarius, and the temples of Fortuna and Mater Matuta.

Livy, History 24.47.15–16

112.5 Triumvirs were elected [in 212 BC] to rebuild the temples of Fortuna and Mater Matuta, located inside the Porta Carmentalis; the temples had burned down in the fire of the preceding year.

Livy, History 25.7.5–6

112.6 Lucius Stertinius returned from fighting in Farther Spain [in 196 BC] and, without even making a claim for the award of a triumph, deposited 50,000 pounds of silver in the Treasury. Out of the booty he also erected two arches in the Forum Boarium in front of the temple of Fortuna and Mater Matuta, and one arch in the Circus Maximus, and he placed gilded statues on these arches.

Livy, History 33.27.3–4

Notes: Holloway, in *The Archaeology of Early Rome and Latium*, 10–11, challenges the common identification of the S. Omobono area temples with the temples of Fortuna and Mater Matuta, finding no evidence in the sources that these temples were right next to each other. His interpretation, however, overlooks Ovid's passage [112.1] (though one could conceivably argue that by locating the two temples in "the same site" Ovid meant the Forum Boarium) and perhaps misconstrues the topography of Livy's fire [112.4]. The Salinae were either old salt-flats or probably salt warehouses where the Aventine rose from the Forum Boarium, and the Porta Carmentalis was a gate in the Servian Wall at the base of the Capitoline; this is to say that the fire pretty much burned down the entire area of the Forum Boarium. The next four sites of burned real estate mentioned by Livy do not express the entire extent of the fire (in which case, as Holloway argues, the two temples in question would be distant from one another as separate coordinates) but are rather bunched together in the corner of the Forum merging with the Capitoline (the Aequimaelium being a section of this hill) and extending towards the Forum Romanum on the Vicus Jugarius, which the twin temples abutted.

Interestingly, the ancient animal remains of cattle, sheep, goats, pigs, and dogs found in the sanctuary at S. Omobono show that the majority of sacrifices were newly born animals (Holloway, p. 75).

113. Forum Boarium

COMMENTARY

Although the whole area along the river between the Capitoline and the Aventine fell under the name of Forum Boarium, it seems there was also an open part of it more properly given over to trade in cattle, which gave the square and then the larger riverside area its name, as explained by Varro (*boves*= cattle). Alternately, as argued by Richardson (pp.162–3), no section of the Forum Boarium was given over to cattle trade (the Campus Martius being more suited for that business); in this view, the forum got its name not from trade in cattle, but from the bronze statue of an ox set up here. Although such a statue could well have been erected because of the prevalence of cattle here, Ovid [113.2], as I read him, specifically says that the statue gave its name to the area.

The Arch of the Argentarii was a monumental gateway into this area from the direction of the Forum Romanum, located where a cross-street from the Vicus Jugarius joined the Vicus Tuscus and the Clivus Victoriae that headed up the Palatine from the Forum Boarium. The name of the arch is a modern derivation from the name of one of the groups (the *argentarii* or "bankers") who dedicated the arch to the reigning Severan family. The inscription [114.1], however, reads *argentarii et negotiatores boari huius loci*, "bankers and cattle-traders of this place." Consistent with his view mentioned above, Richardson (p. 29) interprets *negotiatores boari* as simply "merchants in the Forum Boarium," although this reading would make the addition of the phrase "of this place" redundant. Claridge, noting that the elaborate sculpture on the piers of the gateway began well above head height (from the ancient street), speculates that the lower travertine blocks of the piers were kept plain because the passing cattle would have rubbed against them.

The higher sculpture on the Arch of the Argentarii faced its own threat, in an instance of *damnatio memoriae* familiar from the much larger triumphal arch of Septimius Severus in the Forum Romanum, where Caracalla had his brother Geta removed from the attic inscription [45.1]. Here, Geta's name and two others have been erased from the inscription, and their figures have been obliterated from the inside reliefs of the arch.

SOURCES

113.1 Merchandise of the same product can provide the distinguishing name to a part of the city, as in the case of the Forum Bovarium.

Varro, *The Latin Language* 5.146

113.2 Between the bridges and the Circus Maximus you'll find
A bustling square that takes its name from the statue of an ox.

Ovid, *Fasti* 6.477–8

113.3 I think the beginning of Rome's foundation and the pomerium that Romulus established can be reliably traced as follows. From the point in the Forum Boarium where the bronze statue of the bull stands today (appropriately, since this is the species which is yoked to the ritual plow), a furrow was ploughed to designate the city limits. It ran first to the Great Altar of Hercules.

Tacitus, *Annals* 12.24

114. Arch of the Argentarii

114.1 IMP(eratori) CAES(ari) L. SEPTIMIO SEVERO PIO PERTI-
NACI AUG(usto) ARABIC(o) ADIABENIC(o) PARTH(ico) MAX(imo)
FORTISSIMO FELICISSIMO PONTIF(ici) MAX(imo) TRIB(unicia)
POTEST(ate) XII IMP. XI CO(n)S(uli) III PATRI PATRIAE ET IMP. CAES.
M. AURELIO ANTONINO PIO FELICI AUG. TRIB. POTEST. VII
CO(n)S(uli) I[II P(atri) P(atriae) PROCO(n)S(uli) FORTISSIMO
FELICISSIMOQUE PRINCIPI] ET IULIAE AUG(ustae) MATRI
AUG(usti) [N(ostri)] ET CASTRORUM ET [SENATUS ET PATRIAE ET]
IMP. CAES. M. AURELI ANTONINI PII FELICIS AUG(usti) [PARTHICI
MAXIMI BRITTANNICI MAXIMI] ARGENTARI ET NEGOTIANTES
BOARI HUIUS [LOCI QUI INVEHENT] DEVOTI NUMINI EORUM.

To Septimius Severus [literally: To the Emperor Caesar Lucius Septimius Severus Pius Pertinax Augustus Arabicus Adiabenicus
Parthicus, the greatest, bravest, and most fortunate, the Pontifex Maximus, with tribunate powers for the 12th time, a conquering general for
the 11th time, consul for the third time, father of his country] and to
Caracalla [literally: and to Emperor Caesar Marcus Aurelius Antoninus
Pius Felix Augustus, with tribunate powers for the seventh time, consul
for the third time, father of his country, proconsul, the bravest and
most fortunate prince] and to Julia Augusta, mother of Caracalla
[literally: mother of our Augustus and of the Armies, of the Senate, of
the Country, and of the Emperor Caesar Marcus Aurelius Antoninus
Pius Felix Augustus, great conqueror of Parthia and Britannica], the
bankers and the cattle-traders of this place [dedicate this arch], out of
devotion to their divine powers.

ILS 426 = *CIL* 6.1035

115. Temple of Portunus

COMMENTARY
    Due to its transformation into a church in the ninth century AD
or earlier, the temple now identified as the Temple of Portunus (formerly called the Temple of Fortuna Virilis and thus a favorite of
Mussolini's) is fairly well preserved, in contrast to the written record

Fig. 55 Temple of Portunus

on the temple. It is well located to be a temple to the god of the river port, the Portus Tiberinus, the warehouses for which lined the left bank under the large brick registry-office built in the 1930s.

The compact and high-podiumed temple of Portunus is set parallel to the river and faced the road leading to the Pons Aemilius. Its precinct housed a market for flowers, many of which, like the animals sold in the Forum Boarium, were destined for religious ceremonies. The present Ionic temple was constructed sometime in the first century BC, replacing one built several centuries earlier. The cella is built of Anio tufa, but its corner columns, the architrave, the porch columns, and the podium are all travertine.

SOURCES

115.1 The Portunalia Festival [on August 17] is named after the god Portunus; it was on this day that his temple in the Portus Tiberinus was dedicated and his holiday was established.

Varro, *The Latin Language* 6.19

115.2 The dedication date of the Temple of Portunus near the Pons Aemilius is August 17.

Calendar Inscription (Fasti Amiterni)

115.3   Many items which lack an intrinsic value gain in worth from their surroundings. This can be observed in the case of flowers and wreaths: they have one order of worth when sold by the flower-vendors in the precinct of Portunus, and another altogether when offered by the priests in a temple.

Fronto, Letters 1.7.2

115.4   Merchandise of the same product can provide the distinguishing name to a part of the city. ... For instance, the area along the Tiber near the Temple of Portunus they call the Forum Piscarium, for its fish ["pisces"].

Varro, The Latin Language 5.146

The Pons Aemilius and the Pons Sublicius ("The Pile Bridge")

COMMENTARY
Intact until C16 floods demolished most of it, the Pons Aemilius across the Tiber exists today in the form of one archway, called the Ponte Rotto ("the Broken Bridge"), located just upstream of the Ponte Palatino and below Tiber Island. The information about the bridge contained in Livy [116.1] and Plutarch [117.3] has led to a variety of interpretations. One difficulty is that the name of the bridge does not accord with the chief builder Fulvius (although it does apply to his rival Aemilius); Plutarch names a different Aemilius, a quaestor, as the bridge's builder [117.3]. Another question is the exact nature of the work done in 142 BC: did this complete the bridge, or was a rebuilding involved?
The Pons Sublicius (a *sublica* is a wooden pile) had special status as Rome's first bridge across the Tiber. It was further distinguished by a religious ban against the use of metal, including nails, in its structure. The bridge is also famous as the scene of Horatius's heroic stand against Etruscan troops.
Although no remains have been found to indicate the bridge's precise position on the river, traces of ancient roads place it downstream of the Pons Aemilius and upstream of the Aventine Hill, and in some sources not quoted here, it figures as the bridge with the most direct route between the Aventine Hill and the Transtiber region.

SOURCES
116. Pons Aemilius

116.1   The censors Marcus Aemelius Lepidus and Marcus Fulvius Nobilior carried out a number of public works with the money as-

Fig. 56 Pons Aemelius

signed and divided between them [in 179 BC]. … The works contracted out by Marcus Fulvius were of greater utility, including a harbor and piers for a bridge across the Tiber. Some years later [142 BC], the censors Publius Scipio Africanus and Lucius Mummius added the arches to these piers.

Livy, *History* 40.51.2, 4

117. Pons Sublicius

117.1 [Under the king Ancus Marcius, trad. 640–616 BC] the Janiculum Hill was also added to the city, not from lack of space but to prevent its becoming the elevated stronghold of an attacking enemy. It was decided not only to join the Janiculum to the city with a wall but to facilitate traffic across the river in each direction with the Pons Sublicius, the first bridge built on the Tiber.

Livy, *History* 1.33.6

117.2 [Lars Porsenna, an Etruscan ruler near Rome, attempted in 508 BC to retake Rome for the expelled Etruscan king Tarquinius.] When the enemy appeared, all the Romans left the fields of their own accord and came into the city and ringed it with guards. The city appeared secure, protected by the walls in some spots and by the Tiber in others. The Pons Sublicius, however, very nearly gave the enemy a passage into the city—an event prevented by one man alone: Horatius Cocles. On him did the City of Rome rely for her defense that day.

Horatius happened to be stationed on the bridge when he witnessed the Janiculum captured in a surprise attack, the enemy rushing down to the river, and the panicked mob of his fellow soldiers abandoning their weapons and posts on the far bank. He took hold of one man after the other, preventing his retreat, and swearing by the good faith of gods and men that if they abandoned their posts all flight would be in vain: if they left the bridge standing behind them after they crossed, there would soon be more enemy soldiers on the Palatine and Capitoline Hills than on the Janiculum. And so warning them of this danger, he commanded them to demolish the bridge with iron and fire and any force possible; he himself would hold off the enemy, as much as one man could. Then he strode to the far side of the bridge, conspicuous among the other men who were so obviously shunning combat, and there took his stand, armed and ready for hand-to-hand combat. The Etruscans were stunned by his audacity, and shame kept two of his own men by his side, Spurius Larcius and Titus Herminius, distinguished by both their family names and their deeds.

For a short while the three of them together withstood the first wave of attackers and the initial, most violent onslaught. Then, with the bridge behind them scarcely still standing, and with those who were demolishing it calling for them to come back, Horatius made his two companions retreat to safety. Casting aggressive, threatening glances at the Etruscan leaders, he challenged them individually and ridiculed them all: slaves to arrogant kings and forgetful of their own liberty, here they were trying to stamp out the liberty of others. For some time the soldiers hesitated, each of them looking around to encourage someone else to start the fight. Shame then provoked the attack, and raising a shout they threw their javelins from all sides against a single enemy. After all of the missiles simply stuck in his shield, and the obstinate Roman still occupied the bridge with his massive stance, the soldiers were attempting to dislodge him with a charge when in one instant both the loud crash of the falling bridge and the shout of the Romans cheering their success halted the Etruscan attack with sudden dismay. Then Cocles spoke: "Father Tiberinus, I call on you in solemn prayer: receive these arms and this thy soldier in your merciful stream." Then fully armed as he was, he jumped off into the Tiber and swam beneath a shower of javelins to arrive safely by his comrades. Thus did Horatius dare to perform an act of heroism that would find more fame among posterity than credence. The grateful city placed a statue of him in the Comitium, and gave him as much farmland as he could plough in a day.

Livy, *History* 2.10.1–12

117.3 Most writers explain the origins of the word "pontifex" with a ridiculous etymology, claiming it refers to men who were called "bridge-doers" because they *did* [Latin: *fac-*] sacrifices of great sanctity and antiquity at the *bridge* across the Tiber (*pont* being the root for "bridge" in Latin). Moreover, the safe-keeping and repair of the bridge, as with other inviolate and ancestral rites, belongs to the priests, and the Romans consider the destruction of the wooden bridge not only illegal but sacrilegious. It is also said that, in accordance with some oracle, the entire bridge contains no iron and is joined together by wooden dowels. The stone bridge was built much later by the quaestor Aemilius. The wooden bridge itself, it is said, was finished not under Numa but when Ancus Marcius (the grandson of Numa) was king.

Plutarch, Numa 9.2–3

117.4 [Pliny is speaking of wonders of architecture.] At Cyzicus [a town near Troy] there is a large building they call the Council House; built without any iron nails, it is framed in such a way that beams can be removed and replaced without the aid of scaffolding. The same conditions are a religious requirement at the Pile Bridge in Rome, ever since it proved difficult to dismantle during its defense by Horatius Cocles.

Pliny the Elder, Encyclopedia 36.100

118. The Boat of Aeneas

COMMENTARY

Somewhere along the river "in the middle of the city" was an odd exhibit mentioned only by Procopius [118.1]: the boat on which Aeneas was thought to have sailed from Troy to Italy and up the Tiber. Virgil [118.2], in verses worthy of such a memorial, describes Aeneas's journey up the Tiber in two boats, and his narrative locates Aeneas's landing near the Great Altar of Hercules in the Forum Boarium, where the locals, Greek settlers under the leadership of Evander, are celebrating their deliverance from the monster Cacus, killed by Hercules, as re-told in the next section.

SOURCES

118.1 The Romans, beyond any other people I know, are devoted to their city and take great pains to preserve and maintain the city's heritage so that none of the old monuments of Rome disappear. Even under the many years of barbarian rule, the Romans continued to maintain buildings and most urban monuments that managed by the excellence of their construction to survive such an extended period of serious neglect, and they still preserve today [c. AD 550] any patriotic memorial that has survived.

The most amazing example of this Roman passion to preserve the past is what they have done with the ship of Aeneas, the man who founded Rome. Having built a boathouse for it on the banks of the Tiber in the middle of the city, they put this ship inside it where it remains to this day. [Procopius goes on to describe the ship's remarkable construction: its keel and planks are each formed from one piece of timber bow to stern (120 feet); the curved ribs shaping the cross-sections of the hull are likewise each one piece.]

Procopius, *Wars* 4.22.5–8

118.2 [Aeneas readied two ships to travel up the Tiber to Evander's settlement.]

> For one entire night the Tiber calmed its swollen
> Waters, curbing its flow, and ebbed to a silent standstill,
> Stretching across its surface the smoothness of a calm pool
> Or tranquil marsh. The weary struggle at the oars ceased,
> And happy voices sped the journey on its way.
> Greased keels slid through the shallows, and the waves were struck
> With wonder, as were the virgin groves, that painted hulls
> And shields, flickering afar, should swim across these waters.
> The men outlasted night and then the day with rowing;
> Beneath the Tiber's tent of leaves they put long bends
> Behind as they cut through forests mirrored on the river's surface.
> The fiery sun had climbed to the summit of the sky
> When they first glimpsed, far off, the walls, the hill-top fort,
> And the scattered homes that formed the sum of Evander's state,
> Which now, lifted by Roman power, equals the heavens.
> The Trojans swung their prows toward shore and approached the town.
> That day, it chanced, the Arcadian king was performing rites
> In honor of the mighty Hercules and the gods
> In a grove before the city.
> ···

[The settlers, suspicious at first, soon welcome the Trojan exiles.]

> Then king Evander spoke: "Know that these yearly rites,
> This customary feast, this altar to a force divine,
> Are not the urgings of an empty superstition that slights
> The gods of old: we worship where worship is due, my friend,
> In thankfulness for rescue from a savage death.

Virgil, *Aeneid* 8.86–104, 185–189

119. The Great Altar of Hercules (*Ara Maxima*)

COMMENTARY

The cult of Hercules in Rome was closely associated with commerce, so it is understandable that his greatest altar and several temples to this hero-made-god should have arisen in the Forum Boarium. His worship goes back at least to the regal period and may even have been brought by Greek traders, whose presence at this bend in the river can be dated back to the 8th century BC by remains of pottery.

Rome's legendary connection to Hercules was accomplished by inserting a side-labor into his canonical labor of stealing the cattle of Geryon. His confrontation with Cacus, variously monster or thug depending on the version, was a popular tale, told most famously by Livy and Virgil. I have used Propertius's account [119.1] for its brevity, its information about the Great Altar as being off-limits to women, and its topographical details. The legend of Cacus and his thievery of Hercules's cattle not only gives an explanation for the worship of Hercules at the Great Altar and for its location by the ford, but is interesting as well for yet another connection between cattle and the Forum Boarium.

There is a sizeable platform made of ancient stone in the crypt of S. Maria in Cosmedin. This may well have been the foundation of the Ara Maxima, although the identification of these ancient stones is not certain.

SOURCES

119.1 While Hercules, the son of Jove, was driving cattle
>   Back to Greece that he won from Geryon in Spain,
> He approached the flock-filled heights of the mighty Palatine.
>   There he rested his tired herd and his own tired feet
> Where the Velabra collected the Tiber into a pool
>   And a mariner could sail his craft on urban waters.
> He rested in vain: with Cacus as treacherous host, no herd
>   Was safe, and soon this local marauder with triple face
> And triple tongue who carried out raids from a lethal cave
>   Had violated the laws of Jupiter with theft.

> Hoping to cover the tracks of his crime, Cacus dragged
>   The cattle backwards by their tails inside his cave.
> But god was witness: the cattle all but bellowed "Thief!"
>   Enraged, the hero demolished the monster's gruesome doors
> Of bone and clubbed him dead with a blow to each of his faces,
>   Then set the cattle free: "My club's last labor, go
> And sanctify the Cattle Grounds with constant mooing;
>   The Roman Forum will be ennobled by your grazing."

[Parched by his work, Hercules hears a trickling spring, but its priestess bars his way because the spring is in the grove of the Goddess of Women. Hercules, angry again, responds:]
> "May my Great Altar remain off-limits to women,
>   As punishment for your rejection of a thirsty Hercules."
>   **Propertius**, *Elegies* 4.9.1–20, 69–70

119.2 [Virgil's Evander calls the altar to Hercules] "greatest" because it is huge, as one can see today behind the starting gates to the Circus Maximus.

Servius, on *Aeneid* 8.271

119.3 It would not be easy to list everything destroyed in Nero's fire. Among the losses were some of the oldest sacred sites in Rome, including the large altar and shrine that Arcadian Evander consecrated to Hercules for his help.

Tacitus, *Annals* 15.41

119.4 The first fruits of commercial goods are offered up on the Altar of Hercules…and every year [on August 12] the urban praetor sacrifices a heifer upon it on behalf of the state.

Varro, *The Latin Language* 6.54

119.5 A peculiar practice of the ceremonies honoring Hercules is that the participants sit while feasting. … It is also required that all who perform the sacrifice do so with head uncovered.

Macrobius, *Saturnalia* 3.6.16–17

120. The Round Temple

COMMENTARY

The relatively well-preserved Round Temple in the Forum Boarium between the Tiber and S. Maria in Cosmedin, although formerly called the Temple of Vesta and still generally called the Round Temple, was probably one of the temples Macrobius [120.1] attributes to Hercules Victor, although which temple (the one "in the Forum Boarium" or the one "near the Porta Trigemina") is also not certain, since we cannot locate this gate in the Servian Wall with any exactitude (Coarelli locates it near the Round Temple, others closer to the Aventine). A temple of Hercules Olivarius ("Hercules of the Olive Merchants") is mentioned in the Regionary Catalogue near the Temple of Portunus, and an inscription on a statue-base containing the word *Olivarius* and the sculptor's name was found near the Round Temple, leading some to conclude that the Hercules Victor worshipped here was more commonly considered a special patron of the olive-oil merchants. As such, it would be a temple not financed by the military booty of the political elite, but by business people, in keeping with the character of this region of the city.

Whatever its identity, an architectural analysis of the structure reveals it to be a lavish production from the late C2 BC, making it the first surviving temple in Rome made out of marble. Ten columns on the north side were replaced with marble from the Luna quarries in the C1 AD, but the original columns, the architrave, and the cella walls were all originally Pentelic marble from Greece.

SOURCES

120.1   Varro, in book four of his work *On Religious Rites*, considers that Hercules is called "the Victor" because of his victories over animals of all kinds. There are, indeed, two temples to Hercules the Victor in Rome, one near the Porta Trigemina, the other in the Forum Boarium.

Macrobius, *Saturnalia* 3.6.10

120.2   That sculpture was an art-form familiar to Italy even in the old days is indicated by the statue of Hercules they say was dedicated by Evander [trad. C8 BC] in the Forum Boarium; the statue is called Hercules the Triumphant and is carried in triumphal parades draped in triumphal garb.

Pliny the Elder, *Encyclopedia* 34.33

120.3   [Pliny is relating some amazing facts about birds, and adds:] In Rome, neither flies nor dogs enter the Temple of Hercules in the Forum Boarium.

Pliny the Elder, *Encyclopedia* 10.79

120.4   A famous painting by the poet Pacuvius [fl. 150 BC] was located in the Temple of Hercules in the Forum Boarium. He was the son of Ennius's sister, and his high reputation as a playwright gave his painting more fame. After Pacuvius, painting was not considered suitable work for the upper classes.

Pliny the Elder, *Encyclopedia* 35.19

Notes: The identification of the temples to Hercules in the Forum Boarium area is more complicated than my commentary suggests, involving more than selecting one of Macrobius's temples to coincide with the existing round temple. Competing reconstructions of this puzzle can be found in Richardson, 187–189, and *LTUR* 3.11– 25, in the articles by Coarelli and Palombi.

121. The Aventine Hill

COMMENTARY

The topographical sites on the Aventine Hill are especially dependent on the ancient sources for our understanding of them, since no identifiable ruins have been found to any of the sites discussed below. As a result, for all their importance, they are under-represented in many treatments of the city.

The Aventine lay outside the pomerium until the reign of Claudius, but it was settled early and was included in the circuit of the Servian Walls. There are two basic parts to the hill, the Aventine Major, with its taller summit and steep sides above the Tiber, and the less dramatic Aventine Minor behind the Baths of Caracalla, separated from the larger part of the hill today by the Viale Aventino.

Dionysius's passage [121.1] provides the useful reminder to imagine the valley between the Aventine and Palatine as a much more rugged and prominent division before it was developed as a racetrack. More important for understanding the monuments here, however, is the close connection between the Aventine and the plebeian class of Rome, as reflected in the passage on the Lex Ilicia [121.3] and in most of the other sources included under the other sites on this hill.

SOURCES

121.1 The first achievement of the king Ancus Marcius (642–616 BC) was to add a considerable tract of land to the city by enclosing the Aventine inside the walls. The Aventine is a hill of moderate height about two and one-eighth miles in circumference. At the time the hill was wooded with trees of all kinds, but especially with beautiful laurels. Although there remains a spot on the Aventine that the Romans still call the Laurels, today much of the hill has been developed, and includes among its many buildings the Temple of Diana. Originally it was separated from the Palatine (the first of Rome's settled hills) by a deep and narrow ravine, which has since been filled in.

Perceiving that the Aventine would provide a stronghold to an enemy attacking the city, Ancus Marcius enclosed it with a wall and a ditch, and settled the hill with people displaced from Tellenae, Politorium, and the other Latin towns defeated in battle.

Dionysius, *Early Rome* 3.43.1–2

121.2 Ancus took the Latin town Politorium by force, and following a custom of earlier kings who increased the power of Rome by enrolling her enemies as citizens, he resettled the whole population of Politorium in Rome. Since, of the hills closest to the Palatine (the original seat of Rome), the Capitoline Hill was already filled with Sabines, and the Caelian Hill with Latins from Albani, Ancus settled the new population on the Aventine, and when he conquered the towns of Tellenae and Ficana, he made them new citizens and settled them on the Aventine as well.

Livy, *History* 1.33.1–2

121.3 [In 456 BC] the tribune Ilicius introduced legislation concerning the distribution of public property on the Aventine, the substance of which was as follows. The owners of private property that was legally acquired were allowed to retain ownership of it. Land however that had been acquired by force or fraud was to be made back over to the public, after the owners were reimbursed for their expenditures, at a value to be determined by arbitrators. The remaining public land on the Aventine was given to the populace free of charge, to be divided up among them. Ilicius pointed out that such measures would be advantageous to the city in numerous ways, but especially by reducing the disturbances of the poor, who were agitated by patrician ownership of public land.

The law was passed, and is inscribed on a bronze pillar standing inside the sanctuary of the Temple of Diana on the Aventine.

Dionysius, *Early Rome* 10.32.2–4

122. The Temple of Ceres

COMMENTARY

The Temple of Ceres, like the Temple of Jupiter, was really a three-god temple under the name of its leading divinity; it also had some design features in common with the Capitoline temple, as Vitruvius notes [122.9]. In contrast to the prime aerial location of the sky-king, however, and his close association with Rome's supreme citizens in the drama of the triumph, the temple to the earth goddess of grain was located low on the slope of the Aventine and associated with plebeian interests and the succor of the poor. In neither case, however, does the characteristic social register of Jupiter and Ceres (elite and common respectively; the rich do not worry where the next meal comes from) diminish the universal significance of either deity. As the passages by Valerius [122.7] and Cicero [122.8] make clear, Ceres played an important role in the civic life of all Romans.

SOURCES

122.1 [Returning booty-laden from battle with the Volscians in 496 BC, the general] Postumius contracted for the building of a temple to Ceres, Liber, and Libera. He did so in fulfillment of a vow that he had made when food for the army was scarce and there was a great alarm that it would run out altogether, since not only had the harvest failed but the war had blocked off outside markets. Because of this fear Postumius told the guardians of the Sibylline books to consult them, and when he learned that the oracles said Ceres, Liber, and Libera had to be appeased, he made a vow as he was about to lead his army out that if the harvests during his command should be as bountiful as they used to be, he would build a temple to these gods and establish yearly sacrifices in their honor.

Dionysius, *Early Rome* 6.17.2–3

122.2 [In 493 BC] the consul Cassius consecrated the Temple of Ceres, Liber, and Libera, which is located at the end of the Circus Maximus right above the starting gates.

Dionysius, Early Rome 6.94.3

122.3 Tiberius dedicated several temples that Augustus had begun to rebuild after they were ruined by fire or age; among them was the Temple of Liber, Libera, and Ceres next to the Circus Maximus, which Aulus Postumius had vowed when dictator.

Tacitus, *Annals* 2.49

122.4 Varro considered that the word *pandere* ["to open in welcome"] arose because those who were destitute fled to the Temple of Ceres for asylum and were there given bread [*panis*]; *pan-dere* is therefore *panem dare* ["to give bread"].

Varro, from Nonius 43M

122.5 [In 491 BC the following law was passed as part of the measures taken to give the plebeians of Rome a greater share of power in the state:] "Let no one force a tribune of the people to do anything against his will, as if he were an ordinary citizen; let no one ever punish him with the whip or order another to do so; let no one kill him, or command another to kill him. If anyone should perform one of these forbidden actions, let him be declared accursed, and his possessions consecrated to Ceres, and let whoever kills this lawbreaker do so with impunity."

Dionysius, *Early Rome* 6.89.3

122.6 [In 449 BC] the consuls Valerius and Horatius rendered the tribunes inviolate not only with sacrosanct status but by law as well, ordaining that whoever should harm the tribunes or their aediles or the board of ten who adjudicated cases of citizenship, his life would be forfeit to Jupiter and his possessions would go for sale at the Temple of Ceres, Liber, and Libera. ... The same consuls enacted that the decrees of the Senate, which previously consuls had either repressed or falsified as they wished, should be delivered to the plebeian aediles at the Temple of Ceres. ... Although all these measures were carried out against the wishes of the patricians, they offered no opposition.

Livy, *History* 3.55.7, 13, 15

122.7 After the battle of Cannae [in which the Romans were defeated by Hannibal in 216 BC, costing Rome 60,000 soldiers killed or captured], when nearly half of the Roman forces had fallen on that one cursed and treacherous field, and there was hardly a single household which was not in a state of grief, the Senate decreed that the women could not extend their mourning period beyond thirty days so that they could perform the rites of Ceres. And so the mothers and the daughters, the wives and the sisters, wiping away their tears and putting aside the signs of mourning, were compelled to dress in white for Ceres and burn incense at her altar. This constancy of religious observance filled the gods with shame at the idea of tormenting these Romans any longer, whom not even these bitter losses could deter from worshipping them.

Valerius Maximus, Sayings 1.1.15

122.8 "Now, gentlemen of the jury, I am an aedile elect, and I have a course of action mandated by the Roman people: I must carry out, with utmost care and reverence, the sacred games in honor of Ceres, Liber, and Libera; I must see to it that the good will of the mother goddess Flora is gained for the Roman people and plebs by a crowded attendance at the games in her honor; and I must insure that those most ancient of sacred games, the first to be called the 'Roman games,' are carried out with the greatest dignity and scruple in honor of Jupiter, Juno, and Minerva."

Cicero, Against Verres 2.36

122.9 In an araeostyle temple it is not possible to use stone or marble architraves to span the columns; continuous wooden beams must be used. Moreover, the look of such temples is squat, top-heavy, low, and wide, and the pediment is ornamented in the Etruscan fashion with terra-cotta or gilt bronze statues. Such are the Temple of Ceres near the Circus Maximus and the Temple of Jupiter on the Capitoline.

Vitruvius, Architecture 3.3.5

122.10 The first instance that I can find in Rome of a bronze statue of a god was the one dedicated to Ceres, financed from the trust of Spurius Cassius, whose own father had him put to death [c. 486 BC] for striving after royal power [when he proposed agrarian laws popular with the plebs].

Pliny the Elder, Encyclopedia 34.15

122.11 The plebeian aediles Lucius Aelius Paetus and Gaius Fulvius Curvus, using money from the fines they collected from those who illegally grazed their herds on public land, held games and provided the Temple of Ceres with golden bowls.

Livy, History 10.23.13

123. The Temple of Flora

123.1 Tiberius dedicated several temples that Augustus had begun to rebuild after they were ruined by fire or age; among them was the Temple of Flora next to the Circus Maximus, which had been founded by Lucius and Marcus Publicius when aediles [in 238 BC].

Tacitus, Annals 2.49

123.2 [The goddess Flora describes her powers to Ovid:]
"Perhaps you think that my rightful domain is limited
 To delicate wreaths. But my power extends to the furrowed field:
If blossoms bless the grains, then the threshing floor will be heaped;
 If blossoms bless the vine, then the wine will be copious;
And if blossoms bless the olive, the year will glitter with oil.
...
But if we gods are neglected, the price you mortals pay
 Is steep, as even the Roman Senate discovered once.
Sure, the lilies drooped, and the violets withered away
 Before your eyes, and the tendrils of crimson saffron went slack,
But the olive in blossom suffered as well, blasted by gales,
 And the crops in blossom were ruined, smashed to the ground by hail;
The vineyard was full of promise, until a southwind blackened
 The sky and a sudden downpour stripped away its leaves."
...
The reason that so much sex can be had for sale at the games
 That are held in Flora's honor is not so hard to discover:
The goddess has little to do with your men of stern ideals;
 She wants her celebrations to touch the common crowd
And admonishes us to enjoy the beauty of life in its flower;
 Once the rose has lost its petals, the thorn is scorned.
But why, I wondered, are white robes donned for the festival
 Of Ceres, while Flora's worship comes dressed in various colors?
Is it because the crops grow blonde with the coming of the harvest,
 While every color and shape is proper attire for flowers?
The goddess nodded.

Ovid, Fasti 5.261–359, selections

124. Clivus Publicius

COMMENTARY

Most of the evidence suggests that the route of this road, the most important and direct route up the Aventine from the Forum Boarium, followed the course taken by today's Clivo dei Publicii. There are still those who favor its previous identification (still noted on many current maps of ancient Rome) with the smaller alley called Clivo di Rocca Savella today, which heads up towards S. Sabina from the Tiber side of the hill. The location of the road has some bearing on the location of the Porta Trigemina as well (and vice versa), since Frontinus [124.1] places the Porta Trigemina at the base of the Clivus.

The passages by Varro [124.2] and Ovid [124.3] trace the construction and naming of the Clivus Publicius to the characteristic politics of the hill; Ovid's passage shows that the issue of grazing cattle on public lands is not confined to the American West.

SOURCES

124.1 The waters of the Aqua Appia begin to be distributed at the bottom of the Clivus Publicius by the Porta Trigemina (a place which is called the Salinae).

Frontinus, *Aqueducts* 5

124.2 The Clivus Publicius is named after the plebeian aediles (both Publicii) who built it on behalf of the state [from 241 to 238 BC].

Varro, *The Latin Language* 5.158

124.3 [The goddess Flora explains to Ovid the origins of the Clivus Publicius:]

"Custom had come to allow the grazing of private herds
   On public lands, and those who gained from it paid no price.
Without a champion, the common person was losing his share
   As ranching within one's legal rights got the label of lazy.
This flagrant abuse was brought to the aediles of the plebs,
   Publicii both, who acted where men before them shrank:
The people regained control, and offenders were made to pay,
   And the aediles who fought for the public good earned public praise.
A part of the fines was given to me, and to great acclaim
   The victorious aediles used it to found new games in my name,
And with part they financed a road up a slope that was cliff at the time
   But is busy with traffic today; they called it the Clivus Publicius."

Ovid, *Fasti* 5.283–94

125. The Temple of Diana

COMMENTARY

Although no traces of the Temple of Diana have been identified, it must have been an imposing structure, sitting high on the brow of the Aventine, which Martial twice refers to as "the hill of Diana."

Tradition ascribes the temple's foundation to Servius Tullius in the C6 BC, and the circumstances of its foundation as well as the temple's special significance for the plebeians are of a piece with this king's reign. The late kings of Rome modeled their power on Greek-style tyranny, and this included both an appeal to the people (to counter the power of an entrenched aristocracy) and an expansive foreign policy—both features associated with the Temple of Diana, as recounted in the sources below.

Servius's own background as a former slave is also interesting in connection with this temple, and has parallels to the lurid tradition of slavery and kingship at the Temple of Diana at Lake Nemi [125.4], made famous at the beginning of James Frazer's *Golden Bough.*

A likely area for the temple's location is near the intersection of the Via di S. Sabina and Via S. Alberto, which would place it several blocks closer to the river than the square called Piazza Tempio di Diana today.

SOURCES

125.1 King Servius Tullius [trad. 578–534] advised the leaders of other Latin cities to build a temple of asylum in Rome, using common funds; it would, he argued, be a place where their cities might come every year to perform sacrifices individually and in league, to hold festivals on days they might agree upon, and to settle their differences during the ceremonies by submitting any accusations they might have to the arbitration of the other member cities. … [The leaders agreed.] Then using the funds contributed by all the Latin cities, Servius built the temple to Diana that stands on the Aventine, the largest of Rome's hills.

Dionysius, *Early Rome* 4.26.3–4

125.2 Servius Tullius, hoping that Rome's power would not always need to be increased by warfare, tried to expand her rule through diplomacy while at the same time adding some beauty to the city. … He finally persuaded the Latin leaders to have the Latin peoples join with the Roman people in building a temple in Rome to Diana. This was an acknowledgement that Rome was indeed the dominant partner—an issue that had been disputed so often by weapons.

Livy, *History* 1.45.1, 2

125.3 The festival day for servants is commonly thought to be August 13, because it was on this day that Servius Tullius, who had been born a slave, dedicated the Temple of Diana on the Aventine.

Festus 460L

125.4 As you go up the Appian Way from the town of Aricia, the Artemesium (also called the Grove of Diana) is located to the left of the road. … A barbaric and violent element persists in the ritual here: the priest must be a runaway slave who takes office by killing his predecessor. Because of such terms, he carries a sword with him constantly, scanning his surroundings for attacks, always on guard to fight them off.

Strabo, *Geography* 5.3.12

Notes: On Servius Tullius's style of rule, with some further connections to Roman topography, see Cornell, *The Beginnings of Rome*, 146–147.

126. Tiber Ports and Warehouses; Porticus Aemilia (Fig. 57)

COMMENTARY

With the expansion of trade and population following the defeat of Carthage in the 2nd Punic War, Rome needed a new port area to off-load goods arriving up the Tiber. This expansion consisted, Livy writes [126.1], of a quay or market area (*emporium*) along the left bank of the river outside the Porta Trigemina of the Servian Wall, and a covered warehouse behind it for temporary storage and cover [126.2]. This port, storage, and wholesale market area eventually expanded down the left bank of the river to where the later Aurelian Walls met the river, with the bank directly along the Aventine eventually specializing as the port for imported marble (hence the name Marmorata given to this area, surviving in today's Via Marmorata).

An interesting visual remnant of the commercial function of this quarter of the city is the hill of potsherds (35 m., perhaps higher in antiquity) located beside the abandoned stock-yards a short distance from the river. Generally closed to the public now, it used to be a popular tourist destination, and a path to the top was bordered with Stations of the Cross. The hill—Monte Testaccio today (*testa* being Latin for "shard")—is composed primarily of amphora that brought olive-oil to imperial Rome from Libya and Spain. Although the capital had little or nothing to export (of a material nature) and therefore rarely sent such containers back, they were frequently broken down and recycled in various ways as construction material. Apparently those transporting oil were found unsuitable for such uses, and thus were shattered and piled up in a ziggurat of shards.

SOURCES

126.1 The aedileship of Marcus Aemilius Lepidus and Lucius Aemilius Paullus [193 BC] was a distinguished one. They collected numerous fines from people illegally grazing animals on public lands and with that money…built a covered warehouse [*porticus*] outside the Porta Trigemina, fronted by a commercial market [*emporium*] along the Tiber.

Livy, *History* 35.10.12

126.2 [In 174 BC] the censors Quintus Fulvius Flaccus and Aulus Postumius Albinus added a stone paving to the riverfront market [*emporium*] outside the Porta Trigemina, and they fenced the market off with posts. They also contracted for repairs to the Porticus Aemilius, as well as building stairs from the Tiber to the market.

Livy, *History* 41.27.8–9

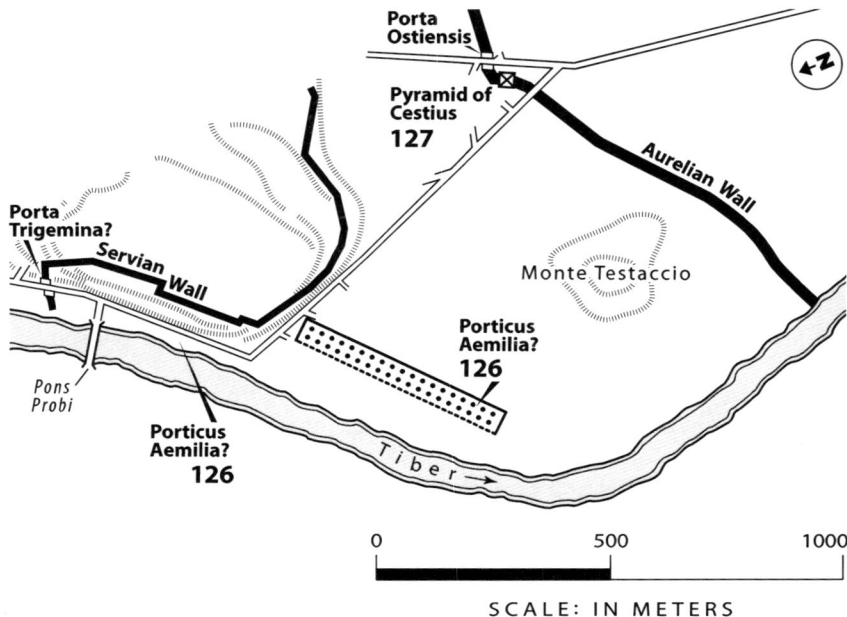

Fig. 57 South Side of Aventine Hill

Notes: The precise location of the Porticus Aemilia is disputed, as is the precise location of the Porta Trigemina. Richardson locates the original structures in the strip of land between the Aventine and the river, while Coarelli *(LTUR* 4. 116–117) and others, utilizing a piece of the Marble Plan inscribed with the letters –LIA, identify it with an ancient complex of warehouses near the river just south of the Aventine, some ruined walls of which have survived. The concrete construction of the walls of these warehouses either dates the structure to the early C1 BC, or, if part of the enhancements of the Porticus Aemilia carried out in 174 BC [126.2], provides one of the earliest examples of concrete construction in Rome.

127. Pyramid of Cestius

COMMENTARY

One of the more curious monuments in Rome is a largely intact pyramid-tomb a short distance south of the Aventine on the road to Ostia, abutting the Protestant Cemetery today. It was built by one Cestius, who died in Augustus's reign sometime before the death of Agrippa in 12 BC, since the latter is mentioned as one of Cestius's heirs in a statue inscription. We know little or nothing more about him than the information given in the inscriptions on the east and west side of

Fig. 58 Pyramid of Cestius and Porta Ostiensis (Aurelian Wall)

the pyramid [127.1]. Apparently he shared some of the fascination with Egypt or Nubia (annexed in 31 and 24 BC respectively) that led to the importation of obelisks in the same period.

The tomb has a brick-faced concrete core, but is sheathed in a veneer of Luna marble. A passageway leads into the small burial chamber that was decorated with frescoes of a later century. In the C3 AD the tomb was incorporated into the Aurelian Walls.

SOURCES
127.1 [Inscription on the tomb]

C(aius) CESTIUS L(uci) F(ilius) POB(lilia tribu) EPULO PR(aetor) TR(ibunus) / PL(ebis) VIIVIR EPULONUM OPUS APSOLUTUM (est) EX TESTAMENTO DIEBUS CCCXXX / ARBITRATU / PONTI P(ubli) F(ili) CLA(udia tribu) MELAE HEREDIS ET POTHI L(iberti).

Gaius Cestius Epulo, son of Lucius, from the tribe Publilia, praetor, plebeian tribune, one of the seven priests in charge of religious banquets [is buried here].

This work was completed in 330 days, in accordance with the will of the deceased, under the direction of Pontius Mela, Publius's son and heir from the tribe Claudia, and of the freedman Pothos.

ILS 917 = *CIL* 6.1374

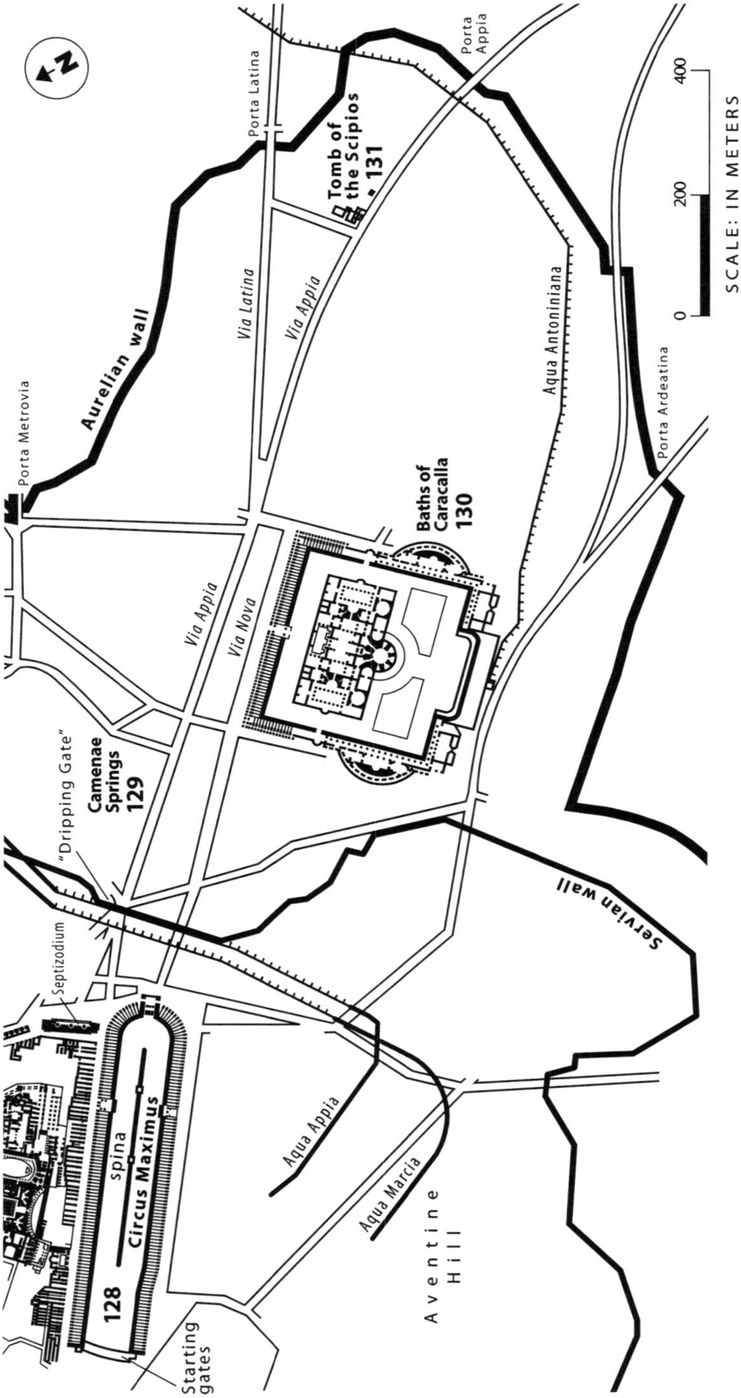

Fig. 59 Circus Maximus to the Tomb of the Scipios

N

SCALE: IN METERS

0   200   400

Porta Latina

Porta Appia

Tomb of
the Scipios
131

Aurelian wall

Via Latina

Via Appia

Porta Metrovia

Aqua Antoniniana

Porta Ardeatina

Via Appia

Via Nova

Baths of
Caracalla
130

"Dripping Gate"

Camenae
Springs
129

Servian wall

Septizodium

Spina

Circus Maximus

128

Aqua Appia

Aqua Marcia

Aventine
Hill

Starting
gates

XI. Circus Maximus to the Tomb of the Scipios

128. Circus Maximus

COMMENTARY

The Circus Maximus was the largest public structure in ancient Rome. Modern estimates of the Circus's seating capacity under the Empire (when the stands were at their largest) vary, going as high as Pliny's estimate of 250,000. By any account, the Circus could hold over twice the audience of the Colosseum, being not so much *in* the valley between the Palatine and Aventine, as a valley in itself with man-made slopes. The Circus is also uniquely and oddly preserved in the modern landscape, being less a ruin than open ground that is neither landscaped as a park like the Baths of Trajan, nor integrated into urban life as a piazza like the Stadium of Domitian (Piazza Navona). The extent of the Circus (it is fully twice as long as Piazza Navona) is certainly well conveyed by the clearing today, although the visible ruins of foundations at the curved, eastern end give little impression of the Circus's exterior architecture, which coins and carvings show resembled the arcade and pilaster arrangements of the Theater of Marcellus and the Colosseum.

Varro [128.1] traces games at the Circus back to the legendary days of Romulus, Rome's king during the abduction of the Sabine women; Ovid perhaps has this in mind when he suggests the Circus as a place to pick up women [128.14]. Livy, on the other hand, ascribes the first proper racetrack and stands to the first Etruscan kings [128.2], and his emphasis on Etruscan origins is corroborated by early Etruscan art of ceremonial horse races.

The Pulvinar, where the emperors often watched the game [128.12], was originally the shrine from which the gods, after being paraded into the arena in statuette-form, would watch the games from a special couch. It then took on architectural definition and became a sort of imperial box, while retaining its religious function. The passages that comment on emperors reading in the Pulvinar show how important imperial appearances at the games came to be in the crucial and uncertain business of relating to the populace of the city, and how a simple act of attention or inattention to the games, broadcast live from the Pulvinar in front of a massive audience, could define an emperor in popular image [128.12].

The passages at the end of the section give some impression of the Circus's place in the life of the city and its inhabitants. The last two are inscriptions. The one describes an immensely successful charioteer's career that illustrates both the details of racing and the Roman passion for the races. The other is the epitaph of a young boy who may have hoped for such a career himself; it was found with the low-relief carving of a boy in a chariot holding a victory palm in his hand.

SOURCES

128.1 The Consualian Games were named for the god Consus. It was during games to this god, being celebrated by the priests near his altar in the Circus, that the Sabine maidens attending the games were abducted.

Varro, *The Latin Language* 6.20

128.2 Tarquinius Priscus's first war was waged against the Latins… . Returning with more booty than reports of the war led people to expect, he put on games that were costlier and more elaborate than those of earlier kings. Then for the first time the ground was marked out for the racetrack which is now called the Circus Maximus. Separate spaces for viewing were designated for the patricians and the knights, on stands propped twelve feet off the ground on wooden braces. Horses and boxers, drawn primarily from Etruria, provided the entertainment. Subsequently, these games, which are called both the Roman Games and the Great Games, have been held regularly each year.

Livy, *History* 1.35.7–9

128.3 Tarquinius Priscus built the largest of the race-tracks, the one lying between the Aventine and Palatine Hills, and was the first to erect covered seating there (until then the spectators had stood), which consisted of benches elevated on wooden scaffolding. He also divided the stands into thirty sections, one designated for each tribe, so that each person watched the games seated in his proper place.

In time this structure was to grow into one of the most beautiful and impressive buildings in Rome. The arena is 2,100 feet long and 400 feet wide. A trench for water, ten feet deep and ten feet wide, has been dug around it on the two longer sides and one of the shorter sides; behind this, stands of three stories are built. The ones at ground level have stone seats on a gradual incline, as in theaters; the upper stories are of wood. The stands extending down the two long sides of the track are joined together by stands that curve in a crescent around one of the short sides, in the manner of an amphitheater. This yields all told a seating area 4,800 feet long, with room for 150,000 spectators. The remaining short side, kept uncovered, has vaulted starting-gates which are all opened simultaneously by one rope.

On the outer side of the Circus there is another portico, one-storied, containing shops with living-space above them. This portico also provides spectators access to the stands, with entrances and flights of stairs alongside each of the shops, such that the many thousands of spectators can enter and leave without inconvenience.

Dionysius, *Early Rome* 3.68

128.4 [Rome's monuments are beyond compare] even if we don't include among our great works of architecture the Circus Maximus built by Caesar when dictator, 1,800 feet long and 600 feet wide, with three acres of buildings and seats for 250,000 spectators … .

Pliny the Elder, *Encyclopedia* 36.102

128.5 [In 329 BC] starting gates were first built in the Circus.

Livy, *History* 8.20.2

128.6 The censors [in 174 BC]… contracted for building starting gates at the Circus, and eggs for keeping track of the laps… .

Livy, *History* 41.27.6

128.7 [As aedile in 33 BC] Agrippa, noticing that people in the Circus had trouble keeping track of the number of laps completed, installed the dolphins and egg-shaped objects to display the number of times the track had been circled in a race.

Dio, *History* 49.43.2

128.8 "Relax, you have arrived in time. The final egg, signifying the chariots are running the last lap in the Circus, has not yet been taken down."

Varro, *Agriculture* 1.2.11

128.9 During festivities for the dedication of the Temple of Venus Victrix in Pompey's second consulship [55 BC], twenty elephants (some say seventeen) fought against African Gaetulians armed with javelins. One of the elephants put up an amazing fight. Unable to walk because its feet had been wounded, the elephant crawled on its knees toward the javelin-throwers and tossed their shields high in the air. To the delight of the spectators, these shields cut graceful arcs in the air on their way back down, as if thrown with artistry and not by an enraged beast. Another astonishing spectacle was an elephant who was killed with one throw of a javelin that plunged straight through its eye into the vital core of its brain.

Banding together, the elephants attempted to break through the iron fencing that enclosed them, which caused such fear among the spectators that Caesar subsequently surrounded the arena with a canal prior to providing a similar show during his dictatorship [in 49 BC], a fence which was later removed by Nero to add seating reserved for the knights. Finally, when Pompey's elephants had given up all hope of escape, they appealed to the crowd's mercy with uncanny gestures, lamenting their fate with a sort of wailing. The people were so disturbed by this suffering that they forgot all about the great general and the magnificent entertainment he had arranged for their sake. In tears, they rose to their feet and called down curses on Pompey, which were soon enough fulfilled.

Pliny the Elder, *Encyclopedia* 8.20–21

128.10 The emperor Claudius refined the Circus Maximus, substituting marble starting-gates and gilded turning-posts for earlier work in tufa and wood. He also provided separate seating reserved for the Senators, who previously had to mix with the rest of the spectators.

Suetonius, *Claudius* 21.3

128.11 When the emperor Domitian celebrated the Secular Games, on the day reserved for the races in the Circus he reduced the number of laps for each race from seven to five in order to fit in a hundred races.

Suetonius, *Domitian* 4.3

128.12 Augustus himself generally watched the games from the upper dining rooms of his friends and freedmen, as on occasion from the Pulvinar, appearing there sometimes even with his wife and children. … Whenever he sat in the Pulvinar, he never occupied himself with other business, either to avoid the bad report that he knew had circulated about his father Caesar for utilizing time at the games for reading and replying to letters and petitions, or because Augustus genuinely enjoyed being a spectator, a pleasure he never denied and often openly professed.

Suetonius, *Augustus* 45.1

128.13 It was customary for the emperor Marcus Aurelius to read, hear reports, and sign documents while attending shows at the race-track— behavior which often, it is reported, made him the target of the people's ridicule.

Imperial Lives, *Marcus Aurelius* 15.1

128.14 [Epitaph:] Gaius Julius Epaphra, a fruit-seller in front of the Pulvinar at the Circus Maximus, sets this stone up for himself and his wife Venuleia Helena, a freedwoman of Caesar.

ILS 7496 = *CIL* 6.9822

128.15 In your search for a lover, don't neglect the noble race-track:
　　The teeming stands of the Circus are rich with opportunity.
Here no need for a code to signal secret thoughts,
　　No need for a nod and a wink to get the message across;
Just sit down next to your lady, there's nothing here to prevent it,
　　Sidle yourself right up and press your hip to hers;
The crowded seating, like it or not, works in your favor,
　　And regulations compel you to squeeze in tight and touch.
Next, a topic of conversation: begin with something
　　Neighborly, delivered in public tones for all to hear.
When horses appear, look excited and quickly ask whose,
　　And whatever racer's her favorite, amazing ... he's yours as well!
But when the parade is passing, with its host of ivory gods,
　　Make sure your loud applause reveals your devotion to Venus.
If any speck of dirt should land on the lap of your lady,
　　As sometimes happens, be concerned to brush it away,
And even if dirt is absent, brush it off anyway.
　　Any service will do to show that you really care:
If the folds of her robe should slip and touch the ground,
　　Gently gather them up and rescue the fabric from filth:
Such service comes with a quick reward: if the girl permits,
　　Your new arrangement of cloth will give you a glimpse of her legs.
Make sure to check behind you as well; with *you* on guard,
　　No knee from the bench above will be jabbing *her* tender back!

Ovid, *The Art of Love* 1.135–158

128.16 Our city is already flooded with the foreign ways of the East:
Even the man whose taste in women runs to hookers
In turbans will find them stationed outside the Circus itself.

Juvenal, *Satires* 3.62–6

128.17 [Women, the poet rants, will plague you with their superstitions.]
　　A woman of lesser means will head to the Circus and race

Around the arcades to learn her future, offering her hand
And cranial bumps to a prophet, clucking at the ominous news.
                                        Juvenal, *Satires* 6.582–4

128.18 [Powerful people are fools and don't know what to wish for.]
But what about the crowd of common people? As always,
They idolize success and save their contempt for losers.
Ever since we lost the right to sell our votes
The people toss their civic cares aside; the citizen
Who once had final say over legions, the fasces, the world,
Contracts himself to the issues of ultimate concern:
Bread and Circuses.
                                Juvenal, *Satires* 10.72–4, 77–81

128.19 The Roman People are kept in line by two things above all: the grain dole and entertainment. Power rests no less upon amusements than upon serious measures: failure in the latter results in greater real damage, but failure at the former results in greater discontent.

The grain dole is not as effective as entertainment in keeping the people content. Grain placates only a person at a time and is targeted to specific individuals; spectacles reach everyone.
                        Fronto, *Letters* (*Preamble to History*, AD 165)

128.20 [So much for the vices of the nobility.] We now [c. AD 360] come to the idle and shiftless plebs. … They spend their entire lives on wine, dice, brothels, parties, and the games. For such people, the Circus Maximus is a temple, a home, an assembly ground, and the focus of all desire. … As dawn approaches on the awaited day of chariot-racing, before the sun is even shining, they all rush in a heedless mass to the stadium, as if engaged in a race with the very chariots they go to watch, many of them having gone sleepless with anxiety over the outcome of their fanatical wishes.
                        Ammianus, *History* 28.4.28–31, selections

128.21 Gaius Appuleius Diocles, driver for the Red Team, from Lusitanian Spain, [retired?] at age 42 years, 7 months, and 23 days. His first race was for the White Team in AD 122; his first victory was for the same team in AD 124. He first drove for the Greens in AD 128, and first won for the Reds in AD 131.

His career statistics: he drove chariots for 24 years making 4,257 starts, with 1,462 first place finishes, 110 of them in the opening race after the procession. In races for which he was his team's sole entry he came in first 1,064 times, 92 of them in the big-money events: he won 30,000 sesterces 32 times (three times with a six-horse team); 40,000 sesterces 28 times (twice with a six-horse team); 50,000 sesterces 29 times (once with a seven-horse team); and 60,000 sesterces three times. In double-entry contests he came in first 347 times, winning 15,000 sesterces four times with a three-horse team. In three-entry races he came in first 51 times.

He came in first or placed 2,900 times, coming in second 861 times, third 576 times and fourth once (winning 1,000 sesterces); he failed to place 1,351 times. ... His career winnings totaled 35,863,120 sesterces. ... He held a lead to win 815 times, came from behind to win 67 times, won under handicap 36 times, won in various fashion 42 times, and took the lead down the stretch to win 502 times (overtaking the Greens 216 times, the Blues 205 times, and the Whites 81 times). He made nine horses 100-time winners, and one horse a 200-time winner.

ILS 5287 = CIL 6.10048, selections

128.22 Here I lie, the little Florus, a two-horse charioteer;
No sooner did I take to chariots than I tumbled to the shades.

ILS 5300 = CIL 6.10078

Notes: Dionysius's description of the Augustan Circus [128.3] as having *stoai tristegoi*, "three-storied colonnades," of which the lowest is stone and the other two of wood, is puzzling. Both of Humphrey's conjectures – "colonnades at the level of the third storey" and "three colonnaded galleries, one above the other" as viewed from the *exterior* of the Circus (*Roman Circuses: Arenas for Chariot Racing*, 74–75)—must be rejected, the former because Dionysius proceeds to include the lowest interior tier in stone as one part of the *stoai tristegoi*, and the latter because he describes the three-storied colonnades as *meta ton euripon*, "next to the canal," in the foremost part of the stands facing the track rather than as seen from the exterior. Dionysius seems to be saying that the Augustan Circus had three tiers of seating, one superimposed on the other, in the fashion of many modern stadiums with upper decks, and not simply three sections of seating on the same gradual inclined plane. Even if such an interpretation is correct, it is possible that Trajan's rebuilding dispensed with these tiers in favor of a single but wider and steeper stone section.

129. Camenae Springs

COMMENTARY

The Camenae and Egeria were originally spring-goddesses who were later associated with prophecy and then poetry as well. Livius Andronicus may have established the link with poetry in the late C3 BC by choosing the Camenae as the Latin equivalent of the Muses in the first line of his translation of Homer's *Odyssey* [129.3]. Their grove and shrine were located a short stroll outside the Porta

Capena, at the foot of the Caelian Hill. Eventually monumentalized, the temple's ruins may be those of a large nymphaeum under the Villa Mattei on the Via Valle delle Camene, although the spring and grotto whose development Juvenal laments [129.5] may have been separate from the temple.

SOURCES

129.1 There was a grove which was watered down the middle by a perennial spring issuing from a shady cave. Because Numa would often come here without any witnesses, as if to meet with his consort Egeria, he consecrated the grove to the Camenae, who (he reported) often held counsel here with his Egeria.

Livy, *History* 1.21.3

129.2 [When the bronze shield, the pledge of Rome's power, fell from heaven,] Numa said that it was necessary to sanctify the spot to the Muses, along with the meadows surrounding it where the Muses were accustomed to meet with him. He further revealed that the spring which watered this spot should be made holy for use by the Vestal Virgins, who were to come here each day to fetch water to sprinkle and purify their temple.

Plutarch, *Numa* 13.2

129.3 Sing through me, Camena, of the man of many moves… .

Livius Andronicus, *Odusia* 1

129.4 Writers have said that the poet Accius, although being quite short, dedicated a tall statue of himself [c. 100 BC] in the Shrine of the Camenae.

Pliny the Elder, *Encyclopedia* 34.19

129.5 When all my friend's possessions were packed on a single cart
He lingered by the ancient arcade and the dripping Porta Capena.
…
We walked on down to Egeria's valley and into the grotto
So painfully artificial. How much more intense
The presence of divinity, if instead of marble
Living rock and green grass bordered the stream!

Juvenal, *Satires* 3.10–11, 17–20

130. Baths of Caracalla (and baths in general)

COMMENTARY

After the Baths of Trajan were built on the Esquiline c. AD 110, more than a hundred years passed before the next of the giant imperial baths was built. These, the Baths of Caracalla (called the *Thermae Antoniniani* in antiquity), contain the most impressive ruins of an ancient bath in Rome, with the possible exception of the central hall of the Baths of Diocletian, which was remodeled into the church of S. Maria degli Angeli by Michelangelo and subsequent architects. Whereas this remodeling gives some impression of the finished splendor of the imperial baths that Caracalla's brick, stripped of its colored stone, stucco, and art is ill-suited to convey, the ruins of Caracalla preserve a sense of the total space and the relation of the many various parts of an imperial bath, in addition to the substantial (but closed to the public) subterranean remains of service corridors among the complex plumbing and heating installations.

The Baths of Caracalla were built on a large man-made terrace that extended the Little Aventine towards the Caelian Hill. The main approach was on the Via Appia, paralleled as it neared the baths by a beautiful new avenue, the Via Nova, which may have formed more of a plaza than a street, bounded on one side by the perimeter walls of the bath. Brick stamps show that the huge central complex containing the open-air swimming pool, the vaulted hall, and the rounded, towering hot-room, was built between AD 212 and 216. The perimeter walls may be the porticoes referred to by the sources and attributed to Elagabalus and Alexander Severus [130.2], but these walls were rebuilt under Aurelian and cannot provide original dating by means of brick stamps.

Public bathing was an integral part of a day of most who lived in ancient Rome, and I have included a few sources here on the bathing experience in general: Seneca's description of the sounds emanating from a Roman bath house [130.4] is justly famous, and reminds us (since his lodging was directly above this bath) that there were hundreds of smaller or larger, spartan or lavish, private baths scattered throughout Rome and incorporated into other structures. The passage by Martial [130.5] humanizes the factors determining which of Rome's many baths to attend, as the short epitaph humanizes the consequences of attendance for one Fortunatus [130.6]. Finally, there is the curious inscription by a man named Ursus, the greatest player but one of the "glass ball game" that he performed in front of crowds in all of Rome's grandest baths of the day. The Verus referred to in the inscription was Annius Verus, consul for the third time in AD 126 and father-in-law of the later emperor Antoninus Pius. Ball playing was a common sport in the baths, but either this version with glass balls (nowhere else mentioned) was a higher-stakes specialty dramatized by this mock-heroic inscription, or possibly an allegory, as some have argued, for the fragile game of imperial politics.

SOURCES

130.1   In Rome, the Emperor Caracalla left behind him the great baths in his name. In these baths is a heated tub-room (*cella solearis*) whose manner of construction the architects say cannot be imitated. The entire weight of the vaulting of the ceiling depends on a gridwork of copper or brass above it, and yet the span of the vault is such that the experts in engineering insist it cannot be constructed in this way.

Alongside his baths (the Antonine Baths, that is) Caracalla also built the Via Nova, the beauty of which you would be hard pressed to find equaled by any other streets in the city.

Imperial Lives, *Caracalla* 9.4, 9

130.2   Antoninus Caracalla dedicated the baths by bathing there and opening its doors to the public, but the porticoes were not constructed until the time of the fake Severine emperor, Elagabalus, and were completed under Alexander Severus.

Imperial Lives, *Elagabalus* 17.9

130.3   [Epitaph:]   Cucumio and Victoria made this monument for themselves during their lifetime [in the C3 AD]; he was a cloak-room attendant at the Baths of Caracalla.

ILS 7621 = *CIL* 6.9232

130.4   I cannot for the life of me see why silence should seem necessary for someone who withdraws to write. Consider my own circumstances: a multitude of noises surrounds me, since I live directly above a bath. Try to imagine to yourself every variety of the human voice that is offensive to the ear. When the body-builders exercise and strain (or imitate someone straining) to lift weights, I hear their grunts as they express pent air, followed by the hisses of their harsh inhalations. When one of the clientele relaxes to a cheap rub-down, I hear the noise of hands as they strike his shoulders, ranging from flat smacks to a cupped blow, depending on the stroke. If a ball-player comes along and begins to count the score, I'm finished. Add to this the aggressive loud-mouth, the thief who's been caught, the person who likes to hear himself sing in the bath, and the bathers who love to make big splashes when they jump in the pool.

In addition to those whose voices are at least normal, listen to the hairplucker keening his presence in a thin shrill tone that never ceases, except when he's found an armpit to pluck, in which case his client yells for him. Top it all off with the drink seller shouting his menu, and the vendors of sausages, pastries, and the cheap-eats from a nearby cook-shop, each of them hawking his wares with his own distinctive call.

Seneca the Younger, *Letters* 56.1–2

130.5 Whatever signs attend a newly acquired friendship,
    These are the signs that Fabius wants me to show to him.
And so I trudge behind him late in the afternoon
    To the Baths of Agrippa, though I patronize the Baths of Titus.

Martial, *Epigrams* 3.36.1–2, 5–6

130.6 [Epitaph:] Daphnus and Chryseis, freedpeople of Lacon, dedicate this to their son Fortunatus. He drowned, age 8, in a pool in the Baths of Mars.

ILS 8518 = *CIL* 6.16740

130.7 My name is Ursus, and I was first among the Romans
To play with grace the glass-ball game with my companions,
Cheered on (I tell the truth) by large applauding crowds
In the Baths of Trajan, Titus, Agrippa, and often Nero.
Rejoice, my fellow ballplayers, gather round my statue
And load it down with leafy boughs, with garlands of violet
And rose, dispense with loving care the pungent scents,
And with the finest wines from my ancestral cellar
Pour libations out for me, though I still live.
Eulogize old Ursus with one concordant voice:
"He was a witty, cheerful, extremely learnèd ballplayer
Surpassing all in strategy, grace, and subtle skill."
But let an old man use this verse to tell the truth:
I've been defeated, I confess, not once or twice
But often, by Verus, three times consul and my patron,
For whom I am content to be called a warm-up act.

ILS 5173 = *CIL* 6.9797

Notes: On the glass ball game and interpretations, see Fagan, *Bathing in Public in the Roman World*, 195–196; on interpretations of the term *cella solearis* [130.1] and its architectural peculiarities, which are much disputed, see Yegül, *Baths and Bathing in Classical Antiquity*, 159–160.

131. Tomb of the Scipios (Figs. 60, 61)

COMMENTARY

    The Tomb of the Scipios, located on a little street that connected the Via Appia and the Via Latina a short distance inside the much later Aurelian Walls, is not only the best preserved tomb of an aristocratic family from Republican times, but contains the sepulchers of a family (the Cornelii) with distinctive burial practices. Preserved along with the tombs are nine epitaphs in all (four of them included here) which both illustrate the ethos of public service among the Republican nobility and preserve some of the earliest Latin verse before the sea-change in Latin versification instigated in part by Ennius, the great Roman poet connected with the Scipio family.

The tomb chamber, cut into the living rock, was probably founded by Scipio Barbatus, consul in 298 BC and the first to be buried here (Tomb A in the diagram, but see Notes). His sarcophagus (or rather a replica; the originals of his and the others are now in the Vatican Museum) is at the end of the central passageway. Tomb B contained his son, consul in 259 BC. Tomb C possibly belonged to Publius Cornelius Scipio, augur in 180 BC but better known as the son of Scipio Africanus (the great general who defeated Hannibal) and as the adoptive father of Scipio Aemilianus Africanus. Livy explains why Scipio Africanus the Elder's tomb is absent from this family site in Rome [131.12]; the tomb of the younger Africanus (so titled for finishing off Carthage in 146 BC) is unattested here or elsewhere, but he may have been interred in a newer chamber tunneled in 2C BC alongside the original and larger chamber. The largest sarcophagus (D in the diagram) in the new section contained the remains of Cornelius Scipio Hispanus [131.7].

About the same time as this addition was built, a monumental facade was added to the front of the subterranean burial chamber (see Fig. 61), with three arched entrances and the three statues of Africanus the Elder, his brother Lucius, and Ennius that both Cicero [131.10] and Livy [131.9] attribute to the monument—admittedly in a conjectural tone, perhaps because there were no inscriptions to confirm these traditional identifications. Ennius was even thought by some to have been buried here [131.11]. His close connection to the Scipios is noted by Cicero and we know of a panegyric he composed to Scipio Africanus. The presence of his statue here may have led to the belief that he was also interred with the family.

Altogether, the burials in this family tomb span the period from c. 240 BC to c. 130 BC, a period during which standard burial practice evolved from inhumation to cremation, revealing the Scipios distinctively conservative in their adherence to the former method. Fashion swung back towards inhumation again in the 3C AD, influenced by practices in the eastern half of the empire that also suited Jewish and Christian beliefs. While cremation was still prevalent in Rome, another type of burial chamber evolved, called a *columbarium* by archaeologists because of its similarity to the dovecotes built in antiquity (a large post-office box would serve as a modern comparison). An example of one survives alongside the Tomb of the Scipios. These structures, frequently subterranean, had walls of many small cubicles containing the ash urns of the cremated, who were typically the slave-staff of imperial families or members of one of the burial societies that were quite popular in the Roman world. The more famous catacombs, most of them further out of town because they were constructed after the Aurelian Walls extended the no-burial zone, are essentially underground dovecotes for corpses rather than ash urns (more like dank sleeping berths trundling through the dark than efficient post-office boxes).

The inscriptions are of interest for both content and form. Throughout they reveal: a) the ambition for glory arrived at by conquest and political office, b) the family pressure to live up to and advance the reputation of the clan, and c) the unstable balance that existed between personal ambition and communal profit that Rome parlayed into an empire, not without numerous civil wars and assassinations. But that came later; the Scipios are stop-framed at a crucial point in this progression, when the competitive aristocracy and the legions at its command were dispatching Rome's last great powers opposing them in the Mediterranean and in the process of opening the provincial world of Rome to the culture of Greece—momentous events in which several of the Scipios played a major role. This is precisely the period, however, to which later Roman moralizers traced the beginning of Rome's decline, which they attributed to prosperity, (Greek) luxury, and growing individualism. There is perhaps a hint of things to come in Livy's observation that Scipio Africanus was the first general to take on the name of a country he conquered [131.12]; such titles became routine under the emperors, as demonstrated by the inscriptions on the Arch of Severus [45.1] and the Column of Trajan [79.1]. Another crucial source for the subsequent and disastrous phase of aristocratic competitiveness would be Caesar's claim [131.8], in explaining his actions that led up to his civil war with Pompey, that he valued his stature (his *dignitas*, a difficult word to translate) more than his own life, and evidently more than thousands of other lives as well.

Finally, the inscriptions document a literary change that was taking place in the C2 BC due to the influence of Greek literature. The first three epitaphs are written in an old Latin meter called Saturnian, of which only 125 lines survive, many of them in fragments from early Roman epics. The most distinctive feature of the Saturnian meter is a strong caesura, or break, near the middle of the verse-line, which otherwise reveals no metrical regularities, and was by later Latin writers felt to be rugged, even crude, and of limited expressive potential. At any rate, a key figure in the demise of the Saturnian meter was none other than Ennius, who broke with earlier tradition and wrote his epic, the *Annales*, in Greek hexameters, the verse form for all subse-

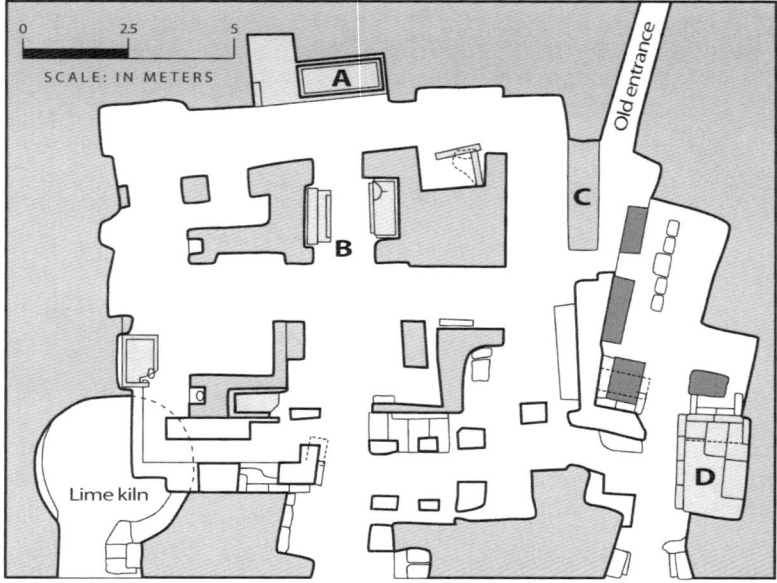

Fig. 60 Tomb of Scipios (after Gismondi and Claridge)

quent Roman epics. The fourth epitaph included below [131.7] represents this literary transformation, being composed in the Greek meter of elegiac couplets, closely related to hexameter. It may also be significant that it is the only one of the epitaphs written in the first person.

SOURCES

131.1 "A dead person," the law in the Twelve Tables reads, "shall neither be buried nor cremated inside the city." This, I suppose, on account of the danger of fire. Still, since the law includes, as a separate phrase "nor cremated," it means that the word "buried" must extend the law to inhumation as well.

Cicero, On Laws 2.58

131.2 [How can you call the dead miserable?] When you leave town by the Porta Capena and see the tombs of Calatinus, the Scipios, the Servilii, and the Metelli, do you really think that they are suffering?

Cicero, Tuscan Disputations 1.13

131.3 Cremation was not practiced among the early Romans; bodies were laid in the earth. But when they became aware that the bodies of those who fell in far-off wars were being dug up, they instituted cremation. And yet many families continued with the old rituals of burial,

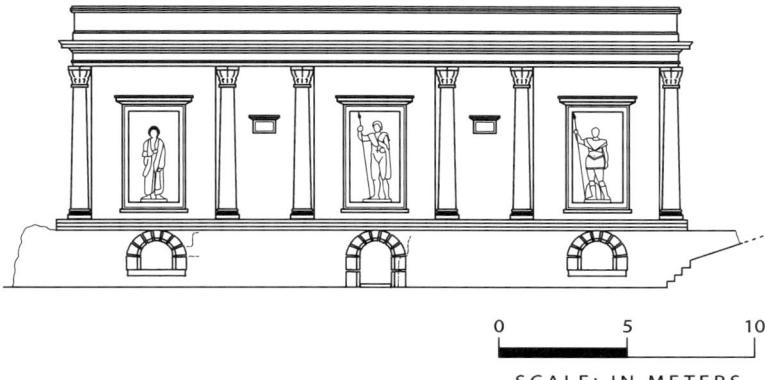

Fig. 61 Tomb of the Scipios, façade (after Gismondi)

SCALE: IN METERS

such as the Cornelii, none of whom, it is reported, were cremated before the dictator Cornelius Sulla [c. 80 BC].

Pliny the Elder, *Encyclopedia* 7.187

131.4   [Tomb A, Figure 26]
Lucius Cornelius Scipio, son of Gnaeus:
Lucius Cornelius   Scipio Barbatus,   [consul 298 BC]
Begotten son of Gnaeus,   courageous man and wise,
Whose physical appearance   was equal to his virtue;
This man among you ranked   consul, censor, aedile,
Captured Samnium,   Taurasia, and Cisauna,
Reduced Lucania whole   and brought back hostages.

ILS 1 = *CIL* 6.1234/5

131.5   [Tomb B]
Lucius Cornelius Scipio, son of Lucius, aedile, consul,
censor:

Most in Rome agree   that he who lies within
Even among the best   was a man preeminent:
Lucius Scipio   son of Barbatus.
This man among you ranked   consul, censor, aedile.
He conquered Corsica   and its city Aleria,
And gave the gods of storms   the temple they had earned.

ILS 2–3 = *CIL* 6.1286–7

131.6   [Tomb C]
You who wore the cap   of Jupiter's high priest,
Death has dealt with you such   that all in life was shortened:
Honor and reputation,   courage, fame, and talents—

Had you been bestowed longer life to use them
Your deeds had surely surpassed all ancestral glory.
Therefore the earth receives you gladly into her lap
Publius, son of Publius, Scipio Cornelius.

ILS 4 = *CIL* 6.1288

131.7   [Tomb D]
Gnaius Cornelius Scipio Hispanus, son of Gnaius, praetor,
curule aedile, quaestor, military tribune twice,
on the Board of Ten for the trial of lawsuits, on the Board of
Ten for the performance of rituals

With noble behavior, I piled still higher my family's glory;
    I continued the line with children and aimed for my father's successes.
I attained the fame of my ancestors: they would rejoice that I
    was born a Scipio. My career has ennobled my clan.

ILS 6 = *CIL* 6.1293

131.8   Caesar informed the messengers that his rank and reputation were his first concern, and more important to him than life itself.

Caesar, *Civil Wars* 1.9

131.9   There are three statues on the burial monument of the Scipios outside the Porta Capena: two of them are said to be of Publius and Lucius Scipio, the third of the poet Quintus Ennius.

Livy, *History* 38.56.4

131.10   Our poet Ennius was esteemed by Scipio Africanus the Elder. In fact, it is thought that a marble statue of him was set up on the tomb of the Scipios. Clearly, however, the praises that literature can bestow distinguish not only the individual being praised, but the name of the entire Roman people.

Cicero, *In Defense of Archias* 22

131.11   The poet Ennius died of rheumatoid arthritis when he was seventy, and was buried in the monument of the Scipios less than a mile outside the city.

Suetonius (in Jerome's *Chronicle*)

131.12   [After his decisive defeat of Hannibal's forces in Africa] Scipio Africanus arrived at Rome and entered the city to the most splendid triumph ever celebrated, and deposited 123,000 pounds of silver in the treasury. … He was the first general who was distinguished by the name of the country he had conquered.

[Foreseeing endless attacks by his opponents, Scipio withdrew from public life in Rome.] He spent the rest of his life in Liternum without any desire to return to Rome, and when he was near death, they say he ordered that he be buried and his tomb erected in that same countryside, so that his ungrateful homeland might not have the satisfaction of his funeral. ... Despite his faults, Scipio's successful ending of the Second Punic War—the greatest and most perilous struggle ever waged by Romans—gained him a reputation second to none.

Livy, *History* 30.45.3; 38.53

Notes: For an analysis of the Scipio epitaphs and historical background, see Courtney, *Musa Lapidaria*, 217–229. Courtney notes that both the poetical inscription preserved on the sarcophagus of Barbatus and the sarcophagus itself post-date the inscription and sarcophagus of his son, and were perhaps motivated by a desire to ennoble, retroactively, the ancestry of a family whose fortune was flagging in the early C2 BC.

Works Cited

LTUR = *Lexicon Topographicum Urbis Romae* (see under Steinby)

Richardson = *A New Topographical Dictionary of Ancient Rome* (see under Richardson)

Aicher, Peter J. *Guide to the Aqueducts of Ancient Rome* (Wauconda, Ill.: Bolchazy-Carducci Publishers, 1995).

Anderson, Jr., James. *The Historical Topography of the Imperial Fora.* Collection Latomus 182 (Brussels, 1984).

Claridge, Amanda. *Rome*, Oxford Archaeological Guide (Oxford and New York: Oxford University Press, 1998).

Cornell, T. J. *The Beginnings of Rome* (New York: Routledge, 1995).

Courtney, Edward. *Musa Lapidaria: A Selection of Latin Verse Inscriptions* (American Philological Association, 1995).

DeGrassi, A. *Inscriptiones Italiae*, 13.3 (Rome, 1937).

de Grummond, Nancy Thomson. *An Encyclopedia of the History of Classical Archaeology*, 2 vol. (Chicago: Fitzroy Dearborn Publishers, 1996).

Dessau, Hermann. *Inscriptiones Latinae Selectae*, in five volumes (Chicago: Ares Publishers, 1979; reprint of 1892).

Dudley, Donald R. *Urbs Roma: A Source Book of Classical Texts* (Aberdeen: Phaidon Press, 1967).

Edwards, Catherine. *Writing Rome: Textual Approaches to the City* (Cambridge: Cambridge University Press, 1996).

Evans, Harry. *Water Distribution in Ancient Rome: The Evidence of Frontinus* (Ann Arbor: University of Michigan Press, 1994).

Fagan, Garrett G. *Bathing in Public in the Roman World* (Ann Arbor: University of Michigan Press, 1999).

Favro, Diane. *The Urban Image of Augustan Rome* (Cambridge: Cambridge University Press, 1996).

Hodge, A. Trevor. *The Roman Aqueducts and Water Supply*, 2nd ed. (London: Duckworth, 2002).

Holloway, R. Ross. *The Archaeology of Early Rome and Latium* (New York: Routledge, 1996).

Humphrey, John H. *Roman Circuses: Arenas for Chariot Racing* (Berkeley: University of California Press, 1986).

Krautheimer, Richard. *Rome: Profile of a City, 312–1308* (Princeton: Princeton University Press, 1980).

Lanciani, Rudolf. *The Destruction of Ancient Rome* (New York: Arno Press, 1980; first appeared in 1901).

Lugli, Giuseppe. *Fontes ad Topographiam Veteris Urbis Romae Pertinentes*, in seven volumes (Rome: 1952–1969).

Moore, Timothy. *The Theater of Plautus* (Austin: University of Texas Press, 1998).

Packer, James. *The Forum of Trajan*, 3 vols. (Berkeley: University of California Press, 1997).

Purcell, Nicholas. "The City of Rome and the *plebs urbana* in the Late Republic," *Cambridge Ancient History*, Vol. 9 (Cambridge: Cambridge University Press, 1994), 644–688.

——— "Rome and its Development under Augustus and his Successors," *Cambridge Ancient History*, Vol. 10 (Cambridge: Cambridge University Press, 1996), 782–811.

Richardson, Jr., Lawrence. *A New Topographical Dictionary of Ancient Rome* (Baltimore: Johns Hopkins University Press, 1992).

Stambaugh, John. *The Ancient Roman City* (Baltimore: John Hopkins University Press, 1988).

Steinby, Eva Margareta, ed. *Lexicon Topographicum Urbis Romae, Vols. I–VI* (Rome: Quasar,1993–2000).

van Heck, A. *Breviarium Urbis Romae Antiquae* (Leiden: Brill, 1977).

Welch, Katherine. "A New View of the Origins of the Basilica," *Journal of Roman Archaeology*, Vol. 16, 2003, pp. 5–34.

Wilkins, Ann Thomas. "Sallust's Tullianum: Reality, Description, and Beyond," in *Rome and Her Monuments* ed. by Sheila K. Dickison and Judith P. Hallett (Wauconda, Ill.: Bolchazy-Carducci Publishers, 2000).

Wiseman, T. P. "Strabo on the Campus Martius: 5.3.8, C236," *Liverpool Classical Monthly*, 1979, pp. 129–134.

Yegül, Fikret. *Baths and Bathing in Classical Antiquity* (Cambridge: Massachusetts Institute of Technology Press, 1992).

Index

Preface pages are in Roman numerals. Arabic numerals indicate source-
numbers—plain for commentary, decimal for citations (suffix *n* = note).
Figures are keyed to list on pp. ix-x.

Guide to the Aqueducts of Ancient Rome
Peter J. Aicher

Aicher's work is a unique fusion of tour guide and archaeological handbook, allowing the reader to view the
Eternal City from the vantage point of an unmistakable
yet overlooked feature of its topography.

Features
- maps
- schematic drawings
- photographs
- reprints of famous line drawings

Pages: xiii + 183 (1995), Paperback, 978-0-86516-282-2, Hardbound, 978-0-86516-271-6

 **Bolchazy-Carducci Publishers, Inc.**
www.BOLCHAZY.com